Originally compiled by Tewie Lord in December 2001
Pedigree Charts updated December 2013

1

The Ralph & Norma Lord

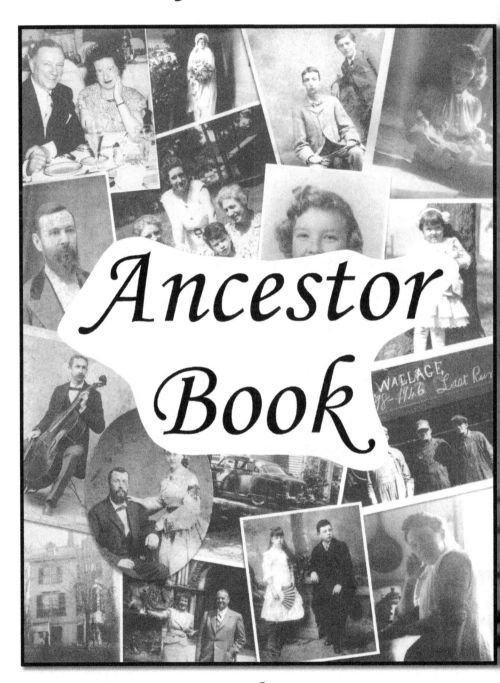

Ancestor Book

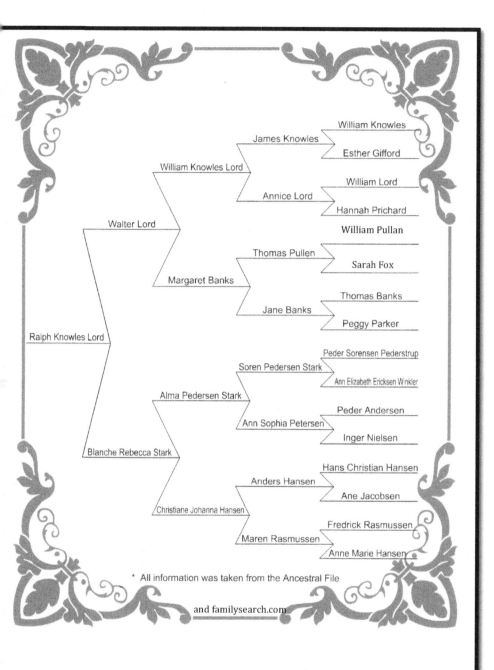

Ralph Knowles Lord

Walter Lord

William Knowles Lord

James Knowles

William Knowles

Esther Gifford

Annice Lord

William Lord

Hannah Prichard

Margaret Banks

Thomas Pullen

William Pullan

Sarah Fox

Jane Banks

Thomas Banks

Peggy Parker

Blanche Rebecca Stark

Alma Pedersen Stark

Soren Pedersen Stark

Peder Sorensen Pederstrup

Ann Elizabeth Ericksen Winkler

Ann Sophia Petersen

Peder Andersen

Inger Nielsen

Christiane Johanna Hansen

Anders Hansen

Hans Christian Hansen

Ane Jacobsen

Maren Rasmussen

Fredrick Rasmussen

Anne Marie Hansen

* All information was taken from the Ancestral File

and familysearch.com

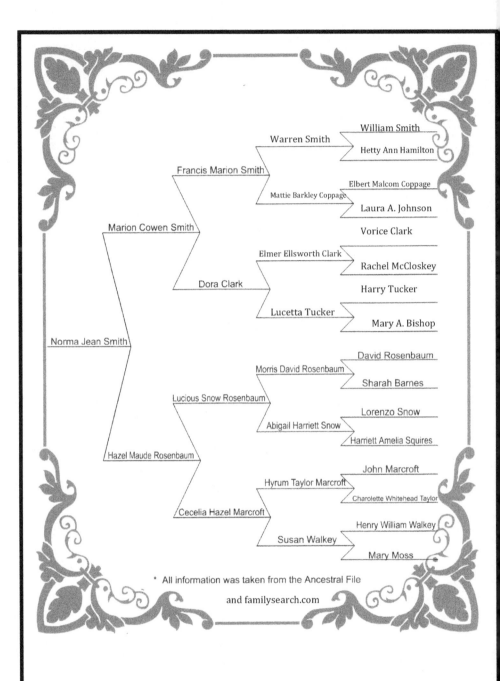

Norma Jean Smith

Marion Cowen Smith

Francis Marion Smith

Warren Smith
- William Smith
- Hetty Ann Hamilton

Mattie Barkley Coppage
- Elbert Malcom Coppage
- Laura A. Johnson

Dora Clark

Vorice Clark

Elmer Ellsworth Clark
- Rachel McCloskey

Lucetta Tucker
- Harry Tucker
- Mary A. Bishop

Hazel Maude Rosenbaum

Lucious Snow Rosenbaum

Morris David Rosenbaum
- David Rosenbaum
- Sharah Barnes

Abigail Harriett Snow
- Lorenzo Snow
- Harriett Amelia Squires

Cecelia Hazel Marcroft

Hyrum Taylor Marcroft
- John Marcroft
- Charolette Whitehead Taylor

Susan Walkey
- Henry William Walkey
- Mary Moss

* All information was taken from the Ancestral File
and familysearch.com

4

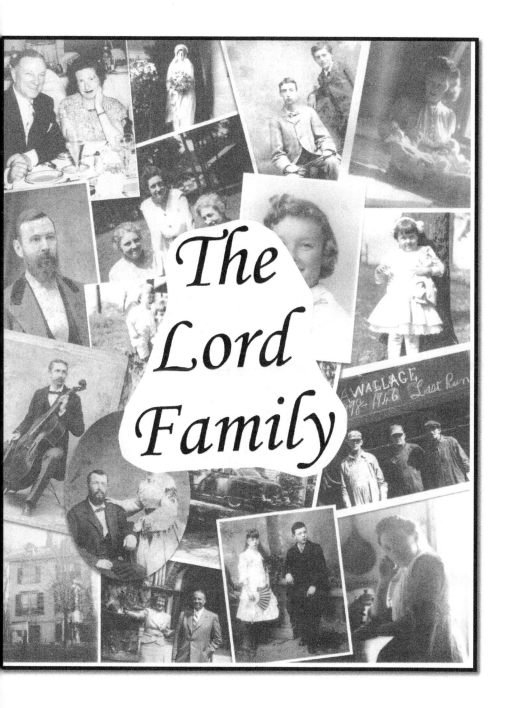

The Lord Family

Ralph & Norma Lord

Hazel & Jose Martinez, Blanche & Walter Lord, Derek Short,
Ralph & Norma,
Elaine Williams, Tommie Lou Geis, Dixie Duncombe, Teresa Martinez

I NEED YOU NOW

This night I want you more my love... Than you will ever know ...
Not just because of circumstance ... Or how the wind may blow ...
Not just because of promises ... That you and I have made ...
Or any thing that might disturb ... Or make our hearts afraid ...
But because it is the time ... I want to be with you ...
When no one else upon this earth ... Can do the things you do ...
I need the comfort of your arms ... The laughter on your lips ...
And all the courage of the men ... Who brave the sea in ships ...
I want you more, I need you more than time and destiny ....
Because you are the only one ... Who means so much to me.

(Poem given to Norma by Ralph)

Ralph Knowles Lord

Father: Walter Lord
Mother: Blanche Rebecca Stark
Born: 12 April 1937
Place: Salt Lake City, Utah, USA
Married: 31 August 1956 to Norma Jean Smith
Place: Salt Lake City, Utah, USA
Died: 1 December 2006
Place: Sandy, Utah, USA

THE UNITED STATES POSTAL SERVICE

presents this certificate to

RALPH LORD

in grateful appreciation for your years of service

Thank you for your dedication

Anthony m. Frank

Postmaster General

U.S. Postal Service

20th

Anniversary

1971-1991

The Post Office Band

The Swanee Singers

Salt Lake
Mormon Tabernacle Choir

*On the Sea of Galilee
Israel Concert Tour 1993
At the Jerusalem Center*

Bicentennial Service
THE CHURCH OF JESUS CHRIST OF LATTER-DAY SAINTS

*July 4, 1976
Washington, D.C.*

Washington D.C. Concert Tour 1995

1st Concert Tour in which Ralph performed

12

You Oral History of Ralph Knowles Lord

Interviewee: Ralph Knowles Lord
Interviewer: Tewie Jane Lord
(Interview conducted 10/19&20/2001)

Q: When were you born and where?

A: I was born on April 12, 1937 at the St. Marks Hospital on Beck Street in Salt Lake City, UT. Delivered by Dr. Woolsey who also delivered my lovely wife when she was born. Coincidence – or maybe not such a coincidence.

Q: What were the family circumstances when you were born?

A: I don't remember I was too young. My dad was a fireman on the railroad. The railroad cut back and he got laid off. He was just working for the CCC, which was a makeshift organization of the government to keep adults employed in something and earn some money to take care of their family during the Depression Era. My mother was having babies – being a mother – she didn't work. She went to work during the war, but this was 1937 – before the war.

Q: Where did your family live first? Where did they move after?

A: We lived in a duplex on Simondi Avenue in Salt Lake City, UT. We were in one half of the duplex and my Grandma Lord and Aunt Edith were in the other half. We were on the East side and they were on the West side. That was when I was about 3 years old. Then we moved over to 9th west – right across from the Fair Grounds parking lot. We lived in a house behind a house. We stayed there about 1-½ years until we bought a home over on 10th West. That's where I grew up. I was just about 5 years old and I started Kindergarten that Fall.

Q: Do you have any preschool memories?

A: The youngest memory I ever had was of somebody getting out of a taxicab. My mother said, "That's your father." He came over to give me a hug and I cried and ran to my mother. I didn't know him because he had just come back from Washington D.C. where he had worked for a year. I was 2 and 3 years old when he returned. Here's this guy that said, "I'm your dad." I thought, "You ain't my dad. I don't know who my dad is." I remember when I was four years old, kitty-corner to our home was our garage and there was a field on the side of that garage in which kids would play baseball. I was standing out in the parking area out in front of my house. A kid hit a fly ball and it hit me on the head. I don't remember if I was knocked out I just remember getting hit with a fly ball.

13

Q: What memories do you have of your grade school years?

A: My very favorite teacher was Mr. Ames. He was my 6th grade teacher. We only had one teacher in each grade and they taught everything. He was fun. Mrs. Pickell was the principal and we used to call her "Mrs. Pickle" behind her back, of course. In 5th and 6th grade we played soccer. We played a little baseball and basketball, but soccer was the main sport. I played marbles. I remember walking around and watching the girls playing hopscotch and jump the rope.

Q: What memories do you have of your high school years?

A: I loved biology. I liked a girl in there (Norma). I really impressed her by dumping ink all over the teacher's permanent notes. I tried to daub them up and then I decided not to so I left a lot of it. Then the teacher come in and asked, "What happened here? Who did this?" I had to impress somebody so I said, "I did it." So I was in the doghouse for a whole year. Math was my favorite. I was the President of the Roller-Skating Club but I didn't attend that often because I was in Track also and they didn't want us to do anything like roller-skating or dancing where you move your feet forward and backwards. They didn't want runners to build up their stopping muscles only their going forward muscles. In track I ran the half mile, threw the javelin and in my senior year I broad jumped. I ran a half-mile in a medley relay down at BYU and we took first place and got a trophy – I got my name on a trophy. We went up to Idaho State University in the fall and I took 4th place in the mile. I had never run a mile before. I went to the awards banquet because I was taking 1st or 2nd or 3rd place my senior years whether it was in running, the javelin or the broad jump. I was a skunk in an assembly. It was a pep rally. Spankey Dixon was the name of the coach at South High School. We were going to play them in basketball or football or something. The pep rally was about the South high basketball team and maybe we were going to "skunk" them. I started playing the flute in the 7th grade and played it through the 12th grade. I was in the marching band 3 years in high school. We marched around the city.

Q: What special lesson and music did you have?

A: I didn't have any flute lessons until I was a senior in high school. I didn't have a flute of my own until I was a senior in high school. My mom and dad purchased it for me. I was allegedly making payments on it when I was first married. They gave me 10 free lessons with a flute player with the Utah Symphony. I took one lesson and didn't go again. I gave up the other nine. I just didn't want to go. That was so stupid. They were expensive and I gave up free lessons. I started taking piano lessons when I was 7 years old from Mrs. Winkler. I took lessons until I was 14. I got past her capabilities and got bored with the lessons. I started piano lessons again after I was married. My teacher was Mrs. Beck who was a good pianist in her day, but she had arthritis. She would try to show me certain things on the piano and it was very hard for her. I'd take lessons and I wouldn't practice until I finally quit. When I quit I would play every day on the piano. It was funny because I would start taking lessons and stop playing and then quit again and start playing on my own. That went on for about 3 years. The pieces I currently play I learned on my own. I learned enough from these teachers that I could pick it up.

Q: What kind of pets did you have as a child?
A: When I was a little kid I had a dog named Duffy. She was a cocker spaniel. She followed my Aunt Shirley home and she didn't know where she picked the dog up at so she couldn't take her back and she didn't want to keep her. I think she was living at home with my grandma and grandpa. So she asked my mother if we wanted it. She said, "Sure." That was my first dog. She had a lot of puppies. One of the puppies we kept and called her Taffy. Now we had two cocker spaniels. We also raised rabbits and chickens. We ate them for Sunday dinner. A little later I got some pigeons. When we got poor enough that we couldn't afford any feed I let some of them go and some of them I killed and ate. These were my pets. I was 16. It was kind of traumatic. I didn't know what else to do. My mother raised canaries to sell them to people.

Q: Who were some of the special friends you had during your early years?
A: I had some special friends who turned out to be not good friends. Some of the kids I ran around with turned out to be "hoodlums." I thought they were o.k. We had fun. When I was finally realized what was happening we were swimming in the Jordan River. We took off our clothes and dived in the water to go swimming. While I was down swimming the kids went through my pants and took my money. I confronted them and nobody would admit anything. Another time we went over to the fair grounds. We always went over to the fair grounds for the rodeos, circus' and state fair. They talked me in to riding my bicycle over. My mother didn't want me to ride my bicycle over there. But I wanted to because the other kids were doing it. It was a brand new bike. I rode it over to the fire station near the tennis courts there and put it in the brush. I went into the fair grounds and when I came out it was gone. I know those kids stole it. That was kind-of the turning point. I finally understood that those kids were not my friends. There were some other friends that I had: David Lindsey and Don Kvachik were good friends. We would go up town, walk up to the capital on a Saturday and also played ball. We "hung-out."

Q: When you were young did you have any medical or dental problems?
A: No. I don't remember going to the dentist all that often. There was an Army dentist that was cheap. We would go to him. I knocked my tooth out in a head on collision on Foothill Drive and Sunnyside with a 15-year-old kid who turned in front of me. This is when I was first married, before Mike was born. I went to this dentist and he put in a false tooth.

15

Q: Did you have to pass through any major epidemics?
A: Polio. We didn't get it. My sister (Dianne) got encephalitis. She was quarantined down at the County Hospital for a couple of weeks.

Q: What childhood fads do you remember?
A: We used to go to the Saturday movies at the Utah Theatre. I remember the serials. They were like a TV show – a sitcom – where it ends one week and begins again the next week at the point where it ended. It was an adventure show – Flash Gordon or Tarzan – they'd show you a half hour of it and continue next Saturday. I'd go there almost every Saturday. They had a spelling bee every Saturday too. I never did enter it but I probably could've won something because I was a very good speller. They'd have the Spelling Bee first and a little program, a little cartoon, the serial movie and then the main movie would come after that.

Q: What kind of pranks or humorous experiences do you remember as a child?
A: I hate to admit this, but when I was a kid we went mud balling. We'd all get a mud-ball, throw it at the door of a house and run like heck. This one guy came out after us. We went running through the backyards of houses. He never caught us. I don't think we did it more than maybe a couple times.

Q: What kind of jobs/chores did you do as a child?
A: Growing up my chores were to do the dishes every other night. On Saturday the kitchen floor was my responsibility. It was a little tiny kitchen. Those were my responsibilities. During the summer's between 8th and 9th grade and 9th and 10th grade, I worked at two different schools – cleaning the schools. We cleaned one school each year. One year I was working alone with the janitor and the next year there were two of us boys working with the janitor. We would oil the desks, clean and oil the floors and wash the windows and then we'd close the door. That room was finished – nobody went in there – because it was ready for the school year. We'd methodically go through the whole school and clean. I did that for two years. In high school I worked in a service station out on Beck Street. I pumped gas and filled propane tanks. My dad worked out at a drive-in movie theater out at the airport (that is no longer there). When he needed extra help I'd go out and help. I'd sell tickets and at intermission I'd work in the booth selling food.

Q: What vacations did you go on that you remember?
A: Our annual trek was up to the Spruces up Big Cottonwood Canyon. We'd go up there as a family and camp out in a camp slot. We'd spend about 5 days up there. Everybody would sleep in one tent. There were 8 of us. That was our annual trek. When I got a little older we went up to Idaho with the Swanee Singers. We decided to take a little side trip to find the farm that my dad worked on up in Idaho and met the people. I don't remember where it was or the people's names I was 15 or 16. That was a nice trip. I got in a fight with my brother (Phil). He'd hit me and I wouldn't want to hit

him back because I'd hurt him. I think we went to Bryce Canyon and Zion's Canyon and Kiabab Forest as a kid. I don't remember a whole lot about it. I just remember us going before we were married.

Q: What were your religious activities?

A: I was baptized into the Church of Jesus Christ or Latter-Day Saints when I was 8 years old. My brother Phil was baptized at 10 years old and he was baptized on the same day. He was afraid or something. He waited until I was baptized. We always went to church. There were no "ifs," "ands," or "buts" about it. Sunday we got dressed and we went to church. Mom didn't have to say, "Come on now get ready." We all knew that Sunday we went to church. It was just a standard thing. I think I was Secretary in the Primary and Deacons Quorum. I was also a Block Teacher (Home Teacher). That was when a kid went with an adult. It was strange because when I was about 12 years old they split the ward right down the middle of our street. They put my family in another ward and I didn't want to go. So I still went to the 29th ward. I was home teaching with a partner from that ward. I still went to all the activities of my old ward. What made me change though was when basketball season came around they wouldn't let me play for my old ward. I had to play for my own ward. I had to go to my own ward to play basketball. I got to know them better. I remember my deacon's quorum teacher had just come back off his mission (Spanish speaking). He gave everyone a card with the Articles of Faith in Spanish if we could memorize the first article of faith in Spanish. And I did: "Nosotros creemos en Dios el Padre Eterno y en su hijo Jesus Cristo y en El Espiritu Santos, Amen." I guess he influenced me. I don't remember any other except some bishops. I had some really good bishops but I don't remember anything about them. I wasn't one who was really gung-ho spiritually. I went to church for friends, for basketball and softball.

Q: Do you have any spiritual experiences that you'd like to share?

A: I saw a couple of spirits. It chokes me up when I talk about it. When I was maybe 8 or 10 we were watching an air show at airport #2. These two guys in this plane were doing loop-the-loops and they came a little too far and couldn't pull out and slammed straight into the ground. This was probably about two or three blocks away. Our car was right straight through the field and we could see them. We could see where they crashed. And I saw the two guys walk away from it. Everyone was running over there to it. There were these real low fences around this great big field. Not the security that they have now. I remember running over to it and I heard people talking and they said, "They both got killed." I said, "No, they couldn't be killed. I saw them. I saw them walk away." I did. Two guys in white – two people walked away from that airplane. Yet when we got there they were not there.

Another spiritual experience was when I went duck hunting. I was with about 4 or 5 other guys. We were 16 or 17. We went up to Farmington Bay area. We went hiking way out to the end of the bay along a ditch. We finally got around to the other side of it and it got dark. We didn't know where we were and we didn't know how to get back. We were going to try to retrace our steps because this ditch with water in it (it was about 30 feet across) was in our way. We didn't know how far we had to walk to get around it. We were going to wade across the water. We were going to take our pants off and wade across and put them back on again. That didn't sound too well. We were Priests – so we knelt down and prayed to find our way back. Just as we ended the prayer and stood up the lights came on in the parking lot about ½ mile away. We thought that if we stay on this side of the ditch bank there has to be a bridge across somewhere along the way. And it happened that way. We just kept heading toward the light and there happened to be a bridge and we got across.

When I used to visit mom before we were married, it got to be late and instead of walking home I'd hop a train. I'd catch onto a train at 8th South and get off at North Temple. This one time when I hopped a train for some reason it started speeding up. I didn't realize that it was speeding up until it was time to get off. I jumped off and started tumbling toward the tracks – I was going to get run over if I didn't do something. Something in my mind told me to, "Spread out." So I spread out my arms and legs and stopped tumbling. I got up and got home. Otherwise I would've lost an arm or leg, head or torso.

Q: What kind of association did you have with your brothers and sisters?
A: My oldest was Dave. He is 8 years older than me. He was born in 1929. I don't remember much association. I was so young. All of us brothers were avid hunters. We'd go hunting together sometimes. Dave, Jim and Phil played softball for the ward and city/county teams. I remember them playing ball and once in a while throwing the ball with them. We were all pitchers. One time Dave and Jim wanted me to fight a boy next door. They were egging me on, "Come on, Ralph. Hit him." Just to have a fight. All my brothers and I would go over to the fair grounds and throw rocks at the windows. We broke some and would come running home.

Elaine played the violin. I don't know that she took lessons. My mom probably taught her. She also played the piano.

Jim played basketball. He played the trombone. He was in the ROTC band. He also sang. He was in all the assemblies and operettas in high school.

Phil played softball. He also picked up playing the guitar, as he got older. I had the closest association with Phil. He is 1 year 11 months and 3 weeks older than me.

Diane played the piano and she also played the cello. Diane was 6 years younger than me and had her own friends down the street.

My siblings ignored me for the most part – except Phil because I had to sleep in the same bed with him.

Q: How would you describe yourself as a child?
A: I was quiet … timid. I wasn't a real outgoing person. Which I still am.

Q: What was the child rearing philosophy of your parents?
A: My dad was kind of a quiet person. He didn't discipline at all. My mom did all the discipline, which she sometimes did with the wire handle of the fly swatter on my arms. I remember one time I didn't want to do the dishes, it got late … I didn't want to do them. She hit me several times. I finally did them. I had to do my chores on Saturday but I don't remember any specific rules. They didn't sit us down and tell us the rules it was just a courtesy that we followed.

Q: How would you describe the neighborhood you grew up in?
A: When our house was built, there was a field across the street. We used to play over there. We'd dig out the foxholes and pull up this "cheat" grass (a thicker blade grass that had seeds like wheat that would stick in your stockings) that had a big glob of dirt on it. That would be our "bomb". And we'd heave it over at the other guys and they'd get covered with dirt. I was probably 10 years old. When the houses came our field was gone. Everybody stayed pretty much to themselves. I chased with a kid named Doug.

Q: What were the difficulties faced by your family?
A: We never had a lot of money. We never had a good car. The first car I remember we had was a '34 Pontiac or something. Another car we had we bought from Mr. Winkler (husband of my piano teacher). It was a '38 something. Then we bought a '41 Pontiac that burned as much oil as it did gas. You didn't put gas in it you put in oil. "Give me two gallons of oil and check the gas." We lived on my dad's postal wages. Which weren't the best, but we got by. He got a job, through a senator, with the Bureau of Mines as a night watchman, but it was in Washington D.C. That was when he had to leave and I was probably 2 years old. So when he came back after that year (I was about 3) that's when I didn't know him and I cried. He got transferred back to Salt Lake City working for the Bureau of Mines up on the University of Utah campus. From there he took the test to get into the Post Office. He started working for the Post Office in 1940. He stayed there until he was 66 years old (1964). I'd been at the Post Office for 8 years. Once in a while I'd work with him. I was clerking then I went over to the carrying side. He delivered parcel post for a long time. Finally he got a job in the business area. That was a good job – you'd have a big glob of mail for bigger businesses. When I was substituting I'd get a job for a day and we'd be in the same area. Not side-by-side but real close.

19

When my sister got encephalitis that's the only time my family prayed together other than Sunday dinner. We didn't pray together. We didn't study the Gospel together. We didn't have Family Home Evening. We'd listen to conference. We'd go up to conference. I saw my favorite prophet, Pres. George Albert Smith. He was the prophet when I started understanding the Gospel. At that point he was my favorite. I remember going up to the tabernacle and watching conference as a family. That's when there weren't a whole lot of people going to conference.

My mom worked at the Arm's Plant during World War II. That's the way she got extra money. She would pack parachutes and put bullets in the belts, etc. The men were in the war and the women had to go to work. The Arm's Plant was at 17th South and Redwood Road. She worked there a couple of years to contribute to the war effort. Then she would work at ZCMI during Christmas. During the war I also remember the rations. We had a coupon book we got in the mail and you couldn't buy anything without a coupon. If you needed a quart of milk or a gallon of gas, sugar, flour you needed to present a coupon. You couldn't find any grease. When we'd cook meat we'd save the grease and give it to the war effort. They would collect it at school. We also brought cans to school – for the metal. You couldn't get rubber. My mom, aunt and my grandma would trade coupons back and forth if they needed a certain item. That must've been a very expensive program. They had to know the size of your family so they would know how many coupons to send you.

Q: Did you ever serve time in the military?
A: I just about did. I went to sign up but the sergeant wasn't there that night. I was going to join the Military Police. I was probably a senior in high school. There were 3 or 4 of us that went up to the National Guard Armory next to the University of Utah campus. They lost out on some recruits because he wasn't there.

Q: Did you go to college or technical school?
A: I took some classes before I was married. I took them because I was supposed to. I didn't do any more. After I was married I took some Math, a Physics and Psychology classes. I took some computer classes for my work. I took a class on the IBM 1401 at Mountain Fuel Supply. It was a card reader machine. We had to write a program and keypunch it and run it through the computer. Later on I took some more computer classes through the Post Office at the Trade Tech (Salt Lake Community College). I took an H&R block class and if we scored so high on their final test they would offer a job to us in one of their facilities in the valley. I did a lot of classes through the Post Office. I went back East to Washington D.C. and to Denver, CO, Norman, OK and San Francisco, CA for some management type classes.

Q: What vocations or careers have you had?

A: When I got out of high school I worked for Western Rock Bit Corp. I worked
for them for about a year. We hardened the mining drill bits. My job was
after the bits had been heated up in an oven they were put on a conveyor
belt that had water running over it, which tempered the ends of the bit so
they could drill into the ground. In the meantime I applied for the Post
Office. I took the test. I got hired on July 14, 1956. I got married August 31,
1956. I had a permanent job when I got married. I worked there until 1992
– for 36 years. I did everything there was to do in the Post office. I was a
carrier, a clerk, a Postmaster up in Heber City. I worked in the Registry
Section, which handled millions of dollars everyday. I was in the Opening
Section. I was in the Transport Section. I'd take the money down to the
RPO, which was the railway train, when I was in the Registry Section. I'd
take a 38 pistol with me because I had millions of dollars with me. Since the
train wasn't there yet sometimes, I'd lay in the middle of these pouches of
mail and go to sleep. I wouldn't do that now, but back then nobody did
anything. I worked in Accounting, Window Section and Box Mail Section
(post office boxes). When they first started the electronic weighing of mail I
was one of the first people who started that. I went from there into
Management in 1970. I was the Supervisor at the Airmail Field. I was the
Supervisor of the Out-going Section on the owl shift. Then from there I was
picked to be an Auditor in 1972. There were only two auditors in the whole
Salt Lake office – Bill Oblad and myself. We spent a couple of years just
auditing our stations and branches. Then they expanded the program to
post offices – the outlying offices. About that time Bill Oblad retired so they
picked 4 auditors. I was picked to be the Senior Auditor over that group. I
had a contingency of 5 auditors. We went around to different offices. About
3 years later, in 1975, the Office of Manager Mailing Requirements and
Mailing Classification opened up. I bid on that job and got that job. All
these are steps up. I managed the mailing requirements, which is part of
the bulk mail unit, which is where you handle all the advertising mail (junk
mail). Plus the front office where we took care of all the permits to mail and
all the meter settings, permits for postal meters, claims sections and
passports. All that was under my jurisdictions. After that I wanted to know
something about the Budget Office, so I transferred into the Budget Office. I
stayed there a couple of years. I didn't like the guesswork of the Budget
Office. I like hard facts. Things I can see and I know. One of the auditors'
positions opened up again. I went to do auditing again. I had 2 guys under
me. One went down to Accounting and the other went out as a Postmaster.
I was instrumental in getting one of the guys, that used to be in the Bulk
Mailing Unit, into one of the auditing positions. All he did was 2nd class mail
and I wanted him to help on audits out in the field. He went out a couple of
times with us to do audits on 2nd class mail. He finally got a job as an
auditor. We kind of hung together and did stuff together as auditors. That
is it and I retired in 1992. My favorite job was as an Auditor. I like
numbers. I can see numbers. I can do numbers. I know this stuff
backwards and forwards. As Mailing Requirements Manager I had to teach

21

clerks how to accept mail and how to verify. If somebody comes in with a sack of mail and you say, "How much you got there?" "Well, I don't know." Well, we have to compute how many pieces there are based on a sample of how many pieces there are in a pound. Then we'd weight the whole thing and we could fairly accurately compute how many pieces there are. I trained a lot of Postmasters and a lot of clerks. I went to Denver, CO to the Regional Mailing Requirements Office – this was for the whole Western United States. I sat with those guys and helped create a training program. Then we went out into the field and did this training. I was training people in Montana, Idaho, Utah and Elko, Nevada. I liked training. If I had to pick one job and stick with it, it would be auditing. I'd make headaches for other people. I just want to tell you on record that I taught a class down at Southern Utah State University. I'm not a professor but I taught a class. It was on Postal Acceptance of Bulk Mail. It was on campus and we got a room free and it was a select group of people. But I can always say that I taught at Southern Utah State. I also went to school at Oklahoma University for 3 weeks for postal classes.

Q: What was the affect of your job on your family?
A: Kind of mixed. I was gone away from home a lot, when I was doing audits. I'd travel up into Idaho and I couldn't come home at night. Once I was there I'd spend a whole week. I would head out Monday and come home Friday. I wouldn't do that every week. I'd try to go out a week and be home 2 or 3 week before I'd go again. Valerie talked about me being gone a lot of the time and Clint talked about going with me on my trips. Part of the auditing job was swearing in new Postmasters. Transferring offices from an out-going Postmaster to an in-coming Postmaster. So we'd have to audit the whole office and making sure everything was there and the Postmaster hadn't absconded with anything, including property. I'd have to count everything and the new Postmaster coming in would have to accept all this. Then I'd have to physically swear him in. Just like you see on TV when they swear the President of the Untied States in – it's the very same oath of office. The only change, I'd swear him in as Postmaster of _____ instead of President of the United States of America. Very same dialogue. When I did transfers of postmasters I took what kids I could take. (Valerie speaking) I remember it being fun when you were out of town. Not that you were gone, but that we did things differently. We had faster food. We would sleep with mom. We might stay up and watch a movie. That's a child's view. It was almost like a vacation.

Q: What memories of courting and marrying?
A: I met my future wife in biology the first day of class in 1952. I really impressed her by spilling ink on the instructor's permanent notes and not cleaning them off. I saw her all during the year. We had one class together. I didn't have a date with her the whole year. One summer a couple of guys from the band and myself – there were 4 of us – we were just hanging out and talking together and one of the guys said, "Let's go pick up some girls."

I said, "O.k." I didn't know who I was going to get. They already knew, because they'd been dating and I hadn't. I called Norma and said, "Hi. Would you like to go for a ride?" She said, "Yea." So there are four boys and four girls and one car. Eight people in the car. I didn't know what was going on, we were just riding around. Then these guys drove up to what we called "Passion Flats." We were in the back seat and Pete Marthakis and his girl in the front started necking. I thought, "That's interesting." Mom says, "Let's go for a walk." So we got out and went for a walk. That's all we did. I called her the next week for a date. She said, "No, I'm busy." Next week, "I'm busy." Called her a couple weeks after that ..., "I'm busy." So I thought, "That's the end of that." All of my junior year I didn't even see her at all. In my senior year I was still kind-of interested in her. I had a good friend who was a flute player in the orchestra and I was in the band as a flute player. They would need an extra flute player in the orchestra or in the band and we would get together occasionally and got to know each other fairly well. Our senior year I thought I'd transfer into orchestra and at the same time he decided to transfer into band. We got together one time and he said, "Why don't we double date?" There was only one girl I really liked so I called her up in October and said, "How would you like to go to a movie with me?" She said, "Yea." (Gulp) We went to the Center Theatre and saw a good classic show. From that time on we dated. I asked her to go steady with me and she said, "Yea, I'll go steady with you, but I've got a date for New Year's Eve." Going steady means that you exclusively only date that other person. A person is asked, "Would you like to go steady?" After that we went steady 'til the end of the school year. On graduation night I took her over the state line – it used to be a law that it was illegal to take a minor over the state line. We went to the State Line Casino in Wendover, NV and had a drink of soda or something. We dated through June to the next January or February and I bought a car. Well mom's girlfriends were all getting rings. When I bought that Buick she was hopping to get a ring like all her girlfriends were getting and she thought she wasn't getting one because I had bought a car (with 300 dollars she had lent me) instead. On April Fool's Day which also happened to be Easter, I took her up to "This Is The Place Monument". We were going to Sunrise Services up at the Capitol, but it was cancelled due to a snowstorm. So, up at "This Is The Place Monument" on April Fool's Day I popped the question to her. We had an understanding that we were already going to get married, but here I popped the question and gave her her ring at about 7 o'clock in the morning. She grabbed it. I put it on her finger and she wouldn't take it off. We've been married for 45 years plus.

Q: Your children?

A: Michael Lord – my 1st born boy was a joy. "I got a boy! I got a boy! I got a boy!" He was a very happy outgoing person. He never stopped. He was a constant mover. I don't know that he ever stopped until he was actually in his crib sleeping. He grew up that way. He was always a mover. He started walking at 7 ½ months. He liked mountain climbing. We bought him a mountain climbing rope as his graduation present from high school. He was one of the first people who repelled down the side of Hillcrest High School gymnasium wall. There were about 4 or 5 kids who repelled down the wall. He was the first one down and didn't get in trouble. He was also in a photography class. He like photography. He bought a nice 35mm camera and did a lot of photography work. He studied the piano and he got to be a pretty good piano player. He could sing well and he's got a good voice. He also played the drums. He had a little band group – a couple of kids played the guitars and he played the drums. They never did go out they would just play downstairs. In 1979 – 80 he went to the Sydney, Australia mission. He came back in November and married the next May. He ran around with a group of kids – good LDS kids. Everyone had a date for a dance and he didn't. He was trying to figure out what to do. This girl (Debbie) was part of the group and Mike said, "Debbie, do you have a date for the dance?" – just off hand. She said, "Sure I'll go with you." He said he went on that date and things just clicked. They didn't see each other anymore as just friends. When he was getting close to the time when he would go on his mission he didn't want to leave a girl. He didn't know how to break off with Debbie. He kind of broke off with Debbie and started going with this girl up in Logan. Her name was Karen. (Mom speaking) What happened before he left was he went up to Rick's College, where Debbie was, and he came back and said, "You know, I still have feelings for her." Before he left on his mission he broke up with Karen. They were both at the farewell. He had broken up with Karen and he knew Debbie was it, but he didn't want to leave her as a girlfriend – he wanted her to be able to date. (Dad) Then when he went on his mission, he only wrote to Debbie as a brother, using words like, "Sincerely" instead of "Love." (Mom) What happened was she came to me and said, "I don't know whether to go to the airport or not. He hasn't asked me to come." So I wrote him a letter and asked him if she should come and he said, "Well, sure. What's the question?" In his mind he was going to marry her but he never let Debbie in on the secret. (Dad) When they got home they just picked up where they left off. It was love. They have 6 six children. We went deer, pheasant and duck hunting together. This is what fathers and sons do. I ordained him to the Aaronic and Melchezedeck priesthood through all the positions. That was neat for me. Here's my son progressing in the Gospel.

Valerie Anne Lord that was what she was named. That wasn't the name when she was born. She didn't have a name. (Mom) Nobody has a name when they're born. (Dad) Anyway, she was our pride and joy because "first daughter". Now I have a boy and I have a girl. I have one of everything. So we were very very excited about her. She was just the opposite of Mike. She was such a docile sweet little girl. Didn't go anywhere. She would play for hours just sitting in one spot. She walked at 13 months. She wasn't interested in going anywhere. I wanted my girls to wear what they're supposed to wear and that's dresses. She is a girl – she wears dresses. She wore dresses all growing up – until everyone started wearing pants. Valerie was a very sweet girl until she hit 11 ½ -- 12 years old. Very very difficult time. From then on she was very hard to get along with. Just like a teenager she didn't understand her parents. She thought we were old fashioned or we didn't know what we were talking about. I tried to have a heart to heart talk with her once in a while and she didn't seem to want to. She is a very sweet girl right now. She also took piano lessons and she was our best sight-reader. She played the clarinet. She took one year of orchestra or school band and a few piano lessons. Another one of her talents is art. She used to draw. I don't remember her doing any singing. Here again she has a nice voice. She's sung with the family in different things. She played a lot of solitaire. She liked being alone. Her bedroom is now the toy room and she'd shut the door and just be in there alone. She was a very smart girl and she was in the International Club in high school. Once a month they'd meet and have food from a different countries and talk about that country. Valerie met Saeed at a dance. There was a "French" kid that met her girlfriend at the dance. Here's this guy from another culture. I told Valerie, "Everything is different than America ... da, da, da, da ..." "Well, we're only friends. There's nothing serious between us. We're just friends. We're going to the dance again next week." Then she said, "Oh, we're getting married." What could we do. They're getting married. So, I started planning a reception. We were talking with her, "We don't have a lot of money to go to a reception center so let's just fix up our back yard." So we started talking about what we could do to fix up our back yard. In the middle of the plans The Choir went to Japan for 3 weeks. When we came back Valerie says, "We got married." She got married while we were gone because Valerie didn't want to have a reception. So she figured I was going to insist on a reception so to settle the problem she got married. I felt a little disappointed because I wanted to at least be at her wedding. I've accepted it. It's in the past now. (Mom – talking about telling dad that they were engaged) I got out of the shower and there was a note on my pillow and it said, "Saeed and I are engaged." I shut the door and knelt down because I thought, "Oh, I don't want to say anything." Because in my experience with my mother-in-law I didn't want to do the same thing. Ralph was at Choir. I took the note to church and when they started passing Sacrament I handed Ralph the note. Ralph's face went red. He didn't say a word. That's how he found out. It gave him a while to calm down before he said something he'd regret. (Dad) What could I say during the Sacrament Service. They've been happily married for 19 years and have 3 lovely children.

Nolana Jean Rice – when she was born I was kind of hoping for a boy. So it would be boy, girl, boy, girl ... Well, I got a girl. "Well, that's o.k." I like girls too. I've got two girls and a boy. She was boy-crazy when she was growing up. When she was little she was probably in the middle of Valerie and Mike – she was active but not as active as Mike. She loved being in charge. She liked to act even when she was a little child. All the kids would get up on the fireplace – that was their stage. Valerie instigated it. They would get up and do their little acts occasionally. She was fun. She wanted lots of friends.

She also played the piano, but she didn't get as far as the other two kids did. She also was talented at writing poems. She used to write all kinds of poems. In high school and Snow College she was in drama and in all kinds of plays. In Snow College the drama team put on this presentation to the local schools. That was real exciting for her. She loved to do that. Nolana wanted to get away from the house. She wanted to be her own boss. After she graduated from school, she and a friend or several friends would get an apartment. Then something would happen where they'd have to leave the apartments. Then she'd come home for a while and eventually get a group again and go out and rent an apartment and get away. She did this several times. We'd make accommodations. One time we had a kid in each bedroom and she came home. We strung a wire from wall to wall downstairs and put up a piece of polyester material. That was her bedroom and she liked it. She went to Snow College and met a boy (Dave) she was crazy about. They were thinking of getting married. Finally, I think he broke it off. (Mom) What happened there was another kid she really had a crush on in high school. She came home. They were going to get married. I had bought the material for the bride's maid dress. She came home and said, "I just had to make sure. I think I'm in love with him." I guess she went out with him and it didn't work out, but she told Dave she wasn't sure if she wanted to get married. Once she'd said that, he went to another girl for consolation and by the time she'd gone back he was already involved with this other girl. It broke her heart, but she broke his heart too. (Dad) Then she left Snow College and come back home again. Then she just went up to institute to sing with the Institute Choir. Stuart Rice was also singing in the Institute Choir. They are married and have a lovely daughter.

Charlinn also was born at a very young age. She did have a major problem when she was born. She had a cleft lip and cleft palate. When I first saw her I just swore that I was going to get the best doctor in the world for her and we did. Dr. Broadbent was the best doctor in the West. We took her to him. Between him and his associate, Dr. Wolfe, they fixed her up. Maybe that's why I've always felt like I've had to protect her. She had about 17 surgeries in her life. About 10 in her first year. She took some piano lesson but they didn't seem to work. Piano just wasn't her thing. In elementary the kids had to run around the school for some reason. She always came in first place. She always beat everybody in running around the school. Charlinn did drama probably because her sister did it. Her sister encouraged her to get into drama. Because they didn't do a final surgery on her lip or nose until she was a senior in high school, that contributed to her being shy and being in drama helped push her to be more outgoing. In high school during her sophmore and junior years she ran track. She ran the ½ mile, just like her dad did. She was good. She ran the crosscountry in the Fall and track in the Spring. When she did a regional track meet, she took first place and broke the record for the ½ mile run. She had the record for the ½ mile for several years until it was broken again. That was one of her accomplishments. She didn't do anything in State in her junior year. In her

26

senior year she decided not to run again because she didn't want to maybe be worse than she was in her junior year. She thought that she'd hit her peak. She didn't even run. But that was her choice. After high school she went to Snow College. She and Nolana were down there about the same time. They were in the plays. A kid named Dick Aagard was also in one of the same plays that Charlinn was in. That's how they met. They just started talking and things started getting kind of serious and I don't know why Charlinn worried about it but, Charlinn came home. She quit Snow and came home. She didn't want to get serious because he was getting ready to go on a mission. She came home and they still wrote and phoned. He went on his mission. In the meantime she was 21 and said, "I want to go on a mission too." She went to the Seattle, Washington Mission. She got home before he got home. It worked out perfectly. That really helped her be more outgoing. Her nose was tucked down all during school and I guess the kids made fun of her. When they did the final surgery, they fixed the nose really good and she was a really pretty girl. I think that helped her a whole lot her senior year. I'm sure she got a lot of comments because she wasn't a really pretty girl because of her problem. She took a lot.

Clint – When he was born, "Finally got another boy – Hurray!" He was a rambunctious kid. He didn't run around as much as Mike. He wasn't as dare-devil as Mike. Clint – he wanted to know everything about something before he did it – everything. "What's going to be the result, before I do this?" He was a very very cautious child all the way growing up. He was just the opposite of Mike in that area. He did a lot of things and tried to see what the results were. He wasn't afraid of do something after he understood it. At age 7, I had a good friend in the budget office and I was in Mailing Requirements, and he was a "computer geek". I was down in San Diego for three weeks and I bought my first computer. I called my friend on the phone to make sure it was a good computer and he said, "If you want a good computer, that's a good computer." When I brought it home I set it up and learned how to do it and Clint was interested. So, I taught him how to program one or two lines of words. It was a start and he loved to sit there and do all this. It wasn't a very big computer. That was his introduction to computers. I had a computer at work. Sometimes I'd bring my laptop home. I'd bring my laptop on my audits with me. I would let him play around with it. I had to transmit some data occasionally, so I'd hook it into a telephone line and transmit from my little laptop. I showed him how to do that. He played around with the computer. I'd take him to work once in a while and he's play around with the office machines while I was doing some work there. I introduced him to the different office machines – the typewriter and the copying machine. We introduced him to the piano and he took some lessons. We thought he was taking piano lessons. I'd drop him off up here to take some lessons and he'd walk through the carport to their back yard and I'd drive away. Unbeknownst to me he wouldn't go in. He'd stay there or walk around for a little while and walk home. He was taking lessons until we found out he was doing that. We thought, "What's the use of taking him up there if he didn't want to take the lessons?" So he quit lessons. Through this computer work he got involved with some kids who were – are they "freaks" or "geeks"? I didn't know what he was doing. He'd talk about computers and the things that were happening. He'd ask, "Can you take me to this kids house?" – like on Saturday. So I dropped him off at least one time to a house in Rosepark and another time at a house in South Salt Lake somewhere. I just thought they were talking. Unbeknownst to me he was getting involved with providing information to people who were using that information in an illegal manner. He never did use it himself. When I finally found out about it I talked to him at great length that he shouldn't be doing it. "Well, we're not doing anything bad. We're just doing things ..." I just kept talking to him. Finally, he heard that some kids got arrested or something and that got him thinking. Finally, he gave that part of it up. He still liked the kids, but he realized they were doing things illegal. He stopped doing that but he stayed with computers. Then I bought a good computer. He just went to town on that. He just loves computers. In junior high he met a girl named Tewie Jane Holmes in 6th grade. In 9th grade they were "good friends". He got kicked out of choir because he talked too much. When they had Christmas or Halloween programs in Kindergarten the teacher would always put the microphone real close to Clint because he had the truest and loudest voice and he would keep everybody else on pitch. Clint always seemed to have perfect pitch. When he sang around here I could just hear he would never waver. That was one of his assets. Another one of his assets was he loved education. He loved to learn. In high school he took a lot of AP classes. He was Sterling Scholar for Jordan High School in Science. He loved to experiment – he made pipe bombs, etc. We were oblivious. He got scholarships to the University of Utah and BYU. He was going to go to the U of U because he loved the "U" and he didn't like BYU. But he heard that a certain girl was going to BYU that year. So, he gave up his University of Utah scholarship and took the BYU scholarship and lost it because he and that girl played around too much and didn't study. He went on a mission. He went to the Canada, Halifax mission. He tells me that when he stepped off the plane to meet the President, the President said, "You'll be one of my AP's." He was eventually. He was a District Leader, Zone Leader and then he was an AP. He loved that. He loved going around and telling the guys what to do. He loved to be in the office. He networked the computers in the office. He loved both his mission presidents. Well the first one was worldly, but he gave them everything they wanted. He was a multi-millionaire and he would buy them everything they needed. The second mission president was very spiritual. He grew to love them differently. He loved them both. In the meantime, this girl, Tewie, they had an understanding. Let me back up a little bit. We went to California to see Val and stay there for a few days and while we were there we went to see Phantom of the Opera. We invited Tewie to go to Phantom with us. Mom and me and Clint and Nolana. We picked up Tewie from San Diego and went up to L.A. to see Phantom of the Opera. The next night we went to Balboa Island and Tewie and Clint went walking down the beach. We were really worried because we didn't know where they were and I was responsible for this girl. We finally came and found them. On the way home I felt like it was kind of sealed there – That this was the fate of these two kids. They will be together. While he was on his mission, Tewie decided she wanted to go on a mission. Tewie left in March and Clint came back in October. He hadn't seen her for his two years of his mission and when he came home she was gone for another 10 months, so it was almost 3 years that they hadn't physically seen one another, but when she came back it was as if nothing had changed. They started where they had left off. They've been married for 6 years and have 3 lovely children.

Q: Tell me about the houses you lived in when you were married?
A: Our first house was 702 South 9th East in Salt Lake. It was a back apartment of a rambler house. Our entrance was in the back of the house. We had a front room, a kitchen and a bathroom. We had a garage that we put our car in. But my car was too big to fit very well in the garage – I only had a little bit of room. So I took a board off the entrance to the garage and I was really lucky that the whole thing didn't fall down because it was one of the structural beams that held the garage up. We lived there for 3 or 4 months. We moved because it was in back and dark and mom was coming home at night when it was dark. We just didn't like it. So we found an apartment on 128 G Street. It was a second floor apartment. It had a big front room and fairly good sized kitchen and our bedroom. We had to walk up a flight of stair every time to go up. We also had a garage that we had to pay 5 or 10 dollars for. That was nice. We lived there for 6 or 8 months. We moved because my Aunt Edith died and gave her piano to Elaine but Elaine said, "Give it to Ralph. He's the piano player in the family." So, she gave it to me and we couldn't take the piano up to the second floor, so we had to find another apartment. We just about rented a basement apartment, but it would've been hard to fit that piano down there. We found an apartment over on 128 Williams Avenue. It was a duplex with a main level and ½ basement. It had a nice front room and not too big a kitchen area and not too big a bedroom but the piano fit in there. We stayed there for 2 years. We met the Corsi's. They were in our ward. They lived over in the trailer park. They had a little trailer. We kind of chummed around a little bit and we were talking about buying homes eventually. One day mom and I were going for a ride. We got on 13th East and come cruising out for a nice Sunday drive, we came to 94th South and stopped. This was way out in the boonies. Nothing is around us. As we looked down over the little hillside over there there were 6 little new homes. We thought, "A subdivision out this far? Who would ever want to come out this far to live?" We drove down there and took a look at them. We walked through one of the homes and thought, "Nice home" but, man alive, it was so far out – 94th South. We kind of dismissed it. About 1 year later we come driving out again. We come upon this subdivision again and it had several streets in it now. People are buying homes out here. We went through the homes again and kind of looked them over. They still were nice and there were more people

29

out here but it was still so far away. We were looking for a home to buy. We went out to Elaine Avenue (40th West 38th South) to look at new homes. We thought, "These are really nice homes. They are nicer that the ones in White City, but, man, are they expensive." We couldn't really afford a whole lot. These were some options. We were talking with the Corsi's and we came to the decision that we were going to buy a home in White City. The Corsi's said, "We're going to buy a home. I think we'll buy a home in White City." We said, "Maybe we'll buy a home too." We decided to buy homes next door to one another. We came down and signed up to buy homes in White City. We came out to see the progress every few weeks. When we came out the first time they were putting up the walls. We asked, "Where's our fireplace?" They hadn't built a fireplace in. We said, "We definitely want a fireplace." They says, "You can't have a fireplace here because we've already got the basement dug and there is no provision for it." We says, "We want it." They says, "We'll have to give you another lot." We said, "We want a lot on the same street." They says, "How about the one on the other side of Corsi's?" That house was marked for split-level. They had to change all their fittings and markers to accommodate us and put that fireplace in. They weren't too happy but I wasn't too happy either. But they did accommodate us. We got the home that we have now.

Q: What is your philosophy of child rearing?
A: (Joking) Get a real strong stiff belt. I used the belt a few times and I'm really sorry for doing that. I would say, "No. Don't ever do that." You know, as you get older you get a little more mellow and smarter. My philosophy was not terribly strict but kind of strict. I don't know. It was kind of strict. You kind of allow things occasionally to go by the way side. If I had to raise children now it would be a lot different. There would be a lot more love and a lot more gentle persuasion than the strictness. I didn't spank too many kids. I used the belt a few times which I'm really sorry for. I didn't do a lot of hitting. My girls got away with murder. "They're girls. You don't hit girls – girls cry."

Q: What was the daily routine of your family life?
A: We'd get up in the morning – breath in and breath out. We'd try to have family prayer and scripture study. That didn't last too long. We didn't do this every year. Then I would go to work. I had to be to work at 8:00. Sometimes I'd drive and sometimes I'd take the bus because it went right past the post office (4th South and Main). I'd come home about 5:00. At night I would go play basketball or softball. I didn't have a computer so I didn't do anything like that. I had to keep active one way or another. In 1976 I joined The Mormon Tabernacle Choir and that took care of all my sports because in my Stake the sports (basketball/softball) were held on Thursday night and that was choir night. I also was getting to the age where I didn't want to do it anymore. When I first joined the post office they had a band for the carriers. The carrier's union sponsored the band. They asked me to join. I joined the band in 1956 and stayed with them until

I joined the choir. There was a conflict there so I dropped out of the band. My dad sang for the Swanee Singers and I used to go with him and sit in the audience while they rehearsed. They rehearsed at a church at about 9th East and 18th South. I was interested in singing. My brother Jim joined the Swanee Singers and stayed a couple of years. I decided that I would join. I had to sing a solo. I had never sang a solo in my life. I had taken one lesson from Rod Zabriski in our Stake. I asked him what I should sing and he suggested the piece, "Suddenly There's a Valley". We went through it for about ½ hour. That was the limit of my preparation for this solo. I sang it for the Swanee's and they accepted me into the choir. I sang with them for 10 years until I auditioned and applied for the Tabernacle Choir in December of 1975. In February 1976, I was accepted into the Tabernacle Choir. I sang with them for 20 years. I had 30 years of singing and one lesson. I love singing.

Q: Your adult medical experiences?

A: Don't ask. In 1986, this was about the time that Pres. Regan had cancerous polyps in his colon. So, it was on everybody's minds. I just had a feeling and I asked one of the doctors in the choir. He said that I should get a colonoscopy. I was referred to another doctor and he found a little bit of blood in my stool. He referred me to another doctor – Dr. Hughes. He did the colonoscopy and he said, "Yea, you have some cancer up there. We'll have to get it out. How about a week from Friday?" I said, "I have cancer. Why can't we do it tomorrow?" He was going to go out of town for that weekend. I had about 18 inches of my colon cut out and everything was o.k. after that. The funny thing about it is that I was still in the choir and I didn't tell anyone about it. I took 2 days of sick leave and 2 days of vacation and then I went back. I still was very tender. Your not supposed to exert very much force and I didn't. I never told them because they would've had me reaudition with Joanne Ottley to see if anything had changed or affected my singing. The lady that took attendance questioned why I would take off 2 days of sick leave and 2 days of vacation in a row. I never did tell them. There was a guy in the choir that worked at St. Mark's Hospital and gave me a blessing. He never told anyone either.

In 1991 I was having pain in my leg when I would walk from my car to choir. That's the longest I would walk. I decided I had better find out what's wrong. I went to the doctor and he said, "This artery is blocked. We'll have take a vein and replace it or clean it out." When he was in there he decided not to replace it but to clean it out. Right afterwards my foot started going bad. There was a piece of something that went down lower into the artery and blocked it. I went back to Dr. Jones and he told me that this was just the body getting rid of the clot. I believed him. He did this for 6 weeks. My foot was going black. My big toe was black. My foot was dying. It hurt like mad and the doctor kept feeding me prescriptions of Percodan and Percocet. After 6 weeks I said, "We've got to do something. We can't just keep doing this." He says, "Well if you want a second opinion

31

you go ahead." I thought, "Great. After 6 weeks he tells me to get a second opinion." He referred me to Dr. Albo. (Mom) He was scared. He didn't have anybody else in the office with him when I thought he indicated there was nothing else to be done for your leg. (Dad) He told me that the veins down in the foot were too small to work on. We went up to Dr. Albo. He took a look at my foot walked out of the examining room and I think he called Dr. Jones. In about 15 min later he came back in. (Mom) He said he had called Dr. Jones. (Dad) When he came in he started talking about the options. He did a graft of the artery in the ankle area of my foot. He did about 3 operations in that same area and nothing helped. The only other alternative was ... he said, "Your foots dying. We've got to take it off. Is this what you want to do?" "Yes." The way he took it off was a new procedure. "First we're going to freeze your foot. After we freeze it it is gone. There is no reversal." Mom went out and got some dry ice. He packed the dry ice around my foot up to about mid-calf. The pain went away. People tell me that I slept for 24 hours just because I had been in so much pain and had gotten so little sleep up to this time. He was going to operate on me on Sunday March 31st. I said, "Dr. Albo I would rather that you not operate on me on Sunday. I'd rather that you wait until the next day." He consented. So, he operated on me on April Fool's Day. That's when I had my amputation on my left leg. I had to learn how to use crutches and a prosthesis. If you ever think it's easy for people with just one leg, try to get into the bathtub with just one foot.

In 1998 I took the TV back in to the house after we came back from a trailer club trip and my back started hurting and it wouldn't go away. It was that way for a couple of weeks. I finally went to Dr. Kesler (Chiropractor) and he did a couple of adjustments but that didn't seem to help at all. The day after one of the adjustments I was sitting down and I leaned forward and I got the most excruciating pain I have had in my whole life. I couldn't move. I hollered at mom, "Call 911." They came out and drove me up to Alta View Hospital. All the time they were driving the guy couldn't get an IV in me. So I was in the excruciating pain and no pain medication. At the hospital they gave me morphine, which didn't help. Finally they gave me Demerol and it did affect the pain. I went from Alta View to Cottonwood. Mom got in touch with Dr. Robert Horn. I was there for a week before Dr. Horn operated on me. (Mom) I think he didn't know what to do. I think he was watching and deciding what to do. He was diagnosed with multiple myeloma and the disease deteriorated two of his vertebrae. I asked the oncologist, "What's the prognosis." She said, "Six months to two years. Govenor Mathison had it and he died in 6 weeks." (Dad) I didn't hear any of this. They finally operated on me. He got bone from a bone graft to take care of my two vertebrae, which had went to mush. He put the bone in and three rods to hold everything together. For 6 weeks I had to have a "turtle-shell." It is a solid piece of plastic that goes over your front and back. I only took it off to take a spit bath. Right after that I got a blood clot in my leg and I went up to St. Mark's Hospital. I saw Dr. Weiss who was on call in the E.R. We really liked him and he became my oncologist. He's very forthright and he'll tell you what you want to know. I told him, "The other doctor told me that I have 6 months to 2 years to live." He said, "Oh, that's rubbish. Nobody knows. I've got a patient who's had this stuff for 8 years. It just depends on you. Let's see what happens." Now I've been on Thalidomide for about 7 or 8 months and it's showing really good progress. The doctor says, "We're going to stay on this until further notice." I've had 3 or 4 blood clots in my legs. This past year my coumadin levels have been very hard to control. In 2001 I have had pains in my chest, dizziness, memory loss and a suspect heart attack and my arms and shoulders ached up until the first week in September. We wanted to go with the trailer club every month this summer and it would come close to the time to go I would feel lousy and we couldn't go. In September I started feeling good and they are through camping for the year. I'm feeling good.

Q: What was your religious participation during your adult years?

A: I thought I would become an atheist, but I know better, so I can't become an atheist. My affiliation is a member of The Church of Jesus Christ of Latter-Day Saints. I baptized all my children into the church. I'm glad they all accepted and they continue to accept. All my children are active and all their families are active. They found good spouses. As far as positions. When we lived on Williams Avenue, I was called to be first counselor in the YM organization. Back then it was called "Mutual." When we were in the Sego Lily 8th ward they asked, "Can anybody play the piano?" I asked the bishop, "Can I take a hymn book home? I know how to play and I'd like to rehearse. I'll be your piano player." I played hymns for the Priesthood. When we were in the 9th Ward I was called to the Stake Aaronic Priesthood Committee, which I only did for 3 or 4 months because it wasn't compatible with my job at work. I was called to be the Sunday School President. I had that for about 1-½ years. We moved over into the new building. That's when I was called to be the Finance Clerk under Bishop Elroy Jones. I've seen the finances go from a 4-part typed copy right up into the computer age. I was instrumental in getting our ward on the computer before any other wards in our area. The finance clerk calling started 10 years before I joined the choir. I had that position for 24 years. They finally decided that 24 years was enough. I argued with my bishop that I couldn't take any other position because I was with the choir. I can't take a position where I would have to do something on Sunday. Or, even during the week because we rehearsed on Tuesday and recorded on Monday, Wednesday and Friday. This was the best job in the whole world for what I was doing. But he says, "The Stake President says I should release you." I was released. I was a member of the Tabernacle Choir for 20 years. That's a missionary calling. I have a letter signed by the President of the Church calling me to the position. I was released from choir in 1996 and was called to be YM President. I had that job for 18 months. That was a fun job. It was fun working with the kids. We'd go canoeing and hiking and fun things. I was released from that job and called into the High Council. I was in there for 10

33

or 11 months then I was released. Then I was called as the Stake Employment Specialist. In certain areas it's a good job and sometimes there is not enough activity going on. You have Ward Employment Specialists who do all the work. The Stake Employment Specialist just advises and gives materials to the Ward Employment Specialist. Before the High Council I was called to work in the Extraction Program. I said, "I'd rather just do the data entry because I have a hard time understanding all the old script lettering. I'm good at the typewriter. I can type 65 words per minute. This is what I want to do." He says, "Fine. We'll call you to data entry." So, when I was called to the High Council I said, "I'm a data entry person, but I'm not going to give it up. I'm going to do that job as well as the High Council position." So, I still do that data entry. That's where I stand at this moment. I also was a Ward Specialist in the area of Church and Civic Relations. We would find out what we could do to help the community out as a church. We made a program that in an emergency we would get 10 minutes notice from Edgemont School and we'd get someone over to the church (across the street from the school) with a key to open it up and the kids would have a place to be in case of fire, earthquake or bomb scare. These were the types of things we were involved in.

Q: What are your hobbies and interests?
A: I don't have any hobbies. My interest is music. Playing the piano. Singing. Dabbled a little bit in the guitar. I collect coins. I am collecting all the state quarters.

Q: What are your reading habits?
A: I don't read a lot. I read the Book of Mormon and the scriptures. I don't read much. I used to read a lot when I was a kid, but I got out of the habit when I got married. I read the newspaper all the way through. That's the only thing I actually read a lot of. I also read some of the Ensign stories.

Q: What are your best abilities?
A: Understanding finances. Numbers and music.

Q: Do you have any allergies?
A: I had hay fever when I was in my early 30's and I had it for several years and it went away. After 6 or 7 years it came back again and after 2 years it went away again.

Q: Preferences and dislikes for food?
A: My preferences are spaghetti, hot dogs -- I'll eat most anything. I could care less about steak. I'll eat it but I'm not gung ho about it. When we were dating or first married we would go to a restaurant and I would order a glass of buttermilk. I liked buttermilk. It's been years since I've had it.

Q: Preferences and dislikes for music?

A: All my piano lessons were involved in the classics. I grew up on the classics and I like them. I don't like the rock and roll stuff they have now days. I like the 40's and 50's dance music. I like popular or well-known classics the best.

Q: Preferences and dislikes for books?

A: I've read the entire set of Sherlock Holmes mysteries and all of Edgar Allen Poe's stories since I've been married. The Sherlock Holmes book was my dad's. I like mysteries.

Q: Preferences and dislikes for movies?

A: Musicals and good love stories. Sleepless in Seattle, An affair to Remember, While You Were Sleeping, You've Got Mail, Casablanca, High Road to China, etc. I dislike anything with sex scenes or bad words. Can't stand them. I turn them off and walk away.

Q: Preferences and dislikes for TV?

A: You've got to be very selective in what you watch now days on TV. I like Poirot. That's a mystery and there are some good stories. The old Sherlock Holmes TV stories. Basil Rathbone was the best Sherlock Holmes there was. I watch The Pretender. I like the games shows. I like Wheel of Fortune, Jeopardy and Who Wants to be a Millionaire? I watch those three just to see how much I know or don't know.

Q: What are your memorable travels?

A: (First Part Family Travels)
       The most memorable trip we ever took was up to Seattle. I belonged to the Post Office Band. The Post Office Band is supported by the Letter Carriers Union. Whenever they would have a convention we would be invited to go along and represent them as a marching and concert band. This was a national convention with a parade of the delegates and the bands would march with them and play. During these conventions we would have opportunity to play at a hotel or parks for about an hour for the general public. It was for advertising. Each band would be in a different place at a different time. It was just a nice thing we were doing. We took everybody but Clint, because Clint couldn't walk yet. We left him home with a neighbor girl. We took our camper and went up to Seattle. There were 4 or 5 families that drove together through Idaho to Washington. The kids still talk about the trip. Our group from SLC was scheduled to be housed in the Washington Athletic Club. Valerie was in a room with some girls so she didn't have to stay with mom and dad. Mike was in a room with some other boys and he didn't have to stay with mom and dad. It was just Nolana and Charlinn that were with mom and dad. Mike and Val had a little more freedom. They played around. Mike and his friends were dropping a hard ball out of the window from 6 stories above. They wanted to see how high it would bounce and they would eventually catch it and run up the elevator

again and throw it out the window again. One time Mike dropped the ball and he turned around to talk to another kid and while he was talking another kid shut the window. Mike turned around to look out the window and put his head through the window. It didn't cut him, but the windowpane was pushed out onto the sidewalk and shattered. We got told about that. The manager of the place said he would never have anybody from any convention stay with them again. We felt bad. We ate out everyday. The convention lasted for 5 days. We were always with other people. We would sightsee and do the convention activities together. After the convention we took a ferry through the San Juan Islands, which is off the coast of Canada by Washington. We took it over to Vancouver Island and drove down to Victoria and stayed there one night. The next day we drove up and took the ferry back through the San Juan Islands and down to Washington.

We also went to Lake Powell with the boat. I've always wanted a boat. When you look at how much fun the people appear to have when they have a boat you think, "Boy, it would be nice to have a boat." I like to fish too so I thought, "This would be something I could do if I had a boat." But we didn't do hardly any fishing. Whenever we took the boat it was for water-skiing and boating around.

(Second Part Post Office Band)
The first trip I went on was memorable because it was the first trip I went on. We went over to Denver and we stayed in the YMCA. I'd never been on a trip before. We only took the kids on the trip to Seattle. Just mom and I went on the others. We also went to Miami Beach. We went on a train for 2 nights and 3 days all the way down. We took the UP (Union Pacific) to St. Louis, switched to a Southern Line down to Miami Beach. We packed food so we wouldn't have to buy anything on the train. These conventions are 5 days. We marched and gave mini-concerts around the city. We went to the dog races one evening. Our guide asked us if we wanted to go. I'd never seen a dog race before. They were greyhound dogs chasing that mechanical rabbit around the track. We pooled our money (a dollar a piece) and bet on one dog. We didn't win but it was fun. One little thing about mom is that she would put up her hair in curlers at night so that she'd have pretty curls in the morning. But once we were out the door within a half hour in the humidity she would have straight hair. She finally went into a beauty shop and had them cut it into a "Pixie" (a very short hair cut). We swam in the Atlantic Ocean at night. We didn't even think about sharks. The hotel had it's own beach area with fence lines going out into the ocean for about 150 feet or so. We had fun. We also went to Detroit. We got off the train in Chicago and we were waiting for another train to get over to Detroit. We had plenty of time because we got in early in the morning. I was with a couple a friends both from Riverton. We were walking across this wide road. The light was green and we got half way across and I saw a car coming and I had a premonition and I started slowing down my walk. The car came through the red light and hit my friend (Merlin Danzie). The hit

36

was a glancing blow that broke his pelvis. It spun him around in a circle and he fell down. The car stopped and there was a park across street that had a program going on. There was a policeman there that saw what had happened and called an ambulance. I went with him in the ambulance to the hospital. We had to leave him to go to the convention to play. We saw him when we came back from the convention. He had to stay there a whole month and they flew him out on a National Guard plane (because they had so many hours they had to fly). The band went to Hawaii, but we didn't go. Mom said, "Hawaii is like Miami. It's hot and humid."

(Third Part Mormon Tabernacle Choir Trips)
I got in the choir in February 1976 and they had planned a bicentennial tour. It was the 200th celebration of the birth of the nation. We went to Boston, New York, Washington D.C., Philadelphia – all the cities that made this country. We flew into New York and then we took a train up to Boston and then sang and stayed over night. Then came back to New York and sang in Carnegie Hall. I can say that I performed in Carnegie Hall. We stayed in Marriott Hotels the whole time. I think they were donated by a very generous man. When we were in New York we were right across the street from Central Park. They told us not to go anywhere at night except in a large group. But, this one night, we did go in a large group. Some of us decided to take the subway. Subways are scary at night in New York City. But with 15 of us together we felt safe. We took the subway over to the ferryboat to Staten Island. Here it is 1:00 in the morning and we took the ferry to Staten Island. While we were on the ferry we saw the Statue of Liberty as big as life and we started singing, "Give me your tired, your poor, your huddled masses yearning to be free. Send these, the homeless, tempest tossed, to me. I lift my lamp beside the golden doors." We sang that to the passengers on board. To me it was real spiritual. It was a real good feeling. We were singing to Lady Liberty and the passengers. Up in Boston we did something different. Usually when a concert is over the audience clamors for encores so we have to stay and sing 2 or 3 encores. The final one being, "The Battle Hymn." In Boston we didn't have a lot of time, because we had to get to the train in a hurry. So at the end of the concert we started singing a single encore and as we were singing the back two rows started walking off as we were singing. We actually walked out while we were singing because we had to get going. It was quite fun to do it that way. It's never been done since. We also sang on "The Mall" between the Washington and Lincoln Monuments on the 4th of July. They estimated that when we sang there were one million people there on "The Mall". You would look out and all you would see were heads. They were packed so close. After our concert it was getting to be night fall and they were going to have the fireworks and they decided that since there were so many people that if we stayed we would be bogged down in traffic and would miss our plane. So they bussed us out before the fireworks began. We only got to see them from a distance as we took off. One thing I did see as we were traveling were fireflies. I'd never seen a firefly before. Fireflies are lit. They

have a little light. I've never seen one since. I did see some fireflies then. So we got on a plane and went home.

We went to Japan (in about 1979). The choir announces where we're going about 4 or 5 months ahead of time. Usually some dignitary would come and tell us where we were going. We were anticipating where we were going and all of a sudden out came a member of the choir dressed in a kimono as a Geisha Girl. They played Japanese music and she danced and we knew where we were going. That was really a neat way to tell us where we were going. We went in August and it was our first encounter with The Orient. Everything was different. We stayed at one of the best hotels in Tokyo, the New Otoni. All the signs were in Japanese so it was hard to get around. They have a great subway system. It is 4 or 5 levels in some places. They are all color-coded too. The names of the subway exits were in Japanese and English so it made it a little easier to get around. We sang for the general public. One of the things the church does is allow the missionaries to give away some tickets to investigators. They would come to the concert and the elders would knock on the door and say, "Hi. How did you like the concert?" That was a way of getting into them and touching them with the spirit in a different way. We would get report after report of the missionary effort skyrocketing after the choir has been in an area. Our music brings the Spirit. We had a report of one of the CEO's of a big company who came to the concert and after the concert he was so touched that he bought enough tickets for his whole management staff to come to the concert the next night. He was so touched by the Spirit. We did not sing in Japanese. We had in some other languages learned maybe a folk song. A guy in the choir could write the words phonetically so that we could memories the sounds with the tune. We would sing at least one song in the language. After Japan we went over to Korea and sang at least 1 or 2 concerts. That was different. Japan was clean as a whistle. We went over to Korea and it was dirty. It was entirely different. The last day we were in Korea they gave us a banquet with a lot of raw fish. Most of us didn't eat a whole lot of it. One time when we were going through immigration in Korea it was really slow. The guy was really scrutinizing things closely. He happened to see someone with a tag that said, "Mormon Tabernacle Choir." And he said, "Are you guys with the Mormon Tabernacle Choir?" We said, "Yes." He says, "O.K." And he didn't even look at us, he just stamped the passports and sent us quickly on our way. Our reputation preceded us. One interesting thing about this trip was that the TV station that sponsored our trip gave every choir member a pearl. I had it in my drawer for 10 or 15 years. We decided to do something with it, so we took it down to a jeweler and had it mounted in a ring for mom. That's a memento from Japan. It was a long flight over to Japan. They had two crews on the airplane. They had an area sectioned off for one crew to sleep while the other flew. We tried to sleep. They gave us blackout goggles and earplugs, but it didn't work real well for us.

In about 1981 the choir was invited by the State Department to go to Brazil. We were to represent the US in a program to "Save the Children." (To help orphans and kids who were roaming the street alone.) We were down there for about 4 days. Ertha Kitt – one of the 40's "bombs" – was on the tour. I've always liked her voice – very low and sensual. She was on the concert tour too and I got her autograph. During the tour we were supposed to sing at another place and we were waiting for the buses to pick us up from the hotel. They didn't come and we were waiting and it was getting late. We started asking the members how we could get there. They volunteered to take us, but they had such little cars. They could only take 2 or 3 people in a car. So one of the guys brought a dump truck. A bunch of choir members got into the dump truck and took us over to the concert. They were speaking Portuguese and we had no idea what they were saying. There was a bunch a people who could speak Spanish and 1 or 2 people who spoke Portuguese. Here we had 350 people trying to get to a concert and only 2 or 3 people being able to communicate. Between all of them we were able to decipher what was being said and we got to the concert on time. At night when they pull up to a red light they will turn their headlights off and as soon as the light turns green they turn their lights back on and start driving. We stayed on the Temple Grounds in San Paulo. There are some apartment houses built for people who are coming from a distance to do temple work. Now the average Brazilian person is 5'6". I am 6'0" and my brother is 6'2" and we had a lot of other tall people. We were sleeping in these beds built for 5'6" people. It was pretty interesting. I was on the lower echelon of the choir so I had to be on the top bunk. Spouses didn't go because the State Department sponsored us and only choir members were invited.

In about 1983 we went to Scandinavia. We flew over to Bergen, Norway and stayed on the university housing there. We gave a concert. We took a train up into the top of the mountains over into Stockholm, Sweden. There we got on a cruise liner and boated to the different places in Denmark, Finland, and Holland. We'd give the concerts, get back on board, go to sleep and the boat would take us to the next port while we were sleeping. This was really neat because usually we would have to have our baggage outside our doors by 5 AM, or sometimes midnight so they could pick it up and transport it to our next destination. That was about 600 bags. That's a lot of bags so they had to start early. On the cruise liner we didn't have to do that. We didn't have to worry about being on buses. The dinners were fun. We could order whatever we wanted. We had a screwy waiter. No matter what you ordered he would bring you whatever he wanted to bring you. They closed the bar and gambling casino. They didn't make any money off us. We took 2 cruise liners as a choir. One of the boats burned to the water and the other went bankrupt. We were hoping it wasn't because of us. We didn't give them any extra money. As we were heading towards Copenhagen my brother (Jim) started getting pain in his lower abdomen. We have doctors with us all the time. Most of them are choir members.

They thought that it was appendicitis. We were out in the ocean hoping it wouldn't burst. They called ahead to Copenhagen and when we came into port he was the first one off. They took him to the hospital and they performed surgery. He stayed there for about a week. A relative of one of the choir members took Marlene in as a guest during the time Jim was in the hospital. They took her to the hospital everyday and treated her with the red-carpet treatment. The funny thing about it was that at that time the law stated that foreigners got their medical needs taken care of for free. So his surgery and stay in the hospital were free. We got home before they did. After Copenhagen we went to Holland. Going over to Holland we had to cross over the North Sea. The North Sea is very rough. During that time we were rehearsing in the ballroom of the boat. So the boat is rolling side to side and up and down and you could see every once in a while somebody would get up, hold their mouth and head out the door. They were seasick. I never did get seasick. In Holland the choir went to the concert hall and the spouses got to go sightseeing. This is what happens all the time. While we were out we saw a Baskin Robbins and choir members love to eat so about 100 or us headed over there. We all ordered ice cream and she was fine with that, except when we went to pay for it we all had big bills and she didn't have enough change. I don't know if we pooled our money or what, but it all worked out. She got rid of a lot of ice cream that day. Then we flew in to London. We gave a concert at Royal Albert Hall. Not many people have sung in Royal Albert Hall. That's where <u>Les Miserable</u> the concert was recorded. We knew we were going to be in London and my Uncle Willie lived outside of London. We had written letters inviting him and his daughter-in-law and her two kids to the concert. The daughter-in-law was sick so she couldn't come. But, Uncle Willie and Judith and Jeff came to the concert. Afterwards we met them, because I'd never seen him before, and we took them back to the hotel and had dinner. Afterwards we didn't know what to do or where to go, so we invited them up to our room and chatted about things. I remember that Uncle Willie had the same mannerisms as my dad. He talked a lot like him and looked a lot like him. During our visit the World Cup Championship was on that night so we turned on the TV and let the kids (Jeff (16) and Judith (18)) watch the tournament. That was real memorable because that was the only time I'd ever met him. After London we flew home.

In about 1986 we went back to Japan a second time.

In 1988 we went to New Zealand and Australia. I know it was 1988 because I had a sweatshirt that says, "New State '88", because they were celebrating the 100th anniversary of the new state of Sydney. We flew over to Hawaii and stayed one night. During that night we went to the Polynesian Cultural Center after it was closed. They gave a special performance just to the choir members and their families. It was so late and we had flown for 8 hours that many people were falling asleep during the performance. We flew over to New Zealand and gave several concerts. Then we flew over to Australia and gave 4 concerts – one concert in each one of the big cities. We ended up in Sydney and sang in that big concert hall that you see with all the arches that represent sails on a ship. In New Zealand we were waiting in the airport and we were stuck. We had to get over to a concert in another town that evening. We couldn't go anywhere because it was so overcast that they stopped all the planes from flying. It was getting later and later. They had no idea how we were going to get over there, so we decided to put it in the Lord's hands. The choir staff members went into a back room and knelt down and prayed that we could get out and give this concert. They came back and all of a sudden the clouds parted and there was a hole that we could see the sky. They announced that they were going to let a few planes out. So they said, "Choir members only head out to this plane really quick and let's get on it and get out." And we did. As soon as we were up in the air flying the clouds started coming back together. It was several hours before the spouses could get out. We got to our concert. We gave the concert. Some of the people were dressing as they were walking into the concert hall. We didn't have out baggage with us. That was quite a spiritual trip. On the way home we stopped in Hawaii again and stayed overnight. We went through immigration there and went home.

I had my amputation in 1991 and that's when they went on the Russian tour. I had my operation in January hoping that I could go. But, it never came to be because I had my amputation in April and they took off in June. I didn't get to go, but I swore that I would meet them when they had their first rehearsal when they came back. And I did. I got my prosthesis and everything worked out ok and I was there for the first rehearsal.

The last big tour I went on was to Israel in about 1993. We went right before New Years. We flew to Jerusalem. When we left from here we went on the Israeli airlines. Their own people were scrutinizing us. They would ask, "Have you had your luggage in your sight all the time? Has anybody asked you to carry something in your luggage for them?" Maybe somebody put a bomb in your bag and they had to ask these questions. We were told ahead of time not to let our luggage out of our sight. It was really tight security. Even just getting on the plane in Salt Lake. We were told ahead of time to take goulashes and rain gear because we were going during the rainy season. We never used it. That's why we called it "The Miracle Tour" because every place we went it didn't rain. It would rain where we had just been or where we were going to but never where we were, except at night. When we drove up to Tel Aviv to give a concert it would rain in Jerusalem (where we had just come from). This is the way it was the whole trip. It always rained in another place. Never on us. We went across the Sea of Galilee to the shore on the late afternoon and the lighting was pretty dull. About the time they wanted to start video taping, the sun would come out and they'd have enough light. We would sing a couple of songs and they'd say, "Cut." Then the sun would go behind the clouds again. This happened a couple of times. While this was happening the place where we were going was being rained on. Just miracles. The only thing that we saw of the warring factions was one of the buses got a few rocks thrown through the windows. They weren't throwing them at the choir they were just militant people. We were up on top by the other buses. We always had Israeli police with us and they said, "O.k. everybody back in the buses quick." We got in and we followed a police car. There was one behind us and one in front of us. We went through the back parts of Israel. We got to see where the people actually lived. We went many places that they claimed the Savior had walked. We walked down the path the Savior took when he made his last entry into Jerusalem. We went to the Shepherd's Fields, where the angels told the shepherds that Jesus was born. We went to the Mount of Olives and the Garden of Gethsemane. We didn't sing there. We just took a tour and saw what could've been the actual tree where Jesus prayed and sweat blood. They don't know if these are the exact spots because the Romans came in and destroyed Jerusalem. We also went to the Dome of the Rock. Where some very important events happened to Mohammad. Several different religions have different monuments there. One of the choice experiences we had was going to the tomb where Jesus' body was taken. It is now owned by some religion out of England. We sang at the tomb. We sang, "When I Survey the Wondrous Cross" which is a tearjerker anyway. Singing in the Garden Tomb was especially touching. They were videoing this while we were singing and about 30% or 40% were crying. When you have tears coming down it's hard to sing.

As a choir we also went to Toronto and down through the mid-west – Ohio, Missouri, Illinois, etc. We went up to Vancouver for a worldwide program up there. Mom didn't go on any one of those. In approximately 1995 we took the last concert tour back east to Washington D.C. Mom went with me on that tour. It was a tour and some concerts. We sang the first concert of, "An American Requiem" in the John the Beloved Cathedral. We went to a play in New York. We went up the Empire State Building. Whenever I see "Sleepless in Seattle" or "An Affair to Remember" I think, "Hey, I've been there." We went to the Statue of Liberty and Ellis Island during this last tour. That was the first time we had been there.

Q: What was it about the choir that you really enjoyed?
A: Number one I got in the choir because I loved the music. I didn't know how much I loved the music until I got in there and started singing the music. When you've got 300 people around you that know how to sing well, it's not like a ward or stake choir, it was just a fantastic experience. You get to know the people themselves. They are all good people. They are all worthy of holding temple recommends and each year their bishops would have to recommend them to continue. They were all good humble, nice people. That's nice to associate with such a good group of people. You don't have a lot of social interaction here at home. The most social interaction is on tour. On tour you don't have to get home so your sitting around socializing and sightseeing together, dinner together. That's where you really get to know

42

the people. I enjoyed the people, the music and the reason we were out there. We are actual missionaries. We bring the Spirit to the people. On a couple of tours we were able to pass out <u>Books of Mormons</u> to the people and proselyte.

Q: What is your life like now that you are retired?

A: My life has slowed down. I used to travel a lot with the Post Office and I was very important. But now that I am retired I am no longer in the forefront and I am no longer privy to a lot of information that I was privy to while I was auditing. I was an auditor and I had to know this information so I knew everything that was going on. Now I am out of the loop. It didn't hurt me, but it felt strange that I no longer knew what was happening. I felt a little bad that I don't know what's happening out there anymore. Like everybody says about retirement, "With all the things I'm doing now how could I ever work?" I don't do as much as other people do. At one time in my retirement my time was filled up with my family. So, I thought, "That's true. How do I have time to work when there is so much to do? Helping my kids with their houses and children." My life has slowed down – naturally. I enjoy it. I enjoy my family. I enjoy being able to go visit them. And if somebody calls – Jessica calls and says, "Can you come pick me up?" I'm there. I'm available. I have mixed feelings about pulling my trailer to Yuma for the winter to spend 2 or 3 months. I don't think I want to go. I don't want to be away from my family because I feel that they need me. Maybe they don't need me, but I feel that way. I just like my family. I like to see them.

Q: What historical events did you pass through?

A: World War II (Dec 1941) – I was 4 years old when Pearl Harbor was attacked. I don't remember a whole lot about it. I remember we were on rations. You couldn't get tires. Rubber was needed. I remember my mother having a little coupon book. Once you used your coupons you couldn't buy anymore – gas, flour, etc. 1953 The Korean War – in 1952 I started high school and met my future bride. I was too young to participate. 1963 The Vietnam War – I had 2 children and was exempt from participating. I didn't have to go to war even though I tried to. Desert Storm (1991) – My son participated in a MASH unit for 6 months in Rehad, Saudi Arabia. The only causalities they had were broken bones from soldiers just playing and a few cases of appendicitis. They had a few scud missiles come within a few miles. It was kind of scary. The Terrorism War (9/11/01) – I think that when you read <u>The Book of Mormon</u> the talk of the Gadianton Robbers that this is just a repeat of history. It's going to be this way for years. In <u>The Book of Mormon</u> some of these conflicts lasted for 40 years. I don't think that it's going to be a quick thing. My whole opinion of the whole business is stay true to the gospel – live the gospel and I think you'll be protected.

Q: Would you share your testimony?

A: From the very first recollection of my life I've always known that what my parents had taught me about the gospel and what was being taught to me in church was true. I never had a doubt that it was true. I always knew. I always knew that Jesus was alive and that God was alive and this was the church that He established. I've not had any doubt of this all my life. Right to this day I know that this is Christ's Church. He is in charge of what is happening on the earth at all times. As I said, if we just stay true to the faith and do what we can to help Him on this earth to spread the gospel that whether or not the terrorists kill us, we'll be safe anyway. He will protect us to live longer on this earth or He will take us up and we'll be with Him again. This is the true gospel and true church. This is His church and His works.

Q: What have been your greatest joys in your life?

A: Meeting my wife. Getting married in the temple. Michael, Valerie, Nolana, Charlinn, and Clint and their marriages to each one of their spouses and each one of their children. These are my greatest joys. My joys are my family.

Q: What have been your greatest sorrows in your life?

A: That I didn't study more. When I was growing up I never doubted that the gospel was true, but I didn't do a lot of studying. I went to seminary, but I only went for a short while. Now they kind of push you to go to seminary, but they didn't do it back then. I started 8th and 9th grade seminary and went a couple months and dropped out. I didn't go to seminary in high school. Marion Hanks was the director over the seminary at West High School and my brother Jim was the president. When I finally read The Book of Mormon I was an adult. That was one of the things I wished I would've done. I've probably read The Book of Mormon more in the last 10 years than all the time before that.

Q: What council do you have for the rising generation to live successfully?

A: Be morally clean, be honest, be faithful to the gospel and do everything the Lord wants you to do. You won't know what He wants you to do unless you study. It's all in The Book of Mormon – everything He wants you to do. Study The Book of Mormon and pray that you can learn the truths contained in it and can live those truths and share the messages with others.

Words to the "!!!" Song
By: Ralph Lord

As I was walkin' down the beach one bright and sunny day,
I saw a great big wooden box a-floatin' in the bay.
I pulled it in and opened it up and much to my surprise
Oh, I discovered a ! ! !, right before my eyes
Oh, I discovered a ! ! !, right before my eyes.

I picked it up and ran to town as happy as a king
I took it to a friend I knew who'd buy most anything
But this is what he hollered at me as I walked in his shop
"Oh, get out of here with that ! ! !, before I call a cop"
Oh, get out of here with that ! ! !, before I call a cop.

I turned around and ran right out, a-runnin' for my life
And then I thought I'd take it home and show it to my wife
But this is what she hollered at me as I walked in the door
"Oh, get out of here with that ! ! !, and don't come back no more
Oh, get out of here with that ! ! !, and don't come back no more.

I wandered all around the town until I chanced to meet
A hobo who was lookin' for a handout on the street
He said he'd take most any old thing, he was a desperate man
But when I showed him the ! ! !, he turned around and ran
Oh, when I showed him the ! ! !, he turned around and ran.

I wandered 'round for many years, a victim of my fate
Until I chanced to come upon St. Peter at the gate
But when I tried to take it inside he told me where to go
Get out of here with that ! ! !, and take it down below
Oh, get out of here with that ! ! !, and take it down below.

The moral of this story is: when you're out on the beach
And you should come upon a box, and it's within your reach
Don't ever stop and open it up, that's my advice to you
'Cause you'll never get rid of the ! ! !, no matter what you do
Oh, you'll never get rid of the ! ! !, no matter what you do!

Norma Jean Smith

Father: Marion Cowen Smith
Step-Father: Jose Emilio Martinez
Mother: Hazel Maude Rosenbaum
Born: 2 November 1936
Place: Salt Lake City, Utah, USA
Married: 31 August 1956 to Ralph Knowles Lord
Place: Salt Lake City, Utah, USA
Died: 8 March 2010
Place: Sandy, Utah, USA

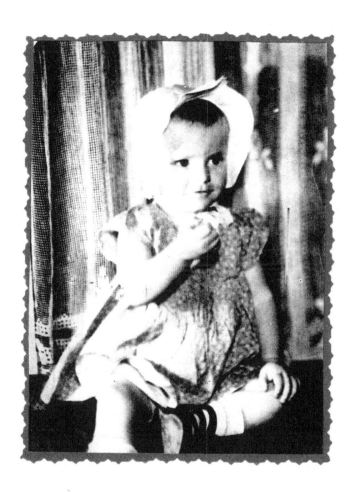

Norma's Birthday cards

given to her by her mother (Hazel)

Oral History of Norma Jean Smith Lord

Interviewee: Norma Jean Smith Lord
Interviewer: Tewie Lord
(Interviewed on: 11/2001)

Q: When and where were you born, and who were your parents?

A: I was born in Salt Lake City in the County Hospital on November 2, 1936. My parents were Hazel Maude Rosenbaum Smith and Marion Cowen Smith.

Q: What were the family circumstances when you were a little girl?

A: My dad was out of work. I don't know if we were on welfare or how we were living. It was a hard time. It was 1936, and it was the end of The Depression so it was a hard time for everyone.

Q: Did you have any other siblings?

A: My dad died when I was 3, and I was the only child.

Q: What were some of your preschool memories?

A: I remember my childhood being pleasant. I don't have a lot of memories but I feel I had a happy childhood. I always felt very loved. When I was older we had a little puppy. The dogcatcher would come house to house to get you to buy a license. My mom knew he was in the neighborhood so she put me in the closet and told me to keep the puppy quiet or he would take the dog away, because we didn't have enough money to pay for a license. We never got caught.

Q: What memories do you have of your dad?

A: I have a couple memories of my dad. I remember when I was little, I can't remember how old I was, but we had a fireplace in our house and my dad brought home two chocolate hearts. One of the hearts was bigger and that was my mom's and the small one was for me. I remember he let me see them and let me touch them, but then he set them on the fireplace where I could only look at them. The one thing I remember of my dad is his legs.

50

Q: Did you have any preschool friends?

A: I probably had the same friends that I had all my life cause we lived on the same street. I had a friend named Sandra that I played with when I was little, I don't think I strayed from the house much when I was this young.

Q: What are your memories of you elementary school years? Teachers? Classes?

A: I had a kindergarten teacher, Mrs. Ervine, who I thought was the most beautiful woman alive. She was older but she was so nice and I felt she really loved me. In the 2nd Grade I had a teacher that called me Donna all year long, instead of Norma. I also remember in the 3rd Third Grade we were going to put a dance on for the school so we had to practice dancing with our little boy partners. I had Mrs. Chipman. One day I asked Mrs. Chipman if I could go to the bathroom and she told me that I should've gone at recess and refused to let me go. So during the dance I wet my pants! And the little boy I was dancing with, his name was Dickey, put his arm around me and told me that it wasn't my fault. Most boys would've grossed out. I will never forget him. I was so mortified, but he was very nice to me. As I got bigger I did a lot of tricky bars, hopscotch and jump rope, some of the things of the day. Hopscotch was my favorite. When I was in 6th grade they would have contests on jacks and I was very good at playing jacks. I won the school champion one year for jacks. We only had one Negro in our whole school and she was my competition, we would play jacks everyday at recess.

Q: Did you have any little crushes in grade school or in junior high?

A: When I went to 7th grade there was a boy in my class named Danny. I thought he was the most gorgeous creature. He was blonde. He was very moody. At that time I just felt I wanted to make him better. He was a nice kid. In the summer, I think I was 14. I had my first date. I think his name was Donny Hale. He took me to a seminary dance at the university institute on the bus, and we came home on the bus. He was 2 years older and I think I had a crush on him. In the 9th grade one of my friends introduced me to a boy named Dave White, who I didn't really care for but it was a free date. Sometimes I would tell him that I wouldn't go out with him unless he got a date for my girlfriend. He would get a date for my girlfriend! If he couldn't find a date then he would pay for her way. He would take us both. I really didn't like him. I think he smoked when I wasn't there cause I could smell the smoke. He was in high school. I went out with him the whole 9th grade, off and on. There was a kid named John Eagan in my school that I had a crush on. He couldn't see me for dirt, but I thought he was wonderful.

Q: How were your teachers, classes in junior high?
A: I had a gym teacher and his name was Mr. Durrant. He had size 15 or 16 shoes. He was our Gym teacher but he couldn't come in to the girl's dressing room. He was so fun. He was probably the funnest gym teacher I had. He was a great big guy. It was the only time I ever had a guy gym teacher. He would only teach us to play games and such. The kids had to mark the role, I remember that really well. I remember an English teacher. I can't remember her name, but I went up to her and said, "I ain't got no pencil." She just about fell to pieces. She got after me in front of the whole class. Another time I had to recite the Gettysburg Address. I had a pencil in my hand and when I leaned over the pencil got stuck in my lip and it had to be pulled out. I had a mark there of graphite for years and years 'til it finally went away. I don't remember the teachers so much. I remember I liked school. It was very fun. When I was young I didn't let anyone push me around so I had many fights over hopscotch and tricky bars. I would stand up to the bigger kids trying to push me off the hopscotch. I was a child of no fear. I'm glad that I don't have children like that. (see Hazel Maude Rosenbaum's Oral History for more)

Q: What memories do you have of your high school years? Teachers? Subjects?
A: I loved high school. I remember Mr. Snow. He was my Biology teacher. I remember that class because on the first day of school in walks Ralph, and he knocks over ink on the teachers

desk, accidentally, on his way in. I thought, "Man he is cute. I would like to get to know him." Another thing that impressed me was when the teacher asked what had happened at his desk. Ralph raised his hand and told him he accidentally knocked it over. I thought, "Wow he is a neat guy." But he wasn't the only one. There was another kid named Jon Carlson who walked in. He was tall and had dark hair. I didn't date Ralph that first year. I went with a kid named Gale McCurdy. The summer before that I went with a kid named Radell Hunt. I always had a boyfriend. I wouldn't date a bunch of guys, but I always had a little boyfriend. My Junior Year I got to be in Pep Club. That was fun traveling around with the teams. We would cheer for basketball, and football. That was a fun year because we got to travel with the team. I belonged to the Swim Club, which I didn't ever go to. I belonged to the Roller Skating Club, which Ralph was the president of. That was our Senior Year and that was fun. I loved going to the Roller Rink. I was a pretty good roller skater of course Ralph was a better one. I also answered phones in the office because we would get extra points for that. The building was away from the main building and so if the teachers got a phone call they would transfer it over there and then I would take the message and take it to the teacher. We would get points for the Award Banquet and if you got points for the extra activities, you could go to the Awards Banquet. I liked Health, and I loved Child Development. There was a great big huge scrapbook I turned in there. I loved History and I like to read. I liked the literature part of English not the grammar part. I loved school. I don't remember the education part so much, I just remember I loved the social part. There were 13 girls in our group. We would go to games together. This was the year I was in Pep Club. We would go to all of the games together and go to school functions together. There was always enough of us that we always felt like we had someone to go with to do something. We would eat lunch together. I loved school.

Q: What was the religious climate in your home like and what things did you do as family and individually. What were your beliefs at that time?

A: There were no religious teachings. We would maybe bless the food at Thanksgiving. Nobody went to church. When I was eight years old my parents said I could chose any religion that I wanted. At that time I had been going to a Catholic Church with my little friend Lillian. The priest would pick us up in a van and take us to Catechism and then drive us home. I fell in love with the priest. I went to Catechism. It is more intense than Primary because you had to learn it and then take tests. Catechism is learning that when you sin it is bad. In the book it says that as you sin your heart gets darker. They don't have Catechism any more but it was a book that just taught you things. It was more intense teaching than Primary and you LISTENED. In Primary you're lucky to get their attention. When the nuns talked to you, you were quiet and you listened. I was baptized into the Catholic Church when I was eight because my folks gave me a choice. I had my Confirmation when I was 12. Once you are confirmed you can take the Sacrament up until then you can't. You have to go confess to the priest before you have the Sacrament. You don't take it unless you have been to confession. Then he would send you out with your rosary and you would say a prayer. He would tell you to say three "Hail Mary's" and four "Our Father's" or a set prayer. One day I went into the priest to do my confession. At 12 I didn't have a lot to confess, just things like, I was mean to my brother and little things like that. Then I went out and was kneeling there doing my rosary and I thought, "Why do I have to go to the priest to talk to my Heavenly Father. Why do I have to? Heavenly Father knows all. He knows what I have done. Why do I have to confess it to the Priest?" That was the start of it. That was making me think. I couldn't understand why I had to go through him. That was the thing that made me fall away. Then I had another girlfriend that was L.D.S. Her name was Thomasine Guise and she invited me to go to her Mutual. I was almost 13. I went and I loved it. It was fun and that is where all of the nice boys were too. They didn't swear and they didn't smoke and they were nice boys and that was appealing. Everything was great. I was fine going to Mutual and then my friend invited me to go to Sunday School. So I did. The first time I went to Sunday School the teacher was giving a lesson on the Godhead. When you have been taught that the Godhead is three in one for all of those years and it is ingrained in you. It was very hard for me to accept that these are three individual beings. I felt like he was tearing my God apart. That is how I felt as a 13 year old girl. So I decided I would never go back to Sunday School. Mutual was OK but no more Sunday School. But then about a year later my friend again invited me to go to Sunday School and I did and again the lesson was on the Godhead! Was the Lord trying to tell me something? I started attending Sunday School. One young missionary gave me an old Bible that he had. I still have it. One thing lead to another but I was still not a member. I had missionaries at the neighbor's house before I met Ralph. Then I met Ralph in high school and he was active L.D.S. and he didn't push me. I always went to Sacrament. Isn't that funny? But not Sunday School. So we would go to Sacrament at my ward. Sunday School was in the morning, then Sacrament in the night and Primary and Mutual were on another day. Ralph didn't ever push me. He set a really good example. We talked about it a little bit but he really never pushed me. We dated all through our Senior Year. That summer, that July after we graduated, I was baptized. At that time I didn't realize Ralph could baptize me or I would have had him baptize me. But my Sunday School teacher baptized me. He had taken the time to explain and teach me. Tithing, he had found in the Bible where tithing means 10 percent. Because my folks were a little tight on money, they didn't believe you should give that much. But he found it so I showed that to them and that explained tithing. My mother was a member so she kind of knew a little bit about it but she hadn't been active since she was a little girl. Then she started coming to Sacrament, her and her sisters came about the time I was baptized. They would just go to Sacrament they never went to anything else.

Q: What was your parent's philosophy of child rearing?

A: That they were to be seen and not heard. My mother was a
       good listener. They were the parents and we were the children.
       A good swat or whatever was necessary they didn't hesitate to
       deliver. I really was pretty obedient, other than being a feisty
       little fighter I was obedient. I didn't give my mother any
       problems. As a matter of fact, she said to my little sister
       several times, "Why can't you be like Norma? Why can't you
       obey like Norma?" So I must have been a pretty obedient child.
       I think being who I was, it was easier to obey than to be in
       trouble. (see Hazel & Joe's Oral Histories for more)

Q: Who are your siblings and what kind of relationship did you
       have with them. Go right down the line.

A: Alfred is 5 years older. He joined the Service when he was 17. I
       remember he would be told to tend us. He would leave and
       say, "You do the dishes and you do this while I am gone." If we
       didn't he would get after us with a broom and hit us with a
       broom and be mad at us. He'd swear if we ever told our
       mother we would be dead meat. But he just left us. I don't
       remember a whole lot about Alfred. He repaired cars. That
       used to be his hobby. One day he caught his finger in the fan
       belt and had part of it cut off. He quit school and went into the
       Service. When he got home he married a girlfriend that he had
       had before he went in the Service for four years. But by the
       time he got home she had been married and had 3 kids, well 2
       kids and one on the way. But she was divorced so he went
       ahead and married her. Then they had one little girl. But he
       lost his two sons when they were just young. The one little boy
       was just a little bit retarded. The one that she was pregnant
       with and the other boy got in an accident and drown in the
       Jordan river. But he has two daughters that are still living.

       Judy – there are 5 years between us. She is younger. She was
       very, ornery and went her own way. I think it is interesting
       but as I grew up I never thought I was pretty and as she grew
       up she never thought she was good enough. I don't remember
       my mother doing this to her as much as she would do it to me.
       She would say, "If she (Judy) were just as good as me she

would have a better life." I would hear, "If you were as pretty as Judy you would have it made." We both had this feeling that neither one of us were up to par, I guess. Except I was loved. Never, ever in my life did I not feel loved. But my little sister did not feel loved. She has had different problems in her life because of different things that happened in her childhood. We didn't do a whole lot together because there were so many years between us. We thought differently and we acted differently. We had different kinds of friends. So we really didn't have a whole lot in common that we were close sisters, which is sad. She got married at fourteen so, I have no idea what her hobbies or talents were. She was so young when she got married. We ran in different circles. We slept in the same bed and that is about the only thing we had in common. She used to wear my blouses after I had ironed them. Because we had 100% cotton back then so you would wear them once and you would have to iron them. You never wore them wrinkled. She would put them back in the closet but I could tell they had been worn. She was always taller than me so she couldn't wear my skirts. This was when we were teenagers. I was smaller than her.

Raymond has always been macho. He is so much like my stepfather. "Joe the tough guy." He is 6 years younger than me. I didn't have anybody close to me I could do things with; because by the time my sister was 14 I was 19. He was very macho. He played the guitar. He loved to fish. He never went into the Service. He quit school. I think he got married at 18. I left home at 19 and he was 6 years younger so he was only 13 when I left. Being so far away and then my mother died so early we didn't have the family things where we got to know each other as adults. He lived here. I lived out in Sandy and didn't have a car to go visit. We didn't see each other a whole lot. I think if my mother had lived longer we would have had that adult relationship.

Q: Did your family move often?
A: We moved but on the same street. I can't remember if we had 5 or 6 houses. I counted them once. We moved from house to

house and each house would be a little bit bigger space wise. That is why we would move. A landlord owned all of those houses. One landlord owned the whole block. We would just move from one house to a little bit bigger for a little bit more space.

Q: What was the neighborhood like?
A: It was Wonderful. As a kid I didn't know that I was poor. That block was our whole life and the neighbors were very nice. Sometimes when the people are poor they are more giving than the people who are more affluent. Our neighbor had an old swayback horse and he would take kids for rides on it. We had an old garage out there, which was home base. We would play baseball out in the backyard. There were no fences the whole block was one big backyard. There was no grass back there, just weeds. Clothesline and things like that. We used to play ball over by the old shed. Good relationships, people were good to each other and if they had something they were willing to share. I remember how my neighborhood reacted to Pear Harbor. I was very young. I was probably 5. I remember everybody going out into the street and talking about it. Anytime, anything big happened on the radio the neighbors would congregate and discuss it and talk about it, which you don't see that anymore. If anybody had a problem or was sick we were there to help them. I think I've just noticed, especially since I have gotten older, that the poorer people are more willing to give what they have. I think the more affluent we get we are afraid that we might give something away that we might need. I felt it was very good until I got bigger and realized what a bad area it was. I didn't know this but when I got in 10th grade they used to call me "The Beauty of the Slums." Because it was a very poor area. There was a lot of fighting of parents, I'm sure, because of the finances and the situations that they lived in. But as far as me personally as a little girl it was a pleasant area for me to live in. Until I got in high school and then I realized I was poor.

Q:	What kind of vacations or travel did you have?

A:	None. We never went on vacation because my mother was ill all of the time so my father would take his vacation leave to pay for doctor bills or hospital bills. There were always bills to pay. I don't ever remember going on a vacation. We used to go on Sunday drives once we got a car. I was older, maybe junior high. My brother was gone because the three of us would sit in the back seat and sing songs, as we would drive around or go up the canyon. But that was really the extent of any vacation we took. Until I married Ralph I did not go out of the state of Utah.

Q:	What other kinds of things did you do for fun?

A:	We had a neighbor who had a truck that he could put wood slats on the sides to make them higher and then we could stand up. He would put as many of us in his truck as he could and then we would go up the canyon. Our parents weren't always with us. There would be some parents there but my parents didn't go. We would go up to the canyons and hike. It was wonderful. We thought it was great because none of those kids got that far away from home because there just weren't the finances. When we were little on payday, and I don't know how often on payday but I must have been in junior high, we would go for hamburgers at Bill's Drive In. I think they were 10 for a dollar sometimes 15 for a dollar. We would go there and, "Wow", what a treat to go out and buy hamburgers that was a real treat. That was one of the fun things that we did.

Q:	Did you go visit you grandparents?

A:	We never did go see my grandparents. My grandpa (Lucious) came and visited us occasionally. Once every two months or so. But, no, we didn't ever go visit them. We had aunts and uncles that came to visit us at Christmas. We would go visit Roy and Fay. They are the only ones I remember going to visit besides June and Donna who, of course, lived right on the street. They just lived on 30 something south. That wasn't too far away. I remember my cousin had a bedroom that was a walk in closet. I didn't know it was a closet at the time. There was bed and a little walkway and a little dresser that was the whole bedroom. I was so envious that she had her very own room. As a child all 4 of us slept in the same bedroom. At one time we all slept in one bed but then as we got bigger we had 2 beds. When I got to high school we got a house where me and Judy shared a room and Raymond had his own room, which was really something for us because we had always shared a bedroom.

Q: Did you have any medical or dental problems as a child?

A: I had a rotten tooth and at that time, of course, we didn't have any money but you could go to the police station and there was a dentist there you could go to and he would take care of your teeth. I don't know if he filled teeth because the only thing he did with mine was pull it. I was around 10 years old. I remember taking the bus up to Salt Lake to the police station and had my tooth pulled and, of course, I was bleeding. Then I had to go catch the bus to go back home. At that time there were drinking fountains on the street and I would go rinse out my mouth because it was so full of blood. I had a hanky that I held on it during the ride home. I had pneumonia when I was little. Other than that I never went to a doctor when I was little. I was not ill as a child. When my dad was dying of tuberculosis I got pneumonia. I was in the same hospital as him. It was the County Hospital, which was for welfare patients. My mother had to go between me and my dad. My dad didn't know I had pneumonia because it would have been hard for him. I don't know what happened but mother swears that the nurse left the window open and my dad got pneumonia. Pneumonia is what killed him instead of tuberculosis.

Q: What were some childhood fads that you remember?

A: We wore dresses. We never wore pants. I remember in junior high we used to wear pants on the weekend but we never wore pants to school. Valerie was in grade school when the kids could start wearing pants to school. There were Joyce and Jantzen, which were big brand names in school. They were brand names like Eddie Bower or whatever. They were very expensive. I used to have Joyce shoes because I worked. They were very expensive and I remember asking my dad to buy me a Jantzen sweater. I usually would buy my own with any money I earned because I did buy my own clothes. He said, "Yea, we will get you one on payday." So on payday I went with my dad to Woolfe's Department Store. Which was an expensive store. We went in and it was a lime green sweater that I wanted. I tried it on and I liked it. He said he was going to buy it. When they told him the price, I thought his chin was going to hit the ground but he bought it. I know now that that was a real hardship for him. At the time, being a teenager I wanted it. He said he would buy it for me, so, he didn't ask how much it was. We wore pantaloons in high school underneath our full skirts and then real full crinoline petticoats. I couldn't afford a crinoline petticoat so I took a sheet and I made a big full petticoat and every Saturday I would wash it and starch it and set it on the floor in my room to dry. The starch would last a good week, then I would wash it and starch it again. When you would walk down between the desks you had so much petticoat it would make noise as it hit the desks. It was fun. Poodle skirts were really big. They were made of felt usually and then they had a little poodle with a chain. Poodle hairstyles were in style. It was a tight curl, a perm; many older women have them now. Where you just get a perm and then comb them out. That was called "a poodle." In junior high I remember my coat practically dragging the ground because that was the style. There were saddle shoes with the tie. I never wore the saddle shoes so much. I didn't care for them. They looked too boyish to me. I used to polish my white shoes and put them in a sack to carry them to school. I would wear my dark shoes to school in the winter. Because wearing white shoes in the winter was a big deal. They would get dirty if you walked to school in them. So you polished them, put them in a bag, then changed once you got to school. Because my hair was so thin and the style was curly I would leave my curlers in with a bandana over them until I got to school and then I would take them out at school. I would go to school about an hour early to fix my hair and put my white shoes on. I was very clean and neat as a young teenager. We had lockers just like they have now to put my things in. We had a gym locker and one in the hallway.

Q: Any humorous experiences or pranks that were either performed on you or someone else?

A: I don't remember any specific experiences at this time, but I have always been very gullible. My friends would tell me things that weren't true and I would believe them. One time my friend Sandra, who was my same age, went out to dinner. We would go for our birthdays over the years. She once told me I reminded her of Betty White off the show "The Golden Girls". I had never seen the show before so I watched it and I wasn't too impressed with what she thought I was – kind of an airhead. I think I have been teased a lot because I believe what I am told. I didn't go toilet papering as a kid, but once I became a youth leader I did. I would take my Mutual girls out. But I would call the people ahead of time to let them know. My girls didn't ever know I did this. So I never went toilet papering without the people knowing it.

Q: What was your social life as a teenager? Dances, dates,

A: I went on dates but I didn't go to too many dances. I went to parties. The Gold and Green Ball, which was a church sponsored dance, which they had every year. Usually in the fall. I went on dates to the movies. We went to old houses on Halloween and scared ourselves to death, things like that.

Q: Besides your dates with Dad, which date was your favorite?

A: I went with this kid named Danny Evans. We went to Antelope Island. I think it was on a holiday like the 4th of July or something. One of the kids that was with us had an uncle who worked on a ranch there. That was real interesting because I had never been there. I can't remember what else we did, but it was fun because it was the first time I had been to Antelope Island.

Q: What chores did you have as a child and then what jobs did you hold?

A: Our chores were on Saturdays. We had to mop all of the floors and wax them. We dusted too. My mother always did the washing because it was a one day-all day thing. If we were there we would help her. My jobs when I was young were: I would baby tend. The one job I had in high school was I baby tended 4 little kids. One of them was a new baby. I got $3.00 a day for nine hours. Then at night I tended for another lady with 4 children and I would tend at her house. I would catch the bus and go up to Phyllis'. That was an interesting thing because my mother didn't know this other lady. I got the job through the high school. They would list different jobs on the bulletin. I tended there for months and months. I'll bet it was 10 months I baby tended there. Then one night I came home and I said, "Guess What Smitty gave her?... a T.V." My mom asked what for and I said I didn't know. My mom asked, "What does Phyllis do?" She worked nights. I said, "I don't know." But she would always sent me home in a cab. Different guys would bring her home and would want to take me home but she would never let them she always sent me home in a cab. I guess she went to bars. Her husband was in prison. She had had a baby since he had been put in prison. But I didn't connect that. Then my mother started questioning me. Of course she didn't like any of that so I had to quit tending for her. She would pay me .25 cents an hour and after midnight I got .50 cents an hour. That was very good money. She didn't get home until 2 or 3 in the morning. Once I graduated from high school I went to work at Young Sign Company. It was just before I was married. I was 19. I was a payroll clerk. There weren't a lot of fast food places to work at as a teenager. Dees had just opened up on 21st south and there were some other carhop places but I never worked at any of them.

Q: What were the jobs you had as an adult?

A: Right after high school my first job was at Arrow Pickle Factory. I had run around looking for a job and just couldn't get anything. Then Ralph's dad was a mailman. As a matter of fact, he was a mailman by my house. He was the mailman for the Arrow Pickle Factory. It was only about a block from my house. He said to go by there and check on a job. I would stick pickles in a bottle. You stick the middle pickle in so it would fit. I couldn't eat a pickle for years. I worked there about a month. Then my friend had an aunt who was the manager for the Young Electric Sign Company and that they were looking for a payroll clerk if I wanted to go down and apply. I got the job there. As an adult Ralph and I cleaned banks and we did a newspaper route for a while. I was a TMC manager for the Deseret News for a while. They gave a free paper on Tuesdays and Thursdays. I managed and hired the young men to throw the papers. I quit because it went to Sundays and I didn't want to work on Sundays. I worked there for about a year. I worked at three different Albertson's. One in Sugarhouse, one in Midvale and one in Sandy. All three I worked in the bakery. I was a sales girl. I tried to work shifts that Ralph didn't work so one of us was home with the kids. After I quit the sign company I had Mike and we moved out to Sandy. Then when Val was about 6 months old I went to work for Albertson's. Later on I worked at a daycare for about 12 years. I worked for a woman named Eva Dial. As she had surgery I would go spend the whole day there or I would work so she could get out and do the things that she needed to do. I also worked as a temp. We did janitorial work at different places. I worked at H & R Block as a receptionist. I worked at the candy shop for Diana. My favorite job was as the payroll clerk at Young Electric Sign Company. I loved that job. I liked the paper work. Right after I left they brought computers in. So I didn't learn computers. It was about a year after I had Mike they computerized the company. I wish I could have been there to learn computers.

Q: What kind of educational classes have you taken as an adult?
A: For years and years I took Institute classes. Cheryl Bullock and I took many classes. I went to Education Week a lot of years.

Q: How did your working affect the family?
A: I don't know that if affected them. They were always anxious for me to come home. Even though their dad was there I don't know how much time he spent with them. I really didn't work

that much when I had the kids. I never worked full time once I had children. We tried to work it out so one of us was home. When I sold Avon Judy Thomas tended Charlinn. I only went out for a couple of hours or so. I remember coming home one day and Charlinn said, "Mom I don't want you selling Avon anymore." So I quit that. But other than that I don't know the kids were affected by it. I only worked part time and that was sporadic. I really tried to work it out that I was here when they came home from school.

Q: In your own words, what was your courtship like with dad and your marriage?

A: I told you already that I had met him in Biology and that I thought he was really cute and that I wanted to date him. At the end of school I had written in his yearbook, "I hoped I would see more of ya." hoping that it would have an effect on him. During the summer him and some other boys were going to go for a ride and they decided to get some girls so he called me and I was really excited. He was someone I really wanted to go out with. So we went for a ride and he took me up to Passion Flats, which is above The Capital. It was the kind of place that you just didn't go to because it was a place that you went up to too park and neck. I was really surprised. He parked the car and the kids around us started necking and I said to Ralph, "Lets go for a walk." So we went for a walk and talked and looked at the lights of the city then went back and he drove me home. I told my mom that night, and even wrote it in my diary (which I have since lost), "I will never go out with him again. I can't believe he took me to passion flats blah ,blah, blah. . . He must not think to much of me etc." But the next week he called me and wanted to know if I wanted to go do something and I said, "NO!" No explanation, just, "No!" Then he called again in another week and I said, "No." And he gave up and didn't call me again. Then my Junior Year started and it was fine. I was really involved and busy. I don't hardly even remember Ralph I was too busy. But then my Senior Year, I answered the telephone at this building across the ball field for a job. One day I saw him walking across the ball field with all of his friends and I thought, "He is so cute. How can I get him to notice me?" At first I played it really cool and just said, " Hi" when I passed him. Then pretty soon I started making a point of meeting him at these stairs that you had to go down to the basement to to the other building. I would hear him coming with his friends so I would stay near the stairs until he came and then I would walk just in front of him. Slowly I started talking to him and eventually it got so we would meet and walk and talk together. Then once I told him that I am in this certain room working and that if he had any time to come down and talk to me. So he did and it evolved from there. He asked me out. We went to the Rialto Theatre to see a movie with some of his friends. I remember he put his arm around my chair and just left it there. From then on we kept dating and then we went to a Gold and Green Ball and he asked me to go steady at a party after the ball. I told him I would be happy to go steady but that I already had a date for New Years Eve. He was very upset. Then I found out he had asked my friend Tommy Lou if she thought I would go steady with him before he even asked me. I went out with Gail on New Years Eve and from then on Ralph and I went steady. We got married a year out of high school. Ralph had borrowed some money from me to pay for a car. I was a saver. I don't know what he did with his money, spent it on dates I guess. Anyway he bought a Buick. I lent him $300.00. My mother was upset because I didn't have him sign a note or anything and there was no commitment between us. But he let me buy clothes on his ZCMI card to help pay it back over time. On Valentine's Day about 4 girls in our ward got engaged and we had talked about getting married so I thought for sure he would propose but he didn't. I was a little disappointed. Actually I thought I might get it at Christmas. He gave me a present in this little box and told me I couldn't open it until after midnight. I took it to my bedroom and very obediently waited until 2 minutes after midnight. I opened it but it was a watch. I was really disappointed. Then in February when everybody got engaged people were asking me if Ralph gave a ring and I had to say, "No." But on Easter Sunday, which happened to be April Fool's Day, they were having a Sunrise Service at "This is the Place Monument." It was a real cold wintry day and it got cancelled. So there at the monument he proposed to me and gave me the ring. We met some friends, Don and Angie Horsley who were engaged. We went out to breakfast with them. (Even though it was Sunday.) I went home and showed the ring to my mom. She said, "It's Angie's." I told her, "No it's not." She told me she would believe it when I kept the ring overnight. She didn't believe that I was engaged until I had the ring the next morning. We were sealed in the temple on August 31, 1956.

Q: Tell us about your children.

A: MICHAEL
Michael was my firstborn. He was born September 20, 1958. The first time I picked the baby up he would lift his head off of my shoulders and look around and act interested in everything around him. I remember thinking, "This is a newborn?" There was such a joy in taking him home and having this overwhelming feeling of love and thinking, "This is MY Child." He was always busy. Always looking for what was around the next corner. Always wanting to climb the next mountain. He walked when he was very young. He was always a very happy little boy and a goer. He was very good-natured. A little bit stubborn sometimes, but always looking for a challenge. Once one challenge had been conquered he was looking for another one. He was always looking for something new and different. He loved life. He was a happy teenager, as far as I could tell. He still is a lot like that. He still wants to try something new. That is who he is. Always looking for something around the next corner, something new. When he was little I remember putting him to bed at night and I would be out on the couch making Barbie clothes and he would come out and say, "HI". I would talk to him for a minute and then put him back to bed and pretty soon he would come back out and say, "HI". He was so happy it was hard to be stern with him. When he would come home from school I would find notes in his pockets all the time from little girls. I can't remember real specifics it was so long ago. Basically, he was just a joy. When he was little he was full of it but as he grew and became a teenager he was a

joy to raise. He was not a problem. I enjoyed raising Mike. It was fun. He would go on a date I would be waiting up for him and he would come and sit in a chair and tell me about his date. I'm sure he didn't tell me everything but he told me what he wanted me to hear about the date. We would sit and talk in the dark. It was enjoyable because I felt like he was sharing some of his feelings. He wasn't afraid to talk to me and tell me how he felt and what was happening in his life. I was always a little worried with Mike. The scariest was when he went on a long hike up over Lone Peak. He was going with a friend of mine's husband, Ralph and a couple of friends. I remember telling my friend before they left that I was concerned about Michael because Mike will finish this at all cost. I just had this feeling that no matter what happens he will finish this. She said, "What will happen if they have to come down?" I said, "He won't! Mike is going to finish this. This is something he is trying to prove to himself." And of course it did happen. Ralph and Mark Sadler had to come home because of health problems. Rick Bullock was beat. When they went to bed that night, Rick told Mike that they were going home in the morning. But Mike got up in the morning and took off. Of course Rick was furious at him because he had to follow him. He couldn't leave Mike up there by himself. But I was concerned about this strong feeling that he had. I just knew that he would finish it at any cost and it turned out to be right. I would also get a little worried when he was going spelunking in the caves. But that was what he liked to do. He always liked to try new things. He did some photography in the basement and other different things. But when he was finished with them it was over and he was on to the next thing.

VALARIE
Valerie was a beautiful little child. She was so sweet. I used to think, "I wonder if she will be here very long?" I had that feeling all the time because she was SO good. It was almost unbelievable. She didn't cry. She was easy to get along with. I would sometimes worry because people would stop me and say how beautiful she is and there sat Mike at the back of the cart. When she got to be 12 she went through some real trials

in her teenage years. She didn't like us very well. But as an adult she is wonderful. I couldn't ask for a better daughter. She is there for us at the drop of a hat. I don't think I could have gotten through all I had to with Dad's sickness without Val. She has been there. Other than her teenage years when she had a real trial and didn't like us, which is probably really typical. My first one didn't do that, so it surprised me. As a little girl she was a little bit coy (like Joy). She was all girl, every bit. She was so feminine. She never learned how to ride a trike. We would sit her on it and she would just sit there and smile. She just wasn't interested. Daddy wouldn't let her wear anything but dresses until she got older. I finally said she had to have some pants. She was pleasant and fun. I remember one Christmas I had gotten her a wind up toy. I would get it out during the day, wind it up for her and let her watch it and chase it then I would put it away and gave it to her for Christmas. She was a darling little girl. I don't remember her talking a lot and as a teenager she didn't share. I guess that was hard for me because Mike had. I wanted her to share and it just wasn't something she wanted to do. I probably handled it wrong because she is a blue and I am a white and I probably could have handled it a lot better.

NOLANA

She was a real spunky little girl and Nolana wanted her way. I don't know that she was particularly spoiled, but being the 3rd child she wanted her own way and if she couldn't have it she would cry and hold her breath until she would pass out. That is real distinct in my mind because I was so worried about it. I was afraid she would hurt herself. I would say, "Give her it." just to keep the peace. Then one day I was asking the doctor about it and he said next time she does it make sure she is in an area where she is safe and can't hit her head. Then let her cry and pass out and when she wakes up don't even look at her. So the next time she did it I was in the kitchen. So I let her and it was so hard. I mean, here I am letting my kid pass out on my kitchen floor while I was standing there doing dishes. She woke up, looked at me and kind of had a funny look on her face. She walked away and never did it again. It was like she thought this isn't working anymore. She was a fun, fun girl. She always liked to have something going on. She was always in charge in her group of friends. She loved boys. She liked fun and loves life. She has a lot of yellow in her. She always wanted more. I would ask her, "What's more?" And she would say, "I don't know. I just want more." She was a fun girl to raise. I worried a little bit about her because she was so boy crazy. She dated a lot and always had a boyfriend. She was very involved. If there was something going on she was always in the middle of it or probably in charge of it. I know her friends used to say, "Well what are we going to do?" Like she was the one to do all the planning. She had a lot of talent. She has a beautiful voice. She is very good at theatre. She was involved in theatre quite a bit. She loved to take dance lessons. There was a point in our lives that we couldn't afford dance lessons and she was the only one who acted disappointed that she couldn't have them. I felt bad that we couldn't give them to her. She was a pretty happy girl. My concern mostly was she just liked the boys more than I would have liked her to. But she was fun with a lot of talent. The thing to do to Nolana if you really wanted to break her heart was to take her off of the phone and ground her. I could do that to Val and she could care less, but it was Nolana's lifeline. I was always frightened while I was raising teenagers. I was always scared that they would go off on the wrong track. I think sometimes I didn't enjoy them as much as I could of because I was so frightened always thinking they might do wrong. She calls me every single day. If she doesn't call then I call her because I think something is the matter. She is real good to call us and keep in touch with us. I appreciate that.

CHARLINN
Charlinn was a very sad birth. I didn't see her for 3 days. She was born with a double clef palette and a double hair lip and the doctor wouldn't let me see her. After 3 days I said to the nurse, "I want to see my baby." She said. "The doctor has a hold on her." I said, "But she is MY baby." She called the doctor and he gave a release. She was beautiful with great big blue eyes but, of course, with the problem. It was very sad and hard emotionally. I think Nolana suffered a lot as a little girl because

she was only 2 ½ and I spent a lot of time in the hospital to feed Charlinn. It took a lot of time. I had to feed her with a little basting syringe type thing because she didn't have a roof in her mouth so she couldn't suck. We spent a lot of time with Charlinn in surgery. I remember taking the camper up there to stay overnight because I would be up there from the time she woke up until the time she went to bed. Which meant Nolana was here with a babysitter, which wasn't fair. Charlinn has been through a lot of surgeries. She is my most spiritual child. She relied on the Lord a lot. She was very very independent. She would always say, "Me do it myself." My dad even called her "Misses Independent." That's how obvious it was that she wanted to do what she wanted to do. Before she went to school for the first time we had a lesson for Family Night on how people are different. She had a little friend, Lisa Thomas, who had really thick hair. The kids used to tease her about having "fat hair". So we used that as part of the lesson. We said some people have fat hair and some people have this or that and Charlinn has a flat nose (because of the surgeries). She came home from Kindergarten the first or second day and she said, "Some kids asked my why I have a flat nose and I said, 'Because I ran into a door.'" I thought, "She will be OK." But then when she got into junior high it was more dramatic. She had two really good friends. She grew up with Kathy and Lisa. She ran track, was very good at it. She was in drama. She set a record in track for the region. I think it was about 5 years before someone broke it. She was very good at it. She relied on the Lord a lot I think. I remember one time, I can't remember what was happening, but I was being very negative and she said, "But mom, what would Jesus do?" I said, "I don't know what Jesus would do, I'm not Jesus." She probably didn't tell me as much about what was going on in her life. Charlinn didn't talk as much. She talked more than Val, but not as much as Mike and Nolana. Some of the kids at school would say, "I hate my parents." And she would think, "I wonder why I don't hate mine?" It was fun to watch Charlinn grow. She had a little bit of an obstacle to overcome. She probably had a lot of emotional upheavals, which teenagers have enough of those already without having other problems. That was probably why she relied on the Lord so much. Overall she was a delight to raise. I would describe her as independent and spiritual.

CLINT

Clint was born 3 weeks late. He weighed 10 lbs and was 22 or 23 inches long. He was a great big boy. The nurses called him their football player because he had such a pair of lungs and he would wake up the other babies in the nursery. But that pair of lungs, as time went on, turned into a very good voice (which he doesn't use). But he had a very good voice. In grade school during the programs the teacher would put the microphone right by him because he had pretty near perfect pitch and he would help keep everyone on pitch. I wish he would use his voice more. It was fun to have him later because I had no children at home. It was almost like a first child again. I got to spend a lot of time with him. He was very bright. He was very curious. He wanted to know, "Why?" on everything there was. You couldn't pacify him by giving him a flat answer. He learned a lot because of his curiosity or thirst for knowledge. He was a fun baby to have later on because I had the time for him. We used to go on special dates. Because he was so much younger than the other kids, I felt like we needed to have time to do his thing. He would choose his special days. It was fun because he would choose things that were interesting or fun like museums. Things that were interesting to me too. We usually did it in the summer once a week. In the winter we didn't do it quite that often. He got a chemistry set and used to try all sorts of things in his bedroom that I didn't know about. I thought he was using it like he was supposed to. When he was little he had a little Commodore computer. His dad taught him how to use it and he has had a love for it ever since. He has never stopped loving the computer or what you do on the computer. He was always trying little things – learning. When he started on the computer he started hacking, which at the time I didn't know hacking was bad. He did a few things which he probably shouldn't have done on the computer which again, we didn't know he was doing. He was never a problem. He was always easy to get along with, EXCEPT – the lawn. Sometimes I would be so frustrated with him because I wanted him to cut the lawn and he would keep saying, "I'll do it." Finally he would be out there in the dark. He was a procrastinator. He is very bright. I remember when he was in high school he would have a report to do or something and he would procrastinate. He had an English teacher that would let them turn in their reports up until 10:00 at night. More than once we were driving there at 5 minutes to 10:00 to turn in his report. He was a joy to raise, never a problem. He was always interesting to talk to. He has a fantastic memory. When he learned something he could retell it so well. He had a lot of knowledge. He wasn't very interested in girls. He met a little girl in the 9th grade that he liked. He couldn't see past her. That was Tewie. I think he went to a couple of school dances on dates. Then one of the teachers in his Senior Year said that if he didn't ask a girl to the Senior Prom that he would dock his grade. (See Ralph's Oral History for more)

Q: What were your family finances like?
A: Ralph was the provider. I worked part time for things like dirt for the backyard, fences and all the extras. Ralph worked at the Post Office most of our married life. We did cleaning on the side – banks, etc. We did watches and pens while Mike was on his mission. We would check the watches to make sure they were working and put pens in these calculators. We didn't get very much but we could do it in the home. Mostly Ralph provided for us.

Q: Could you tell us about the house you lived in, the neighbors and close family friends?
A: We bought this house after when we were married about 3 years. We would come out and take pictures of it while it was being built, which was very exciting. When we moved in it was a huge house. We were used to a one bedroom apartment so we though, "How will we ever fill up this house!" We have had wonderful neighbors all the time. Never any bad ones. We have lived here 42 years. We watched a lot of the houses being built and have had some neighbors move away over the years. Many have moved in and out. The Cummings, who were across the street, they were very good friend. They moved away. The

Crofts moved away, too. Our neighbors on both sides of us are the ones who moved in originally. Our neighbor Mac Corsi, we were with him one day riding around and we came over the hill on 13th. We had been riding for miles and there were no houses and all of a sudden there was this subdivision. We bought houses right next to each other. I'm not very good at keeping in touch with people. I'm not good at letters. This is the only house we have had other than the apartment, which Ralph talked about. So this is the only house we have had. It has been a wonderful neighborhood. We have been in 3 or 4 wards without ever moving. The wards have all been good wards with good people in them.

Q: What is your philosophy about childrearing?
A: I still believe that if a child needs to be spanked they ought to be. I believe that you can talk to a child until you are blue in the face, but if he is not listening they need a swat on the behind to get their attention. I believe in listening to children. If they want to tell you why they did something. I think having a listening ear is probably the most important thing you can have with teenagers. Being there to listen. Don't judge them, sometimes they say things that you are choking over, but try to be calm so they will come back the next time a tell you what they are doing, or at least part of what they are doing. What they care to tell you. But you should really listen. I believe they should have certain jobs that they should do because I think that builds character. I think that they should buy some of their own stuff. If they have finances I think they should save their money to buy things they want. This is something that Clint did. All of his friends would want skateboards and things like that and Clint would say "NO. I'll buy a desk, or I'll buy..." Always very practical in things that he wanted. One more thing is sometimes they don't know that you love them. I don't have a real good ability to share my inner feeling and so sometimes I would think, "I hope they know that I love them." But I don't say that a lot. It would be nice if I had that ability to express those emotions.

Q: What was your daily routine of your life?

A: When I had a wringer washer there was a washday. I would do it on Saturdays, because I worked. But when I got the automatic I do wash when clothes are dirty. I do mop once a week. I vacuum once a week now I used to do it a lot more when I had kids. Usually Mondays, at this point in my life, is when I clean. If I have company during the weekend I want to clean up after they are here not before.

Q: Did the kids have chores?

A: Yes, we had a little chart. They did dishes. The boys had the yard work mostly. They had to keep their rooms clean on Saturdays. We had our difference with getting their rooms clean. I didn't have jobs waiting for them when they got home from school. I don't believe that children should go to school and then have to come home and have chores. Because I think they have been to school all day and they have homework and need to play. So I would do the stuff pretty much during the week, except the dishes. I wish that I would have had each of the girls take a night that was their night to cook. So I could have taught them how to cook. It was just easier for me not to have the mess but I wish I had done that. I don't think they had a lot of chores except on the weekends.

Q: What was a normal day like?

A: Get up in the morning, then get the kids up, feed them breakfast and get them out the door to school. Clean my house, visit with the neighbors and tend the children that were still home. It was just a typical housewife life. I didn't have a car so I didn't go very many places. Now a days it seems the parents are in the car as much as they are home. It was a simple lifestyle because I didn't have transportation. I was on the phone a lot. I called my mother everyday. At night we seemed to sit around and talk a lot. We didn't watch T.V. During the weekdays when school was in. Only on the weekends, but not on school nights. We had Family Night, not every Monday, but as often as we could.

Q: What did you do for birthdays?

A: We usually let the children choose what kind of cake and icing they wanted and what they wanted special for their birthday dinner. That was pretty much it. But we always celebrated birthdays. It was important. That day was theirs! Sometimes we had interesting cakes. One time Mike wanted purple icing. It was a little bit hard to eat but that is what he wanted. They liked the "1 2 3 Cake." It was Grandma Lord's recipe. They always got presents. It was a big deal day for them. I'm not a big party giver, so they didn't have very many. They did have some parties but not every year. As they got bigger they had more parties with their teenager friends. Mainly their parties were with our family.

Q: Did you have any traditions for High School Graduation?

A: It seems like we took them out to dinner for graduation and we bought them a graduation gift. I don't remember anything else. They usually went to the dance or graduation party they didn't necessarily care if they were with us. Mainly they wanted to be with their friends.

Q: What were you family traditions for Christmas?

A: The kids used to help decorate the tree. We used to make things out of marzipan. It was an almond paste. They loved doing that. They would make them into the shapes of pears, and different fruits or vegetable. We would sit around the table and make them. They loved doing that. That was a favorite Christmas tradition. We also made lots of candy. Dad's specialty was divinity. I could never make it very well. But dad makes very good divinity. We don't do any of that any more because dad and I are the only ones here and if we make it and the kids don't come over then I end up eating it and I don't need it. Another tradition is the kids get to open one present on Christmas Eve (usually new pajamas). We would read the Christmas story and we would make the Christmas cookie. On our films you can see that on the cookie we would put the date so that when you watched the Christmas film you would know which Christmas it was. It was one big cookie made out of a whole batch of dough. Then we would set it out for Santa. Of course Santa couldn't eat it all so the kids would get some in the morning. We called it the, "Christmas Cookie". We would do some kind of service every year. When the kids were little they weren't involved but as they got older we would include them. If we had picked a family in our ward then we wouldn't tell the kids either. By the time the kids were involved with us, Mike and Val weren't home, it was with the other three kids more. But we would pick a family, find out what they needed and take it to them. One Christmas that I remember the most was that a car had hit Valerie in her car. It was his fault and he had damaged our car. He had no insurance, no driver's license but he worked at a gas station so he said he would fix it for us if we wouldn't press charges. We left the car there and when we got it back he had put a lot of miles on the car and was full of beer cans. We decided to do this man for Christmas. We bought him a turkey and a box of food and we had the kids take it to his door and ring his doorbell and run. Nolana said at the time she couldn't understand why we would be so good to this man after what he had done to us. That is probably why I remember this the most was because it had such an impression on Nolana. Dad and I always did a Christmas service, but we didn't always tell the kids because it was usually people the kids knew. Another tradition was the kids had this thing called, "The Plan." They would draw out a picture of the house and draw out a plan of how they would sneak upstairs to spy on Christmas. They loved it, especially the little ones because the bigger ones were in charge. It was always the youngest ones job to shut our bedroom door. Most things were wrapped but sometimes there were bigger things that weren't wrapped. They would follow the plan and come up and look at Christmas. We, of course, knew that they were up. One year we had gotten Mike a drum set for Christmas and so I told Michael that I was going to make it so he couldn't get upstairs. He said, "There is no way you can keep me from sneaking up." So that made me more determined not to let them into the front room. So I set up a booby trap at the kitchen door. I put a chair with pans and all sorts of things on it that would crash if he tried to open it. I did the same thing at the front door. That night he DID NOT get up here. I guess it was because he said he could, where, before, I knew that they were sneaking upstairs, but this was a challenge. It was fun to try and stop him. Other that that, it was basically, "Don't wake us up until time." Then we would line them up oldest to youngest down the hall and then we took pictures of them as they came around the corner to see what Santa brought. We probably spent more money than we should have at Christmas but it was a fun time.

Q: What other holidays do you have definite traditions with?
A: At first for Thanksgiving we would go out to Elaine's for Thanksgiving. But then I just felt like I wanted to have it here so we started having our own. The kids were still quite young. I would have my own family and then invite my dad or anybody who didn't have a place to go come. But sometimes I would ask my dad and he would say, "Yes." Then my brother would call him and invite him and so he would tell me he couldn't come or that he could only come for an hour. He was afraid of hurting one of our feelings. It would have been better if he had just said, "I'll come out to one house this year and the next house next year." On Halloween we would always build a fire in the fireplace. We would have the TV in here and watch scary movies. The kids would go trick-or-treating and get lots of candy or go to parties. For Easter we had an Easter egg hunt. We would hide the plastic eggs with a number in it. The number would tell them what prize they got. They were just cheap inexpensive things but the kids loved it. Then as the kids got married and the grandkids came my kids suggested that we do that for them also because I still had kids at home. So we are still doing it to this day. I think the grandkids enjoy it and look forward to it. We divide the little kids from the big kids. The big kids now hide the eggs for the little kids and the adults hide the eggs for the older kids. I think it is fun because it is just tradition because the prizes are not that big or great.

Q: What were your family traditions of a religious nature? i.e.
        FHE, family prayer etc.
A: We had prayers in the morning. We weren't very good in the
        summer. We were better in the winter because it was more
        structured. We would have to get them off to school. But we
        had family prayer and then scriptures in the morning. We
        went to church on Sunday. One Sunday they surprised me and
        called on Valerie in Relief Society to answer the question, "Why
        do you go to church?" Val was a little older and had come to
        Relief Society with me for some reason. But Val's answer was,
        "Because that is what we do. There is no discussing it we just
        get up and go to church on Sunday." I thought that was
        interesting. She had no other reasons to go to church other
        than because that was just what you do. For FHE we were not
        real consistent, but we tried. Once I asked the kids how they
        felt about FHE. One of the things several of them said was that
        they remembered the FHE we had on movies. So often the kids
        would say, "The movie was really good except one little part or
        a few swear words." One mother had likened the bad parts to
        manure. "The movie was really good except for a little
        manure." So I told the story and then for dessert I had ice
        cream with crushed up graham crackers on it and I told the
        kids that the cracker crumbs were manure and asked them if
        they would still want the ice cream. The kids remembered that
        lesson. They were impressed with the fact that I tied the
        dessert in with the lesson. Of course they ate the ice cream
        because they knew it was just cracker crumbs but they got the
        message. Another time Mike was sitting in the chair and Val,
        who was 14, was sitting over in a chair with her arms folded
        with the look of, "You just try to teach me something." Then
        there was Charlinn in the corner standing on her head. Clint
        was a very LOUD 18 month old and was playing at my feet.
        Nolana was sitting by Ralph who was giving the lesson and
        looking at him like he just knew what he was talking about. I
        looked around at that crowd. Then Mike got out of his chair
        and laid on the floor and was asleep in 5 minutes. I looked
        around at that crowd and I thought, "I wonder if this is what
        the Brethren had in mind when they introduced FHE?" But we
        were obedient and doing it and wondering if anything was ever

getting through. Another lesson I remember was we had a FHE on, "What if we had to give up one of the children? If we had to give one away which one would we give up?" Then we went through all of the children and told why we couldn't give up that person. Later Nolana said, "I remember thinking, 'I hope I'm not the one they can give up.'" But the lesson was on how important each one of us are and how we all fit into the family and how we couldn't give any of them up. That is another thing I remember when I was having babies. I kept thinking, "How can I love this baby as much as I love my other children?" It was a hard thing for me to comprehend that I could love another child as much as I loved my other children. It was always amazing that when they put that baby in my arms I would think, "Man, I've got love for this baby too." Your heart just opens up.

Q: What is your adult medical history?

A: I was really pretty healthy until I was in my 40's. I got this bronchitis stuff. I would go to doctor after doctor trying to get cured. I couldn't talk. I couldn't breath. I was coughing constantly. If I talked I would cough. But every doctor could never find anything wrong. So I went on a cleansing program with this herbologist. It was a 3-day cleansing program that made you feel like you were going to die because it made you so sick. When I was about 50 I got diabetes. Just before the diabetes I found out I had high blood pressure. I was overweight. I have arthritis, diverticulitis, I had my gall bladder removed. I had my appendix removed when I was in my 40's. I had an attack one day. I think maybe it was on a holiday because we were having a barbecue outside with all of the kids. I didn't feel well so I went in the house to lie down. I fell asleep and when I woke up I was in excruciating pain. I called and called but know one could hear me. They were all in the backyard. Finally someone heard me. They came in gave me a blessing and took me right to the hospital and they removed my appendix. I had arterial fibrillation. I have asthma, and high cholesterol. So I take a bunch of pills but I'm really not to bad. I swear by cayenne pepper. When the doctors couldn't find anything wrong with me I started taking

80

cayenne pepper pills twice a day. The lady at the herbologist told me about it. Then when Val was pregnant and bleeding with her baby I put her on cayenne and it stopped her bleeding. So it is good for a lot of things. I am a firm believer in cayenne. The pioneers used it if they got an open cut and they could find a plant. They would put it on it and it would stop the bleeding. It aerates the blood they say. Then I had an angiogram and had a stint put in a couple of years ago. The asthma affects me the most. It gets to the point where I can't function. It makes me very tired and I have lots of phlegm. It gets bad in the winter. I think that is all that is wrong with me. Most of it has come since I was 45.

Q: What is your religious attitude?
A: I cannot imagine life without the church. I think about the life my parents lived because they had no guidance. Every night in my prayers I'm so grateful for the fact that I found the truth. I may not be perfect, but I'm able to know what is right and try to live right. I have had a lot of jobs in the church. I have spent probably around 25 years in the Mutual. I have loved every minute of it. It was fun working with the girls. I taught Primary maybe 3 years, not a lot. I've been in the Relief Society about 7 years. I have been in presidencies several times. I think I have been in 3 different presidencies. Not consecutively but with different presidents. I was Compassionate Service Leader, which I really enjoyed. I've been everything in the Mutual except be president. I was in the Stake Relief Society. But then Ralph got his cancer and needed care full time so I was released and they put me in as Supervisor over visiting teachers. That was a piece of cake job. I have been that about 3 years. I was just released.

Q: What was your favorite job in the church?
A: At the time I was in Mutual I enjoyed that the most, but then when I was put in Relief Society I enjoyed that the most. I don't really feel like there was any job that I enjoyed more than another. There were different times in my life. I remember when I was in Mutual I was so busy I could hardly breathe. I was always so busy. But I loved it. I had the girls to my home a

lot. That was when we could have parties and sleepovers in my home. They don't allow that anymore, I don't think. I loved the girls. I have several of the girls that I taught as Beehives who are now 43 and 44 who are in my ward. I loved the mutual. I was frightened when I had to conduct. I've never been good in front of people. I'm good in a group but not when I am up there in front. I have a real problem with that.

Q: In what ways do you think your callings helped you to grow?
A: I had to learn more and study more so I would know what I was teaching. I had to pray a lot especially in a presidency and especially working with the girls. Each girl needed something different and I wanted to know what each girl needed. You have to do a lot of praying when you are in charge. The thing that amazed me in Relief Society was that I felt a love for every sister in the ward. There was like a mantel placed on me and I loved even those who were hard to love. Yet when I was released within a few weeks I didn't have that feeling that I loved them all like I did when I was in the presidency. You are given a mantel that helps you love and appreciate those sisters, even when they are not loveable.

TESTIMONY

I have a testimony of the Gospel of Jesus Christ. I love the Lord. I am so grateful for my children which He has given me to raise and I'm so grateful for the good job my children are doing of raising their children in the church. The greatest joy in my life is the fact that all my children are active in the church. That none of them have strayed. They are all good people, honest people. I am grateful to the Lord for that. I am grateful to have the gospel in my life to help me stay on the straight and narrow path. I think it would be real easy sometimes to do things that the Lord wouldn't want you to do if you weren't going to church or partaking of the Sacrament. When you are renewing your covenants you are promising Him to be good and I think that is wonderful to be able to do that, instead of only being able to do that when you have confession, or once a year when you have Easter. I'm grateful to the Lord for me finding Ralph.

That is one of the greatest blessings in my life. I've had a very very good life. He has been very good to us. I think about what might happen in the future and, you know, no matter how much He has done for us we want Him to do more but I'm grateful for the wonderful life that I have had because of the gospel.

Q: What are your hobbies and interests?

A: I love to read. I'm not good to read the scriptures like I do books but I love to read. I have belonged to a book club for 11 years. I used to like to knit. I knitted sweaters for Ralph and the two little kids but I don't do that anymore. I can't read directions. I need to have somebody tell me if it is something unusual. I used to crochet a lot. I would crochet things for the backs of the couches and doilies. I don't do that any more. I could never read directions. Somebody always had to tell me how to do it. I love to sit and embroidery. I did a lot of embroidery as a young woman. Now I mostly like to read and crochet little wash clothes and do hats for the Humanitarian Section of the church. I like to talk and I like to listen. I don't have a lot of great talents.

Q: Have you been involved in any social or civic activities?

A: I have been a room mother for all of my children. That is part of the PTA.

Q: What are your best abilities?

A: I'm interested in people. I really like to listen to people's problems. Not always to give advice but if they ask for advice I give it and sometimes they don't like the advice I give. I don't usually give advice unless they ask me. I'm a great conversationalist. I keep a nice house. It is not always spotless but it is always clean. I remember Charlinn bringing Dick home and she said she was so glad that she never had to worry about bringing someone home and not having the house in order. It surprised me because I didn't realize it meant anything to the kids. My best accomplishment is that I raised 5 good kids.

Q: Do you have any physical handicap?

A: My memory! I have a terrible memory. I would have people call me and remind me about things. This is not just since I have gotten older; I've never had a good memory.

Q: What are your preferences and dislikes for food?

A: I don't like spinach, cabbage and pizza. I really don't like anything spicy because it burns the roof of my mouth. Everybody looks at me funny when I say that but even when I was a little girl and we would have Spanish food it would burn the top of my mouth, onions too. My mother used to say, "Onions cannot burn the roof of your mouth!" But they did and I would taste them for hours after I ate them. So anything spicy I don't care for. I love breaded veal. That is probably my favorite meat. I like vegetables. I like broccoli, I love all vegetable except cabbage. I liked casseroles because when I was raising my family that was the cheapest way to feed them. I used to like steak but I am losing my taste for that. It seems like there are a lot of things I don't like but I can't think of them now.

Q: What kind of music do you like?

A: I like the 50's music. I like the ballads. I like Country music. I like Johnny Cash and I love Roy Clark. I love his gravel in his voice. I like Tony Bennett, and the music from the big bands. Classical I like but I wouldn't turn it on special. I love to hear somebody playing the piano, especially the old songs. I don't like rock or rap. I don't like loud guitar and drums. I don't like music that intermixes. I don't like high soprano. I love a contralto. I like quiet. I like nothing on just to meditate. I think it keeps you balanced if you can take some time with no outside influence.

Q: What kinds of books do you like to read?

A: I love biographies. I love mysteries. I like "clean" books. I hate to get into a book 50 pages and then feel like I have to take it back to the library because it has bad parts. I like fiction. I like religious books in story forms. The kind that are based around true historical events but with fictional characters. Like, The

Work and the Glory, I like when it is a story. I don't think there are any books I dislike if they are good. I like to read. I feel like I can become apart of the book. I get engrossed, like it is me in the book. It is an escape for me. There are several authors I like. I like Mary Higgins Clark, because she is clean and they are a mystery. But I'm to the point I can read part of it now and know how it will end. That is one of the reasons I have loved the book club. Because all of us are so different that we always pick up different books. I've read books I probably would have never read otherwise. In that way the book club has been good for me.

Q: What kind of movies and television shows do you like?
A: I like musicals and I like romances. I like comedies and adventure. I think I like most of the movies unless they are gory or are violent. As far as television goes, I watch The Pretender with Ralph everyday because he watches it. When Charlinn was a baby and it took so long to feed her I would watch Dark Shadows while I fed her. It was a soap opera about vampires and ghosts and it had a beautiful witch in it also. It wasn't the typical soap opera but nonetheless it was a soap. I got hooked on it. Everyday at 2:00 I made sure it was time to feed the baby.

Q: What are your memorable vacations or travel?
A: I had never been on a trip until I married Ralph. We went to Yellowstone Park for our honeymoon. We had very little money. The first night we went to a hotel called "The Palm". It was the first time I had ever been in a hotel. Then we went to Yellowstone and stayed one night in a room that was in a section that was being added on to. There was no heat. You could have all the blankets you wanted. IT was very cold. The bathroom was down the hall. You shared it with everyone on the floor. Our room did have a sink. We had a hot plate so we made popcorn. We ate spaghetti from a can and different things like that. We usually ate out breakfast, but then ate what we could warm up on the hot plate. The second day we were up there we had some friends come up that had been married about a month. We were so strapped for money our

friends said we could sleep in their tent and they would sleep in the back of their truck. So our third night together was in a tent. But it was still fun. We got a camper when Charlinn was about 2. We took the camper to South Dakota with the Swanee Singers. We saw different things along the way. We saw Mount Rushmore. That was very exciting for me. Ralph had the philosophy that you make memories and I had the philosophy that you use it to put a new bathroom floor in. But he said, "No one will remember what your home looked like but they will remember the things you did together." We went on trip up to Washington State with the Post Office Band. We camped in the camper all the way up there and once we got there we stayed in a men's athletic club. We went to Seattle. The kids loved it. Mike and Val were in another room and the two little girls were in a room with us. Clint stayed home with a babysitter. He was under 1 year old. I remember calling home just as we were going to go on a ferry ride up to Canada. As soon as the baby tender answered the phone I started crying. So I gave the phone to Ralph to ask how the baby was. It was a fun trip we went over to Van Couver Island. We bought a boat when Mike was seventeen. Clint was about 2. We went to Lake Powell twice a year. We went to Utah Lake. After we bought the boat our vacations were boating because we were making payments on it and we felt like we had to use it. Now Mike's family has it. They bought it from us and his family has used it for many years. We went camping in the camper. I went with the band. It was just Dad and I. We went to New Orleans on the train. I was pregnant with Nolana. We stayed on Bourbon Street. Which was real fun. Dad got some wax in his inner ear and it made him not so happy. Everyday I bought myself a nut roll candy bar while Ralph was at rehearsal. That was my craving while I was pregnant with Nolana. We also went to Florida with the band. We stayed on Miami Beach in a very nice hotel. We went swimming at midnight out on the beach because it was busy. I understand the phrase, "Moon Over Miami." It is so big and beautiful. It looks like it is going to touch the ground. It was a fun fun trip. We followed the band around as they marched in parades. The whole family would go to the parades. Sometimes the girls and

I got to march in the parade behind the band. One time we made these yellow dresses that matched. It was while we were in Seattle. The parade got delayed and Charlinn being the independent soul she was decided she had waited to long and that she was tired and she didn't want to march. So she and I sat on the curb in our beautiful yellow dresses.

(Just for the record, mom has kept a journal of the choir trips which is at the end of her section.)

Q: Out of ALL of your trips, choir trips included, which one was your most favorite?

A: Probably Israel. It was very very spiritual. That was the most thrilling because we were right there in Jerusalem. When we took the tours they were so wonderful even though everything was supposedly the way Jesus was. Supposedly where Jesus got the crown of thorns because they could only speculate, but it was incredible. It was a fantastic trip. You could feel the spirit so strong. The thing about going with the choir was that when you heard the choir sing you could feel the spirit there so strongly. It would bring you to tears. Yet I can go up to the tabernacle every Sunday and not get the same feeling and I don't know why. You could tell that the Lord was with that choir and touching the people that were hearing it. When we went on choir trips it would open doors. The missionaries would say they would get lots of referrals after the choir had been there because it was a cultural event. So many would go, then feel the spirit and want to know more.

Q: What has the impact of your and Ralph's retirement been on you?

A: I just think it is nice to spend so much time together. We spend all of our time together. We don't know how many years we will be together. Usually if one of us has to go to the store the other one will go also. Unless one of us is ill. Financially, it hasn't been a burden. I think because we have stayed out of debt and didn't owe a lot of bills. The house and cars are paid for. I think that is the secret to retirement. Make sure you get out of debt before you retire. It would be nice to have a little money saved. We didn't have very much. It is also nice to have the time if the kids need us. When he first retired Ralph was there to do anything anybody needed and could make sure everybody was taken care of. Because of health we can't do that as much now. It has been a real blessing that we do for our kids and have the time to do it. I enjoy this part of my life. In fact I can't think of a time in my life that I didn't enjoy. I have had such a good life. I better cross my fingers the devil is probably listening. We have had our trials but overall I couldn't ask for anymore.

Q: Any comment on any historical events that you have passed through.

A: I think we talked about the tokens you had to have during the war. My aunts would exchange their coupons. So we were never really out of anything. That was during World War II, doing food rations. I remember going to the store using the tokens. I don't remember going without. I don't remember going hungry. My mother believed in letting you be a child and not burdening children with adult worries. Maybe that is why I don't remember the hardships. During the Korean War I was a teenager. During the Vietnam War I was busy raising kids and no one I knew was directly involved with it. During the Kuwait War Michael went to Desert Storm and, of course, I didn't go through what Debbie did. But at that time Ralph had to have his leg amputated from the knee down. I was busy with Ralph's physical problems and so I wasn't as aware of what was happening to Mike as much. My concern was Ralph. There again I had something else in my life that kept me focused instead of on the war.

Q: What comments do you have about our current War on Terrorism? Do you think this is "the end"?

A: I think we should finish it. I'm sorry if some of the civilians get killed but we can't stop doing it. We've got to find the terrorists. We have to destroy that whole group. Because if we don't--We are a paper tiger. We keep threatening to do something. This is the first time that we have had a president that believes in God and looks to God for help and he does things about it he doesn't just talk. He is not afraid of what the people are going to say. My only concern is that we will get tired of it and we won't want to keep going because we are too spoiled. If it is going to put us out any we don't want to do it. No matter what happens they will be after us and if we don't destroy them. . . I'm just glad the Lord is in charge. I keep telling myself that. He knows the beginning from the end. There is not a whole lot we can do about it as individuals but we need to support our president. I do think we have to do this until the end.

Q: What changes have you seen throughout your lifetime in fashion?

A: Women didn't wear pants. My mother always wore a dress. I wore dresses all the time. I was in junior high the first time I put on a pair of pants. I remember wearing hats and gloves. You never went to town unless you got dressed up in heels and gloves and a hat. It was like an event. That has changed a great deal. Hairstyles have changed tremendously. You would roll your hair a lot and put pins in it. I had a haircut called "the poodle." They also wore their hair long and rolled at the bottom. Then came "the bouffant." The teasing. The clothes went from modest to terribly immodest. Skirts used to be to the knee then they went up until they barely cover your bottom. Sweaters used to be called "sloppy joes" They were really big. Now they are skintight. Full skirts, pantaloons. I think like we used to say in Mutual if you do have pants on you don't act like a lady.

Q: What changes in morality have you seen throughout your lifetime?

A: There has always been immorality but it is very accepted now. People justify it and make it seem OK. When I was young, to have a baby and not be married you were considered awful. Now movie stars do that all the time. People do it all the time. The fact that people live together to see if it will work is ridiculous. I think people used to do it in the olden days. The rule was if you lived together with someone for 7 years you

89

had a common law wife. I think the attitude about morality has changed. It used to be more hushed.

Q: What has changed in diet?

A: Years ago when we were poor we ate a lot of starch and less vegetables. Now they are more accessible, canned or frozen. We didn't have frozen foods when I was a kid. There is more variety to pick from now, so you can eat healthier. Cooking has really changed. When my mother would cook dinner it was an all-afternoon affair. But now all it is, come home take it out of the freezer and put it in the microwave. It is a lot faster. Valene and I went to Sam's Club today. She was looking for a big can of kidney beans to make chili. The only way I have ever made chili was by soaking and boiling the beans all day. I didn't even realize you could make chili with a can of kidney beans and the regular other ingredients. So now you can make chili in an hour what used to take you all day. Things are so much faster, but women are out of the home so much more. They are not there to prepare the meals like they used to. Eating out at restaurants has changed. They specialize now in more healthy food. There are so many restaurants to choose from, so many varieties and food from all countries. Dee's opened when I was in high school. There was a Dee's on 21st south when I was in High School and I graduated in 1955. So it was opened probably in 1953 or 54. That was the first fast food. There were privately owned stands but you didn't have the big chains like you have now. Most kids brought a home lunch. They had school lunch. You didn't buy tickets but you brought your lunch money everyday. It was expensive so most kids brought a lunch.

Q: What about health practices?

A: They have learned so much so they have improved. I think if my mother had been alive now she would not have died. She wouldn't have died as young as she was. Now it seems like you can die and they can bring you back, a new heart, a new liver, etc. The Lord has really opened up the knowledge to us.

Q: According to you what brings good luck or bad luck?
A: I don't believe too much in good and bad luck. I don't have any superstitions.

Q: Any nature signs that shows the weather.
A: I have a foot that I broke years ago and whenever there is low pressure in the air it aches. I can, with the asthma, tell when there is an inversion or a problem with the weather.

Q: What kind of home cures do you use for remedies such as hiccups?
A: Drink a glass of water, hold your breath, etc. Toothaches-Ambesol. Sore throats or colds – Collodial Silver if you take it right at the beginning it seems to take care of it. It is not a homemade remedy but it is a natural remedy. Bronchial pneumonia – cayenne pepper everyday. It helps me in general. Arthritis – Heat.

Q: As an adult what are your customs for specific occasions like: weddings, births, April Fool's Day and funerals?
A: We have the normal customs – a wedding breakfast and wedding showers. On the Lord side all of the aunts are in charge of and give showers for the nieces and nephews. For births again, on the Lord's side, the aunts give showers for the first baby, and Ralph and I have a tradition of buying a dresser drawer for the first grandchild of the each family. On April Fool's Day Ralph usually plays an April Fool's joke on me every year and every year I fall for it. It is usually something normal like setting the clock a different time. It takes me a while to get it. And for funerals we have food at the ward after the services.

Q: What are the nicknames that you have had?
A: My brothers called me "Jeanie", short for Norma Jean. My neighbor friends used to call me "Smitty", short for Smith.

Q: Are there any other stories that you wish to tell?
A: My Dad used to come home for lunch and he would buy his boss tobacco chew. He would send me over to Kelley's, which was a café and a bar. I was little but I would buy the chew for

him. I can't believe they would sell it to me. But I would have to do a nursery rhyme first. My mother had taught me all of the nursery rhymes. So I would go over to get the chew and I remember sitting on the bar stool and twirling round and round as I told the nursery rhyme. I was little. 7 or 8 maybe.

Q: What has been your greatest joy in your life so far?
A: My children. The joy is that they are active in the church and that they are good honest people. Ralph, of course, too.

Q: What has been your greatest sorrow in your life so far?
A: It would have to be when my mother died so young. I was 25. I had her for 10 years longer than the doctor told me she would be around. Every time she went to the doctors he was always surprised to see her. She had told him that she would live until her children were raised and she did. It was hard because I was like Nolana. I called my mother everyday just to talk to her. She was my really good friend. I could tell her anything. I took it for granted. When she died I remember looking outside and everybody were just doing their thing. It was like I was upset because MY mother had died and these people were going about life. I thought life should stop. I felt like she was gone too soon.

Q: What counsel would you give to the younger generation to live successfully?
A: You should have some sort of religion and God in your life to be happy. It doesn't matter how much money or success you have if you don't have the Lord you have nothing.

Norma's Journal
Of the
Mormon Tabernacle Choir Tours
Written by: Norma Jean Smith Lord
Typed by: Nolana & Stuart Rice

<u>JAPAN TRIP</u>

Sept. 2, 1979 Sunday

We flew to San Francisco from SL and then boarded a 747. You can't believe how big this plane is. It even has a lounge for about 16 people, of course that is in the first class section. But because this is a chartered flight we can roam all over the plane.

We are traveling at 540 miles an hour at about 35,000 feet. They gave us post card to send home. We had a delicious lunch. It had some green noodles that were not to hot though.

Sept. 3

Lost in time zone.

Sept. 4, 1979

We arrive at Tokyo airport at 4:15 Monday. We then had a bus ride through the down town city from the airport to the New Otani Hotel. The rooms are nice but very small. The bathrooms are very compact. The cost of a room with a double bed is $95 per day. Breakfast is about 1600 yen or $8 American money. We had four meals the first day we left home. We certainly won't go hungry with the choir. From our room we can see a crew of men building something below. They are very clean people, even the construction workers. When they spill dirt they are hauling on the cement, they sweep it up. The dirt is covered before it leaves the yard.

We will have breakfast in the hotel this morning.

When we arrived at the airport we had to go to a line marked aliens, it was a funny feeling to think we now were the aliens.

93

Sept 5, 1979

Yesterday we went on a sightseeing tour of Buddhist Temple and Shinto religion. The difference was really great. The Buddhist was very colorful with drums beating and chanting. The guide said when these religions started there were no moral lessons to be learned but little by little they are being put into the religions. A lot of mythology is a part of religions. The Japanese people used to believe that the Emperor was a God and until General MacArthur came and conquered Japan no one was allowed to see the Emperor face to face only a picture which they had to bow to every time he passed.

They believe in many Gods there is a God for everything in nature. The Sun, The Trees, etc. I think he said that each person would be a God when he died. I'm not sure though. It's about 5 A.M. here. The "S" religion is very quiet and serene. They go to the Shrine and throw in some coins and then bow twice one small one deep and clap their hands twice say the prayer once a year on January 2. The gong is sounded 108 times and you may be cleansed of all your sins if you put money in before the last gong. It is so crowded that they cannot all get up to the front so they throw the coins from wherever they are standing. The huge pillars of wood and the top of the building is marked with the places the coins hit and make dents in them.

We went to the Ginza to shop today but we didn't do much shopping it is very expensive over here. I can't believe the prices. Something that you think might be a couple of dollars is about $6 or $7. Today we go to the Yohahoma for a tour and then the choir has a concert. It is so humid here in Japan that you are damp all the time. The city of Tokyo is a mass of buildings right next to each other for as far as your can see.

Sept. 6th

We started walking this morning after breakfast just on our own and we came across the old Japan. Behind all the modern buildings there are very narrow streets-little shops right next to each other. The fish stores with fresh fish next to China shops-etc. The people that own the shops live in back of them or above them, one shop you could see into the home because it was early and they were just opening up.

There was a beautiful garden. Very small but it was part of the front room.

They do not plant many garden in Japan with flowers because that symbolizes a short life but evergreens symbolize a long life so the Japanese garden are all evergreen plants.

We stop for a brief look at the new Tokyo Temple. We couldn't believe where it is located right in a residential area. We wonder if it will have any land to landscape. It is right off the sidewalk. The Japanese people have in one part of Tokyo 40 thousand people per square feet that would mean barely standing room if they were all standing on the ground together. This was amazing though because the street were not really that crowded. The traffic is awful though, you go about 2 miles an hour it seems like.

Their homes are tenements rising out of the ground with about the average number of floor being 16 stories high. They hang their beds and clothes out on a balcony. It's quite a sight to see. The average home has bedroom 6X9 only enough room for their bed. Which is hung out to air out very often. They kind of look like a sort of air mattress from the bus. Our guide's home, which is in a building, cost him 100 thousand dollars for small front room, two bedrooms, small kitchen. There is it seems no space in Tokyo for expanding but new buildings are under construction all over the horizon. You can see nothing but high rise apartments and business buildings from our hotel.

As the guide for our bus said goodbye, he told us he had been a guide for 17 years serving all kinds of people but if he may say so we were a different people, he couldn't put his finger on it but we were different than most Americans. He wondered if it was our religion. He was a fantastic guide and knows his country well. He seems as if he loves to learn and study. He almost bore a sort of a testimony to us. It was a very special experience. Maybe someday if the missionaries come to his home he will listen because of the contact with the choir.

When we arrived at the hall which the choir was going to sing there was a reception committee with signs and singing Come Come Ye Saints. It was a very touching scene. We didn't get to see the concert because it was sold out. It was held in Kanaguwa Kenmim Hall in Yokohama. The spouses that wanted were bused back to Tokyo.

Before the choir got off the bus they sang God Be With You Til We Meet Again to the Guide. I think it touched his heart. He then asked if that was the choir's goodbye song. The guide said he was not interested in any religion when we met him but I'll bet he will be at least interested now, in learning about the Mormons.

Sept. 7th – Nagoya, Tokyo

We went at 8:30 this morning to the oriental Bazaar with a fellow in the choir who was on a mission here about 12 years ago. It was an exciting trip, we changed subways in route. It was a quaint little store with three levels, it was closed for the day. But the door was open so Dave opened it and talked to the owner and told him how important it was for us to see his shop as we're leaving the next day. So he let us in, there were only six people in our group. But other choir members who had heard about the place keep filtering in. We bought the music jewel boxes there and the picture for Grandma and Barbara. As we left we were very happy with the purchases. I still haven't bought me a fan yet, maybe in the next shop. I'll be glad to have a different breakfast Sat at the new hotel, a pancake sure sounds good right now.

We were able to see the afternoon concert today, it was very special. I had no idea how much influence the choir had. It was a wonderful concert and the people clapped and clapped for encores. They ask for choir member's autographs and many gave them gift for their autographs. They stood in crowds outside to shake hands with us. It was tremendous. After the concert the choir members were each given a long stem.

Marlene and I walked over to the swimming pool that was built for the 1964 Olympic Games. It was closed. It is right in the middle of town. The dinner we had was a boxed lunch that no one could eat. Breakfast is the only meal we know for sure is eatable. We had 3 kinds of seafood Oyster, Crab and salmon. None of it was too tasty. It ate a piece of oyster and almost heaved. (awful stuff)

Sept. 8, 1979- Nogoya, Osaka Kyoto

We again had the same breakfast as we have had for the whole tour and went directly to the Bullet Trains. We were in route for exactly three hours. When we got off we were in the Subway the whole of Japan is catacombed. When they say the Japanese people live on top of each other they really meant it. There are shops running all over under ground. Regular dress shop, shoes, drug stores etc. There are about four levels of Subway. We went out on the subway to see Nagoya castle. It had two moats, an outer moat and inner moat. Two gates outer and inner. This was to make it almost impossible for the enemy to penetrate. There is one castle still privately owned. We went with a Brother that was a history teacher so it was very interesting. I got the cramps while we were there so I came back to the hotel and spent the rest of the day in bed. The food in Nagoya was the best we have had on the trip. They even made a hamburger on two slices of toast. The president of TV station that is sponsoring the choir in Nagoya gave each member a pearl as a gift.

We had a very good breakfast and again traveled on the bus to Osaka to give two concerts. As we boarded the buses the members from a stake were lined up to shake hands and say goodbye. They were giving flags to the choir members. Ralph got one to take home.

We had lunch in the hotel. It was a box lunch without the box. Then we got a group together that wanted to go to doll street. One of the Japanese members gave us instructions on how to take a cab there. But some one insisted she go with us. She kept looking at her watch and then saying something to the young man that spoke better English. We couldn't understand why she had a troubled look on her face until she pull out a ticket to the concert and handed it to the young man. She was going to give up her ticket just to be polite to us. I'm sure she saved up to buy it. We of course wouldn't let her go take us. We found our way to doll street and Marlene bought a doll for Janet. We had tickets for the night concert so we went to it, it was really good. The Japanese people could teach us a lot. They come to the concert early and do not get up until it is finished. They hardly moved during the whole concert. We them bused to the Holiday Inn in Kyoto.

Sept. 9th Kyoto

We had breakfast in the hotel. Then went on a tour of a couple shrines and castles. Some of the members purchased little flying bird. One of the Castles had a hallway all the way through the building that sounded like nightingales sing. This was built so that the Shogoan (a General) could always be aware if someone was coming. You couldn't walk anywhere without the floor singing. (maybe Kon FU) It had the rooms as they were then, nothing in them in the way of furniture, just mat for sitting. The table was moved from room to room as needed. The Castle was 400 years old, but the paintings were still very colorful that were on the ceiling.

We went to sacrament meeting at a big building called Nappon Serbuhan. Afterward they had a beautiful fireside. They did some of the oriental dances for us and had the Primary children sing for us. It was quite a night. The people keep saying what a great sacrifice it was for the choir to come over here, but the real sacrifice has been for the people of Japan. Some of the students have sold 100 tickets each. The spirit of the Japanese people is so great it makes your feel ashamed of yourself. They have 20 families to home teach each month.

Sept. 10th Kyoto

This morning at breakfast we sat by a young couple who had been talking to a Japanese man who lives in Los Angeles and had some connection with the T.V. System that brought the choir to Japan. He is not a member but has been traveling with us through out Japan. He was asking all kinds of questions about the church. He knew nothing about it while living in California. I am overwhelmed everyday by the impact the choir has as a missionary tool for opening the hearts of the people. One man said the world has hardness of the arteries and the choir must soften them. Mrs. Ottley mentioned that if the choir only knew what is in store for them in the next few years they would be overwhelmed.

We went to Toodaiji Temple it has little island with trees all around it. This represents turtle and cranes. Both have long life. There was a grave of a man who had built a boat of stone and drowned. It was his marker. Buddhism is a form of self discipline. And enlighten back to nature. Shinto is worshipping nature and heros. Shinto has no written book. The Japanese people are of both faiths most of the time.

Sept. 11th Koyoto, Tokyo

We left the Hotel early and traveled most of the day to Tokyo. We went directly to the concert hall. It was called the Lumon Kan Hall. It was so big I can't believe it. It looks like it's a block wide and it had a balcony as big. There was a beautiful curtain with a picture of Mt. Fuji. I went to the concert tonight, it seemed as if the choir was tired. The voices just didn't project, the first half but they pulled through the second half.

While the choir was practicing today, Marlene and I walked down the street a little ways and we came across the most beautiful hand painted vase and teaky wood stand. She had only 2 so we bought them. The artists name is Goshia and he's from Koyoto.

We had cookies afterward at one of the first concerts. They had soda crackers because cookies means soda cracker in Japan.

Sept. 12th

We have tangerine orange juice at every meal, it tastes a little different than the regular kind. There are huge bowls of tangerine oranges peeled for breakfast.

The Japanese people seem to be more group oriented, where in the States we are more individual. Most of the school children we have seen have a uniform to wear to school, white top blue skirt or pants.

We spent most all day shopping and riding the subway. Ralph and Jim have the system figured out as long as we are under ground. No we really found each place we set out to. The luggage must be put out tonight, so this is goodbye to Japan. Hello Korea

Sept. 13th 1979

We are flying to Seoul this morning 4 of the choir members packed their passports in the luggage and had to wait until the trucks unloaded the luggage and then find their passports. I can't believe how smooth this trip has went with all of the people involved it has went. They had a crew of 4 Japanese men that worked full time just putting together the risers. The behind the scenes people that handled the luggage and all the other things. As we left the hotel this morning we were given one gift per couple from the member of one of the stake. One lady received a pearl tie tack and cuff links and pictures of the family that gave the gift. One night at the concert the President of the T.V. station gave each choir member a pearl that has been drill for mounting. It is worth between $25 and $45 dollars.

We went to the night concert tonight and a young Korean Girl started to talk to me. She is LDS was baptized 9 months ago. She comes from a family of eight. She is 19 or 20 years old. Very child like sweet as a can be. She doesn't speak English very well but she said she is majoring in Music at the University here. She is coming to Provo BYU next year. She teaches little boys 8 and 9 years old piano. She has a grandfather in Sydney Australia who is not a member. She asked for Mike's address so she can tell him to help her baptize her grandfather. She lives in the 9th ward over here.

Sept. 14th

We went on a tour of Korea this morning, for about 1 hour. The people that we meet in Korea are a lot different than in Japan. Someone said the two countries do not like each other very much. We then were let loose to shop in the ETAWON area. Things here were very reasonable and they would take American or Korean Won. Every one had spent most of their money in Japan, so they were borrowing money from who ever had any left and writing checks out to those people. They would not accept check or Master charge or Visa. We didn't buy much here. I wish we would have had more money and more time, you could get a three piece set of luggage for about $25 it was the soft vinyl kind.

We then were bused to the airport in Korea. The airport there is under tight security. The fellow checking us out at emigration was asking everyone what they were doing in Korea and he was hesitating in letting us go through. It took about half and hour for two people to go through and finally the lady in front of me, took my badge that had Korean writing on it and showed it to him. He then smiled and said "oh you mormon" and we started to go through a little faster. Not to many of the merchants of Korea or Japan had ever heard of us.
One note of interest, the missionaries say they baptize young girls and they're active until they get married and then they are afraid to tell their husbands that they are members.

Joke learned in Korea- Lady says, I have a yen to spend but my husband has no won to.

WE went this morning on the tour. A young Korean girl who was in the same ward as Park Sewng Nim. This girl conducts the music and Sewng Nim plays piano.

The flight home takes about 13 hours total. I'm sure we will all have jet lag. We left Korea at 5:00 Sept. 14 and will get into the airport in Salt Lake at 5:00 Sept. 14th. Everyone almost is sleeping, it was so busy coming over and so quiet coming home.

SCANDINAVIAN TRIP

June 5, 1982 Saturday

We left the Salt Lake Airport at about 7:45. We had a tail wind of 110 miles per hour. So we made good time to Bangor, Maine. Refueled and headed towards Norway. The plane is a DC8 Stretch, sat about 253 people. The air conditioning was not working and we were all roasting, even Ralph. It seems in the 10 or 11 hours we are in the air all we do is eat. We have had three meals already. I guess the choir does travel on its stomach.

We didn't get much sleep last night. It was hot and there isn't much room to move. It started to get light at about Three o'clock so we didn't have much of a night. The isle is very narrow and is always crowded. So we stay in our seat unless we have to go to the bathroom.

June 6, 1982

We lost about eight hours of night. We arrived at the Campus of the University Fantant Hotel about 4:00 Sunday. On the way from the airport we saw ladies in swimsuit enjoying the sunshine. The temperature is about 63 degrees and the people seem to think it quite warm.

Jim and Marlene got a room with only one narrow bed in it so they had to make up another bed for them. Ralph and I really lucked out we got a double bed. We also have a front room. So we have two rooms while many choir member only have one room. Everything is made out of wood in the two rooms, couch, bed, desk. The wood hasn't ever been painted. We have lots of drawer space. The shower is a beauty. It's a curtain on a round ring and a shower hose you hold. There is no distinction between the bathroom and shower area. The hose to the shower will come from under the sink.

The country is beautiful, all green with lots of trees. We didn't have to go through customs, it was waved because of who we are (Tab Choir)

The doorknobs are even made of wood. We walked up the road from the Hotel about 4 blocks to see an old church. It was a church the Vikings had built 800 years ago. They used it for (sacrifice blood) human. It is now used as a Christian church. It's still in use today. It's made of all wood and is still in tact. The cross is made of rock.

June 7th 1982 Bergen, Norway

The breakfast here was really different. It consisted of a roll and two slices of bread, cheese, jelly and butter. We ate the whole roll and one piece of cheese and then made a sandwich for lunch. We're on our own for lunch. We took the bus into town, went past the fish market, they told us they had a tank of fish that you can choose the one you want and they take it out and hit it in the head to kill it for you. (what a way to catch a fish)

We rode a boat called the white lady up through the fjord. It was about a four hour trip and cost $27 or 180 kroner. The largest island has about 7,000 people on it. The fjord are connected by bridges and kind of look like a small version of the Golden Gate. It was a nice trip although it was a little too long and much too expensive. We went to Rosenhantz Castle built in the 1300. It had a steep winding staircase, leading up to the top rooms and steps adjoining each room on every floor. I can't imagine what it was like to take a candle up and down those stairs. We even went in the dungeon and Ralph turned out the light. It was pitch black except for an air hole which didn't give any light. It would be awful to have been in it for 10 minutes let alone days or weeks. Each chamber had three or four windows and a carved out fireplace for heat. I wouldn't have wanted to live in those times even if I were a king. Bathing had to be an enormous undertaking just getting enough water upstairs to bath with. The people in Norway speak a little English. I tried asking four of them for information about where to get pads. (Kotex) and was twice sent to the cosmetic counter for cleansing pads for my face. I got so embarrassed that I finally gave up. Marlene finally got one of them to understand and I was saved. We have seen a lot of sunbathers here the last few days. Norway doesn't have very many cloudless days a year. But the last two weeks have been sunny and warm. (unusual)
They have checked back for 100 years on the weather and they have averaged about 7 clear days a year. We have been very lucky. The concert was in a huge arena. It was absolutely beautiful. It brought tears to your eyes. The people just clapped and clapped and didn't want it to end. Ralph and I both wore our blinders last night. I got up at 1:00 am and it was barely dusk. I guess you get used to sleeping in the light.

June 8th 1982

We had breakfast of bread, cheese and jam again. They say eggs are about 40 cents a piece over here, so I don't believe we will have any on this tour. A cinnamon roll is $2 a piece. A soft ice cream cone is $1.30. Everything seems to be very expensive.

We went on a bus tour of Bergen this morning. We went to Greig home, he is a famous composer from Bergen. Most of the people are cremated.

1. The children only have two months vacation from school.
2. 90% of the people have blue eyes.
3. Most or many are born blonde and turn darker later.
4. Taxes are about 35% to 45% of ordinary peoples wages, and as high as 80% of the ones that make a lot of money.
5. Hospitals are free and dentist are free while children are in school.
6. Bergen is a city on the seven mountains.
7. The whole of Bergen seems to be made of stone. And telephone polls are placed on the ground and then was hooked up into the rock.
8. The Vikings were a superstitious people. They believe that their God Thor had to feed daily. So they made a woodcarving and every night they placed food in an opening and when it was gone in the morning, they believe he had eaten it. Really the mice and other animals ate it.
9. Even when Norway became Christian they still kept a symbol of the Viking on their churches just in case.

We spent the afternoon shopping but came with nothing except some chimes. The sweaters were as much as they are in the states or more.

June 9th

We got up at 4:30 this morning and had to be in the train station early. We have a 14-hour train ride. We could smell brakes burning, they found out the problem was the baggage car was too heavy. So the choir members formed a line, and they put the luggage on two cars. The women watched and sang "Put your shoulder to the wheel" and "I've been working on the railroad". The highest point of Bergen is 4,200 feet. It was such a contrast as we traveled on the train from lush green everywhere, to frozen lakes and snow piled 8 feet high against the tunnel we had to go through. The tunnels were built so the train could through in the wintertime. The choir got off the train in Oslo and gave a concert and then flew to Stockholm. The train had to stop because the car with the luggage was so heavy, it couldn't go on. Then after the choir member left we came about half way to Stockholm and there was a wreck on the track so we were delayed a while longer. While waiting for the train to leave again, we went into the train station to use the restroom. The train was going to leave and I was caught in the bathroom but I made it.

June. 9ᵗʰ Sweden

We finally got on the boat after a 17-hour train ride, it was about 1:00am and we were all very tired. We got to bed at 3:00 am and we got up at 6:00. I really miss not going to the concerts. I'm not on a spiritual level that we were on on the Japan trip. We had a short tour of the city and when we got back they had been paging us all morning. The Andus Pedderson family whom Sherry Wallin is related to were waiting for us. It was quite exciting. We talked for an hour or so, and they said they would like us to come to dinner tonight. So they're picking us up at 4:30. We went to the island they live on, and it is so beautiful words cannot tell. She fixed a dinner of Swedish meatballs, ham, fish, cheese, grapes and crackers. Marlene asked them about a certain church, and they go to it every week. It was unreal we didn't believe our luck. It was the church Marlene's great grandparents are buried at. She was very excited after we went to Andus' sister's home. Her name is Annetta Lundstrom. She had a huge plate of pastries, all delicious. She also had a bottle of some berries that she had put up herself. So I poured about a half a glass and took a drink, it was excellent. And then they told me I was supposed to put just a little bit in the bottom and fill the rest up with water. We all had a good laugh about that one. They are marvelous people they are so hospitable. The wife's name is Ahelena, the 16-year-old boy was Per, the 6-year-old girl was Maria. They have a view from their front window of the sea and they see every ship that sails out of Sweden each day. The sea isn't very far from their home. The little girl Maria has a little playhouse and so do most of the little girls on the island. The children are so well mannered. Per could understand and speak English the best. So we called on him to help us a lot. He gave Marlene and I a lilac from their bush. When they met us on the ship Berit brought us flowers of red white and blue and yellow and white to have the colors of each country.

June 10th-

We went on a tour of the Wasa Ship, it was under water for over 300 years. It was one of four battle ships the king had built to protect Sweden, but it never got out of the harbor. No one knows why it sank. Some say it was built too narrow and top heavy. There is an old story that they had 30 Seamen run from side to side to see if it was sea worthy and after several trips it just tipped over in the water and sank. The front of the ship was very ornate with animal and scary faces to scare the enemy and give the sailors confidence. After the ship was hoisted up it was washed, it was full of mud and each piece had to be cleaned with a special solution. Before they could lift it they had to build a tunnel under the ship through the mud to see if the sea would let go of the ship. They had a spray going 24 hours a day for 18 years with a special solution to clean and preserve the ship and now they are restoring it to almost the original. The Pedderson family took us shopping this afternoon. I bought a crystal candle and a plate and a picture of trolls. The chimes are just like Norway's so we didn't get any. I don't know how we spent so much money and didn't get any gifts. We gave the Pedderson family a tape of the choir.

June. 12th

Last night we saw the light in the Pedderson home from our boat and Ralph got a flashlight from one of the crew and signaled back. Several people on the deck whistled and shouted hoping that they could here us. I guess the concert didn't go as well last night. The choir got Jerry's signals mixed up and half were standing and half were sitting. We are now at sea and are just waiting to go to lunch. There is not a lot to do on board. Some people brought games but we forgot to. The first day on board, the eating arrangement was hard on the crew. People were drifting in and out for several hours. Now if your more than 15 minutes late you can't get in, they close the door.

We had a fire water drill and were told where our life boat was in case. We all put on our life jackets and went on deck, it was kind of fun.

June 12th 1982 Finland

We were at sea all day until 5:00 and when we were docking the choir members were standing on the bow singing the National Anthem of Finland. It was such a thrilling experience. The members at the dock were very happy.

We went on a 2 ½ hour tour of Finland and went to a special church that is made right in the rock. Just the roof is man made material. About 93% of Scandinavians are Lutheran, 3% are Greek Orthodox.

The water is so cold in the winter here they have a special black ship for breaking the ice so the ships can sail.

In the warmer weather the women bring their rags down to the sea to wash them and then they have special places to dry them.

They say this will keep the colors bright in them.

A flat of 3 rooms and a kitchen cost about 60 thousand dollars.

The state owns the one and only TJ stadium $120 a year for license for TV

The hospital is $5 a day.

Everything closes Sat at 1:00 and doesn't open again until Monday. So we went into an underground Subway store and looked around a bit.

Finland imports most of its things so we didn't see many things made in Finland except dolls.

Some people set up shop on the dock, they had a silver fox and this kind of thing for hundreds of dollars. But on the next stop were some knifes and dolls so we bought them. The knife is for Clint because he likes the one Ralph had from Germany. The little doll has reindeer fur on it.

I should tell a little about the ship. It is about 1:00 a.m. so I will tell about the people running the ship tomorrow. There are four thousand members in Finalnd.

June 13, 1982

It's Sunday today. We set our watches to Denmark time last night but the ship is on Finland time until 12:00 p.m. tonight so we missed breakfast. Ralph and Jim are in charge of blessing and passing the Sacrament. So they have been busy with that.

We just went to lunch and sat at a table where the waiter gave you a choice of main dishes and just brought whatever else he wanted you to have. There was extra salad so he just poured it in Ralph's salad dish. If he brought the wrong thing out he just said "no problem" and put it on your plate. He couldn't speak English hardly at all. Out of 4 people that ordered veal, I'm the only one that received it. He was very friendly and tried to keep everyone happy.

We just returned from an hour Sacrament meeting, it was very good, it was bearing of testimonies. Members told of hardships in health and family problems, financial problems. Satan was working over time for some of them. But no matter what the health problems they seemed to gather needed strength for the concerts.

At the concert some times there are people handing out anti-Mormon papers but many people just read it and look disgusted and handed it back to the giver.

Dennis, a member of the choir was once traveling to Russia with some religious literature about Joseph Smith. He was told he couldn't take it into Russia so he thought he had given it all to someone in Finland. As the police checked his luggage very carefully they found an announcement of a religious play and took it from him and asked if he had anything else. He said no believing that he didn't, but as the police checked his journal, Dennis saw as he opened the pages one by one the three pamphlets that he had forgotten. The police past over them almost without seeing them and Dennis heart was nearly stopped. At this point he felt the Lord had blessed him and that these pamphlets were meant for someone in Russia. He didn't know how to get them to individuals so he felt he must leave them. He went to a church in Russia and felt impressed to leave one by the door that the clergy left by, and another at the entrance of the church and at the train station. Before he left he saw a woman over in an area by herself. So he went over there and started to straighten out his camera case carefully taking everything out and them putting it away again, all except the tract and when he left and came back in about 5 minutes it was gone.

Several choir members told of how many years it took them to get into the choir and of music lessons they took so they could get in. Some waited for a year or more on waiting lists and they speak of having a hard time staying in the choir. Ralph has been blessed, he didn't have to wait long to get in and has loved being a member and has seemed to have no problem staying in. Sometimes when you loose the spirit everything bothers you, unimportant things.

This ship rocks all night long and I was dreaming we were on our boat at home at Utah Lake.

June 14, 1982

This ship is something else. The meals are great. There is one waiter we had last night that would take your order and then if it was more than was needed he would just put it on someone plate and say "no problem". Ralph must have looked hungry because he got two salads and two main dishes. The lady next to me got two ice creams. It seems he has a harder time than the rest of them with his English so if one person orders something he just brings one for everyone. It was a riot.

Ralph isn't feeling well this morning. I don't know if it was too much food last night, lack of sleep, or motion sickness. Jim became ill today with a great deal of pain. Marlene wanted some Mallox for him and while she was trying to get some she asked Dr. Wilson for some and he said he would like to check Jim first. When he did he thought it was appendix and had Dr. Barker give a second opinion. He agreed. So they called Copenhagen to have an ambulance ready to take him to the hospital. It took about four hours in the hospital before they did the surgery. By then the appendix has broke and Jim was full of puss and stuff. They cleaned him out and he should be fine.

June 15th 1982

We arose early and started for the hospital about 7:00 a.m. We walked to the hospital because we didn't know how much a taxi was. It took about half an hour. When we got there we found out Marlene has went back to the ship last night. So we waited for her to come back. While I was there the doctor came in and checked Jim. We asked how long he would be in the hospital and the Dr. said eight days. Arrangements have been made for Marlene to stay at members houses while she is here and their flight home will be taken care of by the Church. They passed a law in Denmark two years ago that all hospital even for foreign people is free so that is great.

Marlene is very upset about staying here. I don't blame her but the Church will take good care of her. The choir members have been so good to them, helping wherever they could. I'm so grateful to be a member of this church.

I spent the evening on the boat. My feet are so tired. We had dinner at 12:00

June 16, 1982   Oalborg

We were at sea all night until about 11:00 a.m. We had lunch and then went on a sightseeing tour. Oalborg is famous for its shnops. This is a type of liquor made out of potatoes. The factory makes potato chips for the first three days of the week, and shnops the last two.
As we drove along we saw these huts made out of wood or tin. They were the place where pets were kept because they do not allow them in apartments.

Colony Cottages look kind of like slum area. But are summer homes. People grow their own garden and stay in the cottage during the summer.

Houses in Oalborg are about 120 thousand, cement sculpture, Noah Ark.

Give for tobacco-Goose Girl

We went in an old church it was called Abby of the Holy Ghost. Originally took in people that needed a meal or rest. Now a rest home for aged. Paintings on Ceiling.

Most or 90% of the houses are heated by hot water. St. Anthony was sent into the desert and was tempted by a beautiful young woman and fell from grace. The paintings of the lady have her feet on wrong. And that's how you could tell she was of the devil.

We went to a Viking Cemetery that dated back 500 years before Christ. All the Viking graves were shaped like a boat so the dead could get back to Val Halla.

The thing was to burn the ship with their body left on it but all did not own a ship. But they were all cremated. They had Danish sheep that looked like goats and these were used as the lawn mowers for the graveyard.

I had a chance to go to the concert last night and it was very good. The Danish members of the choir each gave a short speech in Danish and this helped warm up the people.

June 17, 1982

Today half of the people on board were sick. The North Sea was kind of rough and the deck chairs were filled with people trying to get some air. There was one fellow who was so sick he carried a big bucket with him all day. There were little cartons on the end of each rail in case you couldn't make it to your room.

June 18, 1982

Today we went to see the famed Floriade flower show. It was held 10 years ago and was such a success. It has taken them five years to get it ready. It is on reclaimed land. The water had to be pumped out and then prepared for planting. Much of the land in Holland was at one time covered with water. Holland is quite a bit below sea level. That's why they have the dikes.

When they build houses along the canals, they have pilings under the house. The old wood pilings have rotted and some houses are on an angle, so all the furniture goes to one side. Not real safe to live in.

You may buy as many apartments as you like or houses. But the government decided who can rent them, you have no choice.

The canals freeze in the wintertime and they ice skate on them.

The sewage from the city is drained into the canals and every week the old water is let out and clean water replaces it. Holland smelled like a farmyard when I first got off the ship, that's probably why.

The houses are built with narrow, sometimes curving stairways, so they have hooks up on the top of the building to put ropes around furniture and bring it through the windows.

June 19, 1982

All of the countries we have been in have to pay a license for having a T.V.

June 19

We flew to London.

We toured the London area which is only 1 ½ miles and has about 11 millions people living there. The old buildings in London have many old Raman ruins under them.

There used to be a wall around London that was closed at night fall and if you weren't in before that and had to spend the night outside, they were most often murdered.

During one war everything around St. Paul's Church was flattened the enemy thought if they could destroy the church it would destroy the moral of the people but the church was never hit.

Even today when the Queen comes to London, the Mayor of London meets her at the spot where the Wall used to be and escorts her into the town.

85% of England is farmland. On the bus coming into London it was beautiful rolling hills and quaint farmhouses.

London Taxi drivers have to study for 2 years and pass a test before they can drive a Black Taxi. They then must take at test every 3 months. They must know where everything is just by name of the place.

At the palace in London Parliament pink and green tents for lunch.

The Pope is trying to save money so he bought a Volkswagen. They say he has a Chauffeur who is very pompous and is not too happy about the new car.

Owen Victoria has many building and statues in her name and Prince Albert's. But the people dislike her. She was always such a sour puss.

When Prince Albert died she mourned him for 42 years wearing black all the time. She also had his valet lay his clean clothes out every morning and put them away each night.

We flew to London an arrived about 6:00. Ralph's uncle called soon after we arrived. Ralph called him Uncle Willy and was told his name was Bill. Uncle Willy and Jeff and Judith came over about 8:30 and we chatted for several hours. We invited them to church in the morning but they declined. But they are coming to the concert at 3:00.

Jeff is a Book Keeping in a garage and Judith works for a Travel Agent.

June 20, 1982 Sunday

The mission President Ford talked to us. He expressed how happy he was to have the choir there because of the exposure it would give the Church. The people as a whole only know about Polygamy. They think we are not Christian but believe in Joseph Smith only. They think we are sort of a cult. They ask, "Where are the Gold Plates? Why didn't the Lord take the gospel to Russia they need it worse than us?" The paper once had an add that read "Beware of Mormon wolf in sheep clothing" " Watch out for the Church of Joseph Smith, it's a fraud." 120 thousand member in England.

This afternoon is the concert in Royal Albert Hall. We bought tickets for Uncle Bill and Jeff and Judith. I saw them come in and kept an eye on them during the concert, they were very reserved at first but as the concert progressed they warmed up. At the end of the concert when they sang "God be with you" he took out his hanky to wipe his eyes. The spirit in the hall was overwhelming. After the concert we took them on the choir bus back to the hotel. They were a little self conscious. We took them to dinner at the Beefeaters Restaurant and then went up to our room. Ralph's Uncle Bill talked about the songs he remembered singing when he was a member of the LDS church and he sang two old songs that are no longer in the hymnbook. He remembered them both all the way through. He chatted until it was getting quite late about his youth and his feelings on the world as a whole. Ralph finally said it was getting late and we had better break it up. It was a very pleasant evening.

June 21, 1982

We got up early this morning as we are leaving for home at 11:00 a.m. We were going to take the tube to town but only one track was in use. They're having a strike on the subway. We walk into town and were

114

there before the stores even opened. We were looking for a music box for Nolana. We finally found on at Herrods. This is the store where the Queen shops. We just made it back in time to catch the bus to the airport. Those that missed the bus have to take a taxi to airport. And it's about 1 ½ hour away. It took about 12 hours. We stopped in Michigan to go through customs and then they didn't even open our luggage. But as we began to board the plane again our carry on bag went through the x-ray and Ralph was stopped and had to empty out the bag. Some cheese slicers we bought, looked like a weapon. Ralph was a little upset with them.

When we arrived at the airport, we were greeted by our beautiful family and boy did they look good. The first thing Valerie said was "Saeed and I got married yesterday" it was quite a surprise. I really wish she would have waited until we got home and were able to be there with her. But that was not her desire I guess. I think her father feels worse than I do, but what is done cannot be changed.

ISRAEL TRIP

Dec. 26, 1992

We took our luggage out to the S.L. Airport about 2:00 p.m. and were asked several questions about our luggage and where it had been lately – if we had left it unattended after packing it, were we given any packages or letters to take to someone in Israel, etc. We then went back to Sandy and waited until Saeed took us to the airport and dropped us off. We boarded our plane which was a 747 when we took off they played the William Tell Overture as we ran down the runway. It was a riot.

We were 15 hrs getting here - 1 hr refueling in Amsterdam while we were not allowed to leave the plane.

We arrived in Tel Aviv at about 6:00 pm Dec. 29 and were taken by bus to the BYU Jerusalem Center for a sacrament meeting. The opening song was "Israel Israel God Is Calling." I could hardly sing it was so emotional. I have sung that song many times but never felt like that.

The sacrament meeting was wonderful. There was such a peaceful feeling in the BYU Center. It was hard to stay awake because my body thought it was 2:00 am.

Dec. 28

The next morning we went back to the Jerusalem Center and Truman Madsen and his wife told us some about Jerusalem. It took 15-17 years for the church to acquire the property. They finally found a spot not far from where the Center was built and were not real happy with it but they were lucky to find any spot for sale in that area.

Pres. Kimball and Pres. Tanner came to see the sight and were not too impressed – it was kind of down in a crevice. Pres. Tanner walked up the mountain to the choicest part with a wonderful view and said something like "this is the spot." Pres. Holland started to tell him why they couldn't purchase this spot. Pres. Holland tried to explain that no one could buy it especially Mormon, and Pres. Tanner said "Don't tell me your problem just purchase it."

When Pres. Kimball got up there he said, "This is the place. I like it. Everyone who likes it raise your hand." Pres. Holland said he didn't want to argue with a Prophet but still thought it was impossible.

The Jews lost a generation to the Holocaust and are afraid of losing a generation to a Spiritual Holocaust.

The stones for the center are of limestone and all hand chipped. It took 2 years of round-the-clock labor to complete.

On the bus tour we took today one of the buses were stoned. No one was hurt but some windows were broken on the bus. Some of the people didn't get up to the Mount of Olives – we did. I got off the buss and was going to buy some post card from some Arabs who were selling pictures and other things. I asked how much and he said 2 dollars. I asked if he had change for a $5 he said yes grab the $5 and put 2 packages of post cards into my hand and said 2 for $5 and ran off. It was quite an experience.

Because of security reasons, we had to come down from the Mt. Of Olives by a different route – so we were able to go through the Arab part of Jerusalem which most tourists do not get to go through. It was very interesting. We had security all around us. My arm is too sore to write any more tonight.

Dec. 29, 1992

We went on a walking tour of Old Jerusalem. We walked on the street where Jesus was thought to have walked. They have churches and other shrines to mark the places where Jesus fell. We went under the streets that are used now. Some of the churches are built over the original streets. We went into the only Christian church that was left standing in the Arab section, St. Annes. We (the spouses) sang "I am a Child of God inside the chapel. The acoustics were unbelievable. You really didn't want to leave. I took a picture of the only original arch left from the time of Jesus – the peddlers are very aggressive. We stopped at one shop for about 15 minutes. The prices were very high – not many people bought anything. I saw a manger set for $200 a little high for me. I'm having trouble remembering how to spell. I wonder what is wrong.

We left at 1:30 for Caesaria but en route the Guide asked if we wanted to stop at Israel Diamond Center which has a museum. We went through the museum and they explained how they cut the diamond but only if it was a clean cut. Otherwise they cut them the way they have for many many years. We then went up to the jewelry store and looked at the different jewelry. I didn't see anything that I really liked that much. But just then I saw a white gold ring that was only white gold on the top part of the ring and yellow gold on the bottom half of the ring. I tried it on and for some reason didn't take it off. I put off buying it until the last minute. I have wanted a dinner ring for a long time but have never seen one in white gold – so I did it.

The ring didn't fit so they said they would size it and deliver it to my hotel – Jerusalem Hilton - by the time the concert was over. I didn't quite know how to tell Ralph what I had done. It was so unlike me. But on the 2 hr trip home to the hotel I told him. He was very happy and was pleased I had bought myself something nice. That was a relief. Now we got to the hotel and asked the desk if they have a package for me in the safe. The answer is no they do not accept jewelry for the safe except for guests wanting to put valuables in the safe.

This was very scary because the place I had bought it at was 2 hrs away – or so – I was very upset. When Ralph and I had our prayer I asked a special blessing that all would be right in this matter. I couldn't sleep much worrying about this. I began to think I had been taken but Ralph said we would contact the Visa people and tell them what happened. But in the morning there was a letter left under my door. So I followed the directions on the note. I called the security people who the note said had the ring in the safe. They said they had no package for me. I was sick. I call Udell to see what to do – but he couldn't help me. I called back security again and he said "didn't you just call." I said yes and told him my story he said just a minute. About 3-4 minutes later he came back and put someone else on the phone yes they had found out where it was and I could come downstairs and pick it up. That is how Weds. Dec. 30 started.

Dec. 30th

We went back to Old Jerusalem through the Dung Gate (it got this name because the garbage was dump[ed] over it on the time of the Romans). We went to the dome of the rock which is a mosque of the Muslim. It was filled with stain glass windows that were so beautiful with the sun coming through. This is the 3rd most important site for the Muslims. We were able to spend the afternoon touring together. Ralph did pretty well the first part of the tour. His leg got pretty tired after the first couple of hours. We went back to the bus and stayed there until the tour was over. It was nice to spend time together. The choir is very busy and we don't see much of them so far.

My arm is still tired I can't write a very long time.

We went to the upper room where they think the last supper was held. The guide asked us to sing another song. This time we had choir members in our group and we sang "I stand all amazed." It was again very emotional for me. It sounded wonderful. The Tour Guide whose name is Zeev (meaning Wolf) was touched by the singing and told us so. He seems to be a tough enough character and it was nice to think he felt of the spirit.

While we were at the Dome of the rock or "distant place" where Mohammed was supposed to have descended into heaven. He told a couple of other reasons that the rock had been important (This was where Abraham took Isaac to sacrifice him. I can't remember the other but one of the Muslim chastised him and he told the fellow he could say whatever he wanted.

I had a ticket for the concert tonight at Binjanie Ha Ooma but I was exhausted and gave my ticket to Udell Poulson and went to bed. The reviews from the concert were great.

Dec. 30, 1992

New Year's Eve – We went to the Jerusalem Center and had a wonderful slide presentation. Bro. Chadwick told us about finding the top of the arch from original East Gate of the Temple and showed us a picture he had taken by putting his camera down a hole and taking a picture.

There is so much excavation going on all the time. They have found a lot of new things (or old things) in the Last 20 years.

We climbed up to Orson Hyde Memorial. They told us the Land of Jerusalem has been dedicated by many people but never been dedicated for proselytizing. I thought that was very interesting. We then went to the Garden of Gethsemane. It was an olive tree orchard – at one time had an olive oil factory. Church of all nation now stand on the sight of the Rock that Jesus sat on.

We then went to the Holocaust Museum. We didn't have much time there. Ralph and I went through the Children's Museum. It had pictures of small children suspended behind some glass. It gave them an unusual look. They had light Thousands of them surrounding the room and beautiful sad music playing in the Background and the names of the Children and Where they had lived were said with a very flat tone. It was very impressive and emotional.

We had lunch at the 7 Arches Hotel – guess what we had – Hamburgers and french fries – The Hamburger was huge the Bun was an extra large roll there was no way you could have gotten a Bite out of it so we ate them separately. At Lunch we sat with Bro. Talbot and he told us of a sister who was in a store admiring an expensive Statue. The owner saw her badge and asked if she Was a Mormon, She said yes. He told her if she didn't have enough money for the Statue she could put some down and send him payments when she got home. He told her he has only met one Mormon who was not honest. That he has done this Kind of thing many times. There is another shop here called Omars who has made statues of olive wood of the people of the Book of Mormon. The choir has about wiped him out. He will also let you take things back to your hotel or home and pay him later – It's quite a feeling to think the LDS people have such a great reputation for honesty. I hope no one in the choir changes this Trust.

We haven't had a chance to go to any of the olive wood shops yet – But Tomorrow we will go.

Jan. 1, 1993

We left for Tel Aviv at 9:00 am. We went to a museum Called Diaspora Museum. It was about the history of the Jews. When we got to the Concert Hall there was a lady from Israel who was standing by the stairs outside the Concert Hall who approached another sister and I about buying our tickets to the Concert – as they were sold out. I gave her mine but the other Lady sold hers for 50 sheele or $20. I couldn't not believe she would do that – But she just said well I need the money. I don't know her name but she came with one of the Ladies in the Choir. So now I had 2 hrs to kill. We found a mall and it was just like in the states. My feet were about to drop off by the time we went home and Ralph and I sleep through most of the ride. We arrived home about 11:30 or so.

Jan. 2, 1992

Saturday is the Israel Christian Sabbath over here so we were going to attend Sacrament meeting after a boat ride on the Sea of Galilee. We Went to a restaurant that had St. Peter's fish. The fish is served with head and bony fins still on it. It was very mild fish and I enjoyed it. These are said to be the same fish that Peter caught in the time of Christ.

The Sacrament was a real rich raisin bread and it was hard not to enjoy the Bread for its flavor and forget what it represented. Elder Faust said "What has happened here will never have an end". I wrote the quote down and lost it so this isn't exactly right.

We saw a Kibbutz – It's Kind of a commune that seems to work well for these people.

We saw a Bedouin tent on the mountain side. They will invite any stranger into these tents for 3 days and after that it is time to leave.

Jan. 3, 1993

We went to Shepherd's Field for the choir to tape and then we went to an olive wood factory. The young men were carving with a device that finished the olive wood statues. They wore no goggles and the dust was really bad. The olive wood has to dry for 5 years to dry out. There was an outlet store on top and that is where I bought 5 Moses and one Flight to Egypt for the kids and me. Later that day we went down to a street that I'm sure was a tourist section but it was fun to walk around.

We haven't heard all the Good the Choir is doing but we have heard some Wonderful feed back. I'm sure we'll hear more on the way home and after we get there.

Jan. 4, 1993

We went to the Shrine of the Book. This is where the dead sea scrolls are housed. It had the scroll on a pedestal of some sort encased in a round glass thing. You had to walk around it to look at all of them. If anything happens (earthquake fire etc) the pedestal is lowered into the ground to protect the scrolls. They had the Vases the scrolls were found in on display too. It was quite a feeling to Know How old the scrolls were and to see them. They have been studying them for 40 years and haven't released all that is in them.

We also went to the garden Tomb and saw where Jesus was laid after he was hung on the cross. I read the scriptures. Now I will have a different feeling for them.

Jan. 5, 1993

We traveled to Masada today and on the way we saw many Bedouin Camps. They live much like they did hundreds of years ago. Its tents made of skins or something.

We first went to the Dead Sea and had Box Lunches (Dry Bread with a small piece of Beef or some Kind of cheese.) Dad and I put our hands in the Dead sea. It was very oily. It is 34% Salt. Nothing not even Bacteria can live in it. It looks very thick almost like you could walk on it.

We then went to Masada. It is a flat mountain about 5 times higher than Timpanogos. We went up in a tram and then had to go up 85 more stairs. I told dad he shouldn't go up but he said he wanted to so we went. It took us a little longer than most but we made it. With just a few stops. Mike Fitzgerald who has M.S. pretty bad made it too. It took him a little longer. It was well worth the climb. For as far as the eye could see it was <u>desolate</u>. I mean <u>desolate</u>. Not a bit pretty. I'm amazed they survived in this wilderness. The ruins were very interesting. The bath the way they got Water from the rain in cisterns.

We could see the caves where the Dead Sea Scrolls were found – it was quite a feeling to think things were preserved for so many thousands of years.

It was a Very Wonderful experience. I'm grateful I had the chance to go to Israel and see the history that is there.

I Know the choir had a marvelous effect on the people of Israel and they now know who the Mormons are.

Dead Sea – Lowest spot on earth

Never rains in the wilderness out side of Jerusalem

Olive trees are almost immortal – they can live for thousands of years. The olive is bitter to the taste when picked. Put under pressure the olive oil is sweet.

Psalm 37. The Jews kept religion even when they were scattered and had no place to worship.

Israel – has a music Service once a year at Christmas time when all Religions can sing their music. The Choir changed the word in

Many times the Choir felt it had angelic help – Because they know they weren't doing it on theire own. They sang in 6 Languages English, Hebrew, Arabic German, Russian, Latin.

Requiem – Mormon Choir singing a Catholic Mass to a Jewish population.

Critics Raved about the choir – Said it sounded like angels from Heaven. The critics in Israel are usually quite hard on people and give bad reviews more often than not

There was a reporter from New York sent to Israel to cover the demonstrations that were expected against the Choir. Just for the sensationalism for the papers back east – He left very disappointed.

Jerusalem has been dedicated 8 times to the Return of the Jewish people. But never has it been dedicated for proselyting.

Before we left for Jerusalem we had to sign a paper saying We would not answer any question about the Mormon Religion. The only answer we were to give was "I can't talk about my religion." Orson Hyde dedicated it in 1841 to the return of the Jews. But it has never been dedicated to proselyting. 60 years before the gathering of Israel.

The Jews have already lost one generation to the Holocaust – They fear losing another through what they see as a spiritual Holocaust.

The most important thing to the Jewish people is the education of the children – about the Jewish religion.

The Shabbat service for the Jews is on Saturday everything is closed down in the Jewish section the elevators are put on automatic so you didn't have to press the buttons. They stop on every floor on Saturdays. They do not drive cars on the Shabbat. They set their TV on timers so they don't push the button.

The Choir was sent to Israel to "speak Comfortable words to her people."

The Choir was not able to proselyte but showed Love through Music. Telling people of God's love for them. The people of Israel felt this love and felt comfortable with it.

Helaman 10:4-5 Blessing for Choir – Elder Faust

The prophecy in Israel was fulfilled.

"Speak peace to the people in Israel."

The people felt the spirit of the Lord when the Choir sang and it brought peace to them.

A prominent PLO Arab Said to Pres Holland – "There is such a feeling of peace – your choir has done in one hour tonight what we have been unable to do in 50 years. (Have everyone in one room Without fighting – Palestinians – Jews – Arabs – Orthodox Jews etc.) Sing with the spirit – But can't speak of Mormonism.

Robert Conic has been here 13 months and never seen the Concert Halls filled – and never had there been so many curtain calls. The patrons usually started leaving as soon as it ended --The Choir got 3 to 5 curtain calls every time.

The mission of the choir was to sing of love in a city where everyone hated each other.

Mount of Olives – Where Jesus wept over the unrighteous of Jerusalem – How does Jesus and HF feel? Does he weep over our sins? (Church of all Nation built on site).

Garden Tomb maintained by the Methodist from England – They are sent on 3 month missions to help people who Tour it.

Shepard Field – Owned by Franciscan Monks. Have a monastery there. No one has been allowed on the land for 100 years – They let the Choir film there because they Knew they Would Testify of God.

Buildings in Jerusalem are of white lime stone – when the sun shines on it it looks kind of like Gold – "City of Gold" Sunsets make the city glow like Gold.

Aid to the Mayor came to choir practice March 14 and said the impact of the Choir was like an earthquake – and Israel is still feeling the after shock. They are requesting the music on the radio and Video and on TV.

There was a patriarch in Choir who had opportunity to give patriarchal blessings to 15 members in Tiberius Bro. Winters.

[attached page]
1.

Before the choir Left for Israel we had several meetings cautioning us that we would be watched very carefully. We were not to say anything about the church even if we were asked. That we were not to wander off for our own protection. That there might be the Orthodox Jews trying to break up the concert – etc. By the time we left we were a little nervous. Not Knowing What might happen – with all the turmoil in Israel. Every time the choir had something – that they might protest.

2.

It took 15-17 years for the church to acquire Property. They finally found a spot not far from where the BYU Jerusalem was built. They were not real excited about it but felt lucky even for any spot in the area for Sale.

Pres. Kimball and Pres. Tanner came over to see the site and were not impressed it was kind of down in a crevice between two hills. Pres. Tanner – walked up the mountain to the choicest part with a wonderful view he said "something like this is the spot."

Pres. Holland tried to tell him that no one could purchase that spot especially the Mormons.

Pres. Kimball came up the hill and said – "This is the place. I like it everyone who likes it raise your hand." Pres Holland said he didn't want to argue with a prophet – But Knew it would be impossible to purchase – this choice piece of property.

The building of the BYU Center had many problems. They had a time period to finish the Center in So they worked round the clock – different Sabbaths.

We went to an olive wood factory.

There were young men carving with a device that finished the olive wood statues. They wore no goggles. Their eyes looked so sore from all the dust.

It takes 5 years after an olive tree is cut to dry out enough and carve it.

We went to the "Shrine of the Book" this is where the Dead Sea scrolls or keep. The scrolls were on a pedestal of some sort. If anything happens such as an <u>earthquake</u> the Pedestal is lowered into the earth to protect the scrolls.

They had been studying the scrolls for 40 years and haven't released all the information that was in them.

We Went the spot that they believe was the upper Room – Where the last supper took place.

Went – We sang "I stand all amazed." It was very emotional. To be standing where they think the last supper was held.

We saw Bedouin tent on the mountain side just as in the time of Jesus. Their custom was back then and still is that any stranger may share their tent and food for 3 days after that they will ask you to leave – their tent are made of skins.

The Dead Sea is very oily it is 34% Salt not even Bacteria live in it. It looks Very thick almost like you could walk on it.

Masada is a flat mountain about 5 times higher than Timpanogos. A group of Jews went there to live in peace and practice their religion. Away from the Romans. It was desolate as far as the eye could see – not one twig no vegetation they caught their water from the rain.
[end inserted page]

Sweden

90% are Lutheran. 3% go to Church.

It Sweden 24% of it is green – They have 8 months white winter 4 months green winter.

Church with organ – graves with stone covers fill the floor.

There is one area where you can buy the house but not the land its on – because it's Royal Land. Very exclusive.

One of the spouses said she paid $2600 and found out on the plane she couldn't sit with her husband when she got to Bergen, Norway – they had twin bed – so no sleeping – The concerts were sold out so she couldn't go to them and the last straw was one night in Bergen they told the spouses to wait and eat after the choir members.

When we came abroad the Ship some Choir member saw his room on the lowest deck on the boat with Twin Beds and said "Oh Hell" and his wife just looked at him and said – No that's one deck below.

One lady said an ashtray full of orange peeling – was a Mormon ashtray.

A Choir member went out to take a suntan in Sweden and a beautiful Swedish girl put her towel next to his and began to undress she had on Bikini bottoms. But when she took off the shirt she had nothing on. He didn't know what to do so he just stayed there for a while.

The cow Puncher standing in the middle of desert holding a rope – Didn't Know if he had lost his horse or found a rope –

One in four have one foreign parent. Finnish people can usually understand Swedish but the Swedish have a harder time understanding Fins. 24% of Sweden is green.

Japan

Custom
Cover water cover most things
Dust Cars – Wash once a week. White gloves. Wash fronts of stores and shops. Home everything is so very clean.
Put tickets to concert on installment plan under developed - $200 month - $400 Bonus at end of year
Japanese do not like to bargain prices on each piece.
Korean – no prices on things, will bargain.
Self discipline – Didn't talk or move during concert

128

History of the Introduction
of Norma Smith to the
Church of Jesus Christ of Latter-day Saints
Written by: Norma Smith (18 years old)
Transcribed by: Tewie Lord (2001)

I was born into the great land of Zion but I never knew of the wonder of the Church until I was in my early teens; and even then I didn't realize how beautiful the Gospel was until I was a few years older. I started coming to Mutual at the age of 13 only because my girl friends went. Before this time I went to a Catholic church for 6 or 7 years. I joined it at the age of 10 or 11 not knowing and not caring what the church taught. My girl friends happened to be Catholic and that was enough for me. All my life I had done what the others did not because I believed in something, but because it was what the other girls did.

When I went to Jr. High school and there I met the best friend I have ever known. By this time I was going to be pushed. I attended the L.D.S. church for several years just going to Mutual not attending the other organizations. This friend asked me to attend Sunday School. I went not intending to go more than that once. As it was I had a teacher who could put over the Gospel so wonderfully that I started attending regularly and soon was intensely interested. I attended all my meetings and gained everything I could from each one. Soon I was baptized by the Sunday School teacher who first arose my interest in the church. I am now Secretary of the M.I.A. I'm trying to become a Silver Gleaner with the help of my wonderful teacher.

Walter & Blanche Lord

Walter Lord
Father: William Knowles Lord
Mother: Margaret Banks
Born: 16 June 1898
Place: Nelson, Lancashire, England
Married: 5 Februrary 1928 (to Blanche Rebecca Stark)
Place: Salt Lake City, Utah, USA
Died: 3 July 1982
Place: Salt Lake City, Utah, USA

The Family of Walter & Blanche Lord

(back row)
Phil, Ralph, Elaine, Jim and Dave
(in front)
Diane

Walter & Blanche's 50th Wedding Anniversary

Walter & Blanche

Ralph & Norma   *Dick & Elaine*

Jim & Marlene   Dave & Gloria   Roy & Dianne   Phil & Marge

Row #1 – Valerie Lord, Kevin Shaw, Jim Lord, Ralph Lord, Dave Lord, Greg Lord, Roy Shaw, Duck Williams, Phil Lord, Cammie Lord, Craig Lord

Row #2 – Caroline Lord, Brian Lord, Marlene Lord, Norma Lord, Gloria Lord, Walter Lord, (on lap) Stephanie Shaw, Blanche Lord,

Row #2 (continued) – Dianne Shaw, (on lap) Marilee Shaw, Elaine Lord, Marge Lord, Carrie Lord, Alan Lord

Row #3 – Clint Lord, Nolana Lord, Charlinn Lord, Janet Lord, Allison Shaw, Gordon Shaw, Paul Williams, Chad Lord, Curtis Lord, Todd Lord

133

Walter Lord

Ralph, Diane & Walter Lord

H.M.S FORESIGHT

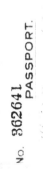

Benjamin & Louisa Bell
Walter & Blanche Lord
Children: Dave & Elaine

No. 362641
PASSPORT.

SIGNATURE OF BEARER

Walter Lord

DESCRIPTION OF BEARER

Age
Place of birth
Profession
National status
[spouse details]

Height 5 feet 5 inches
Forehead
Eyes
Nose
Mouth
Chin
Colour of hair
Complexion
Face
Any special peculiarities

Walter Lord's Passport

PERSONAL HISTORY OF WALTER LORD

June 16, 1898 – July 3, 1982

I was born on June 16, 1898 in a little house on a street called Bradley View in Nelson, Lancashire, England. When I woke up and looked around, I was so surprised, I didn't speak for almost a year. I was 1 year and 9 months old when my father died. My younger brother William E., was born 6 months after my father died.

One year and 3 months after my father (William Knowles Lord) died, a lady, my mother's cousin (Elizabeth A. Banks), came to live with us and to take care of us three children, Edith, Willie and myself, while my mother (Margaret Banks Lord) went to work. We always called her Aunt Lizzie.

She had a little money so after a while, she bought a little grocery store. It was all right for a while, but she had to give it up. She let too many customers buy on credit and they never paid her, so she closed it up.

I was about 3 or 4 years old and I remember she used to take us kids into the store on Sunday (the store was closed) and let us pick out a candy bar.

We moved from there to the end house on a row of houses called Throstle Street in Nelson and lived there about 13 years. Mother went to work all this time as a winder in a cotton mill. We kids all went to school.

Oh, I forgot to mention "Granny." She was my mother's mother (Jane Banks). She lived with us also and after we moved to Throstle Street, she got sick and went to bed and stayed there for about 8 years. We had a 4-room house (2 up and 2 down). Grandma slept upstairs and mother and one or two of us kids slept in the same room.

In the daytime, when she wanted to attract our attention, she used to tap on the floor with a walking stick. Then one of us would go upstairs to her.

136

Grandma lived to be 83 years old and is buried at Kirby Malham in Yorkshire. All or us kids were christened there. It is an old parish church dating back to Cromwell.

I was not too much interested in sports such as soccer, cricket, etc. and I had a chum about the same so we used to go hiking, fishing, picking blackberries, bird nesting or swimming in the old swimming hole in our spare time.

As we grew older, (12 years old) we went into the cotton mill to learn how to weave cloth half a day in school and half a day in the mill. When I reached 13 years old, I went all day to the mill. I would start at 6:00 AM and work until 8:00 AM, then have a half hour for breakfast. Then I would work from 8:30 AM to 12:30 PM and have one hour for dinner. Then I would go back to work at 1:30 PM to 5:30 PM and then go home. I would work half a day on Saturday. How I hated that job.

When I got to be 17 years old, I quit the mill and went to work on the railroad as a locomotive cleaner. It was always my ambition to be a railway engine driver. When I got to be 18 years old, I started to go on the engines as a fireman when anyone was sick, or they put on extra trains for the vacations in summer. When I reached 21 years old, I was promoted to regular fireman. I enjoyed that more than any job I've ever had.

I used to like to go to dances. Our family was noted for their dancing. I had an Uncle who died dancing (on the end of a rope.)

I was a member of the church, mother joined before I was eight. I was baptized when I was 8 years old.

I remember going to a town about 4 miles away on the streetcar. Boy, that was a big event.

We did not have much opposition to the church in our town. Every so often, a play would come to the local theater. "A Mormon and His Wives," or "A Victim of the Mormons," were the name of a couple of plays. After the show was over, the elders used to deliver tracts to the people as they came out.

In 1914, war broke out with Germany but I was only 14 years old so I could not join the armed forces. When I worked on the railway, I was exempted from military duty, but one day in November 1917, I went and joined the navy. I then went to my boss on the railway and told him what I had done, but he let me go anyway, with a promise I could have my job back when I came home from the war.

In January 1918, I was drafted to the Eastern Mediterranean Sea. That was a cold journey. I got on a troop ship in Italy and continued to journey by sea. While passing through the Aegean Sea, around Greece, the ship was torpedoed and sunk. There were 600 men on board and 300 went down with the ship. I was lucky.

The night our ship was torpedoed, it was hot and my buddy and I didn't want to sleep inside the ship so we got some hammocks and went up on the deck and set up our hammocks and slept in them in the fresh air. Early the next morning the ship was hit. Since we were up on top, we escaped almost certain death. I jumped overboard and managed to get on some wreckage and was picked up about 8 hours later. The survivors were taken to a little island called Mudras. I was later transferred to a ship called H.M.S. Foresight. And stayed there until the war ended.

The Mediterranean Sea is beautiful in good weather but it can get pretty rough. You see some of the most beautiful sunrises and sunsets you ever saw.

We traveled the length of the Mediterranean two or three times, from Gibraltar in Spain to Alexandria in Egypt and visited places in several countries but it was nice to get back to England.

My younger brother, Willie, had to go in the army of occupation in Germany after the war ended. My older brother, James was in the army also, in the trenches in France and had several narrow escapes, including being gasses. He was blind for a week. My mother went over to France to see him. They though he would not pull through, but he did.

Jim came home after the war his lungs were damaged by the gas, but he gained fairly good health again. He went to some training the navy or government gave him, and learned to be a wireless operator and was put on a merchant ship.

His health wasn't entirely all right. He had to get work where he could have plenty of fresh air and sunshine. The sea air did him some good.

He had gotten married to May before he left England. They had no children. He was on this job before the Second World War and then Germany started the war and England went to war with them, his ship was torpedoed. Jin was sending our messages that they were sinking and that is how they said he drowned.

My mother and sister Edith came to America and my brother Willie stayed in England. We moved into a house in the 28th Ward. I met a young lady of that ward named Blanche and we started going together. We later married.

I worked on the railroad but when the Depression hit, I lost my job. I worked where I could. I got a job with the CCC (government-sponsored job). One of the things our group did was build Stillman Bridge. This is located at the mouth of Parley's Canyon.

In the latter part of the 30's, I got a job with the Bureau of Mines as a night watchman. I had to work for them in Washington D.C., so I had to leave my family. I worked there for more than a year. Finally, a job opened up at the Bureau of Mines in Salt Lake City. I was transferred to Salt Lake City. I was with my Family again.

Some Early History of Walter Lord
as told to daughter
Dianne Lord Shaw on July 4, 1973

Walter Lord was born 16 June 1898 in Nelson, Lancashire, England. A son of William Knowles Lord and Margaret Banks. His father died when he was about 1 year 9 months old. He has no recollection of his father at all. His younger brother, William, was born a few months after the father's death. The family consisted of an older brother Jim and an older sister Edith. After the father's death Dad's mother's cousin (they called her "Aunt Lizzy") Elizabeth Banks came to live with them. She had a little money and later tended the children while the mother went to work in the mill. When the children became about 12 years of age they went to work in the mill. I asked Dad if Aunt Lizzy was a member of the church and he thinks she was the one who first let the missionaries in the house. They joined the church before Dad was 8 years old.

One of Dad's earliest recollections is of his kindergarten class. The teacher told them, "Let's all be very quiet and a little mouse will come out of the hole." So they were all very still. The school he attended was rather large. Grades kindergarten thru 8th grade was housed in the school. Dad quit school at the beginning of 8th grade to go to work in the mill at about age 12. At first he worked just half a day and made the wage of about 50 cents a week. After a time he worked full time – 6 AM to 5:30 PM – 5 ½ days a week for a wage of about $1.25 per week. For about the first year they were a man's helper, then they were given 2 looms of their own and later 3. The mill contained about 700 looms. The place was extremely noisy and lip reading was learned quickly. To make a person hear your voice you had to shout in his ear. Dad remembers he hated the work.

At age 17 he quit the mill to begin work on the railroad. At first he washed down engines then learned the trade of a fireman. When the war broke out he joined the Navy (about age 18). At the end of the war he was given his old job back on the railroad and became a fireman. This he says was the most enjoyable job of his life. It consisted of feeding coal to the fire, keeping water in the boiler to keep the steam up. There was one fireman and one engineer on each engine. He traveled over Northern England. He worked for the railroad for a total of about 5 years.

In 1921, Dad had been active in the church and knew a family who was coming to America and said they would take him too. They were Ben Bell and wife Louie with baby. He was on shipboard about 6 days and landed in Montreal. Then he traveled to Salt Lake by train. He arrived in Salt Lake 2 days before his 23rd birthday. He lived with this family at first. Dad said he couldn't find a good job for about six months. He worked in the kitchen at LDS hospital for a while and also on a ranch in Idaho milking cows and working the fields. Then he got a job on the railroad. His mother and sister came to Salt Lake about four years later.

After having been in America only a short time, he was fishing on the ranch property not knowing a license was needed, and was arrested and taken to jail in Park City. He spent a couple of hours in the jail before his boss came and paid the $25.00 to bail him out.

Experiences told to me, Dianne L. Shaw, by my father, Walter Lord, in May 1974:

When dad was about 17 the 1st World War broke out and he quit work to join the Navy. He received his training and then was put aboard a troop ship to be delivered to an island in the Aegean Sea just off the coast of Greece. While traveling to that destination, the ship, the H.M.S. Louvain, was torpedoed by an enemy submarine. Dad was supposed to sleep below deck that night, but because it was "too stuffy" he decided to sleep on deck. About 9 o'clock he was in his hammock in the front part of the ship when a shell hit the back part. Immediately the ship began sinking. In about 5 minutes the ship was completely gone. There wasn't time to launch any of the lifeboats. He and his pal did go to get in one of the boats but Dad decided it was too packed and would most likely sink when it touched the water, and so he lost track of his pal and later learned that he had been crushed between the side of the ship and the boat and was in the hospital in Malta. Dad swam around in the water for several hours before being picked up by their escort destroyer. Dad says as soon as the ship was hit this destroyer started sailing around the ship in a big circle dropping depth charges. He doesn't know if they got the enemy submarine or not. As a result of being in the water so long, he contracted typhoid fever and was in a hospital at Malta for quite a while. I can remember him telling of being delirious a good part of the time.

He didn't learn until later that his pal had been in the same hospital. Later he went back to visit him. Of the approximately 600 men on the ship about half of them were lost. Dad says the ones in the engine room and below deck didn't have a chance. He later wrote a poem about his experiences and sent it to the newspaper in his hometown and they published it.

After Dad got out of the hospital in Malta, he was assigned to an escort destroyer. They were at sea a great deal, but saw no combat. They were the ones that escorted important persons from place to place. Dad was chosen to be one that manned the small "whaler" boat that was sent to pick up important people. They had to dress in their sparkling white and be ready at all times to be sent off. Being on this crew he used to miss out on some of the hard, "dirty" work aboard the ship. When they had to load coal on their ship, the whaler crew would be sent to a small, nearby island so they would not get dirty. If they were needed, the crew would hail them. He can remember escorting an important General, who later had a part in the liberating of Palestine and also helped a Russian Prince to escape from the Bolsheviks.

Dad also told about some of the experiences of his older brother, Jim. He had several narrow escapes. Once in combat they needed some men to man a machine gun and Jim was to be one of them. But for some reason he got left behind and a few minutes later the machine gun position was hit and all were dead. Later in France, the enemy gased Jim. Many of the men died, and they thought Jim wouldn't live, so his mother was able to go to France to visit him in a hospital. But Jim did survive, although one of his lungs was completely stopped up and he had much pain. Dad said he came back to England, but because of his lung condition he couldn't stand to work inside in the mills, and so he took an exam to be a wireless operator on a ship. He passed the exam and went home to wait to be assigned a ship. For some reason they forgot about him and he waited for nearly a year at home. After being in contact with the representative in Parliament, he was sent for and took the exam again. After being away from it for nearly a year, he passed the exam again.

142

This time he was assigned a place as a wireless operator aboard a merchant ship. He traveled all over the world on the ship. One time he was docked in California and he traveled to Utah to see his mother, sister and my father who had in the meantime all immigrated to the U.S. My mother recalls meeting Jim and saying he was a handsome fellow and she liked him a lot. This was when my brother Dave was a baby.

On a later trip, at the beginning of World War II, it was to be his last trip aboard ship. He was going to quit and open a small store in England after this, but his ship was sunk without a trace. A Message was received from the ship – something like, "Being attacked, ship sinking" – and that was all. Since Jim was the wireless operator on board, he probably sent the message.

POEMS AND SONGS
BY WALTER LORD

CHRISTMAS HYMN

Oh, Christmas time is here again
Bringing it's joy to the hearts of men.
For lo, a holy sign is given
To bring the souls of men to heaven.
With joyful giving and merry tune
Knowing that Santa will be here soon.
A lovely child was born on earth,
A holy, though a lowly birth,
And in a manger, there he lay,
His bed a layer of new mown hay.
And then do Angels start to sing,
All Hail to Jesus, new born king,
Hosanna, to the Holy One,
And Peace on Earth, Good Will to Men.

HYMN OF PRAISE

"Jesu" Lord of all creation,
Gently we beseech thee now,
Fill our hearts with glad emotion,
As we humbly kneel and bow,
Grant us peace and understanding,
Of Thy sojourn here on earth.
Of thy sacrifice on Calv'ry
And Thy lowly gentle birth.
May we at this Christmas season
Think of all that Thou hast done,
To redeem the world from darkness,
That the victory might be won.
Glad Hosanna's sing the Angels,
"Peace on Earth", "Good Will to Men,"
Spread the news through all the nations,
Man, though dead, shall live again.

AN EASTER SONG

1.   Bright is the dawn of Easter Morn,
      All nature is in tune,
      For Christ has risen from the dead,
      And triumphed o'er the tomb.
      Glad voices raised on High,
      Sing out in glorious cry.

         Chorus
      Hail to the risen Lamb,
      Who on this earth was slain,
      That man from sin should ere be free,
      God's glory see again.

2.   The ages dark have passes away,
      And light on earth is shed,
      The Prince of Life to earth has brought,
      Redemption for the dead,
      The Hosts of Heaven rejoice,
      In one united voice.

         Chorus
      All glory to the Lamb,
      Peace on the earth below,
      Man is redeemed from death to live,
      And heaven's wonders know.

PRAISE

1. Praise to the Lord Almighty,
   Hallelujah loud proclaim,
   Creator of the heavens and earth,
   All glory to his name.

2. He is our God, our Father,
   Christ our Savoir, is His Son,
   Supreme in power, He is the source,
   From whom all blessings come.

3. To faithful seer and prophets,
   He has revealed His ways,
   And restored to earth the Gospel true,
   In these the latter days.

4. The way of true salvation,
   Taught by men of olden times,
   Is spreading wide throughout the land,
   Where e're God's presence shines.

5. It tells of Gods great mercy,
   And His love for all mankind,
   And how, if we but do His will,
   Salvation we shall find.

6. Rejoice then in the Gospel,
   In the Saviors glorious plan,
   To redeem the world, and bring to pass,
   The immortality of man.

AT EVENTIDE

1.   Hushed is this hour at eventide,
The stars in splendor shine,
The heavens extending far and wide,
Bespeak the peace that's mine.
And through the twilight clear,
An angle choir I hear.

Chorus
Glory, Glory, to the Lamb,
Peace on the earth below,
Man is redeemed from death to live,
And heavens wonders know.

2.   The cares of life seem far away,
The vesper hour is here,
As heaven comes down to join the earth,
And man to God draws near.
And as the night draws nigh,
A song is heard on High.

Chorus
Glory, Glory, Christ is risen,
Those happy voices sing,
Man is redeemed and sin forgiven,
All hail our glorious King.

DEAR OLD WEST HI.

These walls of old ivy, in your regal attire,
Your crown of achievement rises higher and higher.
Here the pride of our nation in the fervor of youth,
Strives to learn and excel in their searching for truth.
Hear the echoes resounding through the classrooms and halls,
"I can" and "I will" on the listening ear falls.
With their eyes ever focused on the goal of success,
They strive to learn wisdom 'mid the toil and the stress.
Learning and doing with great self control,
They follow the pattern of the great Master's role.
So my God help our children with power from on high,
To ever be a credit to "Dear Old West Hi".

EXCELSIOR (ONWARD/UPWARD)

If you would seek advancement
  In this world of toil and strife,
Then start to climb the ladder
  That leads to a better life.
Work through the day and study
  Nights, an eager mind to gain,
And soon you'll be, crowned with
  Success, aboard the gravy train.
So if you find, the job you seek,
  Is way up near the top.
Don't waste your time and play
  Around, or advancement soon will stop.
And you will find, to your regret,
  The job you had in mind,
Is given to the studious one,
  And you are left behind.

I DON'T KNOW WHY

1.   I don't know why I'm always thinking of you,
I don't know why I'm always feeling so blue,
Since you went away and left me all alone,
Though you almost broke my heart,
When you said, "'Tis best we part,"
Yet I can't forget I once called you my own.

    Chorus
So won't you please come back,
To that little old shack,
Where the honeysuckle blossomed long ago,
When the skies were always blue,
Earth seemed made for me and you,
And the songbirds sang their music soft and low.

2.   I don't know why your face haunts me all the day,
Or why your last good-bye lives in my memory,
I can't forget you, how I've tried but all in vain,
Though each hour has seemed a day,
Ever since you went away,
How I'm longing just to hear your voice again.

MISSING YOU

Many years have passed
Away since first you left me,

How I've missed you, there's no
Way that I can tell,

I live in memory the many times
I've kissed you,

And held you in my arms when
You were well.

How I miss you in the sunset
O my darling,

When I think of happy days in
Years gone by

And I pray that once again
We'll be united

And be happy in our mansion
In the sky.

YOU AND I
Dedicated to my wife

1. It was twilight time in Utah,
The stars were peeping through,
When I had to part, from the girl of my heart,
And we bid a fond adieu.

Chorus

Blanche for you, I tell you true,
There's not a thing in this wide world I wouldn't do.
Though the skies seem dark and drear,
I always know I've got you dear,
And though the road is full of thorns,
I'll come to you.

2. Though dark clouds beset our pathway,
The sun will shine again,
And we'll sing out our song, as we journey along,
So just let's forget the rain.

149

HOPING

1.   I had a dream one sunny day, while coming through the rye,
I dreamt I held you, oh so hard, I almost made you cry.
But how I wish that it were real, because I love you true,
There's only one fills all my thoughts, and that someone is you.

        Chorus
So let us face reality and put all dreams aside,
And sail along the sea of life, and banish the ebb tide.

2.   We'll find the way to happiness and find life's joys anew,
And battle through the storm and stress, for love will put us through.
We'll make our songs of joyfulness reach to the clouds on high,
And think again of happy days as we came through the rye.

IN OLD GLAMORGANSHIRE

1.   When the song birds are all mating; Jenny Dear,
Then I know that you'll be waiting, Jenny Dear,
So I'm coming back to you,
For you promised to be true,
When we said "Good-bye" in old Glamorganshire.

        Chorus
For Jenny, Jenny, I love you more than any,
With your sparkling eyes and shiny raven hair,
Though we are many miles apart,
You will always have my heart,
For I've left it there in old Glamorganshire.

2.   For you know I love you truly, Jenny Dear,
When the apple trees are budding I'll be near,
Soon the wedding bells will ring,
And the old church choir will sing,
When the roses bloom in old Glamorganshire.

CICELIA

On the shores of a bay in Cicily,
I saw a vision rare,
Skin of olive hue,
By the water blue,
Cicelia was standing there.

Chorus
Cicelia, Cicelia,
I give my heart to you,
From my memory nothing can steal ya,
Cicelia, my dream come true.

Such a pleasing sight, neath the bright sunlight,
I could not choose but stay,
For I found a pearl,
She's my dark skinned girl,
By that blue Cicilian bay.

TO THE RAIN

1.   Pitter, patter, fall the rain-drops,
On the grass so tenderly,
Bringing life to field and meadow,
Laving every flower and tree.

2.   Folding every hill and valley,
In a clinging, wet embrace,
'Til mother earth springs forth in blossom,
Like a smile on nature's face.

3.   Every root is gently nurtured,
By the rain-drops from above,
Each leaf and bursting bud remembered,
In God's great and boundless love,

4.   So let us not be melancholy,
As we view the falling rain.
Think upon the coming morrow,
When the sun will shine again.

TO THE SPRINGTIME

1.   The sun is slowly rising,
       Springtime is everywhere,
       The notes of feathered songsters,
       Now fill the morning air.

2.   The blackbird in the bushes,
       The lark up in the sky,
       The thrush out in the meadows,
       Join in the joyful cry.

3.   Oh, nature's sweet harmony,
       Naught can with it compare,
       When birds sing out their joyful lay,
       And Spring is in the air.

THE PRISONER

1. She has spent her young life behind the bars,
This beautiful creature so fair,
Though gentle by nature and tender in years,
What justice to keep her there.

2. She seems blithe and gay as the days pass away,
And her eyes are as bright as the stars,
But who knows the feelings within her breast,
As she looks through her prison bars.

3. She sings with delight, and from morning till night,
Her beautiful voice can be heard,
But that's as it should be, for this creature, you see,
Is my mother's canary bird.

PEACE

By the side of the lane in the valley,
There stands an old Sycamore tree,
And each time I go to the valley,
It brings sweet peace unto me.
I gaze on the star spangled heavens,
And the moon in its glory so grand,
And the stream rushing down from the mountains,
To water the sweet fertile land.

TO THE WILD BIRDS

Purring like a Summer zepher,
Pass the birds in happy flight,
Bringing to us sweetest music,
From the dawn until the night.

Nesting on the leafy branches,
Flying swiftly through the air,
Warbling, singing, ever spreading,
Peace and gladness everywhere.

Trilling, thrilling souls with gladness,
As they fly from tree to tree,
Harbingers of peace and goodness,
In the great Eternity.

MY IOWA

When the weary day is ended
And the moon begins to shine,
Then sweet memories of my Iowa,
Are brought back to my mind.
How the fine old rooster use'ter,
Wake me up at break of day,
Down upon the farm, far away from harm,
At my home in Iowa.

You can sing of coral beaches,
And the waves upon the shore,
But give me back my old home,
With the roses round the door,
With the locusts and the crickets,
Chirping all the Summer day.
In the waving corn, where I was born,
At my home in Iowa.

   Chorus
So I'm going away to Iowa,
Far across the deep blue sea,
Where the waving corn in the early morn,
Waits there to welcome me.
And the harvest moon is shining,
On the fields of new mown hay,
How I often yearn, to again return
To my home in Iowa.

MY MEXICO

1.   When the humming birds are singing
        down along the Rio Grande,
And the mandolins are strumming in that
        dear old Southern land,
Then my thoughts go ever backward to
        the days of long ago,
And the home I left behind me in
        dear old sunny Mexico.

    Chorus:
    My Mexico, dear Mexico, the pride
        of all the earth,
    Where 'ere I be, I long to see the
        land that gave me birth,
    The place where days are sunny,
        and nights with stars aglow,
    I'm coming back, to that little shack,
        in dear old Mexico.

2.   When life seems sad and dreary, and
        friends are hard to find,
Then memories of my Mexico are brought
        back to my mind,
I sit and dream of childhood in that
        God created land,
And I live again in fancy, down along
        the Rio Grande.

I'M GOING BACK TO DEAR OLD CAROLINA

Way down South, where the sun is always shining,
In a dear old Southern town,
Where black mammies croon to little piccaninnies,
And you seldom see a frown,
There my heart is turning ever, though I'm far away,
There the handshakes and the welcome,
Drive all care away,

Chorus
So I'm going back to dear old Carolina,
Past the Mason-Dixon line,
For my dear old Carolina,
All day long I pine,
When the harvest moon is shining, o'er the waving corn,
Then I'm going back to dear old Carolina,
'Cause that's where I was born.

When the shadows of night have softly fallen,
And the stars are shining bright,
Then I see my Carolina homestead
Basking in their silvery light,
Sweetest memories of my childhood then come back to me,
And once again I kneel in fancy at my mommies knee.

BEAUTIFUL HAWAIIAN MOON

Oftimes when night is falling,
And stars are in the sky,
I dream about the long ago when troubles ne'er came nigh,
I see Hawaii's mountains close by the moonlit sea,
The noise of tumbling waves at play comes through the night to me.

Chorus
Beautiful Hawaiian moon,
Shining o'er the silv'ry sea
Youthful dreams of long ago, you bring back to me,
Again I stroll in fancy along that coral shore,
And live again life's sweetest hours,
As in the days of yore.

When life seems dark and lonesome,
And clouds are all around,
I think of dear Hawaii and the ocean's happy sound,
'Tis then I seem to be on old Hawaii's wave beat shore,
And joyous lays of childhood days, come back to me once more.

When birds have ceased their warbling and peace is on the land,
My memory brings the moonlight and the evenings on the sand,
I dream of dear Hawaii and the days of long ago,
And how the years now fly away, when then they went so slow.

MY BEAUTIFUL HAITI HOME

Land of dreams and romance,
My beautiful Haiti home,
In my dreams I see thee, no matter where I roam,
I see the palm trees swaying beneath the silvery moon,
I hear the wind a saying
Come, hear your Mammy croon.

Chorus
Haiti, beautiful Haiti, I often think of thee,
The memory of thy sunny skies will always be with me,
I hear the piccaninnies, and see old Mammy Lou,
I roam the world so weary, so I'm coming back to you.

Home of happy childhood,
Land of skies so blue,
My heart is full of gladness at the thought of seeing you,
I'll roam the world no longer amid the toil and strife,
I'm coming back to Haiti,
To settle down for life.

MY NEVADA MOUNTAIN HOME

When the sun has gone to rest in old Nevada,
And the moon in all her glory starts to shine,
That's the time I long to be in old Nevada,
In that little ivy-covered shack of mine,
Where the snow capped mountains rising in splendor,
Stand as sentinels kissed by the evening dew,
May the gods watch over you my old Nevada,
'Til the day, dear home, that I return to you.

Chorus
So I'm going back again to old Nevada,
When the roses and the honeysuckle bloom,
Where all toil and care will cease,
'Mid the happiness and peace,
Of that little old Nevada mountain home.

All the world seems dark and drear far from Nevada,
And the joys of life have lost their rosy hue,
How I long to go again to old Nevada,
To a place so free from care and sorrow, too,
Where the night birds wing o'er head out in the gloaming,
And the stars shed silvery light on hill and glen,
Hasten on the longed for day of my returning,
To my old Nevada mountain home again.

A UTAH GIRL

I'm a little blue eyed girl,
With a little curly curl,
And I live out West in Utah,
How I love the hills and streams,
And lovely flowers, to me it seems,
There is no place so nice as Utah.

Give me saddle and a horse,
You'll have to lift me on, of course,
And I'll never whip or boot her,
And I'll ride out on the range,
This to you, may seem quite strange,
But it's quite the thing in Utah.

If you'll come out to my house,
You can learn to milk the cows,
And I will be your tutor,
Then the rich cow's milk we'll drink,
And you'll tell your friends, I think,
That you are glad you came to Utah.

So let mother pack your grip,
And start out upon your trip,
To me there's nothing could be cuter,
Than to have a little friend,
All the Summer with me spend
At my home out West in Utah.

SCOUT SONG
Tune: "Marching Thru Georgia"

What teaches one good turn each day,
The BSA, the BSA
What keeps me straight when I would stray
The BSA, the BSA.
A scout's motto is be prepared,
With him distress and woe are shared
To reverent be, at work or play,
Is taught to all the BSA.

BOY SCOUT CAMPING SONG
Music: "Marching Through Georgia"
Words by: Walter Lord

Come gather round the campfire, boys,
And listen to a tale,
Of brawny scout adventurers,
Along the camp fire trail,
Of nights spent in the open,
Underneath the stars so pale,
And lets give a rousing cheer for scouting.
Hurrah, hooray, we're going to cam today,
Hurrah, hooray, we'll soon be on our way,
The weather's right, our hearts are light,
        we're feeling blithe and gay,
So let's give another cheer for scouting.
        "Hurray!"

A SONG OF THE SEA

Out on the sea, with a wind that's free,
And your ship sails boldly on,
It is then that the strife in a sailor's life
Is banished with a song.

    Chorus:
For it's Heave, Ho, steady my lads,
Hurrah for a life on the main,
When the wild winds whirl and the sails unfurl,
And we are homeward bound again,
So me for the life of a sailor, who sails the distant sea,
With the hatches pinned and the offshore wind,
This is the life for me.

Out in the gale, when the leeward rail
Is buried in the sea,
Then the song of the main, and the wind,
      And the rain,
Is the sailor's lullaby.

    Chorus:
For it's Heave, Ho, steady my lads,
Hurrah for a life on the main,
When the wild winds whirl and the sails unfurl,
And we are homeward bound again,
So me for the waves and the perils,
Of the boundless rolling sea,
As we sail once more, for a distant shore,
This is the life for me.

When the sails up above, like the wings of a dove,
Are flapping in the wind.
And your ship sails on,
In the lift of a song,
And we leave the waves behind.

    Chorus:
For it's Heave, Ho, steady my lads,
Hurrah for a life on the main,
When the wild winds whirl and the sails unfurl,
And we are homeward bound again,
So me for the life of a sailor, who sails
      The distant sea,
With the hatches pinned and the offshore wind,
This is the life for me.

THE SINKING OF TROOP SHIP S.S. LOUVAIN, IN THE MEDITERRANEAN SEA.
SUNDAY, JANUARY 20TH, 1918

See the troop ship sailing onward,
Through the sea of azure blue,　　　　1.
Filled with sons of mighty England,
Going forth to war, with will to do.

No sign of fear in any face,
No talk of death on any tongue,　　　　2.
As the order comes, "keep life-belts handy,"
We're coming into the danger zone.

Our guardian ship, a bold destroyer,
Drops slowly, quietly to the rear,　　　　3.
As night falls gently o'er the water,
No sign of lurking death is near.

Within their hammocks the men were
sleeping,　　　　4.
But the watching sentries failed to see,
The lurking shadow off to starboard,
Tossing in the rolling sea.

A submarine was waiting, watching,　　　　5.
And as the troopship hove in view,
Released a torpedo straight toward us,
Sent with deadly aim and true.

Suddenly a noise like thunder,　　　　6.
Woke us from security,
And the good ship, S.S. Louvain,
Settled in the restless sea.

Confusion reigned, no time for boats,
The ship was sinking fast,
Each man, who could, went overboard,
Into the ocean vast.

Below the decks that fatal night,
Two hundred sailors lay,
None gave a thought that nevermore,
They'd see the light of day.

The sea rushed in the engine room,
The boilers blew sky-high,
The black squad standing watch that night,
Were all foredoomed to die.

The sea was turned to angry foam,
Wreckage lay all around,
As, with the proud troop ship Louvain,
Three hundred souls went down.

Their names are writ in purest gold,
On the roll of England's dead,
But nothing can ever compensate,
For the tears that have been shed.

Grim war, the curse of every race,
Oh will it never cease,
To vanish from within our midst,
And on the earth be peace.

A TALE OF THE SEA

T'was on a dark and stormy night,
As to the bulkheads we held tight,
And all around was a foaming sea,
I heard a voice say unto me,
　　　"We're paying off."
I looked around and stood amazed,
As for the speaker long I gazed,
No human form there could I see,
But still the voice said unto me,
　　　"We're paying off."
The speaker must a spirit be,
This is no human agency,
My thoughts ran on in such a strain,

Just then the voice cried out again,
　　　"We're paying off."
I searched the ship both fore and aft,
The lifeboats and the "Carley" rafts,
I searched the decks, foretop and
main,
But still the voice cried out again,
　　　"We're paying off."
I could not solve the mystery,
My thoughts were in a quandary,
Just then out rang the telephone bell,
Alas, I knew the truth too well,
　　　It was only a buzz.

CHILDREN'S POEMS

HAPPY DAY

Written for my daughter Elaine age 8
I went outside the other day,
I walked right through the door,
I just forgot to open it like I've
Always done before.
I slipped and fell upon the step,
How it happened, no one knows,
Instead of lighting on my feet, I lit
Upon my nose.
I lost my hat and looked for it,
"What's the matter," someone said,
And I never felt so silly as when
They said, "It's on your head."
I limped down to the garden gate,
My nose was smarting so,
And just to make the day complete,
I went and stubbed my toe.
I sat right down and hollered, "Ow!",
I 'most began to cry,
Then I woke up, it was just a dream,
There was none so glad as I.

KEVIN

Kevin is a wiggly worm,
He wiggles tall and strong,
I think when I want fishing bait,
I'll just take him along.

Christine is a sweetie Pie,
She's such a darling girl,
That every time I think of her,
My head goes in a whirl.

And baby is a honey-bunch,
To her we'll sing a song.
Can you guess who we'll sing about,
Her name is Allison.

A BEDTIME STORY

A child gazed in her mother's face,
As the stars began to peep.
Tell me a story mummy dear,
Before I go to sleep.

The Mother tucked the child in bed,
And kissed her golden head,
Then took her little hand in hers,
And unto her she said,

"In a village many miles away,
There lived a maiden fair,
And every evening in her room
She knelt in humble prayer.

'O God, the giver of all good,
Who looks down from above,
Someday, send me a little child
To cherish and to love.'

The years rolled by, she loved a youth,
And life was bright and gay,

None was so happy as the maid
Upon her wedding day.

The humble prayers she'd sent above,
Were heard up in the skies,
For an angel came to earth to dwell,
From God who is so wise.

The Mother took the little babe,
This gift from heaven above,
And as it grew she lavished it,
With all a Mother's love.

She tended to its every need,
In sickness and in health,
But the joy the babe gave in return,
Could not be bought with wealth."

The child looked in the Mother's eyes,
"Mums, is that story true?"
The Mother said with a loving smile,
"Yes dear, that babe was you."

163

HALLOWEEN NIGHT

On Hallow'een night the witches fly,
Riding their broomsticks, way up in the sky,
They circle round and round the moon,
Whilst the Hallow'een cats sing a mournful tune..

Then down to the ground they come with a rush,
You'll find them in cupboards, behind tree or bush..
With eyes of green or fiery red,
They look for little children, who won't go to bed.
And "woe" unto these if any be found,
When the witches come from the moon to the ground.

So on Hallow'een night when the tempests howl,
And the Hallow'een cats begin to prowl,
Don't stay out late and roam about,
Or the witches will get "you"
If you don't watch out.

MY DOLLY AND ME

1. I have a pretty dolly, her name is Kate,
   I take her to school, and we are never late,
   And we smile at everyone we see,
   For everyone knows my dolly and me.

2. She stays with me throughout the day,
   And at recess we go out to play,
   We laugh and shout, so gay and free,
   For we are always happy, my dolly and me.

3. We write and draw till the day is done,
   For going to school is lots of fun,
   'Till the bell rings out at half-past three,
   Then we walk home, my dolly and me.

4. We play at house out in the shed,
   And at eight o'clock we go to bed,
   For what makes us feel so good, you see,
   We get lots of sleep, my dolly and me.

5. We wake each morn with smiling face,
   And out to breakfast we both race,
   We wash and clean our teeth you see,
   Then off to school, my dolly and me.

6. And so the days go slowly by,
   Sometimes we laugh, sometimes we cry,
   But we always try to happy be,
   For I love my dolly, and my dolly loves me.

165

DIARY

You have all heard of boys and girls who had a dog or a cat for a pet but I once had a tame dinosaur for my pet. I would like to tell you how I got him.

One night I was hunting buffaloes in the jungles at the back of my house when I heard someone crying. I crept over and there I saw "Dinny". He was guarded by 20 lions, 50 tigers, and 100 wild elephants, and - an - an - an - an 1000 goats, I mean ghosts, but I did not care. I rushed at them. I had a sword in each hand and a pistol in the other, and boy, I mean girl, I waded through them like a fly through a can of molasses. I said boo to the ghosts and they all went home crying. They were only young ghosts and they thought I was a spook. After I had killed all the buffaloes and alligators and wild boars; (what do you say, there were'nt any of these)? Oh well, I would have killed them if there had been. After I had killed all these rattle snakes and boa constrictors, I looked for the dinosaur and I saw him climbing up a tree, I said, hey, you caw'nt do that, come down at twice, I mean at once, he said no, I said yes, he said no, I said yes, he said no, I said yes, he said alright.

When he came down, I took him by the ear, I think it was his ear. I said what is your name, he said, Bertie-Willie, so that is how I came to know his name, Clevah. What? I took him home, and trained him to eat little boys and girls, but don't get scared, because Bertie is on a diet, so he can't eat any more school children; don't you feel sorry for him?

166

Written specially for my daughter Elaine (8)

1. I went down to the zoo one day,
   And I laughed 'till I was sore,
   For I saw more funny sights that day,
   Than I'd ever seen before.

2. I saw a big brown monkey,
   With great big blinking eyes,
   He looked just like a funny old man,
   He'd sit and look so wise.

3. Then all around his cage he'd go
   Then stand upon his head,
   If I did half the things he did,
   I'm sure that I'd be dead.

4. There was Mr. Alli-Gator,
   His mouth three feet by two,
   I think if he ever got me in it,
   I'd be gone in just one chew.

5. There were brown bears and cinnamon bears,
   And bears all snowy white,
   But don't let them get hold of you,
   They'll hug you, Oh, so tight.

6. I went to see the lions,
   And they began to roar,
   I thought they were coming after me,
   So I flew out the door.

7. I saw a baby "hippo",
   He's not pretty like me and you,
   But don't you let his mother hear that
   Or she'll be sore at you.

8. Then next came Mr. Giraffe,
   The tallest in the place,
   You see about 15 feet of neck
   Before you see his face.

A Day At The Zoo - continued

9. I also saw a kangaroo,
    It tickled me to find,
    It had two little short legs in front
    And two long ones behind.

10, And then I saw the squirrels
    They'd jump upon my knee,
    I'd give them nuts, and then they'd run
    And scamper up a tree.

11, At last the day was ended, and so (we)
    Came away,
    But I promised some baby monkeys,
    I'd come again someday.

THE ONE LEGGED HEN

1. A hen was roosting in the coop, she only had one leg,
   She said, I've nothing else to do, I think I'll lay an egg.

2. She hopped right down from off her perch, and sat upon her nest.
   She had never laid an egg before, but she said, I'll do my best.

3. A crowd of chickens standing near, began to cluck and grin,
   You'll never lay an egg, said they,
   You're just a one legged hen.

4. The one legged hen stayed on her nest, the sun shone bright
                                                        outside,
   And then she laid a snow white egg, which made her cluck with
                                                        pride.

5.. The other hens all gathered round, all filled with jealousy,
   To think a little one legged hen, could be as smart as they.

6. The one legged hen stood proudly by,
   And then to them she said,
   I may not have two legs like you,
   But I still can lay an egg.

169

A JUNGLE TALE

1. In by-gone years of long ago,
   In ages passed away,
   There lived a poor old dinasaur,
   Who roamed about all day.

2. He'd eat the grass and chew on trees,
   And when shadows gathered round,
   He'd roll himself into a ball,
   And sleep upon the ground.

3. One day a mean old saber-tooth,
   Thats a tiger don't you know,
   Took a little bite at Dinny's leg,
   And Dinny hollered, Ow.

4. He kicked the tiger in the face,
   Which fairly made him wince,
   And then old Dinny scrammed away,
   And no one's seen him since.

5. But I know where old Dinny went,
   Though I'll not breathe a thing,
   He crawled into a deep, deep hole,
   And pulled it in after him.

6. So boys and girls, if a saber-tooth,
   Ever starts to chew on you,
   Just kick old snarty in the teeth,
   And then you beat it, too.

WOODY WOODPECKER (1965)

Mr. Woody Woodpecker was pecking on a tree.
Said he, "There's no one in the whole wide world
    can peck as good as me."
He preened himself and looked around
    To see who could have heard.
But no one seemed to give a hoot
  About the silly bird.

So Woody, he just pecked away
  As hard as hard could be.
Until he had a nice round hole
  That was a sight to see.
He pecked some more, then looked at it
  Said, "That's good enough for me."
And then he flew and started
  Pecking on another tree.

OUR NEW BABY

Hello there little stranger,
With eyes of azure blue,
You're just what we've been waiting for,
To greet the likes of you.

You're just a darling baby,
Sent down from heaven above,
So we can hug and kiss you.
And smother you with love.
Someday you'll grow to manhood,
But not for quite a while,
For we love to hear you gurgle,
And watch your baby smile.

And when you're getting sleepy,
And eyes begin to close,
We'll lay you in your cradle,
To rest in sweet repose.
And if Mama is not handy,
To hear your baby cries,
And wipe away the teardrops,
From out your baby eyes,

Just start to whoop and holler,
With all you're might and main,
And Grandpa will come and hold you,
'Till you're all smiles again.

THE FOOLISH PIG

Come gather round and hear about a foolish little pig,
He ate, and ate the whole day long, so that he'd soon be big.
He pushed the other pigs away and ate up all the food,
There never was another pig so nearly half so rude.
He strutted round the piggy pen with many grunts and digs.
Because he was much bigger than the other little pigs.
The farmer came to see, one day, how much the pigs had grown,
He said, I want a nice fat pig to take with me to town.
The greedy pig thought, "Now's my chance to show how big I am,"
I want to go to town today with the farmer if I can.
Ther farmer looked at him and said, you're what I'm looking for,
And then he took him into town, into a great big store.
The pig began to grunt with glee, and thought how smart I am,
To get to ride to town today, along with the farmer man..
Just then a man took hold of him, and said that grunt we'll stop,
And the silly piggy ended up right in the butchers shop,
So boys and girls, please be content although you're not so big,
Don't be impatient to grow up like the foolish little pig.

BABY'S FIRST CHRISTMAS

Little Johnny at our house
Is not quite one, you see,
So this is his very first Christmas
So I know he'll shout with glee.

We took him up to Toyland
How his eyes shone with delight
When he saw all the toys and the animals
And the other wonderful sights.

Next we took him to Santa
That fat and jolly old man.
And you should have heard him laugh
When he gaily shook his hand.

So Santa's trip to our house
Will be one jolly treat
When Johnny wakes and
see the sights.

GETTING UP IN TIME ON THE FARM

The barnyard folks awoke from sleep,
Quite early in the morn,
And the farmer's boy rolled out of bed,
So tired and forlorn.

The cows began to move about,
And started in to moo,
What they really said was, "sleep head"
There's work for you to do.

The pigs began to root and grunt,
And this is what they said,
Wherever is that farmer's boy,
It's time that we were fed.

The chickens and the ducks cried out,
With all their might and main,
If you want some nice fresh eggs today,
You'd better feed us some grain.

Fido the dog 'woke from a dream,
Of lovely rabbit stew,
And then he said, woof, woof, which means,
Hey boy, I'm hungry, too.

At last the noise was quieted down,
The barnyard folks were fed.
But by this time the boy had forgotten,
All about his bed.

And so the day began again,
As it always seems to do,
With a cluck, cluck, cluck, quack, quack, oink, oink,
Woof, woof, bow, wow, moo, oo.

173

DINOSAUR, JR.

1. Young Dinny was a playful thing,
   He only weighed a ton,
   And never seemed to have a care,
   He was always full of fun.

2. He'd go and tease the baby bears,
   And steal away their toys,
   For when it came to playing pranks,
   He sure was one of the boys.

3. But one day Dinny got a fright,
   The worst he'd had in years,
   An elephant caught him putting rocks,
   Into her baby's ears.

4. She held young Dinny in her trunk,
   Then stood upon his tail,
   And when he could not get away,
   You should have heard him wail.

5. He said, please Mam, get off my tail,
   It's the only one I've got,
   But she said, I'm going to cut you up,
   And stew you in my pot.

6. Young Dinny's face grew white with fright,
   His eyes began to roll,
   And then to everyone's delight,
   He started in to bawl.

7. Please, nice, kind, Mrs. Elephant,
   Oh, don't do what you say,
   And I'll never play with rocks again,
   After you've gone away.

8. She said, I'll let you go this time,
   Now go straight home to bed,
   But if I ever catch you here again,
   You'll wish that you were dead.

174

AN AEROPLANE RIDE

I went with Dad the other day,
To the airport we did go,
And I'll tell you all about it,
If you really want to know.
We got into an aeroplane
To fly up in the sky,
But the engine's roar scared me so much,
It almost made me cry.
Then all at once the flying field
Seemed to drop clean out of sight,
But Daddy looked at me and smiled
And held me, oh so tight.
We flew around up in the sky
We could not talk for noise
And everything down on the ground
Looked just like Christmas toys.
Then all at once the ground came up,
I gave a little shout,
And my stomach came into my throat,
It almost came right out.
The people walking on the street,
Looked like a lot of flies,
And the cars they looked so tiny,
I could scarce believe my eyes.
We touch the ground and gave a bounce,
Like sailing on the sea,
And when we stopped I climbed right out,
And said, that's enough for me.
But now I'm safely home again,
I laugh at what I said,
And when Dad takes me to fly again,
I won't be the least afraid.

175

You have all heard of boys and girls who had a dog or a cat for a pet but I once had a tame dinosaur for my pet, I would like to tell you how I got him.

One night I was hunting buffaloes in the jungles at the back of my house when I heard someone crying. I crept over and there I saw "Dinny". He was guarded by 20 lions, 50 tigers, and 100 wild elephants, and - an - an - an - an 1000 goats, I mean ghosts, but I did not care, I rushed at them, I had a sword in each hand and a pistol in the other, and boy, I mean girl, I waded through them like a fly through a can of molasses. I said boo to the ghosts and they all went home crying. They were only young ghosts and they thought I was a spook. After I had killed all the buffaloes and alligators and wild boars; (what do you say, there were'nt any of those)? Oh well, I would have killed them if there had been. After I had killed all these rattle snakes and boa constrictors, I looked for the dinosaur and I saw him climbing up a tree, I said, hey, you caw'nt do that, come down at twice, I mean at once, he said no, I said yes, he said no, I said yes, he said no, I said yes, he said alright.

When he came down, I took him by the ear, I think it was his ear. I said what is your name, he said, Bertie-Willie, so that is how I came to know his name, Clevah. What? I took him home, and trained him to eat little boys and girls, but don't get scared, because Bertie is on a diet, so he can't eat any more school children; don't you feel sorry for him?

176

I DON'T KNOW WHY

Words and Music by
Walter Lord

A SONG OF THE SEA

Music and Words by
Walter Lord

1. Out on the sea with a wind that's free and your ship sails bold-ly on. It is then that the strife in a sail-ors life is ban-ished with a song.

2. Out in the gale when the lee-ward rail is bur-ied in the sea. Then the song of the main and the wind and the rain is the sail-ors lull-a by

Chorus

For it's Heave! Ho! Steady my lads, Hoo rah! for a life on the main. When the wild winds whirl and the sails un furl and we're home-ward bound a-

For it's Heave! Ho! Steady my lads, Hoo rah! for the bound-ing main. When the bil-lows roll and we reach our goal and we're off to sea a-

gain. So me for the life of a Sail or who
gain. So me for the waves and the per ils of the

Sails the dis - tant Sea, with the hatches pinned and an
bound - less roll - ing Sea, as we sail once more for a

off shore wind — This is the life for me!
for - eign shore — This is the life for me!

180

Blanche Rebecca Stark

Swimming at Saltair
in the 1940's

Father: Alma Pedersen Stark
Mother: Christiane Johanna Hansen
Born: 17 November 1904
Place: Spanish Fork, Utah, USA
Married: 5 February 1928 (to Walter Lord)
Place: Salt Lake City, Utah, USA
Died: 23 August 1990
Place: Sandy, Utah, USA

Tam-O-Shanters
Entertainers

Audrie Imlay—*Piano*
Wanda Burnett—*Sax*
Wasatch 5111
Hyland 5670

Grace Bowman—*Banjo*
Anna Commans—*Drums*
Blanche Lord—*Violin*
Thora Guill—*Sax*

Music for All Occasions

Something to Write Home About

The Tam-O-Shanter Band Itinerary Kept by Blanche Lord

Tam O. Shanter
Orchestra
Blanche Lord.

Tooele —   1.68
June 25 —
Not much of a town.

June 26
Grantsville   1.32
a very poor place
Played in Opera
house

June 27   2.12
Eureka
a nice town but
poorly advertised

June 28
Nephi   6.00
a nice good town
played at theatre

July 13
Salina   6.23
Nice town, good
time, played at
Liberty Theatre
and at Red Mont
Revoir? dance
hall, very good dance
dance hall on lake.

July 14
Loa.   3.40
Small town, about
20 miles from
Fish Lake

July 15
Visited Fish Lake
Lake, about 3 miles
across, 20 miles long,
very nice scenery
good fishing.
Many people, stormy
weather, poor
roads. About 190
miles from S.L.

July 16 -   .50
Gunnison -
Small town, played
at Theatre, Casino.

July 17 Richfield 11.43
Largest town in
section of country
nice paved streets
nice scenery
Played at Rialto
Theatre, played at
Prairie Hall, an
Ice cr. and dance
hall 5 miles from
Richfield.

July 18 -
Manti   2.09
Nice town, beautiful
inspiring Temple
built on hill, nearby
grounds, played at
Theatre -

July 19 -
Spring City -   1.55
Small city, played
at Third Ward House.

July 20 -   8.41
Fountain Greens
Small city, played
at theatre and
dance hall house.

July 21 -
Ephraim -   1.72
Small town
Played at theatre

July 22   9.04
Fairview City
Small town, played hall

July 24 -   4.80
Coalville -
Nice town, played at theatre

July 25 -
Coalville -   .16

July 26 -
Evanston, Wyo. - 4.8
Nice, good today
played at theatre dance
July 27
Evanston -   4.
Played at town
and dance

July 28
Lyman, Wyo. 4.
Nice cow town
played at theatre
and dance
Big thunderstorm
rain.

July 29 -   6.3
Green River

July 13
Salina   6.23
Nice town. good
[time] played at
Victory Theatre
and at Red Mesa
open air range
hall, very good and
dance hall on lake.

July 14
Loa.   3.40
Small town, about
20 miles from
Fish Lake

July 15
Visited Fish Lake,
lake, about 3 miles
across 20 miles long,
very nice scenery
good fishing. —
many people, stormy
weather! Bad
roads. About 190
miles from S. L.

July 16 —   .50
Gunnison —
Small town. Sunset
at Theatre, Casino.

July 17 Richfield 11.43
Large town in
section of country
nice paved streets
nice scenery.
Played at [Isis]
Theatre [and at]
[Green] Mill, an
open air dance
[and] we [stayed] in
[Redwood]

July 18 —
Manti   2.09

Nice town, famous
[mining] Temple
built on hill. nice
grounds. played at
[Theatre].

July 19
Springville —   1.55
Small city. Played
at First [Ward] House.

July 20   8.41
Fountain Green
Small city. played
at [Amuse and]
[Dance Hall]

July 21 —
[Ephraim] —   1.72
Small [town]
[played at theatre]

July 22   9.04
[Heber City]
Small [town played at]

July 24 —   4.80
Coalville —
Nice town. played at Theatre

July 25 —
Coalville —   .16

July 26 —
Evanston, Wyo - 4.80
[Nice] good looking
played at [stand dance]
July 27
Evanston —   4.12
[Played at theatre]
[and] dance

July 28
Lyman, Wyo. 4.8[ ]
[One roof town,]
[Played at theatre]
and dance
Big thunder storm.
rain.

July 29 —   6.36
Green River

July 30   4.80
Green River
Pretty town, near river. Large river
Played at theatre and at Grandpark.
beautiful mountain scenery.

July 31 -
Rock Spring - 4.80
Wife
First town, about
two... large railroad
center, heavy
mountains scenery.

Aug. 1 -
Kemmerer Wyo. 4.80
Nice cool town, played at Victory Theatre.

Aug 5 $7.32
5.68
Soda Springs.
Ida
Small town with natural Soda springs. Play at...
Aug. 6
Fish Haven -
Ida.
Nice swimming
... cabins.
... every day
to Monday night.

Aug. 7
Afton, Wyo 6.30
Small town,
near mts. nice
scenery. Played

Aug 3
... Wyo 9.80
Logan town, Wyo
at Opera House
Sept. 3
Salt Town
... two ...
on the coast.

...Beach 1.02
Beach...
Bear Lake, Ida
wonderful blue.
Nice Beach.
Slept in cabins.

...American
Theatre, dance
afterwards

Aug. 8
... Ida - 1.6
Small town, played
at ...

Aug 9 -
... Ida -
Small town, farming
district. Play
Opera House and
open air dance
hall.

By Blancheford

Dedicated to

My Baby. Ralph

Little dark head
With your tousled hair
You've gone to sleep
In your own high chair.

Tired of playing
In the sand bar
Making castles of
Sand and rocks

How it tickled a round
with the sun all day
Romping with Fal
And pretty at play.

You've waited & laughed
And sang with glee
And read the story book
Sand with me.

Your beautiful eyes
And closed in sleep
Come, let Mommy tuck you,
Between your white.

Your a gift from God
Out of the skies
That when you got
Your large blue eyes.

And may God always
You safely keep
And guide your feet
Till his kingdom you
reach.

For Mommy love
Will guide you too.
Till god calls them back
to his kingdom too.

187

Personal History of Blanche Rebecca Stark Lord
November 17, 1904 – August 23, 1990

Born of very fine parents (Alma & Christiane Stark), whom I loved very much, and of a wonderful Pioneer heritage, my grandfather (Soren) and grandmother (Ann Sophia) emigrants from Denmark who came here for the Gospel. Also, my Mother's parents (Anders & Maren Hansen) who sent their children one at a time from Denmark, so they could live here where they would have a chance for a better life and to live where the church was gathering their people. I have so much to be thankful for and to thank my wonderful grandparents for all the sacrifices they made for the gospel and to come to America.

The house where I was born in Spanish Fork was an old pioneer house of logs. We lived there for several years on a farm and had all kinds of fowls and pigs and cows and horses. One time when I was very little, mother warned me to not go around where the geese were, as they had nests and the gander was mean and would chase us away and make a very loud noise, which scared me. I didn't listen to my mother and the gander knocked me down and stood over me with his wings flapping and yelling and picking at me. My mother had to come and beat it off me. I guess I learned my lesson and I stayed away after that.

Our hens used to make nests in our haystacks and straw stacks and we had fun looking for them. Sometimes we would find some in a really hidden place with a lot of eggs in it and sometimes with the hen setting on the eggs. We would watch that nest until the eggs hatched and a lot of darling little baby chicks came out of it.

We loved the farm. We had a very large weeping willow tree in front of the house and we used to climb it and our old dog could climb up part way. We had a lively childhood there.

When I was about 5 years old, my father built us another house about a half block away that was real nice. We moved there and had a very nice farm with a large strawberry patch. We would help mother pick them. Father planted an orchard on the hill above our house and it was doing real good but they started building up way above our house in Mapleton and the seepage from the new development ruined our trees. It was a hard blow for our father, as he was very proud of his lovely orchard. Evidently, they hadn't put in drainage by then or perhaps that wouldn't have happened.

When I was about 9 years old, and after I was baptized, my father sold our farm and we moved to Ruby Valley, Nevada onto a very fertile piece of land. We found out later the people who sold it to us didn't have a title to the land and that it was a big land swindle. All the people who bought this land, including us, lost all they had invested in it and all we had left was a homestead (dry farm).

When I was a very small child, I lived in Spanish Fork. We lived on a country road, which was the road into Provo and on to Salt Lake City. About once of twice a year, a large group of Indians would travel down our road. They would camp across the street, a large road, on some vacant land and would stay there for about a month before they would move on again. I remember them well. They used to come to our home and beg flour and sugar and other things from my mother. They had a lot of horses and dogs and the women used to seem to do all the work while the men sat around. I was sort of scared when they come over to our house. Usually it would be one of the braves and they always looked at us and I was frightened and was always glad when they pulled up camp and moved on.

Then another thing I remember while I was very little, was when sheep herders would drive their flocks of sheep past our place and sometimes they would leave very small lambs behind as they couldn't keep up with the flocks and my father used to get these little lambs and we would give them milk and take care of them. We had several, I remember one year.

There was a large empty field in front of our home across the road where my sister and I used to roam around in. It had sagebrush and greasewood growing in it. There was a little pond in it and we loved to see the geese and ducks go over across the road and swim around on it. When I was just a little toddler, mother said I used to go over across the road to the water and she was worried that I would get drowned, so she told me a waterman lived in the pond and that he would grab me or pull me in and he called, "Come on in ..." when I got near. So I became frightened and stayed away from the water. The grasses made some kind of sound and it sounded like they said, "Come on in."

We had a grand old dog that always went around with us and we loved it very much. My father had some workhorses and I remember him putting me up on the back of one of them and letting me ride. I thought that was wonderful. I always loved horses and when we moved to Nevada when I was about 9 years old, I had an old mare I called "Pet" that I rode on all over Ruby Valley. I also rode other horses.

One time I was riding Pet and our dog was with us. When we came over a little hill, I was about 3 or 4 wolves. Our dog was frightened of them and so was the horse, so I turned around and rode away fast from them.

I loved to roam around in Ruby Valley and go to the mountains with my father for cedar posts and wood. One time I found some stones that looked just like diamonds. We found out later that they were a high grade of quartz crystal. They were on a butte on the East side of the valley.

One winter, my sister Mary and I left Nevada and went to our Uncle Moroni's place in Spanish Fork so we cold attend school. I was in the 2nd grade. The following year, there was a school for all of the children in Ruby Valley. We had to ride in a covered wagon like a bus from our homestead to Ruby City, about 20 miles, where the school was located. There were quite a few of us children that rode in the school bus.

When I went back to school in Ruby Valley, I had been graduated to 4th grade but I only spent about 1 week in 4th grade and the teacher decided I had most of the studies and got 100 in everything so they put me in the 5th grade.

We lived in Nevada for about 3 years and couldn't make a very good living as it was so dry and my father and all of us were living on a homestead. The land he had bought in Ruby City was a big land swindle and all of the people who invested in it couldn't get a title to their land that was very fertile and good so many moved away or moved onto homesteads.

SOME SPECIAl EXPERIENCES:

When I was a very small baby, I got a bowl blockage and my mother thought I was dead, as I had gone limp. When some man knocked on the door and it was a neighbor who lived about a mile away and he asked if someone was sick. He said he had a feeling that he should come to our house and that he was needed. He administered to me and I recovered. I was quite frail for a long time and I used to go into our chicken coop and get an egg, make a hole in one end of it and suck out the egg. The doctor told my mother that would be very good for me. She was worried about me doing that but it must have been good for me, as I grew stronger.

Another time I was playing out in our yard and went on top of a shed. I was looking down and lost my balance and fell. Below me was a pitchfork with the tines pointing up and as I fell towards it, my mother said it was like someone pushed me to one side and only the tip of one tine hit me and took a piece out of my eyebrow. My guardian angel surely was watching out for me.

Another time I wandered away from home and went a long way from our house where we had a young orchard. My father had the irrigation water running all over in it. I played by the streams, jumping across them. It is a wonder I didn't get drowned.

One time my older sister and another girl got on a horse with me, the smallest, in the middle. We rode down in a ditch with a high bank and as the horse came out of the ditch, we all fell off and both my sister and the other girl fell on me. It must have injured me as I was sick for several days afterwards.

EULOGY FOR BLANCHE R. LORD

Blanche Rebecca Stark Lord was born 17 November 1904 in Spanish Fork, Utah to Alma Pedersen Stark and Christiane Johanne Hansen. Mother was the forth of 10 children. "About the age of 9, after I was baptized," as mother states in her personal history, "my father sold our farm and we moved to Ruby Valley, Nevada on a very fertile piece of land." They found out later that the person from whom they bought the land was a swindler, and they lost all they had invested. "All that we had left was a homestead (dry farm). We moved into this land and my father built a one-room house and we had a tent that was boarded up to the top of the sides, and we lived there for about 3 years." Mother loved Ruby Valley in the Summers but tells of the hard Winters they had to bear with snow over three feet deep. The family moved back to Salt Lake when mother was in the Fifth grade. After graduating from the Eighth grade, mother went to work. Her father bought her a violin and she began taking lessons. She was very talented and became a wonderful violinist. She became a member of a group called the "Tam-O-Shanter Girls" who traveled around entertaining for parties and dances. Playing the violin was to be a life-long love for her as she performed as a soloist, and in small groups and orchestras much of her life. She instilled that love for music in each of her children, for which we will always be grateful. Through the church and her music, she met a wonderful man, and in 1928, she was married to Walter Lord. Six children were to bless this union, 4 sons and 2 daughters. These now have expanded to include 36 grandchildren and 60 great grandchildren.

Mother was a wonderful cook and homemaker and her flowers were the showcase of the neighborhood. She also enjoyed sewing and was an expert in the nearly lost art of tatting. She made many hundreds of tatted doilies and lace edgings for handkerchiefs for her family and friends. She was a life-long member of The Church of Jesus Christ of Latter-day Saints and has worked in many of its organizations, also serving on a stake mission. She was a temple worker for many years.

Blanche Rebecca Stark Lord will be missed by all who knew her, and we, her children, thank her for her wonderful example as a kind and loving mother and for her many years of concern and unselfish service devoted to them and to others.

POEMS AND A CHRISTMAS STORY
BY BLANCHE LORD

CHILDHOOD

Dear little child, I love you so
You're always tripping to and fro,
You're always happy as can be,
You're always singing songs of glee.

Why is it you can always smile
While folks around just frown and scowl
How can you sing in this drear world
While other folks think it absurd.

And then you smile you're wondrous smile.
And your face with happiness beams the while,
And from your eyes a light divine,
Of perfect love and joy does shine.

And suddenly I realize why perfect joy and love
Are thine, and not a sad disguise.
It is because faith's holy light
Has come to you from out the night.

For the little babe at Bethlehem
Has taught you wisdom and love for man.
Oh! Why can't the folks I pray
Learn from this child the better way.

For when loves holy light does shine,
You'll always find a happiness divine
So of this Child I pray thee read
And live more noble in life and deed.

EYES

Eyes, your eyes are the windows of souls
    They mirror just what we think
    They express what a soul longs to utter
    And binds us together with loves gold links

Eyes there are that are dark as pools
    Hidden deep in the mountains breast.
    That seem to flicker and flame to life
    As a volcano upon its crest.

And when love speaks in eyes of blue,
    They are fair as summer skies.
    And zepher breezes seem to blow
    Their perfumed air, round your true blue eyes.

And eyes of gray when they gaze in brown,
    Have a saintly, mellow glow,
    That speaks of a soul pent up by love
    And a voice that is sweet and low.

There are hazel eyes too that are restless as pools,
    Of hidden imprisoned light.
    That glow as warm as a hearth's firs,
    When their mate says a tender, "Good night."

There are other eyes too which poets say
    Are a beautiful violet shade,
    And some that are black as storm tossed skies
    And some as green as jade.

But give me the eyes that looked on mine,
    When the moon was shining clear
    That pledged to my soul a silent vow
    That they would forever hold me dear.

They were eyes of brown, which were large and deep,
    As the depth of his own noble soul.
    And his heart beat in time with my own wild heart,
    At the thought of wedding bells toll.

And though our paths should go far apart,
    In this world of sin and strife.
    I know that his eyes will look for mine
    When I enter the next blissful life.

So God keep our feet on the narrow road
    Guide us over the slippery road,
    So that the eyes that love may forever find,
    The kindred eyes that can ease their heavy load.

THE CHRISTMAS SPIRIT

"Johnie, wipe all the snow off your shoes before you come in this house," shouted his irate mother. "And close the door quietly after you or you will awaken you father."

All day long Mrs. Slinger had been working to clean and prepare the house for the arrival of her Christmas guests. Cleaning and scowering, baking and scrubbing. Until she was very tired and very cross.

"Why is it you must always be told to do such things, John Henry? Mother gets so tired of always reminding you. What do you think your Aunt Ellen will say when she hears you are such a bad boy? You know she always thought you were such a fine little man. I am sure she will be disappointed in you. Now you come along and get those wet clothes off you and get ready for bed. Tomorrow will be a busy day for all of us. And you must get a good nights sleep." With those words Mrs. Slinger hustled Johnie off to the bathroom, where sounds of running and splashing water mingled with protest from Johnie were to be heard. Before long a fatigued mother and shining clean small boy emerged. Hurrying him to his bedroom, Mrs. Slinger tucked him snugly in bed, kissing him good night, and again hastened to the kitchen to put the last touches on an enormous fruit cake and finish so many small tasks waiting for her hands to do.

"What good is Christmas anyway," thought Mrs. Slinger. "All I get out of it is hard work and worry, while others enjoy it and can rest and take life easy. I wish there weren't any more Christmas' to worry about." With these thoughts in her mind she rushed from one task to another, until the clock on the mantel struck eleven. Then she made her way down the hall, taking a last peek into Johnie's room, where rosy-cheeked Johnie was dreaming about Santa and all the things he was in hopes he would get on Christmas. With a loving kiss, she again tucked him snugly in bed, sighing, went to her own room wondering how such a innocent little child could cause so much worry and work. At last she went to bed where in a few minutes kind sleep claimed her tired body.

Out side the snow was silently falling and the moon came out to make a land of magic dazzling white, huge trees stooping low with their burden of snow. Housetops heaped high. Clotheslines like silver ribbons strung from one ghost post to another. All through the town small lights blinked out from one street corner to another, and in many houses lights still burned where tired mother's were still preparing for the coming holiday, at last all the lights were turned out, first from one house, then another, and the little city slept. And still the snow continued to fall.

When the first streaks of dawn began to show the shrill peel of an alarm clock rang out in the silent house. With a tired grunt Mr. Slinger reached out and shut it off, and turned over in bed. Presently he arose and dressing himself went out to clean the snow from the walk and from before his garage where it was very deep. His wife also arose, dressed, and hastened to prepare breakfast. Then rosy cheeked, sunny faced Johnie came bounding out of his room.

"Oh Mamma, just think Santa will come tonight, I can hardly wait. I hope Aunt Ellen will soon be here too."

"Aunt Ellen will be here about five o'clock," his mother replied. "In the meantime I hope you will be a good boy. I want you to hurry and get your breakfast and run down to the store. I forgot a few things that I must have for our dinner."

"All right Mamma," replied Johnie, and he hurriedly began his breakfast. Mr. Slinger having finished cleaning the sidewalk came to breakfast also.

"We surely have a big layer of snow this morning," he said, "I'm afraid Santa will have to come by airplane this year. He won't be able to get through all this snow any other way."

"Oh, I hope he does," said Johnie. "It would be great to see him come that way. I'm going to stay awake and see if I can see him tonight!"

"You hadn't better," said his mother. "Because they say if he sees any one watching him he will not leave anything for them."

"Aw, see!" I would like to see him come though," he replied. His large blue eyes filled with wonder.

"You'll see him sometime perhaps," said his father. "I must hurry now and be on my way to the office. Today will be a rush to finish up our work so we can have a few days holiday."

"Take Johnie with you as far as Jones' store, will you?" asked his wife. "He is going on an errand for me."

"Sure, come along Johnie," he said, as he got into his enormous fur coat, and Mrs. Slinger helped Johnie into his own good warm one.

"Now hurry back Johnie," called his mother as he and his father rushed out to get into their car. And they were soon speeding on their way to town. The snow had been cleaned away from the streets and sidewalks, and men were busy piling it into large noisy trucks to be hauled away from the city.

"Here we are Johnie," said his father as he brought the car to a stop in front of a small grocery store. "Now hurry and get what mother sent you for and then hurry home. I'm sure Santa will remember you tonight."

"All right, Papa," replied Johnie as he jumped out of the car and waved a good-bye to his father. He hurried into the store and soon was getting the things his mother had sent him for.

"Is Santa coming to your house tonight," asked Mr. Jones with a smile.

"You bet he is," replied Johnie, his eyes dancing with delight. "I can hardly wait for him. He is going to bring me a big sleigh and skates and a lot of other things."

"You are a very lucky boy," said the grocer. "There are some poor little boys and girls that won't get anything I am afraid."

"Oh, do you really think so," asked Johnie, his sweet face filled with sorrow.

"Yes, I have seen some I am afraid won't get much."

"Gee, I hope they get something anyway," said Johnie as he took the things the grocer handed him and went out.

"Have a Merry Christmas," called Mr. Jones as he left.

"You too, Mr. Jones," he replied.

Oh his way home he saw a little boy about his own age, with a bundle of newspapers under his arm. The little boy was very poorly dressed, with no warm coat on like Johnie's, his shoes too were worn and full of holes. All this Johnie noticed as he came toward him, still thinking of what Mr. Jones had said. Then he recognized him as a boy from his own room at school.

"Hello Johnie," Tom replied, looking very sad. "I'm afraid he's not going to come to our house this year."

"Why not?" asked Johnie, his troubled eyes on Tom's.

"Mamma said it was because Papa had been out of work so longs, and then poor little Sis is sick too. Gee! I wish he would bring something to her anyway. She would be so happy for just a tiny doll. I must hurry and try to sell all my papers, then maybe I can buy one for her." So saying he hastened on his way to town, calling good-bye to Tom as he went. Poor little thin faced Tom, his little figure bent, his arms tightly locked around his burden of papers, trying to shield his little thin figure from some of the icy cold wind.

Johnie hurried on his way home, his face no longer happy. His good little soul tormented to think that someone must suffer on this day of days. When he got home he rushed to his mother and told her all that he had seen and all about Tommie and his poor little sick sister.

"I wonder," said Mrs. Slinger, "can it possible be true?"

"I am sure it is," replied Johnie. "At school I remember he was getting free milk and the teacher asked him how his little sister was."

"Something must be done about it. We must go see Santa Claus," said his mother.

"Oh, Mamma, that will be wonderful," said Johnie dancing with joy. So she rushed about her work, John helping her and they soon were getting ready for town. They dressed in their own good warm clothes and hastening out were soon in one of the towns largest department stores. They hunted Santa up and after telling him all he took them to the boys clothing department where they bought a good coat for Tommie about Johnies size. Then shoes, stockings and a cap. Then to the children's department where they got some nice clothes for his little sister, that could be exchanged if they didn't just fit. From there to the grocery department where a large amount of groceries were bought, including everything to make a real Christmas feast, even down to a nice fat goose. Then candy and nuts. Then to the toys where they bought a sleigh and wagon for Tom and a lovely doll and dishes for his little sister. With all these lovely things bought, Mrs. Slinger gave a sigh of relief and asked Santa to please deliver them first on his way out that night. He promised her he would, and after bidding them both good-bye, hastened back to his other labors. She and Johnie hurried home to be there when their guests arrived.

"Oh, Mamma, won't they be happy when they find out Santa hasn't forgotten them?" said Johnie, his beautiful face filled with joy.

"Yes," said his mother. "I believe that Christmas is a good day anyway. If we can do some good we really find out its worth." Her face glowed with happiness, she never once thought of the lovely dress she was to have bought with that money.

Before long her guest arrived laden with gaily wrapped parcels. They greeted one another with hugs and kisses and jolly rebuffs. Johnie, shy when he saw his beautiful little cousin Clair, soon fell to playing with her and showing her the enormous Christmas tree they were to decorate that evening. Everything went on happily. Mr. Slinger arriving home to be greeted by the guests, then all seated around a brightly lighted supper table, shining with snow-white linen and bright silver and laden with everything good to eat. When supper was over and everything tidied and put away, they all went to the living room where the great tree was, to decorate it. What fun they had, on stepladders, hanging shining ornaments on it. Putting the tinsel and presents on it too. The older people laughed and joked while the children played games. At last it was finished and it shown from top to bottom with bright trimmings and lights. A beautiful Spirit of Christmas. Then they all went to their beds to await the arrival of Santa.

Very early the next morning the little people scrambled out of their beds, rosy with sleep, to see what dear old Santa had left them. With shrieks of sheer joy they rushed from one lovely present to another until the whole household was assembled before the Christmas tree. Mr. Slinger caught his wife's hand and drew her aside from the others.

"Margaret," he exclaimed, "your so changed so much more beautiful and tender since last night. Tell me dear, what has happened to make you so different."

"Oh, John dear, I am so happy, something wonderful happened yesterday that has made my life different. From now on I am going to try and do some good every day."

"What on earth happened?" asked her husband, unable to retain his curiosity longer. So she told him all about Tommie, his sick sister, and what she and Johnie and Santa had done. Explaining that she could wait about getting that new gown. "Margaret dear, I am so proud of you," he said when she had finished. Tenderly folding her in his arms and giving her a loving kiss. "I will see that you get that gown anyway, and from now on we will try to shed some happiness among our less fortunate neighbors."

In another home happiness also reigned. Santa Claus had not forgotten them anyway. Little Tommie was so happy for his good clothes – and nice sleigh and wagon. He was fairly dancing with happiness. But he was more happy to see his little sister sitting up in bed, so much improved, just for the good food and clothing and most of all for her lovely doll and dishes. Their mother and father were so happy that tears of joy shown on their kind faces. And they knelt down together and gave thanks to God that their little children were happy again. And they did not forget to ask Him to bless the kind souls that had made such happiness possible.

And at the home of Mrs. Slinger, peace and contentment reigned. She had at last found that the Spirit of Christmas was in doing good to others. To make ourselves happy we must first make others happy.

William &
Margaret Lord

MOTHER

Written by: Walter Lord

Dedicated to my mother

1. From out the past a memory,
   Keeps pace with passing years,
   'Tis like a heavenly angel,
   Sent to silence all my fears.
   I see a thatched cottage,
   Each room so neat and clean,
   And someone there, my Mother dear,
   Kind face and eyes so keen.

2. Her hair which then was golden,
   Has long since turned to gray,
   But all the cares of passing years,
   Can't take her smile away.
   I wish that I could recall,
   Acts of mine that made her sad,
   In carefree days of long ago,
   When I was just a lad.

3. When day is slowly fading,
   And shadows gather round,
   The children all tucked in their beds,
   And no discordant sound,
   Then memories of my Mother,
   Come to me through the night,
   With sweet scenes of happy childhood,
   Which Mother made so bright.

4. And when this life is over,
   She'll return to God on High,
   For my Mother was an angel,
   From the mansions in the sky.
   So let us all unite in homage,
   To the truest friends on earth,
   To the Mothers who watched o'er us,
   Toiled for us, and gave us birth.

William Knowles Lord

Father: James Knowles
Mother: Annice Lord
Born: 31 May 1867
Place: Settle, Yorkshire, England
Married: 19 November 1892 (to Margaret Banks)
Place: Kirby-Malham Ch, Yorkshire, England
Died: 21 March 1900
Place: Nelson, Lancashire, England

Margaret Banks

Father: Thomas Pullen
Mother: Jane Banks
Born: 21 May 1897
Place: Airton, Yorkshire, England
Married: 19 November 1992
(to William Knowles Lord)
Place: Kirby-Malham, Yorkshire, Enland
Died: 26 April 1952
Place: Salt Lake City, Utah, USA

Louisa Bell, Edith Lord, Walter Lord, Margaret Lord, Lizzie Mozley
Children: ?, Edith & Raymond Bell
Taken about 1923 in Salt Lake City, UT

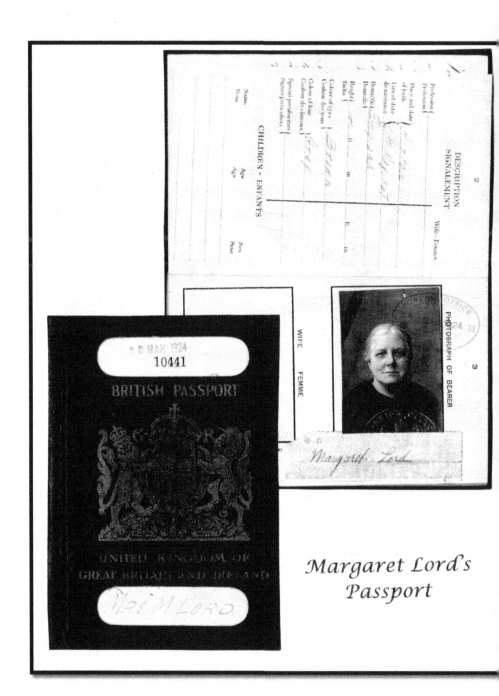

Margaret Lord's Passport

Edith Lord & Louisa Edwards
Best Friends

Edith Lord, Louisa Edwards Bell, Sara Ann Edwards
Raymond Mozley
13 December 1919 - Benjamin & Louisa Bell's Wedding

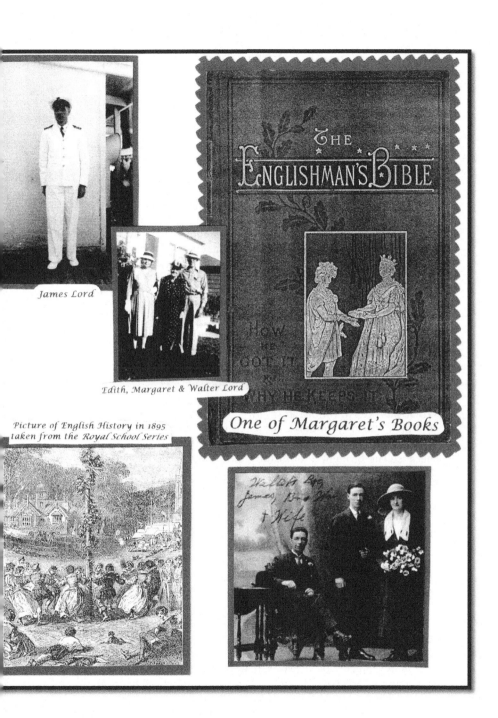

James Lord

Edith, Margaret & Walter Lord

Picture of English History in 1895
taken from the Royal School Series

One of Margaret's Books

Oral History of Margaret Banks Lord
Interviewee: Dave Lord (Grandson)
Interviewer: Tewie Lord
Interview taken on 11/4/01

Q: What were the family circumstances when Margaret was born?

A: She was born an illegitimate child born in England. Her father, Thomas Pullen, had an estate in Winterburn, England and her mother, Jane Banks, was a maidservant on that estate. In fact there is one book that Margaret brought with her that belonged to her mother entitled, Domestic Cookery, which was given to her in 1847. This book tells how to do everything domestic from cooking to home remedies. There is another book, Persuasives To Early Piety, which has the name "Frances Pullen" in the cover. It is evidently some relative of Thomas Pullen. Jane and Thomas were never married. Jane Banks was 38 when Margaret was born. She was an only-child raised by a single mother.

Q: Where did the family live in her early years?

A: She was born in Airton, Yorkshire, England. When she left England she left from Nelson, Lancashire, England which is about 1 ½ hours drive by car away from Airton.

Q: What was her education like?

A: I think it was very minimal. In that area it was typical for the children to go to work at a young age in the textile factories. She must've liked to read because she brought a lot of these little English books with her when she came over. Some of the books are entitled: The Universal Letter Writer: The New Art of Polite Correspondence, A Picture of English History, and Cullegians or the Colleen Bawn.

Q: Did she have any pets as a child?

A: I don't know.

Q: What were her hobbies and talents during her early years?

A: I don't know.

Q: Did she have any medical or dental problems during her early years? Any epidemics she had to pass through?

A: She seemed to be overall healthy in her later years. Not suffering from any traumatic injuries or diseases that she might have had as a child. Jim remembers, "She could have had bad teeth because all her teeth were gone when I knew her. As far as I know, she did not wear false teeth. She was very hard of hearing. I think her memory was failing in her later years."

Q: What were some of the fads of the day that she would've been part of?
A: I doubt there was very much along those lines. Most of the young people quit school and went to work when they were 12 or 13 years old. I doubt very much that they had much of a "night" life or a social life.

Q: Pranks or humorous experiences?
A: Jim remembered, "One time 2 of us kids got in her house somehow when she wasn't home and hid in her front room. When she came home we made funny noises and she kept looking for where they came from and couldn't find us until finally we showed ourselves. We liked to play pranks on her." Another time when Margaret felt in a jovial mood Jim remembers: "One time when Elaine and I were talking to her and joking with her, and this was probably when she was in her 70's, she suddenly said to us, 'Be careful, you might cut yourself.' And we said, 'What do you mean?' She said, 'You're so sharp.' It about floored us. We laughed at the wit of this little old lady."

Q: Job or work experiences during her early years?
A: She worked in the mills. They were cotton mills. They wove cloth. The Western part of England was a heavily industrialized area in terms of clothing mills. That's where the kids went to work at a young age.

Q: Did she do any vacationing as a child?
A: Blackpool was a resort area that was fairly near to where they lived. It was within 50 miles. It was kind of like our old Saltair (1940's). It had a beach an amusement rides and things like that. In talking to Aunt Edith and my dad I know they went there on holiday. They didn't move around very much and it would've been a major undertaking to even go that distance during that time.

Q: What were her religious activities during her early years?
A: I don't know what her mother (Jane) believed, but somewhere along the line she (Margaret) met the missionaries and joined the Church. She was married with children at the time. I do know that the children were baptized at 8 years of age. She has this little set of Common Prayer & Hymns which she got in Christmas of 1887. They probably are Church of England books, but they look like new. She has a book called The Pillar of Fire which she got in 1878. It is a book about Bible stories. She also has The Englishman's Bible: How He got it and Why We Keep it which could be about King James or King Henry VIII, who started the Church of England. She received that book in 1880. It would seem that she had leanings towards religious things. There is a book with Edith's name in the cover about the Latter-day Prophet Joseph Smith. Edith worked in a bookstore for a while when they moved here to Utah.

Q: What was her family life like?

A: She grew up as an only child of a single mom in a very industrialized area of Western England.

Q: Do you know of any of the difficulties faced by the family?

A: Not specifically. She was an only child born to a single mother during a hard time in English history. Even under the best of conditions, unless you were aristocracy, it was a hard life. They had to work hard for their living.

Q: Did she ever serve in the military?

A: No.

Q: Did she ever attend vocational school or college?

A: No.

Q: What vocations or careers did she have?

A: According to Walter's personal history, when her husband, William, died they, "moved from there to the end house on a row of houses called Throstle Street in Nelson and lived there about 13 years. Mother went back to work all this time as a winder in a cotton mill. (The mills were located right across the street from where she lived.) We kids all went to school." Aunt Lizzie took over the care of the children. Walter's personal history tells of his grandmother, Jane Banks, living with them during that time as well. This probably was the main vocation she had in England. When she came over to the USA I'm not aware of any jobs she held. She was mostly a stay at home person and Aunt Edith was the one who worked to support both of them. Aunt Edith did work as a seamstress in a couple of different upholstery factories. I know of one located downtown Salt Lake.

Q: What was the effect of her job on the family?

A: From your dad's history we know that when William Knowles Lord died Margaret went to work at the mills, to support the family and "Aunt Lizzie" (Elizabeth Banks – Margaret's cousin) came in to help take care of the children and her Aunt Jane Banks. Aunt Lizzie had a store that went under due to too many people buying on credit.

Q: Do you have any knowledge of where Margaret met William, their courting, their marriage, what their relationship was like?

A: I don't remember anything being said about that. All we know is that they were married 8 years and had 5 children in that time. One of which died when a baby.

Q: How was the family financed?

A: The only thing I know is from looking at that one picture of William Knowles Lord, my grandfather, standing next to a horse and cart. This would indicate that, maybe, he was involved in some type of delivery work, but I don't know for sure. They lived in the industrialized – cloth-weaving area of England so we can guess that he was involved in delivering cloth or supplies to and from the factories. Or he could've used his horse and cart in some other endeavor – we really don't know. When he died she worked at the mills. (See above)

Q: Where did the family live?
A: In Nelson, Lancashire, England. When Margaret came over to the USA she left from Nelson.

Q: Who were their children? What was their character like? Talents, interests, hobbies, lives...
A: 1st – James Lord. He spent most of his adult life in the British Navy. He served during the 1st and 2nd World Wars. On one occasion he came to Salt Lake to visit his mother and brother and sister when his ship was in port in New York (California). He stayed for, maybe, a few hours. All the other things we know about James are told in Walter's personal history.

2nd – Edith Lord. She was a very talented seamstress. She made us a blanket out of upholstery material remnants during Depression times. It was very heavy. She had a stamp collection. Money was pretty tight back in those days and she used to give each of us kids a nickel each week for an allowance. There were two little grocery stores, Zip Ways and Davis'. We would buy penny candy and we would get a whole bag of candy for a nickel. I would get a huge Hershey's chocolate bar for a nickel. She wasn't very outgoing. She wasn't the type of person you would've been attractive, either in looks or in personality. She was kind and would talk to us as kids. Our family (The Walter Lord family) and Margaret and Edith lived next to each other on Simondi Avenue in a duplex for about 10 years (from about 1931 to 1941). When I was 5 we went to Nevada that was in 1934. I started school in the 1st grade there. When we came back to Salt Lake I was put into Kindergarten. We moved back into the same house when we came back. I would suspect that Grandma and Aunt Edith took care of the house while we were gone. After this house they moved to another one on 5th west. This is the house in which both my grandma and Aunt Edith lived when they passed away. They had a cat. In her latter years she was very much into doing genealogy. She did most of what has been done on this line. She never married. She never had children. She took care of her mom, Margaret, until she passed away.

3rd – William. Died before his first birthday. We don't know of what cause.

4th – Walter Lord. (See Walter's Personal History)

5th – William E. Lord. I knew him as "Uncle Willie", but when we got over there everyone called him "Bill". He was the only person in the family to stay in England. He didn't seem like he was too active in the Church. We couldn't find his baptismal date in the IGI so we re-did his baptism. There is a newspaper article that has a picture of my dad seeing Uncle Willie after more than 50 years. He got married and had one son, Stanley. Stanley had two children – Jeff and Judith. Neither of them have any children and they are both in their 40's. Judith is married and Jeff is not.

Q: What was her daily routine like?
A: Here in Utah she was pretty much sit at home. She would walk from her home on 5th West to ours on 10th West quite often. She was active in the church. She and Edith would go to town together, which required getting dressed up in hats and gloves. We didn't have a bathtub and I assume that they didn't either since they lived in the same duplex as we did on Simondi Avenue. We would take baths in a big tin tub and put cold water in and then boil water to heat and pour into the cold water. I don't remember her visiting or cooking or cleaning. I'm sure she did, but I don't remember any specifics. She spent time with her English friends (Mosleys and Bells). She never owned a car. They did own a radio and I remember it being on, but what they listened to – I don't know. I'm sure they went to Conference at The Tabernacle.

Q: What were the family traditions for birthdays, Christmas, Easter, weddings, funerals?
A: I remember visiting when they lived next door to us, and later when they moved up to 5th West. I think they would come over to our house for the different Holidays. I remember they used to make English toffee and bring it over. It just seemed like they were always there so no specific memories come to mind. Jim remembers, "Grandma and Edith came down to our house on 10th West many times for Thanksgiving and Christmas dinners. She made good breads and cakes."

Q: What were her adult medical experiences? What did she die of?
A: I think she died of old age in 1952. I don't recall any physical problems or diseases or injuries. All I remember of her is a little old lady. And she was little. She was 4'11". She is buried next to Edith in a cemetery off 33rd South and Highland Drive. I think its Wasatch Lawn Memorial Park. Her tombstone is located close to the West fence of the cemetery on the North side on the West side of the road that exits the cemetery on 33rd South above Highland Drive.

Q: What was her religious participation? Callings?
A: They were both very active. They went to the 28th ward when they lived next to us. Then they were in the 16th ward when they moved to 5th West. I don't remember any specifics. She believed in God and had a strong testimony.

Q: What were her hobbies, talents, and interests as an adult?
A: I don't know.

Q: What were her best abilities?

A: I remember feeling loved when we would go over to visit, but I don't remember her that well. Jim remembers, "She was very kind to us and would always give us some kind of cake. I liked her pound cake. I liked her bread also." Jim also shares, "She was generous and helpful as far as she could be. I remember one time when there was scarlet fever in our home on 10th West, and Dave and I went to live with Grandma Lord for 3 weeks during the quarantine period."

Q: Did she have any allergies or physical handicaps that you're aware of?

A: In later years she had a poor memory and poor hearing.

Q: Do you have any idea of her preferences or dislikes for food, music, books, TV, movies?

A: They had a piano. Aunt Edith gave it to Elaine when she died and Elaine gave it to Ralph. He still has it and uses it. I assume that Edith played the piano. She died in 1952 and the TV came out in about 1948 or 1949. I don't think she had a TV.

Q: Memorable Travels?

A: The resort trips taken in Blackpool, England with the family. And when she went to see her son, James, in Paris when he was in the hospital being treated for being gassed during the 1st World War.

Q: Historical Events that she passed through in her life?

A: She went through the 1st World War in England and this directly affected her son. The Great Depression. The 2nd World War she lost her oldest son, James. She has ration books she and Aunt Edith had. These are the instructions printed on the back of the ration booklets:

1. This book is valuable. Do not lose it.

2. Each stamp authorizes you to purchase rationed goods in the quantities and at the times designated by the office of Price Administration. Without the stamps you will be unable to purchase those goods.

3. Detailed instructions concerning the use of the book and the stamps will be issued. Watch for the instructions so that you will know how to use your book and stamps.

4. Do not throw this book away when all of the stamps have been used, or when the time for their use has expired. You may be required to present this book when you apply for subsequent books.

Rationing is a vital part of your countries war effort. Your local War Price and Rationing Board can give you full information. Any attempt to violate the rules is an effort to deny someone his share and will create hardship and help the enemy.

Q: What were the changes she saw throughout her lifetime in technology, morality, fashion, etc.

A: She saw the advent of the telephone, radio, TV, and car. In fashion I never saw my grandmother wear pants. Jeans came out in the 1940's probably due to the war effort done by the women on the home front.

Q: What were her greatest joy?

A: Probably living next to and with her two children and grandchildren in the USA until she passed away.

Q: What were her greatest sorrows?

A: We can assume that the loss of her husband and children (William & James).

Q: Home remedies?

A: I know that grandma and Edith made wine occasionally. I don't know why, but they had it around. Jim remembers, "They also had brandy around for medicinal purposes. We found it one day when we were there alone, but we did not drink any. Instead, we poured some in a bottle cap and set it on fire. The alcohol in it burned for a few seconds. We got a kick out of doing that."

Alma & Christiane Stark

Children: (L to R) Grace, Blanche & Marian

Alma Pedersen Stark
Father: Soren Pedersen Stark
Mother: Ann Sophia Petersen
Born: 19 December 1874
Place: Spanish Fork, Utah, USA
Married: 30 March 1897 (to Christiane Johanna Hansen)
Died: 4 April 1960
Place: Salt Lake City, Utah, USA

PERSONAL HISTORY OF ALMA PEDERSEN STARK (1874-1960)

I, Alma Pederson Stark, was born in Spanish Fork, Utah, December 19, 1874. This is a history of my life as far back as I can remember. My father and mother were born in Denmark. My father, Soren Pederson Stark was born in Reesdalshede, Serup, Sogn, Vilborg on September 5, 1829. My mother was born in Denmark at the town of Shelland, January 5, 1839. Her maiden name was Ann Sophia Peterson. Father died May 15, 1881 in Spanish Fork, Utah. Mother died February 28, 1912 at Leland, Utah.

They sailed for America April 15, 1862, on the sail ship Franklin. They married April 16, 1862 on board the ship. They landed in New York City on May 31, 1862.

I cannot remember much about my father, being less than seven years old when he died. I do remember that I rode a borrowed horse when he cultivated the corn and sugar cane, also when he cut my hair, he said for me to sit still so he could make a good close job, so my mother could not pull my hair. He said I sat and kept my head very still for the job. We only had an ox team at the time. We had a home in town, which he sold. We then moved on to a homestead, located on the northeast side of Spanish Fork, Utah. I well remember the first night we stayed on the homestead. We only had a covered wagon to live in at first. I cried and said to mother, "let's go home". She said that this was our home. Father was out in the canyon getting logs for our new house. He built a one-room log cabin, which was an old landmark for many years. There we were raised on the old homestead, which we loved, located at the foot of a hill and right on the main road to Springville, Utah. Forty acres of the homestead were in the city.

My brother, Moroni was bitten by the first dog, on the arm. I can see the dog now and how we were playing with a hoop, rolling it around. It struck the dog. It grabbed Moroni just above the wrist and kept chewing until it reached his elbow. Father got the old musket gun. I well remember him taking a rest shot, on one knee, at the vicious brute. He took some of the warm dog flesh and put it on the wound.

I remember father came home one evening with logs for the barn. He unhitched the team of oxen and let them loose. One of the oxen picked my brother Nephi up with his harness and threw him over the stockyard fence. He was not hurt, as luck would have it. Father yelled to us to get out of the way. I remember my father milking the cows. They were white ones. I don't remember how many cows we had then, but we had some white cows in the herd for many years. He brought home a wagonload of sheep. I saw him taking them out of the wagon by hand, one at a time.

I remember father and James Higginson bought a molasses mill, which they set up on the west side of the road from our home. We kids were delighted with the mill and would spend lots of our time there playing and watching the building of the mill, where we played many happy hours away, night and day, making molasses candy and watching the hauling in of the sugar cane and the grinding-watching the juice run into the tank. We watched the juice boil being made into fine golden molasses. They took the skimming and made it into molasses candy. My sister Inger, was in charge of the candy making, and she was the best molasses maker in the land. My brother, Moroni was the boss of the feeding of the cane into the mill. I was in charge of taking the rejects away. The molasses making time was about the happiest time of our lives. People would bring in their sugar cane for miles around to get it made into molasses. We also raised a lot of sugar cane ourselves on our lands. I worked in the cane fields a far back as I can remember, planting, stripping the leaves off the cane, cutting, piling and hauling to the mill. We had lots of company then. Kids from all over the country would be there for molasses candy and to play with us.

Father did not live to enjoy the fruits of his toil, too much exposure. He died a young man at the age of 52. Just in the prime of life. He was in his sick bed for a year or more. My father was the first person that I had ever seen dead. The family all stood by his bed when he passed away. Nephi and I said that he was asleep. We tried to wake him, but he slept on. I remember the funeral. It was the first funeral I had ever attended. It was a sad time for mother, out on a farm so far from neighbors, with four small children, the oldest being eleven. Every night when we would gather around the table for the evening meal, for a long time, she could not keep back the tears of her great sorrow for the loss of her beloved companion, husband and father. I was too young to realize just what it meant for a father to die, to be called away, but mother and the two older brothers and sister were heart broken, which time alone can heal.

I remember well when we got our first horse team. We traced our oxen team for them. I don't think children today would be more delighted for a new auto than we were for the new horse team. One of them we could ride. We called him Billy. I was on him from morning until night. I had many a fall until I mustered the art of horseback riding. I finally became quite an expert, especially on one occasion when my life was no doubt saved in a race with a mountain lion.

(This is as far as Alma Pederson Stark wrote about his own life)

ALMA PEDERSON STARK (1874-1960)
By Mary Ann Stark Woodward (Daughter)

Alma Pederson Stark was born December 19, 1874, in Spanish Fork, Utah County, Utah. He was the son of Soren Pederson Stark and Ann Sophia Peterson, early Pioneers in Spanish Fork. He was the sixth child. Soren and Ann Sophia lost their three oldest babies in Sanpete and Sevier Counties, where they were sent to help colonize in 1863.

Being a son of a Pioneer Family, Alma's early days were full of hardships. He lived on his father's homestead, located at the Northeast corner of the town of Spanish Fork. There was plenty of hard work to be done on the farm, taking care of the cattle and crops.

The real hardship Alma passed through was when his father died, when he was only seven years old. That left his widowed mother with four young children, the oldest being eleven years. Their names were Moroni, Inger, Alma and Nephi. Soren was 52 years old when he died of a long infection

216

caused by pneumonia. When Alma was 12 years old, his only sister, Inger, a lovely girl 15 years old, died of typhoid fever. She had been helping some friends. Inger was Alma's playmate and her death saddened him very much.

When Alma was three years old he had the measles, which left him deaf in one ear. This proved to be a real handicap all his life..

Alma often told his children of the experience he and his brothers (Nephi and Moroni) had with a mountain lion. The three boys went with a team and wagon up Spanish fork Canyon to get a load of wood. The boys found a spot to get the wood to load their wagon. It wasn't long before the horses began to appear restless and afraid of something. Soon Alma saw a mountain lion watching them from a cliff. The lion began to slink closer through the shrubs and grass. The horses became more frightened. The boys did not wait to determine whether the lion was after them or the horses.

When Alma was still in his early teens, his mother married again. His stepfather proved to be a cruel man. The two older boys, Moroni and Alma, could not get along with him. They kept away from the farm most of the time. They secured work on the new railroad, being built and at the mines. After the stepfather died, Alma returned to the farm to help run it for his mother. He married Christiane Johanna Hansen in 1897. They enjoyed the farm life together. Alma never had a chance to get an education, as he always had to work. He had a very good mechanical brain. If he had secured an education he could have gone far in this field.

Alma was always kind to little children. He loved his grandchildren. They always loved to play with him. He had an inventive mind. When he was in his late teens, he worked on the railroad. He helped put the railroad into several farm and mining towns in Utah. It was while working on the railroad that he figured out a block signal and other ideas. He confided in a man who promised to help him get them patented. They did not help him, but proceeded to steal his ideas. He just did not have much of a chance in those early days.

Alma and Christiane had always longed for a large farm or ranch. Several times he had planned to go into Idaho or one of the Western States, to file on lands being offered for homesteading, but every time he would discuss the matter with his mother (Ann Sophia) and older brother, Moroni, they would talk him out of it. The years passed and in the meantime his brother Moroni had bought his family plenty of wonderful farmlands very cheap and built a fine brick home on the land at Leland, Utah.

In February 1911 Alma's mother, Ann Sophia Petersen Stark, passed away. Alma's restless soul could not stay on the farm. He wanted more land. There were some land schemes being developed at Delta, Utah and Ruby Valley, Nevada. He was talked into going to Ruby Valley, Nevada, so they sold their farm at Spanish Fork, Utah. Alma and Christiane took a homestead in Ruby Valley and also bought 80 acres of land from the Taylor Brothers, located near Ruby City in Ruby Valley. They lived on a lot in Ruby City. It was terribly cold there and snow came in September. They moved to the homestead, which was about 10 miles southeast of Ruby City. It was much warmer there and very little snow. It was on desert land. For several years, they could raise dry land wheat and hay. That did not last long as there wasn't any water, only in a surface well, and very little rain fell. The jackrabbits were so thick. They would eat the young potato plants and peas and also the young wheat. Mary Ann, Alma's daughter remembers when they first went to Nevada, how good wild rabbit and potatoes tasted. Christiane roasted them in a Dutch oven. Alma would make a fire in a hole in the ground. The Dutch oven was then placed on the live coals. In the mean time Alma and Christiane had lost their 80 acres of land at Ruby City. The Taylor Brothers Land Company had gone broke, and the lands went back to the ranchers. The company sold the land with full water rights, which they never did have title too. It was terribly misrepresented. People came from many states and some from Canada with their families. They all suffered real hardships and all lost everything they had invested in the Ruby Valley land scheme. It wasn't long until they had all moved from Ruby Valley. All the homesteaders also had to leave. Christiane and Alma moved to Salt Lake City, Utah, having lost the lands, which they had longed for and worked so hard to get. They lost their horses and cattle and several thousand dollars, which they had paid down on the lands in Ruby Valley, Nevada.

Alma was a good salesman. He sold nursery stock for Stark Brothers Nurseries of Missouri. He made a good living at it for many years. He was also a salesman for many other things. He was a good carpenter. He worked hard to take care of his large family. Christiane was such a good manager and that helped him plenty.

Alma Pederson Stark lived to be 85 years old. He had good health most of his life. The last 10 years, his eyesight and hearing began to fail him. He was always pleasant and cheerful in spite of his many troubles and hardships. He passed away in Salt Lake City, Utah, April 4, 1960. He was buried beside his wife and his children who had passed away, at Spanish Fork, Utah.

Christiane Johanna Hansen

4 Generations
Christiane, Mary Ann (daughter),
Sanford (grandson), Maren (mother)

Father: Anders Hansen
Mother: Maren Rasmussen
Born: 13 October 1881
Place: Fyn, Vissenbjerg, Denmark
Married: 30 March 1897
(to Alma Pedersen Stark)
Place: Spanish Fork, Utah, USA
Died: 3 April 1954
Place: Salt Lake City, Utah, USA

DESERET NEWS

APR 1954

Christiana J. H. Stark

Mrs. Christiana Johanna Hansen Stark, 72, of 949 Ouray Ave., died Saturday at 3:55 p.m. in a Salt Lake hospital of a heart ailment.

Born Oct. 13, 1881, at Fyn, Denmark, daughter of Anders and Maren Rasmussen Hansen. Came to Spanish Fork at age 12. Married to Alma P. Stark March 30, 1897 at Spanish Fork. Active temple worker. Church of Jesus Christ of Latter-day Saints. Taught in Relief Society 30 years.

Survivors: husband; sons and daughters, Mrs. Charles (Mariam) Woodward, Mrs. Walter (Blanche) Lord, Mrs. John (Grace) Foutz, Mrs. A. H. (LaVern) Wahlen, Mrs. Den (Shirley) Dimmick, Salt Lake; Mrs. Alois A. Stark, Hayward, Cal., and R. L. Stark, San Bernardino, Cal. 26 grandchildren, 25 great-grandchildren; two sisters.

STARK—Funeral services for Christiane Hansen Stark of 949 Ouray Ave., will be held Wednesday at 12:30 p.m. in the 28th Ward Chapel with Bishop Lester J. Lees officiating. Friends may call at the mortuary, 36 E. 7th South Street Tuesday 6-8 p.m. and at the residence Wednesday from 10 a.m. until noon. Funeral directors, Deseret Mortuary Company.

DESERET NEWS

APR 1954

Christiana J. H. Stark

Funeral services for Christiana Hansen Stark, 72, of 949 Ouray Ave., will be held Wednesday at 12:30 p.m. in the Twenty - eighth Ward Chapel Church of Jesus Christ of Latter-day Saints, with Bishop Lester J. Lees officiating. Friends may call at the mortuary, 36 E. 7th South Tuesday from 6 to 8 p.m. and at the residence Wednesday from 10 a.m. until noon.

Mrs. Stark died Saturday at 3:55 p.m. in a local hospital of a heart ailment.

Born Oct. 13, 1881, at Fyn, Denmark, daughter of Anders and Maren Rasmussen Hansen. Married to Alma P. Stark March 30, 1897, at Spanish Fork. Later married in Salt Lake Temple. Active Temple worker. Taught in Relief Society 30 years.

Survivors: husband; sons and daughters, Mrs. Charles (Mariam) Woodward, Mrs. Walter (Blanche) Lord; Mrs. John (Grace) Foutz, Mrs. A. H. (LaVern) Wahlen, Mrs. Den (Shirley) Dimmick, Salt Lake City; Mrs. A. A. Stark, Hayward, Cal., and R. L. Stark, San Bernardino, Cal. 26 grandchildren, 25 great-grandchildren, two sisters, Mrs. Gilbert Olsen, Salt Lake City, and Mrs. Annie Whitehead, Long Beach, Cal.

CHRISTIANE JOHANNA HANSEN STARK
(1881-1964)
By: Mary Ann Stark Woodward (daughter)

Christiane Johanna Hansen Stark, was born October 13, 1881 at Vissenbjerg, Denmark. Her mother's name was Maren Rasmussen and her father's name was Andrus Hansen.

Christiane's parents were early converts to the church and being devout would walk with their children about five miles to attend church, and would stay in church most of the day. Christiane often spoke of the missionaries and how they would look forward to meetings with them. She often told her children how the children at school would point them out and make fun of them because they were Mormons.

When she was old enough to work in a factory, Christiane related that she was put to work in a brick factory at nine years of age, and was charged with separating the bricks to keep them from sticking. She went to school every other day alternating with her work at the brick factory.

Although her childhood was filled with hard work, she also told of the fun she and her sister and friends had going hazelnut picking. One time, Christiane recalled that she was carrying her younger sister, Emma, on her back so she could keep up with the others. They all started to run and Christiane did also even though her younger sister was on her back. Consequently, Christiane fell and broke her arm at the elbow.

Christiane's mother (Maren) had some friends, a family by the name of Carl Grotegut, who had come to Utah years before with their families and had settled at Spanish Fork, Utah. These wonderful friends of Maren had encouraged her to send her children to Spanish Fork, Utah to make their home with them. In response to this generous offer, Christiane's oldest sister, Anne, was first sent to live

220

with this family. Christiane's turn soon came to go to Zion to live with the Carl Grotegut family.

Christiane's parents didn't come to Utah with their children. They sent one of their children at a time to Utah because Andrus Hansen (Christiane's father) was twenty years older than his wife, Maren, and he was unable to travel because both of his legs were crippled as the result of a mad bull attacking him and goring him severely. Consequently, Maren had to earn most of the living for her family in addition to enough to send them to America. She knew there was no other way but to send them one at a time with missionaries. She had so much faith in the gospel that no sacrifice was to great, hence, she parted with her children one at a time to afford them the opportunity of coming to Zion and having the advantages of the gospel and a free land to live in.

Christiane left Denmark on August 10, 1893 and arrived in Utah on September 5, 1893. She lived with her older sister, Anne, at their parent's friend's home, Carl Grotegut at Spanish fork, Utah. She was only twelve years of age when she left Denmark.

Christiane said she worked very hard and was hired out to help with housework, herding cows or working in the fields. Sometimes she received fifty cents a week and stated that the people she worked for were very kind and good to her. During these tender young years of her life, away from her mother and father, she often said that it seemed that our Heavenly Father watches over his children and looks out for them when they put their trust and faith in him.

A short time after Christiane had arrived from Denmark to live at the Carl Grotegut home, she moved to the home of Mrs. Ann Sophia Stark, a widow who had just lost her lovely fifteen year old daughter from typhoid fever. Mrs. Stark took Christiane right to her heart and was very good to her. Mrs. Stark and her three sons, Moroni, Alma, and Nephi, raised some very fine horses on their farm. Christiane enjoyed riding a great deal and could handle horses very well. They had some of the finest buggy and riding horses in the country as well as fine milk cows.

Christiane married one of Mrs. Stark's sons, Alma Pedersen Stark, when she was sixteen years old. They worked very hard on the farm and she frequently mentioned that she enjoyed hard work. She was one of the hardest workingwomen I've ever known and was thankful for the wonderful health she enjoyed that enabled her to carry out her arduous tasks.

Kindness and patience were also qualities of Christiane's character. She went without nice clothes in order to save money so her children could dress well. She also saved money for their needs by raising and selling fresh vegetables and fruits. She would often go early in the spring and summer mornings to water her gardens. Her strawberries were always the largest and earliest on the market. They produced and sold many buggy loads of these beautiful, fresh strawberries and vegetables for the Spanish Fork Co-op.

Christiane also raised fine geese and ducks. People would ask her to save them a goose for Thanksgiving or Christmas and she usually received one dollar apiece for them. Her family surely did enjoy these ducks and geese on holidays.

Christiane worked very hard on the farm. She milked cows sometimes morning and night, and fed the poultry and cattle. She also helped harvest the crops and worked from sun up to sun down and often way into the night. She also made very tasty butter and sold it to the stores along with eggs and farm produce.

Being an excellent seamstress, mother often designed clothes for herself and her small daughters and we were very proud of these beautiful clothes. She was an excellent cook and always had pies and cake on hand to serve to her children and grandchildren.

Although Christiane did not have much schooling and didn't have the privilege of going to school in Utah because of having to work, she never the less, was a well-educated and intelligent woman. She educated herself by reading the schoolbooks her children brought home. She and her children would often write and spell together. Christiane could speak the English language very well and al the Danish language.

Christiane was a wonderful person to make beautiful fancy work of all kinds and all of her children and grandchildren have some of her lovely embroidery work and crochet pieces. It made her very happy to give gifts to them.

Her children enjoyed hearing mother sing our Latter-day Saint hymns, as she had a beautiful voice and was always singing and happy.

Ten children were born to Christiane and Alma and they raised seven of them to adulthood. These children all have families of their own now. Christiane knew the sorrow of burying three of her young babies. In those days midwives delivered the babies and Christiane had midwives for all of her deliveries except the last two, which were attended to by a doctor. She never entered the hospital for a confinement.

Christiane had a firm testimony of the gospel and enjoyed attending church. She loved her Relief Society work and was a Relief Society teacher for more than 25 years. She loved to go to the temple and did a lot of temple work when her health would permit it. She urged all of her children to go to church and was always happy when they were active in the church.

Christiane Johanna Hansen Stark passed away on April 3, 1964 at the age of 72 years.

Annice Lord

James Knowles
Father: William Knowles
Mother: Esther Gifford
Born: 29 March 1845
Place: Settle, Yorkshire, England
Married: 24 August 1867 (to Annice Lord)
Place: Giggleswick, Yorkshire, England
Died: 6 June 1920
Place: Cornholm, Lancashire, England

Annice Lord
Father: William Lord
Mother: Hannah Prichard
Born: 23 December 1845
Place: Settle, Yorkshire, England
Married: 24 August 1867 (to James Knowles)
Place: Giggleswick, Yorkshire, England
Died: 4 September 1879
Place: Settle, Yorkshire, England

Tid-bits about
James Knowles and Annice Lord

James Knowles and Annice Lord were engaged to be married when they started having children. In England during that time it was very costly to get married, therefore they had to wait. During the waiting period two children were born: Jane Lord (born: 24 June 1864) and William Knowles Lord (born: 31 May 1867). The law stated that if two people were not legally married that the children born to them would take on the surname of the mother. Thus, the last name of "Lord" was given to the first two children. They finally had saved up enough money and were married shortly after having William Knowles Lord (24th August 1867) and had three more children, which were given the family's last name of "Knowles." Their names were: Ester Hannah Knowles (born: 25 April 1870), John Knowles (born: May 1873) & Mary Knowles (born: 1878).

.

Grocer Run & Owned by Elizabeth Banks

*Jane Banks, Elizabeth "Aunt Lizzie" Banks
and William Lord*

Jane Banks

Father: Thomas Banks
Mother: Peggy Parker
Born: 24 June 1826
Place: Airton, Yorkshire, England
Died: 22 November 1912

Jane Banks signature in cover
Dated 1847

Tid-bits of Information about Thomas Pullen and Jane Banks

Thomas Pullen owned an estate in Winterburn, Yorkshire, England. Jane Banks was a maidservant on that estate. They had a baby out of wedlock and for that reason was given her mother's surname of "Banks". Jane only had one child at the age of 41. Margaret Banks was born the 21st of May 1867. Thomas and Jane were never married.

Dave and Gloria Lord have a book owned by Jane Banks entitled, Domestic Cookery By A Lady. It could have been used as a reference by Jane as a maidservant on the estate in Winterburn. It contains information about cleaning a house, cooking, and caring for the sick. It is signed by Jane Banks and dated 1847. Also, Dave and Gloria have another book entitled, Persuasives To Early Piety, which has the name "Frances Pullen" in the cover. We don't know who this is, but it is evidently some relative of Thomas Pullen.

This is an excerpt taken from "Walter Lord's Personal History" stating his memory of his grandmother, Jane Banks. It helps to explain the photo of Jane, Elizabeth & William standing in front of the grocery store:

"One year and 3 months after my father (William Knowles Lord) died, a lady, my mother's cousin (Elizabeth A. Banks), came to live with us and to take care of us three children, Edith, Willie and myself, while my mother (Margaret Banks Lord) went to work. We always called her Aunt Lizzie.

She had a little money so after a while, she bought a little grocery store. It was all right for a while, but she had to give it up. She let too many customers buy on credit and they never paid her, so she closed it up.

I was about 3 or 4 years old and I remember she used to take us kids into the store on Sunday (the store was closed) and let us pick out a candy bar.
We moved from there to the end house on a row of houses called Throstle Street in Nelson and lived there about 13 years. Mother went to work all this time as a winder in a cotton mill. We kids all went to school.

Oh, I forgot to mention "Granny." She was my mother's mother (Jane Banks). She lived with us also and after we moved to Throstle Street, she got sick and went to bed and stayed there for about 8 years. We had a 4-room house (2 up and 2 down). Grandma slept upstairs and mother and one or two of us kids slept in the same room.

In the daytime, when she wanted to attract our attention, she used to tap on the floor with a walking stick. Then one of us would go upstairs to her.

Grandma lived to be 83 years old and is buried at Kirby Malham in Yorkshire."

Thomas Banks

Peggy Parker

Thomas Banks

Father: William Banks
Mother: Margaret Redmayne
Born: 14 April 1793
Place: Airton, Yorkshire, England
Married: ? (to Peggy Parker)
Place: Airton, Yorkshire, England
Died: 4 June 1864
Place: Airton, Yorkshire, England

Peggy Parker

Father: Bartholomew Parker
Mother: ?
Born: December 1793
Place: Kirby-Malham, Yorkshire, England
Married: ?
Place: Airton, Yorkshire, England
Died: 16 January 1868
Place: Airton, Yorkshire, England

Anders & Maren Hansen

Anders Hansen
Father: Hans Christian Hansen
Mother: Ane Jacobsen
Born: 27 June 1830
Place: Vissenbjerg, Odense, Denmark
Married: 23 December 1870 (to Maren Rasmussen)
Place: Denmark
Died: 28 March 1912
Place: Denmark

ANDERS HANSEN AND MAREN RASMUSSEN

By Mary Ann Woodward (a granddaughter)

Anders Hansen was born 27 June 1830 at Kreldstrup, Odense, Denmark. His wife was Maren Rasmussen, she was born 18 November 1851 at Vissenbjerg, Odense, Denmark.

Anders was 20 years older than Maren. He had been married before and was a widower. His wife died and left three children. Anders had been in the Kings Navy. He was a kind good man they say. He worked on a farm taking care of cattle. A prize bull there was supposed to be tame but for some reason the bull became enraged and attacked him. It injured Ander's legs so he could not work on the farm any more. This accident made it necessary for Maren to go out and work to support the family. Anders did wood carving at home to help support the family too.

Anders and Maren welcomed the Mormon missionaries in their home. They were baptized and their children were baptized when they were old enough.

Their daughter Christiane said that her mother, Maren and the two oldest children Annie and Christiane would go to the Latter-day Saint Church about five miles away. They would go early in the morning and stay all day. It was a very difficult time for them as they were made fun of and called names.

Anders and Maren wanted to immigrate to Utah and live with their friends who had immigrated to Utah. They could not because of Anders being crippled. They decided to send their children one at a time with the missionaries going home to Utah. Maren and Anders had some very good friends that had immigrated to Utah. These wonderful friends by the name of Carl Ludwig and Kristen Grotegut welcomed their children and helped them find homes to live in.

Christiane was only 12 years old when she came over to Utah. Her older sister Annie was already over here. It was not easy for them, as they had to work in families that needed help. It was real hard work, all kinds of housework and farm work too.

Anders and Maren knew that was the only way their children could come over to Zion or Utah. The only chance they would have to live their religion and to be married in the church. It was very hard on the parents to part with their children one at a time soon after they were 12 years old. Emma, Christiane's younger sister said that her mother would cry and wonder how her two daughters were over in Utah. Emma would cry too. Soon it came her time to go. Anders and Maren sent all of their five children over here. One son, Chris came here to Utah in his teens, as did his youngest sister Caroline. The three eldest daughters married Latter-day Saint men.

Anders Hansen passed away in March 1912 in Denmark. The five children that were now living in Utah sent for their mother to come to Utah. What a wonderful happy family to see their mother over here in Utah.

Chris married soon after his mother arrived in Utah, then her daughter, Caroline, married a few years after her mother came here. Out of the five children sent here to Utah, four of them have raised fine families and have been to the temple. Caroline had a fine family too.

Maren Rasmussen Hansen was Relief society President in the Branch over in Denmark for years before she came to Utah. Mary Ann, a granddaughter, has a sterling silver spoon, a large one that was given to her grandmother by the sisters in the Relief Society to remember them by when she left Denmark for Utah. Maren also brought with her a book with many names of her dead ancestors to do temple work for. She did names and work in the temple for a number of her ancestors on her side and on her husbands side.

One of Mary Ann's remembrances of her grandmother was: "She was a sweet and kind person and appreciated everything so much. We could not understand each other to well, but she always loved to see us." After Maren had been here a few years, she married a fine old man by the name of Jacob Christensen. He was a widower that lived in Pleasant Grove Utah. He made a nice little home for her. They always welcomed their children and grandchildren to their modest little home. Maren always had cake and cookies for us. Jacob Christensen was very good to grandmother. They had a few years of a happy life together.

Maren Rasmussen Hansen Christensen lived to be 80 years of age. She was not called a pioneer, but she and Anders went through many heartaches and hardships in Denmark. Parting with their children was hard, but they knew there was no other way but to send them to Zion with the missionaries.

Maren Rasmussen

Father: Fredrick Rasmussen
Mother: Anne Marie Hansen
Born: 18 November 1851
Place: Skalbjerg, Odense, Denmark
Married: 23 December 1870 (to Anders Hansen)
Place: Denmark
Marriage: ? (to Jacob Christensen)
Died: 23 May 1933
Place: Pleasant Grove, Utah, USA

Maren Rasmussen & Jacob Christensen
Maren's 2nd husband

Soren and Ann Sophia Stark

Soren Pedersen Stark

Father: Peder Sorensen Pederstrup
Mother: Ann Elizabeth Ericksen Winkler
Born: 5 September 1829
Place: Resdal, Serup, D, Denmark
Married: 16 April 1862 (to Ann Sophia Petersen)
Place: On Board the Ship _Franklin_ en route to the USA
Died: 15 May 1881
Place: Spanish Fork, Utah, USA

Moroni Pedersen Stark

Nephi Pedersen Stark

Alma Pedersen Stark

SOREN PEDERSEN STARK

From granddaughter, Marian Stark Woodward, and translated from Danish by her mother, Christiana Johanna Hansen Stark (Mrs. Alma P. Stark)

Soren Pedersen Stark, was born September 5, 1829, at Reesdalehede. Serup Parish, Viborg, Denmark. His father's name was Peder Sorensen Pederstrup. He was born March 1, 1792, in Pederstrup, Viborg, Denmark. His mother's name was Ane Elizabeth Winkler. She was born about 1804 in Fredericksog, Denmark.

Soren was baptized April 11, 1857, at Burop Mosa, Dallerign, Skanderborg Parish by Peter Christensen. He was confirmed by Peter Just. On August 9, 1857 he was ordained a priest by Christopher Folkman. On August 31,1859 he was ordained an elder by Karl Wideborg.

Soren was called to preside over the Forkel Branch soon after being ordained an elder in 1859. He presided for a year over the Forkel Branch. On Sunday, April 8, 1860, he was released and called and set apart to preside over Mols Branch.

Soren met and converted a lovely young woman whom he married two years later. Her name was Ane Sophia Pedersen. From Soren's diary in his own words he has written, "I was sick for some time after presiding at Mols Branch, but the Lord was with me and blessed me. With the blessings from the Lord, many saw the light and joined the church. I worked in Mols until October 1, 1861. I was transferred from Mos Branch to preside at Rouse Souderhalet of North Thereder."

In Soren's own words he says, "We held many meetings and the Lord blessed me and many listened. I bore my testimony to many. The people seemed to awaken and listen to the gospel that I preached to them. In the spring conference I was released from my mission to make it possible for me to go to Zion."

Soren left Aarhus April 7, 1862. They went by train from Kiel to Hamburg, Germany. They boarded the sailing ship, <u>Franklin</u>, on April

8. They raised anchor April 15, 1862, and sailed down the Elbe River for North America. Soren and Ane Sophia were married on the ship on April 16, 1862. They had their bunks below deck. The bunks were so wide that three persons easily could have room in one of them side by side. Eleven lanterns were lighted every night. Some of the Saints carried the measles with them from home and the disease was spread to all parts of the ship so that no less than 40 persons, mostly children were attacked at once. Many of the Saints were also suffering with diarrhea, which caused very much weakness of body. They held a council meeting every night and the sanitary condition of the ship's apartments was attended with great care. Three times a week the decks were washed and twice a week the ship was thoroughly fumigated by burning tar. A spirit of peace prevailed and very few difficulties occurred.

They held at times meetings of worship on the upper and lower decks and every morning at 5 AM the signal was given by clarinet or accordion. At 7 AM and 9 PM a similar signal was sent calling the Saints to assemble in their several districts for prayer. They amused themselves by dancing.

Christian A. Madsen was in charge of 413 Scandinavian Saints on the ship. There were at least 40 or more persons buried at sea, most of them children. (from the measles) From Soren's diary he says, "There was much sickness and death on the ocean voyage. My wife was very ill, near unto death, and the elders administered to her and she was restored to health." That was the beginning of the many testimonies of the power of the Priesthood for them. Soren writes, "We landed in New York, May 31, on June 2 we left the Franklin. (From Andrew Jensen's book, History of Scandanavian Mission, he writes, "During the last few days the chicken pox also broke out among them and 4 cases developed. Arrived in New York May 29. They were not permitted to go ashore because there were a few cases of measles. They remained there for two more nights and a day. They left the ship May 31. Sixty-two of Franklin's company died between Hamburg and Salt Lake.") My wife got her foot caught in the gangplank. That same evening we got on a train to take us to Florence, Nebraska. My wife's foot became very bad from the shaking of the train and from sitting still so long. When we reached Florence, I took her to a doctor who gave me some medicine that helped her very much. I think it was a great miracle that she didn't lose her foot as it was crushed very badly."

They stayed in Florence, Nebraska, until July 14 and while staying there Soren acted as both doctor and nurse to the sick.

On July 14, 1862, with an independent company of 500 immigrants and 80 wagons, they started the trek to Utah. The company was in charge of Christian A. Madsen and Ole M. Liljenquist the wagon trains. After more than two months of hardships crossing the plains, they arrived in Salt Lake City, September 23, 1862. They were sent to Spanish Fork and arrived there September 27, 1862. A friend by the name of Jens Hansen met and helped them to find a place to live in. Lafte Johnson let them have a cellar to live in. They lived in the cellar until January 2, 1863. (Jens Hansen was Soren's brother-in-law, his sister, Mary's, husband).

On January 2, 1863, they were sent to help colonize Moroni in Sanpete County. In the summer Soren built a two-room house and bought their first cow. On September 17 their first child a son, was born and named Soren P. Stark. The baby was blessed by his father in Fast Meeting. But they were not to enjoy their first born for long for at the age of 8 months on the 26th of may, 1864, he died. When Soren and Ane saw that he was near to death, Soren ordained him an elder as that was the custom in that day.

On October 3, 1864, they were blessed by another son. They named him Soren Peder Pedersen and he was blessed by Brother Shephert at Moroni. That winter Soren moved his family again. They were with the first 20 families that settled Monroe, which was first called Alma. They arrived the 14th of March 1864 at Alma in Sevier County.

The Black Hawk War started in April of 1865 and early in 1865 the settlers built a fort at Alma. Soren helped build the fort. During the Indian War the families all lived inside the fort. Soren was a Home Guard during the war.

They lived in the fort for almost a year. While enduring all the trials and hardships of the Indian War and pioneer life, sorrow struck again taking the life of their second son. He died September 16, 1865. This son was also ordained an elder. He was ordained by Wiley Allred.

The Indians drove off the settler's cattle and killed several persons. The settlers had to go sixty miles to the mill to get their flour ground. An accident occurred one time when Soren went. They went in companies to protect themselves from the Indians. Soren was on the return trip coming back from the mill with the wagons loaded with flour and foodstuff. While crossing a river, some of the wagons were swept downstream. Teams and wagons were overturned and several horses were lost. Also, some more lost their lives. Much of the foodstuff was spoiled and lost. Soren had a very narrow escape from death.

The Indian trouble with Black Hawk's band got so bad that the settlers were driven out of Alma. Soren and Ane moved back to Spanish Fork. Soren built a two-room house on a city lot. The house was built on the same corner where James Nielsen's home is now. They lived there for some time. Their sons Moroni and Alma were born there. Soren sold his house and lot to Joseph A. Reese, the father of Alfred Reese. He and family moved again to a lonely homestead that he took up on the lower part of the Spanish Fork bench.

Ane and her small children lived in a wagon box or white top while Soren went into Spanish Fork Canyon and cut logs to build hem a log house. He moved an apple tree that was still in bloom from their lot in Spanish Fork. The tree bore apples from the blossoms that were on it when they moved it. Soren was a great horticulturist. He cleared off the side hill into terraces and planted all kinds of fruit trees. This was quite an undertaking at that time, there were no nurseries so he sent back for seedling trees and then grafted choice fruit in later. They had the satisfaction of sampling some of this fruit. They were not to enjoy this long for when people started to farm the upper bench land and put water on the land above, it ruined the land below. Their fine young orchard and grapes of many varieties were destroyed.

Soren's pioneer spirit did not give up. They put crude drainage in and saved part of the land for short rooted plants such as corn and sugarcane. They were among the first pioneers to plant sugarcane and own their own molasses mill. Soren sent back for machinery for a molasses mill. They were known far and wide for their fine molasses.

Soren would take a wagonload of molasses to Sanpete County and trade for flour and foodstuff. It was on one of these trips that he took a severe cold and that started an illness that he never fully recovered from. It can be truly said that he was a very humble and willing church worker and a true Latter-day Saint. He would get out of bed in the middle of the night and administer to the sick and stay with the sick. Chrisiane, his daughter-in-law, said he had the gift of healing.

Soren Pedersen Stark died May 14, 1881, at the age of 52 years.

INDAIN HOSTILITY BRINGS EVACUATION ORDER TO SEVIER VALLEY IN APRIL, 1867

Soren Pedersen Stark and Ann Sophia Stark, his wife, were among those evacuated at this time.

A Troup of mounted militiamen led the long procession out of the settlement of Richfield on a pleasant April day in 1867. Behind them followed a noisy herd of cattle, sheep and pigs driven by an almost as noisy gang of shouting boys and barking dogs.

A group of townsmen mounted on their horses were next in line to see that none of the livestock got away from the boys and to round up the stock and drive it to safety in case of Indian attack. Then came wagon after wagon loaded with everything the settlers would pile on. Women drove some of the teams because their men were needed for other duties in the caravan.

The little town became deathly still, deserted. With sad hearts, the people in the caravan looked back wondering what would become of their cabins that they had enjoyed for such a short time. Would they ever see them again? They wondered. Previous experience in being driven out of their homes did not make the present loss any easier, they found.

On the advice of President Brigham Young, every settlement in Sevier Valley and at Alma (later called Monroe) was being evacuated in this movement due to the mounting ferocity of the Indian attacks in the area. The mountains east of the valley were the stronghold of the

239

Black Hawk and his allies who were determined to drive the white invaders from the Indian hunting grounds.

Trouble had started soon after the first permanent settlers had come to the valley in 1864. Soon after the first flare-up of the war in Sanpete Country to the North, Col. R.N. Allred rode into Salina one day with a number of Sanpete militiamen. They had followed a party of raiders to this point. Here they learned that the Indians had headed up the canyon. The colonel, reluctant to follow them into the mountains, sent an express to Brigham Young for advice.

Some of his men were too anxious to recover their stolen cattle to wait for instructions. They pushed up the canyon against the better judgment of their leader. About 12 miles up the narrow defile, rocks and trees all around seemed to open fire. One man was killed, another left wounded in the wild retreat back to Salina.

Several other skirmishes were fought in the valley. A number of men, women and children died in Indian attacks and cattle were being driven off constantly during the summer months.

With no hope for peace in sight, the evacuation order came. The Sevier people headed for Gunnison. From there they dispersed to the various northern settlements. Some made permanent homes elsewhere and never returned to their farms in Sevier Valley. A few ventured back in 1868, but found the Indians as hostile as ever. More came in 1870, but found they had to battle not only the Indians, but a scourge of grasshoppers as well. Their crops were destroyed and they nearly starved. As their clothes wore out, they fashioned new ones from buckskin, tents and wagon covers. The women had to begin making their own cloth. It was not uncommon for them to shear sheep and card the wool as well as to spin it and weave it in to fabric.

Peace was finally made with the Indians in 1872. The Sevier Valley people were then able to devote their full energies to the development of the great agricultural resources of the area and to the building of attractive communities filled with beautiful home, schools and churches.

THE ABOVE ARTICLE APPEARED IN THE CHURCH SECTION OF THE DESERET NEW ON MARCH 26, 1960.

Ann Sophia Petersen

Father: Peder Andersen
Mother: Inger Nielsen
Born: 5 January 1838
Place: Berderod, Fredrks., D, Denmark
Married: 16 April 1862 (to Soren Pedersen Stark)
Place: On Board the Ship _Franklin_ en route to the USA
Died: 28 February 1912
Place: Spanish Fork, Utah, USA

Ann Sophia Petersen Stark
(1839 – 1912)

By granddaughter, Mary Ann Stark Woodward

Ann Sophia Petersen, was born January 5, 1839 at Berkerod, Sjaelland, Denmark. She was the daughter of Peder Andersen, who was born May 2, 1811 at Blousterod, Frdrks., Denmark. Her mother was Inger Nielsen, who was born March 28, 1799.

When Ann was quite young, she secured work on a farm estate. It was here she met her future husband, Soren Pedersen Stark, who came as a humble missionary. Soren converted her to the gospel and Ann was told she was no longer welcome in her parent's home when she joined the Mormon Church. About two years later she bade farewell to her family and friends and went with Soren by railroad from Kiel to Hamburg, Germany. They boarded the sail ship <u>Franklin</u> which raised anchor April 15, 1862 and sailed down the Elbe River for North America. Soren and Ann Sophia were married on the ship April 16, 1862.

The ocean voyage was very trying for Ann as she became very ill, near unto death; however, her faith in her husband and in the administration of the elders brought her back to health. Nevertheless, that was only the beginning of the many trials and hardships she was to pass through.

From Soren's diary we find, "We landed in New York on May 31 and on June 2 we left the <u>Franklin</u>. When Ann was leaving the <u>Franklin</u> to board a small boat that led to the dock, she slipped and her foot was crushed between a plank and the ship or gangplank. Her foot became very painful as they traveled by train to Florence, Nebraska. It was a great miracle that she didn't lose her foot as it was crushed very badly." This was always a testimony to Ann of the healing power of the Priesthood.

They stayed in Florence, Nebraska until July 14, 1862 and then started the trek to Utah with an independent company of 500 emigrants and 80 wagons. Some friend by the name of Karn Marie traveled with them. Soren and Ann arrived in Salt Lake City, Utah on September 23, 1862. They were sent to Spanish Fork on September 17, 1862. A friend by the name of Lofte Johnson let them live in a cellar until January 1863, at which time Ann and Soren were sent with some saints to help colonize Moroni in Sanpete County. In the summer they were very busy building a two-room house. They also bought their first cow.

On September 17, Ann was blessed with her first child, a son, who was named Soren Pedersen Stark. They were very happy with this firstborn son; however, they were not to enjoy him for long as he died at the age of eight months, on the 26 of May 1864. Ann would become very sad with trials and hardships of pioneer life. She would long for her sister and friends in the green land of far off Denmark, however, Soren was a good and kind husband and would always comfort her and tell her to have faith in the gospel and put her trust in the Lord.

On October 30, 1864, Ann was blessed with another son, who was named Soren Peder Pedersen. In the winter of 1864, Soren and Ann, with their small son were called upon to move again. They were with the first 20 families that settled Alma, Utah, which was later called Monroe. They arrived in Alma, which was in Sevier County, March 14, 1864. Soon after their arrival in Alma, the Black Hawk Indian War began, in April 1864. Early in 1864, for their protection, the settlers of Alma built a fort with log houses on three sides and a rock was ten feet high on the fourth side. On the northeast side of the same block was built a corral for the livestock. The fort was built in nine days, in the month of February. Before the fort was ready for occupation, may people slept in the meetinghouse overnight, as they were in danger of attack by the Indians. Many of the settlers who built on their lots originally, moved their houses into the fort. Soren helped build the fort and was a Home Guard.

The Indian War proved a great hardship to the pioneer settlers. Armed herdsmen had to guard the cattle by day and night. On April 24, 1864, just before daylight, a guard at Alma discovered Indians prowling about the stock corral. Fortunately, they were frightened off that time but only to return again.

On July 12, 1864, Anthony Robinson of Alma, was found lying in his wagon, murdered by the Indians. Ann often told her children how frightened she was during the Indian War, but she would always pray and taught her children to also do so.

While enduring all of these trials and hardships or pioneer life, sorrow struck again and they were called upon to part with their second son. He died at the age of eleven months, on September 16, 1864. This son was also ordained an Elder, as their first son was, before his death, since it was the custom at that time. Wiley Allred, who was the Bishop at Alma at that time, ordained their second son.

Ann had a daughter, Annie, born August 26, 1866, at Richfield. She died September 13, 1867. Ann's three oldest children are buried in unmarked graves.

The Indians made attempts to steal stock from the corral at Alma. The settlers intended to put in crops in the spring, however, since the hostilities of the Indians were worse than ever before, the brethren were advised to evacuate the settlement. The settlers left their homes sorrowfully, as many had become quite attached to their fertile lands. The people evacuated the fort at Alma in 1867. Soren and Ann moved back to Spanish Fork, Utah, where they lived on a city lot in a two-room house, which Soren built. My uncle, Moroni, and my father, Alma Pedersen Stark, were born there. Ann and her family moved again to a lonely homestead, which was on the lower Spanish Fork bench. She and her small sons were very lonely there. They lived in a white top, or covered wagon, while Soren built them a log house.

Ann helped with the farming. They had a very fine orchard and grapes of many varieties, but they were not to enjoy their fine orchards and fertile lands, which they had worked on so hard and for so long. When people started to farm the upper bench lands, the water drainage soon ruined the lower bench lands, where Soren's homestead was located. Hence, their fine orchards, and vineyards were destroyed. Nevertheless, their pioneer spirit was not daunted. They put in a crude drainage system, which saved part of their lands, for short rooted plants, such as corn and sugarcane. They were among the first pioneers to plant sugarcane and build their own molasses mill. Ann would move her bed to the molasses mill while the juice was boiling and she would not let anyone else do the work, except herself. She was praised far and wide for her clear, fine molasses. She also spun wool and cloth and did much farm work.

Ann Sophia was left a widow in March 1881 (her husband died at 52 years of age) with four children, the eldest one being only eleven. Alma was only eight years old when his father died. Ann had eight children. Three sons lived to manhood, two of which raised large families. Alma was the last one to die. He passed away April 4, 1960 at Salt Lake City, Utah, Ann's second daughter, Inger, died at the age of 15 years. She had been helping a family that was sick. They found out too late they had typhoid fever.

To help for her family, Ann worked at the molasses mill, made butter and raised vegetables, which she sold to the stores in Spanish Fork. She was a good nurse and went out to help care for the sick. For this service, she would never take any pay. She was an ardent church and temple worker in her latter years. She was a Relief Society teacher for 33 years.

Mary Ann, a granddaughter remembers: "She was one of the kindest and sweetest women. She lived with her son, Alma, and his wife, Christiane, a few years before she died. She often told my mother (Christiane) that she loved her and thought as much of her as she would her own daughter."

Ann Sophia Petersen Stark died February 28, 1912, at the age of 74 years.

Peder Sorensen Pederstrup

Father: Soren Jacobsen
Mother: Maren Eriksen
Born: 14 March 1790
Place: V, P, Viborg, Denmark
Married: 31 January 1824 to Ann Elizabeth Winkler
Place: ?
Died: 10 May 1844
Place: Resdal, Serup, Denmark

PEDER SORENSEN (PEDERSTRUP)

Peder Sorensen (Pederstrup) was born 1 March 1790 in Pederstrup, Vinderslev, Viborg, Denmark. The Pederstrup was added to his name when he became older. It is his farm name used to identify him from other Peder Sorensens living in the same parish. His parents were Soren Jacobsen & Maren Ericksen (pg. 24 Vinderslev Parish Register). Witnesses to his christening were Laurids Rasmussen's daughter, Anna Magrete Ericksdatter, Jacob Nielsen, Christen Andersen, Soren Christensen, Mads Andersen all of Pederstrup. His parents had 10 children.

Peder served in the Danish Army in 1820 in Regiment 4B, then another regiment. He received the right to lease land in Reesdal, Serup, Viborg, on 6 October 1828. (Military Levying Roll miscellaneous information).

Peder married Ane Elizabeth Ericksdatter Winkler 31 January 1824. Ane Elizabeth was born 14 May 1803 in Haurdal, Rederiks, Viborg, Denmark. Her parents were Johan George Winkler and Ane Rosine Breuner.

Frederiks Parish was founded by German colonists. Winkler and Breuner are not Danish names. The parish church was built 8 January 1765, but was destroyed by fire 26 April 1809. All of the parish records were lost. A new church was built and the register began in 1804. Records of the Winkler & Breuner family were obtained from census records and Military Levying Rolls. The Military Levying Rolls contain a list of eligible males from birth to about 44 years of age during the period 1789-1849. After 1849, the males were first listed at the age of 14 years and after 1869 listed at 17 years. Each entry on a roll contains the person's name, age, place of birth, residence, height, name of father (if a person is born illegitimately, the name of the mother) and miscellaneous information. One can follow a family from one parish to another through these MLR rolls.

The family appeared in the 1834 Census for Reesdal, Serup Parish. Peder age 44, Ane Elizabeth Ericksdatter Vinkler age 30, Carl Gotlieb age 8, Soren age 4, Johannes Daniel age 1. Peder's occupation is listed as renter and laborer.

They are also listed in the 1840 Census. Peder is now 50, Ane Elizabeth Ericksdatter 36, Carl Gotlieb 15, Soren 11, Johannes Daniel 7, and Sine 2.

Peder died 10 May 1844 leaving Ane Elizabeth to keep the family together without her husband. They were very poor and she spun wool to make a living for her family. At a very young age the children worked for others to help the family out.

On 9 May 1868, Ane Elizabeth was baptized into the Church of Jesus Christ of Latter-day Saints in Silkenborg, Aarhus, Denmark at the age of 65 years (Silkeborg Mission Record). Her marriage to Alfred Theodore Andersen was recorded in a Temple Record Book which was kept by her daughter Maren Hansen but the compiler could not locate the record of her marriage.

Four of their children also joined the LDS Church in Denmark. Their son Soren was the first to be baptized on 11 April 1857. All four immigrated to America.

Ane Elizabeth died in Denmark 13 November 1879.

Their Children:

1. MARIA PEDERSEN born about 1824 and died as a baby. She was probably born in Gerning Parish, Viborg, Denmark, but the records were lost.

2. CARL GOTLIEB PEDERSEN born 17 July 1825 in Borridsolund, Gernig, Viborg, Denmark. He was confirmed in the Serup Parish Church on 26 April 1840. He died when he was just 16 years old on 18 November 1841 in Serup, Vibog, Denmark.

3. SOREN PEDERSEN born 5 September 1829 in Reesdal, Serup, Viborg, Denmark. He added "Stark" to his last name which means "Strong" in Danish. He was confirmed in the Luthern Church in 1844. When he was 16 years old, he left home to work in Brabrund Parish in Aarhus County. At the age of 19 he was found working in Hasle Parish in Aarhus. (MLR) He was at home with his mother in the 1855 Census. When he was 28 years old, he was baptized into the Church of Jesus Christ of Latter-day Saints on 11 April 1857 at Borup Mosa, Dallerup, Skanderborg, Denmark by Peter Christensen. He was confirmed by Peter Just. Peter Just was married to Karen Marie Christensen, sister to Rasmus Peter Christensen who later became his brother-in-law.

He was ordained a Priest by Christopher Folkman on 9 August 1857 and ordained an Elder on 31 October 1859 by Karl Widenborg. Soren was called to preside over the Forkel Branch soon after he was ordained an Elder. He presided for a year over the Forkel Branch. On Sunday 8 April 1860 he was released from the Forkel Branch and called and set apart to preside over Moso Branch. He wrote in his diary, "I was sick for sometime after presiding at Moso Branch, but the Lord was with me and blest me. With the blessings from the Lord, many saw the light and joined the church. I worked in Moso until October 1, 1861. I was transferred from Moso Branch to preside at Rouso Souderhalet of North Thereder." He baptized Rasmus Peter Christensen on 30 January 1860 at the Forkel Branch.

Soren met and converted Ane Sophia Pedersen whom he married two years later. In his diary he wrote. "We held many meetings and the Lord blest me and many listened. I bore my testimony to many. The people seemed to awaken and listen to the gospel that I preached to them. In the spring conference I was released from my mission to make it possible for me to go to Zion."

He left Denmark 7 April 1862 on board the ship <u>Franklin</u> to come to America. While on board <u>Franklin</u> he married Ane Sophia Pedersen on 16 April 1862. He kept a diary, which his granddaughter Marion Woodward had translated into English. In it he wrote, "There was much sickness and death on the ocean voyage. My wife was very ill, near unto death, and the elders administered to her and she was restored to health. We landed in New York, May 31 and on June 2 we left the <u>Franklin</u>. My wife got her foot caught in the gangplank. That same evening we got on a train to take us to Florence, Nebraska. My wife's foot became very bad from the shaking of the train and from sitting still so long. When we reached Florence I took her to a doctor who gave me some medicine that helped her very much. I think it was a great miracle that she didn't lose her foot as it was crushed very badly."

On 14 July 1862 they started the trek to Utah. After more than two months of hardships crossing the plains, they arrived at Salt Lake 23 September 1862. They were sent to Spanish Fork and arrived there 27 Septemeber 1862. A friend by the name of Jens Hansen met and helped them find a place to live. Lafte Johnson let them have a cellar to live in. They lived in the cellar until 2 January 1862 at which time they were sent to help colonize Moroni in Sanpete Couty. In the summer Soren built a two-roomed house and bought their first cow. On September 17 their first child was born and named Soren P. Stark. They were not to enjoy their first born for long for at the age of 8 months he died on 26 May 1864.

They were with the first twenty families that settled Monroe, which was first called Alma. They arrived in Alma, Sevier County on the 14th of March 1865. The Black Hawk Was started in April of 1865 and Soren along with the other settlers built a fort at Alma. During the war the families all lived inside the fort for almost a year. Soren was a home guard during the war. Sorrow struck again taking the life of their second son. He died 16 September 1865 when he was only 11 months old.

The settlers had to go 60 miles to a mill to get their flour ground. An accident occurred one time when Soren went. They went in companies to protect themselves from the Indians. Soren was on the return trip coming back from the mill with the wagons loaded with flour and foodstuff. While crossing a river some of the wagons were swept downstream. Teams and wagons were over turned. Several horses were lost as well as the precious flour and foodstuff.

The Indian trouble with Black Hawk's bands got so bad that the settlers were driven out of Alma. Soren moved his family back to Spanish Fork where he built a two-roomed house on a city lot. Their sons Moroni and Alma were born there. Soren sold this house and lot to Joseph A. Reese and moved to a homestead on the lower part of the Spanish Fork canyon and cut logs to build them a log house. Soren moved an apple tree that was still in bloom from their lot in Spanish Fork. That tree bore apples that same year. Soren was a great horticulturist. He cleared off the side hill into terraces and planted all kinds of fruit trees. This was quite an undertaking at that time. There were no nurseries so Soren sent for seeking trees and grafted choice fruit in later. They were not to enjoy the fruit for long for when people started farming the upper bench and put water on the land above, it ruined the land below. Their fine young orchard and grapes were destroyed. Soren's pioneer spirit did not give up. He put crude drainage in that saved part of the land and grew short rooted plants such as corn and sugar cane. He was among the first

248

pioneers to plant sugar cane and own a molasses mill. Soren sent back East for machinery for the molasses mill. Soren would take a wagonload of molasses to Sanpete County and trade for flour and foodstuff. It was on one of those trips that he caught a severe cold that started an illness that he never recovered from. He was ordained a High Priest 1 February 1874 by Bishop A.K. Thurber. He died 15 May 1881 in Spanish Fork, UT at the age of 52.

Children:

1. SOREN PEDERSEN STARK born 17 September 1863 in Moroni, UT. Died 26 May 1864 in Moroni, UT.
2. SOREN PEDER PEDERSEN STARK born 3 October 1864 in Moroni, UT. Died 16 September 1865 in Alma, Sevier, UT.
3. ANNE S.P. STARK born 26 August 1866 in Richfield, Sevier, UT. Died 12 September 1867.
4. MORONI PEDERSEN STARK born 11 October 1869 in Spanish Fork, UT. Married Sarah C. Hanson on 10 February 1897 in Salt Lake City, UT. They made their home in Spanish Fork. He served a mission to the northern states from 1899-1901. He was president of the 129th Quorum Seventies and a member of the stake board religion classes. A short history and picture is in "Pioneers & Prominent Men of Utah." He kept the Temple Book where temple work was recorded for the Pedersen-Winkler families after his aunt, Maren Hansen, died. He died 1 December 1934 in Spanish Fort, UT. Children:
    1. Anna Elizabeth Stark born 30 November 1897 in Robinson, Juab, UT.
    2. Henry Moroni Stark born 28 March 1900 in Leland, UT. Married Helen Candland 28 March 1936.
    3. Grant Soren Stark born 27 August 1902 in Spanish Fork, UT.
    4. Mark Hanson Stark born 6 October 1904 in Leland, UT. Married Mary Burch 29 May 1936 in Logan, UT. Children:
        1. Wayne Burch Stark born 18 December 1943 in Salt Lake City, UT. Married Charlene Kay Carter 20 January 1961.
    5. Elenor Sophia Stark born 29 August 1906 in Leland, UT. Married Frank Edman.
5. INGER ELIZABETH PEDERSEN STARK born 13 March 1872. Died 14 August 1886.
6. ALMA PEDERSEN STARK born 19 December 1874. Married Christiane Johanna Hansen 30 March 1898 in Spanish Fork, UT. Later solemnized 3 October 1906. Alma worked as a carpenter, farmer and salesman. During World War II he worked at Geneva Steel Co., Hill Air Force Base and Clearfield Naval Supply Depot. When it became difficult for him to do regular heavy work, he began devoting his energies to selling trees for a local nursery. Children:
    1. Marion Stark born September 1898 in Spanish Fork, UT. Married Charles Sanford Woodward 8 June 1915. Children:
        1) Charles Sanford Woodward. Married Lillian Aleen Vowles.
        2) Heber J. Woodward
        3) Norma Mae Woodward
        4) Franklin Stark Woodward
        5) Melvin James Woodward
        6) Ralph Alma Woodward. Married Connie Mae Fackrell.
        7) Marian Stark Woodward. Married Ross Wayne Moody.
        8) Alma Stark Woodward born 16 October 1933 in Salt Lake Ctiy, UT. Died 26 October 1933.

249

2. Alice Elizabeth Stark born 30 June 1900 in Spanish Fork, UT. Died 7 May 1902

3. Alvin P. Stark born 9 October 1902 in Robinson, Juab, UT. Died 22 November 1902

4. Blanche Rebecca Stark born 17 November 1903 in Spanish Fork, UT. Married Walter Lord 6 February 1926 in Salt Lake City, UT. Children all born in Salt Lake City, UT:
   1) Son Lord born 5 February 1929. Died 5 February 1929
   2) Walter David Lord born 5 February 1929
   3) Elaine Blanche Lord born 2 September 1930
   4) Lawrence James Lord born 17 June 1932
   5) Phillip Alma Lord born 26 April 1935
   6) Ralph Knowles Lord born 12 April 1937
   7) Dianne Margaret Lord born 5 August 1943

5. Violet Stark born 19 February 1906. Died 22 February 1906.

6. Grace Christiana Stark born 1 March 1909. Married John Moffit Foutz 21 November 1933 in Salt Lake City, UT. Children all born in Salt Lake City, UT:
   1) Geraldine Grance Foutz born 27 June 1934
   2) Merrilyn Gay Foutz born 29 February 1936
   3) John David Foutz born 6 June 1938
   4) Richard Dena Foutz born 10 January 1941
   5) Linda Margaret Foutz born 27 January 1943

7. LaVern Sophia Stark born 6 March 1912. Married Arvid Hilmer Wahlen 17 June 1928 in Salt Lake City, UT. Children:
   1) Sherry Lavern Wahlen born 3 Mary 1929 in Murray, UT
   2) Yvonne Arville Wahlen born 1 April 1931 in Murray, UT
   3) Mitzie Christiana Agusta Wahlen born 28 November 1932 in Murray, UT
   4) Sandra Myran Wahlen born 24 January 1935 in Salt Lake Ctiy, UT
   5) Arva Maud Wahlen born 19 August 1940 in Murray, UT
   6) Arvid Stark Wahlen born 21 October 1943 in Salt Lake City, UT

8. Alois Anders Stark born 8 August 1915 in Ruby Valley, Elko, Nevada. Married Eleanor Mary Aabagost 24 September 1938. Children:
   1) William Alois Stark born 6 October 1939 in Richmond, CA

9. Ray LaMar Stark born 31 July 1919 in Salt Lake City, UT. Married Glenna .... 1948.

10. Shirley June Stark born 18 June 1924 in Salt Lake City, UT. Married Charles Gribble 3 March 1942 in Salt Lake City, UT (Divorced). Children:
    1) Christie Lee Gribble born 31 January 1943 in Salt Lake City, UT

7. NEPHI PEDERSEN STARK born 9 October 1876. Died 15 December 1919 in Spanish Fork, UT of miner's consumption at age 43. Unmarried.

8. JOSEPH PEDERSEN STARK born 11 May 1880. Died 11 May 1880.

4. JOHAN DANIEL PEDERSEN born 24 September 1832 in Serup, Viborg, Denmark. He was confirmed in the Lutheran Church at the age of 14 ½. A record of him appeared on the Military Levying Rolls for the Danish Army for 1852 when he was age 20 and appearing before the draft. In 1858 he was listed on the Military Levying Roll at Serup at the age 26. He was lost track of after that.

5. MAREN PEDERSEN born 1 April 1835. Died when she was almost 4 years old.

6. SINE PEDERSEN (SENA) born 17 March 1838 in Reesdal, Serup, Viborg, Denmark. (Pg. 35 Serup Parish Register). She married Rasmus Peder Christensen on 28 April 1873. (SEE FAMILY HISTORY)

7. JOHAN ERICH REDERSEN born 4 August 1840. He was confirmed a member of the Lutheran Church in 1855. When he was 18 he appeared on the military Levying Rolls at Reesdal in 1858. He was baptized into the Church of Jesus Christ of Latter-day Saints on 16 May 1874. We do not have a record of when he came to America. He settled in Gunnison, Sanpete, UT. He married Elna Anderson 6 July 188?. Do not have a record of any children. He died 1 March 1892

8. MAREN PEDERSEN born 25 December 1842. She was baptized into the Church of Jesus Christ of Latter-day Saints on 31 August 1858 and immigrated to America on the same ship as Rasmus Peter Christensen who later became her brother-in-law. She sailed on the ship Monarch of the Sea on 16 May 1861 when she was 18 years old. She settled in Spanish Fork, Utah, and married Jens Hansen on 8 March 1862 as a plural wife. Jens was born 13 October 1823 in Otter up, Odense, Fuen, Denmark, son of Hans & Maren Kirsten (Petersen) Jorgensen. Jens died 28 June 1897 in Spanish Fork, UT. Maren died 17 April 1926 in Grace, Idaho, and was buried in the Spanish Fork Cemetery. She was responsible for much of the genealogy and temple work for the Pedersen-Winkler-Breuner family and kept a Temple Record Book where the information was recorded. Her nephew, Moroni Pedersen Stark kept the book for a number of years. Then it was on file at the Family History Library in Salt Lake City, UT for a number of years until it came in possession of Soren Pedersen Stark's granddaughter Marion Woodward. Children all born in Spanish Fork, UT.

    1.   Wilhelmine Hansen born 6 May 1863. Married George MeLellin 25 October 1882. Died 14 December 1938

    2.   Ephraim Sorensen Hansen born 9 May 1865. Married Mary Caroline Moore 2 January 1888 in Spanish Fork, UT. Died 14 March 1941 in Spanish Fork, UT. Children all born Lake Shore, Spanish Fork, UT.

        1)   Flora Bell Hansen born 25 April 1889. Married Lehi Ruben Davis

        2)   John Moore Hansen born 27 January 1891. Married Edna Petersen.

        3)   Leah Hansen born 4 November 1892. Married John Hutchinson. Died 10 February 1942.

        4)   Ephraim Arch Hansen born 12 February 1895.

        5)   Nephi Wilford Hansen born 7 March 1897. Married Erma Jackson.

        6)   Lindsay Hansen born about 1899

        7)   Alden Hansen born 22 July 1901. Died 22 August 1902

        8)   Mary Caroline Hansen born 17 July 1902. Married Ruben Ray Cook.

        9)   Verna Hansen born 13 August 1904. Married Roy Fulmer.

    3.   Nephi Sorensen Hansen born 13 August 1868. Married Mary Jane Monk. Died 6 June 1955. Children all born in Spanish Fork, UT.

        1)   Charles Nephi Hansen born 8 June 1896. Died 12 June 1896.

        2)   Gertrude May Hansen born 18 September 1897.

        3)   Annie Leywood Hansen born 28 October 1899

        4)   Wilford Roy Hansen born 6 September 1901

        5)   Ross Eugene Hansen born 24 August 1907

4. Eleonora Elizabeth Hansen born 5 May 1870. Married Charles Shomaker. Died 17 January 1945.
5. Albert Peter Hansen born 3 November 1873. Died 24 July 1874.
6. Enok Alfred Hansen born 5 May 1875. Died 26 July 1889.
7. Elias Sorensen Hansen born 31 January 1877. Married Elizabeth Moore 3 April 1903 in Salt Lake City, UT. Children:
    1) Ella Hansen born 1 October 1904 in Cedar City, UT. Married William Lee Beezley 12 June 1931.
8. Daniel Francis Sorensen Hansen born 25 February 1879 in Benjamin, UT. Married Leonora Rees 27 May 1903 in Spanish Fork, UT. Died 8 August 1955. Children:
    1) James Alfred born 31 December 1906. Died 7 March 1907.
    2) Grant Lee Hansen born 23 March 1908. Died 13 June 1908.
    3) Ruth Hansen born 18 September 1915. Died 26 September 1917.
9. ?
10. ?
    4) ? (married in 1964)
    5) Ned Boyd Christensen born 14 May 1941. Married Wilma Ann Reynolds 30 June 1962.
    6) Ila Suzette Christensen born 11 March 1952. Married Jerry Sorensen 2 September 1972
11. Forrest Franklin Christensen born 5 September 1915. Married Virgina Ruesch 3 Decmember 1936 in Salt Lake City, UT. Children:
    1) Reed Forrest Christensen born 5 September 1938 in Moroni, UT. Married Myrla Eliason 21 August 1963.
    2) Arleen Christensen born 2 August 1943 in Moroni, UT. Married Terry Lynn Johansen 9 September 1967.
    3) Jeannine Christensen born 9 May 1950 in Mt. Pleasant, UT. Married Larry Smith Hansen 9 June 1972.

The Mormon Church practiced polygamy so Peter took as his other wife Sena Pedersen who was 17 years younger than he was. They were married in the endowment House in Salt Lake City by D.H. Wills on 28 April 1873. Sena was the sister of Soren Pedersen Stark who baptized Peter and Maria in Denmark. She was also a sister to Maren Pedersen who traveled with Peter and family to America on the ship <u>Monarch of the Sea</u>.

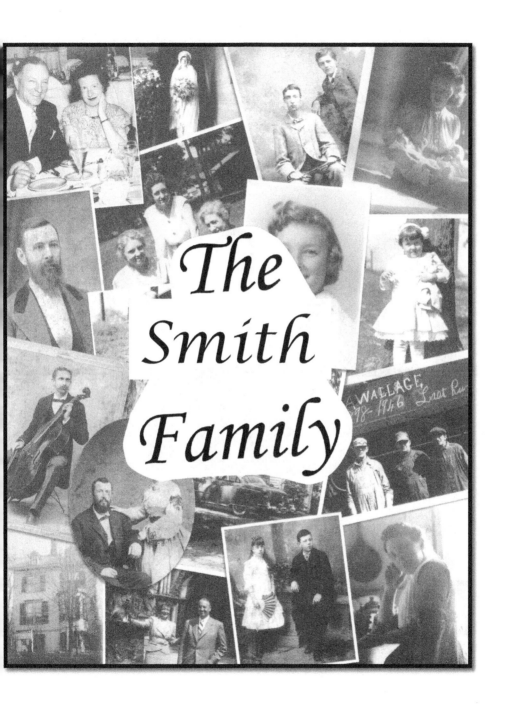

The
Smith
Family

Jose and Hazel Martinez

The Smith/Martinez Family
Alfred Martinez, Norma Jean Smith, Raymond Martinez, Jose & Hazel, Judy Martinez

Marion Cowen Smith

Marion with Harry Smith Harvey
(Marion's Brother)

Taken in Liberty Park

Marion Cowen Smith
Father: Francis Marion Smith
Mother: Dora Smith
Born: 12 December 1912
Place: Hamilton, Ohio, USA
Married: 9 April 1936 (to Hazel Maude Rosenbaum)
Place: Salt Lake City, Utah, USA
Died: 9 February 1940
Place: Salt Lake City, Utah, USA

Letters from Marion Smith to His Wife (Hazel Rosenbaum Smith) and Little Girl (Norma Jean Smith)

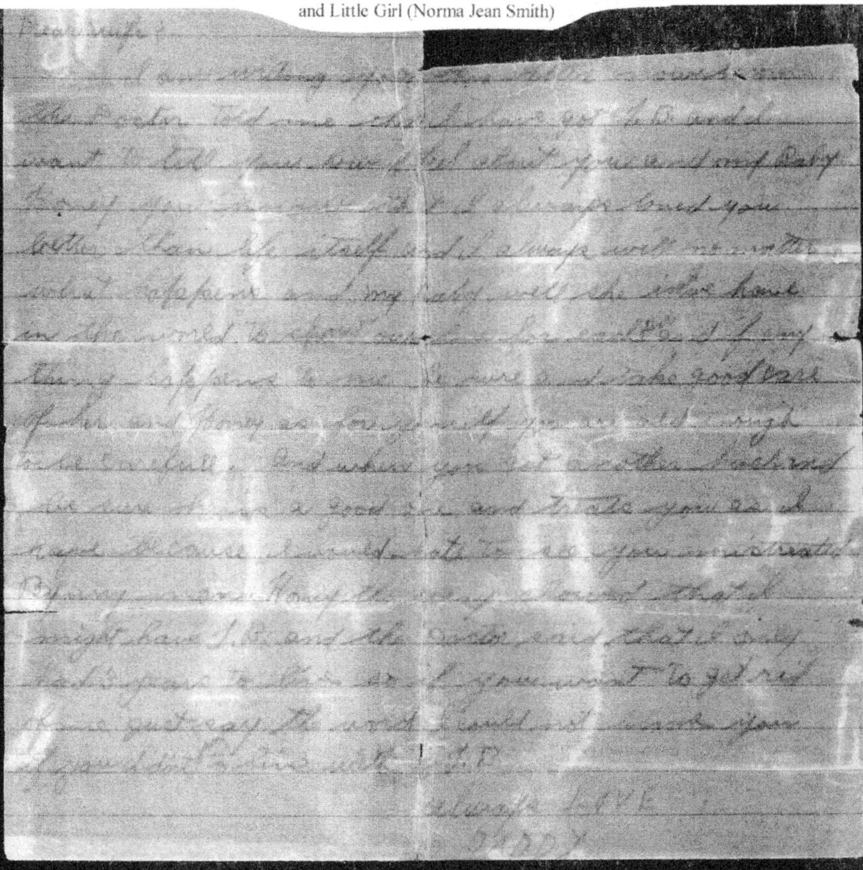

Dear wife:

I am writing you this letter now because the Doctor told me that I have got T.B. and I want to tell you how I feel about you and my Baby. Honey, you know that I always loved you better than life itself and I always will no matter what happens and my Baby, well, she is all we have in the world to show our love for each other and if anything happens to me be sure and take good care of her and Honey, as for yourself, you are old enough to be careful. And when you get another husband be sure he is a good one and treats you as I have because I would hate to see you mistreated by any man. Honey, the x-ray showed that I might have T.B. and the Doctor said that I only had 3 years to live so if you want to get rid of me just say the word. I could not blame you if you didn't want to live with T.B.

Always LOVE
DADDY

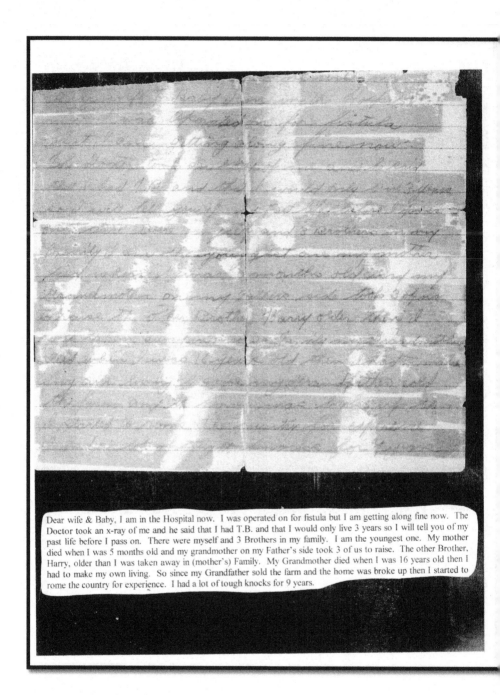

Dear wife & Baby, I am in the Hospital now. I was operated on for fistula but I am getting along fine now. The Doctor took an x-ray of me and he said that I had T.B. and that I would only live 3 years so I will tell you of my past life before I pass on. There were myself and 3 Brothers in my family. I am the youngest one. My mother died when I was 5 months old and my grandmother on my Father's side took 3 of us to raise. The other Brother, Harry, older than I was taken away in (mother's) Family. My Grandmother died when I was 16 years old then I had to make my own living. So since my Grandfather sold the farm and the home was broke up then I started to rome the country for experience. I had a lot of tough knocks for 9 years.

Oral History of Marion Cowen Smith
Interviewee: Norma Jean Smith Lord (Daughter)
Interviewer: Tewie Lord (Interviewed on 10/7/01)

Q: What do you know about your father's birth – where he was born?

A: He was born in Hamilton, Ohio, and his mother died 5 months after he was born. Not to long after that the family was separated. And, I think, the baby (Marion) went with the dad to a farm someplace. He had three brothers. They were all older than he was, he was the baby cause the mother died. And they were all farmed out to different families cause the dad couldn't take care of them. One small fact that we do know is that Marion's grandmother on his mother's (Dora's) side is a full-blooded Cherokee Indian.

Q: Where did Marion go to stay?

A: We don't know.

Q: Do you know how much older the brothers were than Marion?

A: No.

Q: Do you know any of the names of the brothers?

A: Jim and Harry and I can't remember the other brother's name.

Q: Did your mom (Hazel) or anybody talk about his childhood or his early years?

A: I know that my mother and dad went back East to his family when I was just learning to walk. It was on a train and we went back East to visit his family when I was just a toddler. I don't remember any of it. Just from my mother telling me. One thing she did say was that when she got back there they were concerned about her horns. (Because she was Mormon.) Back in those days they thought Mormons had horns.

Q: His childhood was in Ohio – At what point did he leave Ohio?
A: There are four corners there – four states. And we don't know where he moved or how old he was. I know that when he met my mom he was with the CCC (Civilian Conservation Core) and that was during the Depression. They would go around to different states and take the guys around to work. He always said he was a "hoboe" before that.

Q: How old was Marion when his mother died?
A: 5 months.

Q: Didn't Marion go live with his grandmother?
A: Ultimately he went to live with and be raised by his grandmother. In the letter it mentioned that after his mother died he and his older brother went to live with his grandmother. He lived with her until she died. Marion was 16 years old. Grandfather sold the farm and Marion began to roam the countryside for 9 years.

Q: What kind of an education did he get?
A: Not much. He didn't have a high school education. He was probably in school until he left home at 16. Because when he left home he was on his own. If they did go to school back then, sometimes they'd just have them on the farm. And we don't know.

Q: What were his hobbies or interests?
A: I don't know I was 3 years old.

Q: What kind of jobs did he have.
A: Other than the CCC, I don't know what he did for a living.

Q: How about religion?
A: I don't know that he was ever baptized into a religion. He did take the missionary discussions. He was a smoker. When they asked him to be baptized he said, "I think you've got something here. I think this is probably a good religion, but I'm not going to give up my smoking." He refused to be baptized.

260

Q: Did he enjoy traveling or vacations?
A: They didn't have any money. They were dirt poor. They didn't have a car.

Q: During that "9 years of hard knocks" do you know what he did during that time?
A: Just that he traveled all over. I don't know what he did.

Q: What characteristic of you do you attribute to your dad?
A: I look like my mother and my mother never did say anything about me being like my dad.

Q: Did he have any childrearing philosophies or rules?
A: No. He loved me. I remember feeling very good about whoever he was. Because I don't remember him. I remember his legs. I felt very loved by him.

Q: What were some of your earliest childhood memories of your dad?
A: My earliest memory was a chocolate heart. On Valentines Day he brought my mother a big chocolate heart and me a small one and, where ever we lived there was a fireplace with a mantle. He let me see the chocolate heart and he put it up on the fireplace. Because we couldn't have it right them. I just remember his long legs and him putting it on the mantle. I couldn't reach it. If I stood back in the room I could see it. That is my earliest impression.

Q: Your other recollection was when you were hypnotized...
A: At Relief Society Homemaking they had a hypnotist there and I told him my greatest fear was being in front of people. I just go blank when I'm in front of people. So, he took me back to when I was three and he said, "Where are you?" I said, "I'm in a closet." "Why are you in a closet?" I said, "I'm hiding my dog because the dog catcher is here and we don't have any money for the license." I'm talking in a little child's voice. I know I'm doing it, but I have no control. He asked a few questions, "Does your mom love you?" I said, "Yeah." He asked, "Does your daddy love you?" And I just let out a scream saying, "He's dead!" I was just crying. He said, "I want you to bring your daddy into the closet with you." So

in my mind I brought my dad in my closet. He said, "I want you to give him a big hug." I said, "I can't." He said, "Why?" "Cause he's too tall." So he said, "O.K. have your dad kneel down so you that can give him a big hug." So I did that and gave him a hug in my mind. He took me out not to long after that and told me that I would not be afraid and told me to rub my finger together and that would remind me to not be afraid when speaking in public. And for a while I wasn't afraid when I had to conduct.

Q: Did your dad ever join the military?
A: No.

Q: What knowledge do you have about your mom and dad – where did they meet? How they got to know eachother?
A: I don't know where they met. He dated my mom and his brother dated my mother's sister. June Rosenbaum Williams and Harry. Then they were married. My mother had called him "Jim" the whole time they were going together, but when they went to get their license he wrote his real name and it was Marion. That's when she found out that his name really wasn't Jim, was the day they got married. They were married a total of four years. 1936 to 1940.

Q: Did you mom ever describe the difference between them?
A: She said she was really ornery with him. And after he died she felt really bad. He'd want a white shirt ironed and she'd tell him, "I'll have to do it later." She said, "I was kind of ornery with him and I felt kind of bad that I didn't do more for him."

I don't know if I told the story of when I was born. When I was born my dad was so happy to have a little girl, he didn't have a coat, and it was one of the coldest November seconds in years, he didn't have a coat, and I was born at the County Hospital and he was so thrilled that he put on my mother's old fur coat and walked around Salt Lake telling every body that he had had a baby girl and he was so thrilled.

Q: What was daily life like for them?
A: I don't remember. I was only two or three. I played all day. I don't know what they did. I don't remember any arguments or any

262

kind of contention. They must've got along fairly well. With my mother, I think that both her husbands loved her more than she loved them. Not anything against my mother. They loved her with their total selves – both my dads.

Q: What historic events did he have to pass through?
A: The Depression. He was born in 1912 and died in 1940.

Q: Tell me about how he found out he was dying and his death?
A: The only thing I know is that he got tuberculosis and they put him in the hospital (quarantined) because at that time they didn't have all the stuff they have to cure it. While he was in the hospital I got Pneumonia. My mother took me into the County Hospital and I was on the floor below him. I was in the hospital with pneumonia and he was upstairs with TB, but he didn't know I was in the hospital. My mother didn't want to worry him. My mother said that somebody left a window open and he caught pneumonia and that's what killed him not the TB. He died the 9th of February 1940 and his body is buried in the Salt Lake Cemetery. The cemetery was flooded and we don't know where his coffin is.

Q: How long from the time he was diagnosed until he died?
A: I don't know, but it wasn't years it was just a few months.

Q: After that did your mom grieve a lot?
A: I don't remember.

Q: Was there any personal memorabilia that he left behind?
A: No. He had very little. They had nothing.

Q: Are there any other memories of your father that you can remember?
A: Why he named me Norma Jean. My mother told me that when he was back on the farm there was a little girl that he would take horseback riding and he just loved her. When he had me and I was a girl, which he wanted instead of a little boy, he named me Norma Jean after the little girl he used to let ride horses.

263

Jose Emilio Martinez

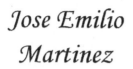

Jose E. Martinez

Jose E. Martinez passed away November 11, 1992 in Salt Lake City, Utah.

Jose was born in Lis Pochecis, New Mexico, a son of Jose and Senarina Martinez. He married Hazel M. Rosenbaum in 1942 in Salt Lake City, Utah.

Jose is survived by his sons, Jose and Raymond Dee Martinez; daughters, Norma Lord and Judy Petramale; sister, Florepa Dupree, 22 grandchildren, 19 great-grandchildren, and many nieces and nephews.

Graveside services will be held Saturday, Nov. 14, 1992 at Mountainview Memorial Estates, 3115 East 7800 So. at 10 a.m.

Norma Jean (daughter) & Joe

Father: Raymond Martinez
Mother: Maya Emada (Indian)
Born: May 3, 1900
Place: Lis Ponchecis, New Mexico
Married: to Gabriel Lujan (1/2 Cherokee)
Married: 31 January 1942 to Hazel Maude Rosenbaum
Place: Salt Lake City, Utah
Married: to Francis
Died: 11 November 1992
Place: Salt Lake City, Utah

Oral History of Jose Emilio Martinez
Interviewee: Norma Jean Smith Lord (Daughter)
Interviewer: Tewie Lord (Interviewed on 10/14/01)

Q: What do you know about your father's birth – where he was born?

A: He was born in Lis Pochecis, New Mexico in April 1899.

Q: What were the family circumstances when Joe was growing up – as a child?

A: He said his dad was very very strict. Extremely strict. He used to do a lot of staying out in the outdoors by himself and run with the deer. He used to chase deer. That's where he learned to run so fast and so good. He would try to catch a deer just running and sometimes he would catch a deer. He left home when he was very young because of the strictness. He was maybe 16. He got a job and married Alfred's mother. As a young child he lived on a farm and his dad was really strict. He didn't ever say much about his mom. Seems like his mother was pure Spanish and he was proud of that – now this is all hearsay.

Q: Did they move when he was young?

A: Not that he ever spoke of.

Q: Education?

A: He didn't have much schooling like in 4th grade. He was still in grade school when he quit school – to work on the farm. Back then they did that.

Q: What were his hobbies and special interests as a child?

A: Running – I don't know of any others.

Q: Did he have and medical or dental problems as a child?

A: No. He was very healthy. They didn't go to the dentist back then. If you had a tooth pulled you pulled it. He was a very healthy man all his life. He had false teeth when he was older.

Q: What kind of jobs did he work in his early years?

A: He said that he had to work hard on the farm and that his dad was real strict.

Q: Do we know anything of his life as a teenager?
A: I think he drank. I think he was probably a wild teenager – just because of the life he led later.

Q: What were the religious activities in his home like?
A: He had nephews that were very active in the Catholic religion. Those are his sister's kids. I'm sure they were Catholic and they probably went to mass. I don't know how active they were.

Q: How many brothers and sister did he have?
A: He had 5 sisters and 1 brother. The sister's names are all Hispanic (May, Flor, Senfirosa & Floripa) and the brother's name was John.

Q: Did he join the military?
A: No.

Q: What vocations and careers did he have as an adult?
A: His first job, when he moved from New Mexico, was working in the mines in Price, UT. Back then the place where the trains ran was very narrow. One time as he was working in one of those tunnels a train caught him and dragged him many feet until he fell into a hole that just happened to be there. It saved his life, but he did end up with a broken shoulder that kept him out of work for a while. Then he moved up to the Salt Lake Valley and took a job at Kennecott. The next job was working in the Cement Plant. He worked for the Utah Portland Cement Company most of his life. He retired from there. I think he worked there for 40 years. It was an o.k. Retirement – 700 a month. He moved from one division to another. There weren't promotions – just changes. His last job was a specialized job. He and another guy were the only ones who did it. He had to make sure that the "clinkers" were the right temperature and stayed the right temperature for the cement. They couldn't be more or less than 2 or 3 degrees difference. He had to make sure everything stayed the same. He also filled up bags on the machine. He did the "clinkers" for a lot of years. I don't know if they're called "clinkers" but that's what he called them.

Q: What were the effects of his job on the family?
A: We knew that he was a good hard worker. He was very reliable. He never missed. Well or sick he went to work. He was very responsible. He worked 8 to 5. He had a regular job. He didn't work shift work. My mom would pack him a lunch everyday. One of the fun things for us kids was when he would bring his lunch home. He'd always save half a sandwich or some other treat. We rotated among the kids and each day it was one of our turns to get his lunch. A bologna sandwich that had sat there all day long tasted wonderful at night. We did take turns as my

house, because if we didn't we'd have probably fought about it. He walked to work. It was about 2 blocks away.

Q: Was he a member of a union?
A: Yes. The Cement Workers Union?

Q: Did he have any associates or friends from work?
A: He had his drinking buddies he went over to Kelley's with. Other than that he really didn't do that much. My mother's two sisters and their husbands and my dad would do things together more than his work/drinking buddies. Donna's husband was named Larry and June's husband was named Evan. They were younger. They would build stuff like a shed. They might of drank but it was a beer here and there. They liked to talk.

Q: Marriage? How many times and who to?
A: First he was married to Gabriel Lujan. She was 8 years older than Joe and had been married previously and had two children – Mary and Phillip. Phillip was 12 years older than Alfred and was in some way mentally handicap. Gabriel divorced her first husband and married Joe. Gabriel and Joe had Alfred together and when Alfred was 9 his mother died of pneumonia. His second wife was Hazel Maude Rosenbaum. At the time when Joe's wife had died Marion Smith died (Hazel's first husband). He lived next door to her when my dad had died and even when my dad was alive he would make sure that she was taken care of – if she had any needs. He'd take care of then. It just kind of evolved. He helped her a lot with whatever needed to be done. He's quite a bit older than her (maybe 10 or more). He was good to her. They were married for 19 years.

Q: How was the family financed?
A: My dad's paychecks. That was the sole income.

Q: Characteristics of children? (See Oral interview of Hazel Maude Rosenbaum)

Q: House lived in – close friends and family? (See Oral interview of Hazel Maude Rosenbaum)

Q: What were his child-rearing philosophies?
A: You minded and if you didn't you got spanked or beat. Not with us girls. He was very strict. He was very good with us girls. He'd just yell at us and we'd cry. So he never had to raise a hand with us. He was very physical with my brothers. He said it and his word was law. I don't know what he beat them with. I'm sure it was a switch. I just remember

267

the one time with the lunchbox (See Oral interview of Hazel Maude Rosenbaum). The man was in charge.

Q: Daily routine of his life?
A: Get up in the morning, have breakfast and be gone before we even got up. My mother would pack his lunch pail. He'd go to work and come home. He was a worker. Even when he was home he was always fixing things around the house. As we moved to different houses on the street, he would build a back porch and a coal bin, if there wasn't a good coal bin. He built back porches on every house we moved into, I think. He was not a lazy man. He worked hard. He had a lot of nervous energy. He had to move all the time. I don't remember him watching TV that much – not until he got older.

Q: Adult medical expenses?
A: None. He was healthy as a horse. He was probably about 80 when he started having failing health. And it really wasn't that bad. It was just age. He didn't have any high blood pressure. There was nothing wrong with my dad except he had "hardening of the arteries". Other than that he was totally healthy and he was 93. He just didn't want to live. He starved himself to death. He wouldn't eat.

Q: Religious participation when he was an adult?
A: He wasn't active in any church. He would go – like when I was confirmed. He'd go to those kinds of things. He'd support the family in those kinds of things. He was very good. Even when I joined the Church he was very supportive. He'd go to mass once a year or so and then I don't know how he was ever baptized in the Mormon Church – I didn't even know he was, but at one time, somehow, he was baptized in the Mormon Church. We didn't know about it. And I don't know if it's true or not. He said he was baptized. He never talked about it. Just one time out of the blue he said, "Well, I was baptized." This was when he lived on Goshen Street. The landlord next door probably introduced him to the church. My dad told us and my dad embellished the true. He told you what you wanted to hear a great deal of the time. When he was in the rest home we know he went to the weekly LDS service. When he died he had a Catholic service. Because Alfred wanted to give him a Catholic service. He was his dad not mine.

Q: What were his hobbies and interests?
A: Boxing. He loved boxing. I think he might have boxed as a young man, but as he got older he loved to listen to boxing on the radio. He would be so into it – you know how somebody watches television and you can't get through to them? – my dad would do that with boxing on the radio. He be sitting by that radio jabbing and cutting. It was fun to watch him

listen to the boxing. His favorite boxer was Joe Lewis. He also loved to go fishing. He was an avid fisherman. He had all kinds of lures. He would fish locally and sometimes take Alfred with him. That was probably his only vacation time he had in his working life. He was a worker and fixed things a lot. He built my first hope chest. It was just a box. I loved it. He built my sister one. We thought it was wonderful. I put embroidered dishtowels, runners – all the things you want to use someday when you get married. I had it here for years and years. It was the Halloween costume box. Then I finally gave it to Val and we painted it orange.

Q: Did he read at all?
A: He didn't read very well.

Q: What were his best abilities?
A: He was a good worker and he was willing to help people too. If somebody on the block needed something, he was right there to help them. He was real good to help anybody who needed help. If he could help out with finances he would. That was not something he did very often. I remember once or twice buying food for my Aunt June. She went to work at Welfare Square because my uncle hurt his back. Aunt June got their food at Welfare Square, but I remember dad giving June money for food. He didn't have a whole lot of money. If he'd of had more he would've been more generous. He was very generous with his time.

Q: What were his preferences for food? Dislikes?
A: Mexican food. Tortillas. He loved meat. He loved lamb. He would have meat with every meal. He cooked sometimes. He would cut up meat and put it with peas – vegetables, but he would have meat constantly. I don't think he ever went a day in his life without meat. Sometimes he'd have it two times a day. He hates pasta. When he went in the old folks home they feed them a lot of pasta because it's cheap and they don't have any teeth. That's when they called me in and said that I couldn't give him any more candy because he wasn't eating. I would take him a pound of hard candy each week. I told the dietician, "It's not the candy, he doesn't like pasta. He hates pasta." They didn't have a lot of meat and he loved meat and they didn't have a lot of meat there. I don't think they ever fixed it.

Q: What were his preferences for music?
A: Spanish music. He liked Spanish music all through his life. He'd listen to the Spanish station even when he got older.

Q: What were his preferences on the TV?

A: I don't remember him watching a lot of TV. Matter of fact we didn't even get our TV until I was in high school, so we weren't in the habit of watching TV. He watched it a lot less than my mother did. When he got older he liked to watch football and sports. He would turn the TV off and say there was nothing good on.

Q: Traveling?

A: He would go to New Mexico to see relatives when they'd have weddings or something and that was about it. He might have went once a year or so with Alfred -- to see his nephews. He had some nephews he really liked. His sisters were down there.

Q: When did your dad retired?

A: As soon as he could (he was 62, I think). What happened is, I guess somebody else took over the plant, and there was a guy there that was supposed to retire and he fell asleep when he was watching the clinkers and somehow he lost his pension. It scared my dad. They wanted him to stay longer and he wouldn't. He said, "I know what they're trying to do." He was very suspicious of people. He retired whenever 40 years were up. After he retired I would take him shopping for his groceries and wash his clothes and pay his bills. That was when he was about 80. He probably worked in his yard between when he retired and when he had to go to the rest home. He also remarried the landlord from Green Street apartments. He lived with her for two years maybe and got a divorce. Her name was Francis. I guess Francis said that, "my mother was always there." My mother always came between them. But in later years, she got ill and they weren't married, but he had her come and live and with him and he took care of her. She died in his care. She would save papers. She'd save them and put them in drawers and my dad would get so upset. He was in his late 70's when he took care of her.

Q: Changes throughout lifetime?

A: Same as my mom. We got a car. My uncles taught him to drive. We were the last ones to get a car out of June and Donna and my mom. Donna always seemed to be just a little ahead of everybody with finances. She only had one child. They got a car first, they got a TV first, and she was the one who gave me the fifty dollars so I could join Pep Club. That was a lot of money back then.

Q: What would you say was his greatest sorrow?

A: I think when he lost my mother. I don't think anyone realized how much he loved her. She was his life. He really loved her. I didn't see a lot of affection. He was very possessive, very jealous of her. I think he liked keeping her home.

Q: What would you say was his greatest joy?
A: My mother and his step-daughter (me). For being a step dad I probably was his favorite. I'm sure my brothers and sisters would say that too.

Q: If he could what council do you think he'd give to this generation?
A: "Work hard." He really believed in working hard and giving it your best.

Q: Did he have superstitions?
A: A lot of them. I can't remember any right now, but he had a lot of them.

Q: Did he have any nicknames?
A: "Martini." My aunts, uncles and mother called him "Martini". Everyone on the street called him Martini, too.

Q: When did he die and how did he die?
A: A year before he died he went on a "no-eating" kick. We (Alfred and I) would take turns and go down and feed him. I would usually do mine at noon and he would do his at night. That would last a couple of weeks and then he was o.k. and came back. But he said he was tired of living. But the next year he did it again, and this time he wouldn't take anything. He was tired he wanted to go. He refused to eat and wasted away in about 3 or 4 weeks. He put no heroics on being sick. They just let him go. We knew he was dying because we went there everyday. I think my brother called me. I wasn't there when he died. He had a Catholic funeral and the Priest spoke. We didn't say anything at the funeral. He's buried at Wasatch Memorial on Bengal Boulevard (up by Val).

Q: What else do you want to say about Joe?
A: I could get almost anything I wanted out of Joe -- if I went about it the right way. He had a hard time telling me, "No." He was real good to me. I probably wouldn't have been treated any better by my real father. He was very very generous with me. I think he really loved me. I was very fortunate to have a step-dad and be a good to me as he was.

271

Hazel Maude Rosenbaum

Norma Jean (daughter) & Hazel

Father: Lucious Snow Rosenbaum
Mother: Cecelia Hazel Marcroft
Born: 6 September 1917
Place: Salt Lake City, Utah, USA
Married: 9 April 1936 (to Hazel Maude Rosenbaum)
Place: Salt Lake City, Utah, USA
Married: 31 January 1942 (to Jose Emilio Martinez)
Place: Salt Lake City, Utah, USA
Died: 25 November 1961
Place: Salt Lake City, Utah, USA

Oral History of Hazel Maude Rosenbaum
Interviewee: Norma Jean Smith Lord (Daughter)
Interviewer: Tewie Lord (Interviewed on 10/7/01)

Q: What were the family circumstances when your mother was born? When was she born? Where was she born?

A: She was born in Salt Lake on 6 September 1917. She was the third from the youngest of eight kids. Her mother died when she was twelve years old. The older sister, Marie, raised the kids. The dad was there, but he was a dad, and he was working and didn't have a lot of time to spend with the kids. My mother's memories of her mother were that they were apparently active in church when the mother was alive because they had a parlor, which they never went into, except on Sunday. They would go up in the parlor on Sunday and they had a cedar chest that had clothes in it. That was their Sunday clothes. They would take them out and wear them and when they came home they would take them off and put them back in the cedar chest. As the kids got bigger and would outgrow an outfit they would take the next oldest child's Sunday clothes. They each had one Sunday outfit. That's all I remember about her (early) life except that they were real poor and pretty much raised by each other.

Q: Where did they live and did they move during her early childhood?

A: They lived in Salt Lake City. I don't know that they owned a home, but I think they pretty much stayed in the same house. Downtown Salt Lake some place.

Q: Do you have any memories of your mother's preschool years.

A: I know that she went up to Idaho. They had some relatives in Idaho I don't know if they owned a store or what, but it seemed like they were a little better off. It was her grandmother, Susan Walkey Marcroft. They used to go up there to her house and she loved going up there. There was plenty of food. When they were home she probably stayed home and I think her mother worked a little bit, even back then.

Q: Education?

A: She did not finish high school. I don't know why.

Q: What were her hobbies or interests as a child?

A: She played. They didn't have any money for anything. They didn't have any supervision.

Q: Did she have any medical problems as a child?

A: She got scarlet fever when she was twelve and it affected her heart. She had a rheumatic heart. Years later when she got pregnant with my little sister (Judy) they told her that she shouldn't have any more kids. So when she got pregnant with Raymond she didn't go to the doctor until she was five or six months along, because she thought they would abort the baby. Once she had Raymond she went downhill after that. Her heart just got worse and worse. Matter of fact the doctor that she was going to when she had Ray said to my stepfather, "The only thing that is keeping her alive is her determination and shear will power to live. Every time I see her I think, 'I wonder if I'm going to see her next week?'" But she said to the doctor, "I am going to live until my children are raised." And she did because of shear will power. Matter of fact they owed that doctor so much money at the time and the doctor waived it. Told my dad, "Forget it." Also, at that time they had a heart specialist in New York that might have been able to do something for her, but the chances of her pulling through it weren't big enough to take the risk. So they didn't do it. She was tired a lot and never really healthy. She died in 1961 when I was twenty-five and Raymond was nineteen. So all of her kids were raised when she died.

Q: What kinds of fads were prevalent during her childhood?
A: They went to Saturday movies. They had a kid's movie on Saturday. It was cheap. She tells the story of one time being in the Saturday movie and her sister Marie had taken a loaf of bread for their treat. During the movie one of the actors or actresses on screen said, "I just need a piece of bread – anything..." because she was starving, and my Aunt Marie jumped up and said, "Here I've got some bread!" She remembers being embarrassed because my Aunt Marie had gotten so engrossed in the movie that she was going to offer bread to the actor or actress.

Q: Who were her favorite siblings?
A: June and Donna were her good buddies. They did everything together. They were her sisters. They were very very close. When they got married they all moved on the same block and raised their kids together, borrowed stuff from each other. None of them had a whole lot of money. Donna probably had more that either one of them. They were very close. They were best friends. We lived in several houses on the same street. My Aunt June, Aunt Donna and my mom moved around three or four times on the same street.

Q: Did she have any pranks done to her or humorous experiences?
A: Not that she ever told. She wasn't a real talker. She was kind of quiet, but very stubborn. She didn't get stubborn very often, but when she thought she was right she would defend it like a bulldog.

Q: Did she ever go to work outside the home?
A: Not that I can remember. And that was one of the things that I liked. When I came home from school, my mother was always there – always. She didn't have any skills and back then women didn't work.

Q: As a teenager did she go to any dances, etc.?
A: She never talked about that at all.

Q: What kind of music did she like?
A: We had an old graphanola that you wound. We had records. I remember "Oh, Johnny. Oh, Johnny. Heavens above" -- it was the music of the time.

Q: What kind of movies did she like?
A: I don't think my mother went to movies. I don't remember my mom and dad ever going to movies.

Q: Vacations and travel?
A: She never went on vacations. I never went on vacations until I married Ralph.

Q: Was there something different that was done during the summer?
A: Our neighbor had a truck. We had a really interesting street. There were no fences in the backyards. It was just one big backyard. This guy who had a truck would load us into the truck standing up, it had sides, and we would go to the canyon. He'd take as many in the neighborhood that he could in the truck and we'd go up the canyon. We'd take some food and hike and picnic. We did that every so often just for the day.

Q: Tell me about your mom's religious upbringing?
A: I think she was brought up in the LDS church until the mother died. Then as the father took over they just kind of drifted away. She didn't have any religious affiliation until I was a teenager and her and my Aunt June and Aunt Donna used to go to Sacrament occasionally. But it was real foreign to them and that was about it. But my mother believed in God. She knew that He answered prayers. There was no formal prayer in the house. I think there was a Bible in my house but we would never open it. But, I know that my mother believed in God and knew that He would answer prayers cause she would tell me that.

Q: How did you come to be Catholic at some point in your life?
A: When I was eight my mother and dad gave each one of us a choice to become whatever we wanted, because my dad was a Catholic and my mother was baptized Mormon. When we were eight we were able to choose the religion we wanted. I had little Catholic friends. They would pick us up in the Catechisms van and I was in love with the Father. So I was baptized with my friend, Lillian Morano, she was my same age. I went every week to catechism and mass. (Would you come home and talk to your mom about what you were learning each week?) I'm sure I did, but she was not that interested. My mother didn't talk to us a lot, as far as asking us what we were doing.

275

Q: Did she have any religious experiences?

A: When she was sick she'd have the Elders come many times to the hospital many times and give her a blessing and she'd recover and she felt it was because of the blessing. I think she believed in the power of the Priesthood, but she was never really verbal.

Q: What was her association with her siblings like?

A: Other than June and Donna – we didn't see them really often, usually on Christmas Day, they were better off than these three, they had cars and they would come down on Christmas Day and bring the cousins and visit for a few hours. It was never a planned thing. My Uncle Claude would come down for maybe an hour. Then my Aunt Faye and Uncle Roy would come down for an hour and I always thought my Aunt Faye was a lady because she carried a purse. You had to be a lady if you carried a purse. I remember she had one brother, Morris, who was very well off, as far as we were concerned because we were so terribly poor. She had another brother named Roy who was a plumber. Plumbers made good money. But none of them were active in church except Marie. She wasn't active when she was younger but she got active early in her life. She had a sister named Cora who when my mom married my step-dad Cora said, "If you marry him (because he was a Mexican) I will never speak to you again." And she didn't. They lived out on Redwood Road and they owned a house (anybody who had a house we thought was rich, cause we rented all our lives). She never spoke to my mother again. But when she died, she was in a coma, and when she woke up from the coma and said to her children, "Please bury me next to Hazel." And she had not spoken to her for who knows how many years. I think that was her way of asking for forgiveness.

Q: When did you see your grandfather, Lucious?

A: He died when we were pretty young too. But he would come down, he was always dressed in a suit and looked very clean and, to me, he was tall. One of the instances my mother recalls with her dad was ... we didn't have telephones back then. One night she was awakened in the middle of the night. My grandpa was sitting on a hope chest in her bedroom. He was sitting on it and smiling at her. She said, "Dad what are you doing here?" He just smiled at her and he got up and left and went in the front room. So she got out of bed and followed him and he wasn't there. The next morning she was telling either June or Donna about her dream and they thought that was strange. About two or three hours later some one came by, because no one had a phone, to tell them that he had died the night before. He was just smiling. She said, "I don't know if it was just to let me know he was happy." He didn't say anything, just smiled. Other than that we only saw him when he would come by. Once every five or six months. He would just stop by and visit. He had three daughters right there on the street.

Q: What were your mother's child rearing philosophies?

A: (laughs) If you spank them hard enough they'll do it right. It was physical. She believed in spanking and punishing and she did. I don't know about her home growing up.

Q: Were there any other difficulties that your mother had to pass through as a child? (Aside from her mother dying young)

A: Financial difficulties. Sometimes they didn't have enough food when they were little. That's why a loaf of bread was a real treat to take to the movies. It was French bread.

Q: What happened to your mom during the time between when Marion died and she married Jose?

A: I don't know how she lived financially – I have no idea. But I know that when she married my dad (Jose) she had another man's baby. My sister Judy is another man's baby. She didn't know that until she got a little bit bigger and that was a real traumatic point in her life. On her birth certificate she has the name "Smith". My dad raised her and married my mom right after she had Judy. They were next-door neighbors and his wife died and my dad died. Joe and my dad were friends before he died. And he said to Joe when he was visiting one day, "Joe, when I die will you please see that my wife is taken care of?" And Joe said, "I will." And he did. This was when he was in the hospital. Joe had a son from his first marriage. When we were kids she (Judy) would always make me aware that it wasn't my dad that it was hers. Little did she know.

Q: What was their relationship like?

A: He was very macho, very "in-charge". He would hang up his clothes when they were dirty and my mom would have to find them in the closet to make sure they were clean. He was in charge. He was the boss. He ran all the finances. We had a charge account at a little grocery store two blocks away. In those days you could charge your groceries and then on payday we would pay it and then you'd have to start over charging cause we didn't have any money. My mother never had any money that I remember, ever. My dad took care of all the money. But, my dad really loved my mother. My mother said to me one time, "Joe will never take the place of your dad. I don't want to be buried next to Joe." I think she was young when my dad (Marion) died so she had this image of it being wonderful. Joe was the boss and she would cow down to him until she thought she was on the right track. Then neither hell nor high water would change her mind. No, I don't remember a lot of affection. I could tell that he loved her and to her it was a marriage of convenience.

On payday Joe would go to this bar across the street from us – it was a café and a bar. He would go over there with his friends and drink beer. I don't know how many drinks he'd have but he'd come home feeling pretty good so he must've had a few drinks. But my mother had said to him, "You've got to stop drinking cause it cost too much and we just can't afford it. I don't want to do

277

this anymore." Of course he said, "I earn the money, I'll spend it how I want." My mother said, "If you got over to Kelley's one more time I'm leaving you." For my mother to take a stand like that was ridiculous. She had nowhere to go and I think he knew it. So, he went over there after work and started drinking and my mother packed me and my brother and sister and took our hands and started walking down the street. My brother Alfred asked, "Where are you going?" She said, "We're leaving. I told you dad." He said, "Take me with you." She said, "You know, I can't Alfred. You're not mine. You belong to Joe." I think Alfred ran over to Kelley's and told my dad. For the first time in my whole life I saw my dad humble. Well, first he wasn't humble. He came when we were only about a block away from home and said, "What do you think your doing?" My mother said, "I told you, Joe, if you left to drink again I was leaving you." He still was a little bit rebellious, but then all of a sudden he knew she meant it. He got so humble. For my dad to get humble was amazing. He just said to my mother, "Don't leave." He was almost in tears. He said, "Don't leave. Don't leave me. I will never do it again." And he never did. He would buy some beers and put them in the fridge, but he would never go to Kelley's and drink on payday. He drank beer. He'd have beer in the fridge. I just remember thinking, "I didn't know my mother could do that." That she could have that much power over him.

Q: How were the family finances?
A: We were poor. But on Easter we would all get new outfits, no matter what. We got new outfits, hats, gloves, everything – every Easter. We ate a lot of fried potatoes, a lot of beans, lot of tortillas – whatever was cheap. A lot of my dad's money went to doctor's bills.

Q: What was seen as a luxury?
A: Some paydays we would go to a place called "Bill's Hamburgers" (on like 17th South and State). We got 10 hamburgers for a dollar. We never bought French fries, but we would go there for a treat in the car. We had to be bigger when we had the car. It had to have been Junior High age or High School. My dad was good to buy me things that I really wanted. One time I wanted a "Jensen's sweater" (it was a fad, they were just sweaters with a brand name that were very expensive) I asked my dad if I could have one. My dad was really good to me – he really was. I didn't ask him very much for anything. He said, "Sure." So he took me to Wolf's Department Store to get this sweater. I don't remember the price but he almost fell off his chair. But he got it for me. I remember that and thought, "You know he really couldn't afford that and it wasn't fair, but I really wanted it." He was good to me that way.

Q: What were the different characteristics of the siblings – talents, hobbies?
A: My dad was really mean to the boys. I remember him beating them with a lunch box – my older brother; I don't know what he had done. We all slept in the same bedroom – the four of us. The girls in one bed and the boys in the other bed. My dad had a terrible temper. But he never struck me ever. He never struck any of the girls. He did the boys.

278

My older brother joined the service when he was 17. He loved girls. I guess he was pretty normal. Alfred liked to work on cars. He lost his ring finger on his left hand in a fan belt when he was young. He did a little smoking and drinking even when he was young. Did a little dancing. He was pretty mild mannered actually, except when he would tend us. When he would tend us and he would be mean to us. I remember being under the kitchen table, which was against the wall (me and Judy were both under there), and he would get a broom and hit us with it because we wouldn't do something he wanted. It was not a loving family. I think that that's one of the reasons why having my family like each other is so important, because I didn't have that.

I was a horror. I fought with everybody. I was angry all the time and I don't know why. I remember at school I would get in fights over hopscotch. I was not real big when I was little. I remember one time I was saving a hopscotch and a bigger kid had pushed me off of it and I had a fight with him -- without even hesitating. I didn't start fights, but if I was in the right, then you better watch out because I had no fear – no fear. Scares me now to think about some of the things I did because I had no fear. My sister would take my clothes and wear them and hang them up wrinkled. I didn't like that. I didn't give my mom a lot of trouble, except for fighting – even with people on the street. I went to the Principal's office a few times. One time there was this black kid, a real heavy boy, who wouldn't let us pass his house. He would chase us and hit us. I said to my friends, there were three of us, "Let's go past his house, and if he comes after us all three of us will jump him." We had to walk an additional block to avoid his house. "O.K., we will." So we get there, guess who jumped him … me. He beat the tar out of me. He beat me so bad I had spots in my hair where he had pulled my hair out. I had scratched his black head. I scratched his face and arms so that there was no skin – it was white. It was a terrible fight. But, you know what, he let us go past his house after that, even when he beat the tar out of me. He won. There was no doubt about that. But he did let us go past. But those other two friends they just watched and took me home. I think my mother dreaded when it was time for me to come home from school, because she never knew what shape I would come home in. I didn't do it all the time, but when I did it was really pretty bad. I was very feisty. Matter of fact some of the kids I grew up with can't believe I'm who I am today – how I turned out as an adult. Once I got into high school, actually junior high, I changed. My hobbies as a young girl were: I bought some knitting needles, I wanted to learn how to knit. I had money for knitting needles but I didn't have any for yarn. Somebody gave me a piece of yarn that had been knitted and so I undid it and would knit and undo that white piece of yarn until I learned how to knit. When I got into junior high I wanted to learn how to sew. I didn't have a sewing machine but my Aunt Donna did. With my some of my baby-sitting money I bought the sewing machine from her for ten dollar and sewed my own clothes. I did have one year of sewing in school, but nobody in my family sewed, no one knew how, so I did that and I learned to embroider. My mother taught me how to embroider pillowcases. I did the sewing just for myself.

My sister was strong-willed and her and I did fight a lot – physical fights. She didn't have any hobbies. My sister was ornery. She loved boys. She was real boy-crazy. She was married when she was fourteen. She was pregnant and had a baby when she was young. There was a lot of anger in her too. We both had a lot of anger.

My little brother was much like my dad – he was very macho. He liked to play the guitar.

Q: What was your daily routine like?

A: We couldn't have school lunch when I was a kid. Unless your mom worked or your mother had to go to the doctor or there was a reason to stay at the school to have lunch, otherwise you had to go home. So, we went home for lunch, and we were at the very far boundaries of our school. We had to run home, eat our bowl of soup or sandwich, and run back in order to get there in time. In the winter, one of the things I always wanted were those brown stockings that the kids wore that they all hated. I wanted a pair of those so bad. I just wanted my legs to be warm. You run home for lunch and it's cold. We lived four blocks from school. Some of those kids would take off their stocking when they got to school, and I'd think, "I can't believe you. I'd give anything for a pair of those stockings." My mother's routine was, she fed us breakfast, she had to have lunch when we came home and then she cooked dinner at night. I don't know what she did during the day. She didn't have a car. She didn't have any money. She had her two sisters and I think that kept her sanity.

Q: What were your family traditions for birthdays?

A: I had one birthday in my life. That was when I was dating Ralph. We invited my aunt's and uncle's (June and Donna and their husbands) and my mother and dad and Ralph. That was my first birthday. I was 18. It was the only birthday party I ever had. It was just a dinner. My mom did give me a card for my birthday. I'm sure she made a cake and gave me a present, but I don't remember.

Q: What are your memories of Christmas?

A: Christmas' were very sparing. My little sister didn't like dolls. I loved dolls. When I was twelve my mother said I was too big for dolls. But my little sister got a doll – guess who played with it? We would get things like bath powder. I have a picture of me sitting there and my Christmas sits on my lap, just a few things. We didn't have exaggerated Christmas'.

Q: What are your memories of Halloween?

A: We went out "trick-or-treating". We had to find our own costumes in the "rag bag". We had this old bag of old clothes. For Halloween we would make make-shift costumes from the clothes in the bag. We only went on our street. When I got to be bigger, as a teenager, I would go to Halloween parties off my street. But, as a little kid we would just stay on the street and "trick-or-treat".

Q: What kind of medical expenses did your mother have?

A: Horrendous medical expenses. Back then they were paying 100 dollars a month for her pills. I think if my mother hadn't of been ill my folks would've been able to buy a house. They would've had a little money. After my mother died my dad said, "I don't regret one penny that I spent on her to keep her alive." My mother used to say, "I think I built that wing of Holy Cross." She was in and out of the hospital constantly. They called us to her bedside at least three times to tell us she just had a few hours, but she would revive. Afterwards she would say, "I'm staying alive until my kids are raised." I remember her having a stroke when I wasn't very big. That was when doctor's came to your house. She had no side effects from it. I remember the doctor coming to the house. They had horrendous medical bills.

Q: What were your mom's hobbies, interest, reading habits, etc. as an adult?

A: She would read "True Confessions". It was a "rag". They were stories about love affairs. I used to sneak them once in a while. She loved birds and she loved flowers. She could make a flower live forever. She loved birds – all of her birds just thrived. She kept canaries. My mother did crossword puzzles all the time. She was good at it. There was no place for a garden. We had a little patch of grass in the front yard and the back yard was gravel. There was an alley in between our house and the next house. We had no "yard". The little patch of grass you didn't get on. It was just to look at.

Q: What were her best abilities?

A: She was a good listener. I just loved her. I don't know what it was about her. Kept a clean house. She took care of the family. She did the washing – she had a ringer-washer – and that was all day long job. She did canning. We had an icebox. It was out on the back porch. An icebox has ice on the top and you put your food on the bottom. When the ice melts it goes down into a tray on the bottom and you have to empty it. The iceman would come by every three days. You would buy ice from him and he'd take it in and put it in your icebox. We would go out and steal any chips of ice and put them on newspaper while he was putting the ice in the icebox. That was a real treat. We didn't have milk as kids. We got milk on payday. In the morning when we would have mush, we would put half canned cream and half water and that would be our milk. It was so neat when we finally got a fridge. My mother didn't have a furnace. We had a coal stove in the front room. Our house had a front room, a bedroom, a bedroom and a kitchen. And the bathroom was off from the kitchen. There was no central heat. We had a coal stove in the front room and we had a coal stove in the kitchen. My brother would have to make sure he had wood in there and coal, to start the fire in the morning. The girls would get dressed in the kitchen and the boys would get dressed in the front room. My mom would be fixing breakfast in the kitchen. Our bedrooms were not all that warm because they were in between where the heat was. So we couldn't get dressed in our rooms cause it was so cold. Then we finally did get a furnace. We moved to five different houses on the street. It would be the same lay out in the house but it was a little bit bigger. Donna and June did the same thing. Donna finally bought a house. We never

281

did, I'm sure it was because my dad spent so much money on medical bills for my mom.

Q: What were her preferences for food or dislikes?

A: I don't know that she had any dislikes. She'd eat about anything. A lot of onions, fried potatoes (4 or 5 times a week), beans. I don't think she had a lot of money to say, "This is my preference – I'll cook this." I think she cooked because she had to feed the family.

Q: Did you listen to the radio?

A: All the time. Back then there wasn't much of a choice. It was music mostly. There were soap opera's, "Helen & Trent", "As the World Turns", etc. On Saturday, if we got our work done, we'd listen to "The Squeaking Door" "The Lone Ranger". We would sit in the front room, just like you'd sit in front of the TV, and listen to all these kids stories. My mother listened to all the soaps that came on. "Amos & Andy" I think was one of her favorites.

Q: Would you describe her as an emotional person?

A: I think she was emotional but didn't share it. If you were having problems you didn't tell anybody. She didn't want to share with us because she was the adult and these were her problems. She didn't want to make us worry. I really think that was part of my mother's personality. You don't make your kids worry. Let them be kids.

Q: What kind of changes did she see throughout her lifetime? Technology? Fashion?

A: The wearing of pants. She wore housedresses. I hardly remember my mother wearing pants. I'm sure she did near the end, but I don't remember much. She usually wore housedresses. We got our first telephone when I was in junior high. The reason we got it was because of my mother's illness. Telephones weren't readily available. You have to get on a waiting list. We were on a party line. The doctor had to sign a paper and take it to the telephone company that required my mom to have a telephone in case she needed to call for an emergency. We got our TV when I was in junior high. That was a thrill. The lady down the street had ten kids. She had a boy that came and lived with them and he bought them a television. On Friday nights there was a scary show on, and each one of their kids could invite someone over to watch this scary show. We were sitting in their front room. There was no room to go to sleep or even fall over with ten kids and ten guest and this little seven inch television. We thought that was heaven. I always wanted Kathy to invite me. They could only invite one. She'd invite me most of the time, but sometimes when she was mad at me she'd invite Sandra. That was so neat. When we got our own television, man, we were really coming up in the world. I think my mom watched game shows – she was interested in that.

Q: What were some of the medical remedies your mother taught you?

A: We had mustard plasters when we were sick. We had to take cod liver oil. It was healthy, good for you – I don't know why we got it. We didn't have to have

282

it everyday. My brother would've drunk the whole bottle. I could hardly stand to smell it. It was good for your health. Mustard plaster you would put on your chest when you were sick (congestion). Also, Vick's mentholated rub – you'd put a pad on your chest and you couldn't hardly breath. I didn't go to a doctor until I was in high school, except for when I was a baby with pneumonia. We didn't go to the dentist cause we couldn't afford it. When I was ten I had a tooth that was rotten and my dad gave me money to take the bus up to the police station to get my tooth fixed – it was free. I remember going up there to get that tooth pulled and afterwards having a bloody mouth coming home on the bus. We had street fountains back then, and I would spit the blood back into the bowl. I was a sight with Kleenexes in my mouth that were full of blood, taking the bus home and I'm only ten years old. I don't think I went to the dentist again until after I married Ralph. That's were we went to get our shots – at the police station.

Q: What would you say was your mom's greatest sorrow in her life?
A: I loosing my dad (Marion) and feeling like she wasn't as good to him as she could have been. She talked about that a lot.

Q: What would you say was her greatest joy?
A: Being able to live long enough to see all her children grown.

Q: Did she have any major turning points in her live?
A: The older she got the more "in-charge" she got. She didn't cow down to my dad anymore. I remember one time, he would come home drunk and yell at my mom and make her cry. One time he made her cry and he went to bed in a drunken stupor and I went out and got a rock that was big. I went to the side of the bed. I thought, "I'm going to kill him, because he can't keep making my mother cry." I remember thinking that. I don't remember how old I was. I remember holding the rock and thinking, "He made my mother cry. He made my mother cry." My mother happened to come in the room and said, "What are you doing?" I said, "I'm going to hit him. I'm going to hit him." She took the rock away and talked to me and said, "Just cause he makes me cry that does mean you want to hurt him." I remember that so vivid – that I was so angry.

Q: Did your mom have any superstitions about what brings good luck?
A: Absolutely. She believed that when there was lightning you had to turn all the mirrors to the wall, turn out all the lights and sit in the dark. Lightning would strike the mirror if you didn't do it. I can't remember more. She was very superstitious about a lot of things. Friday the thirteenth she was very very careful not to do anything out of the ordinary. I can't remember more right now.

Q: Wives tales?
A: For hiccups you could hold your breath, drink water, have somebody hit you or scare you – those kinds of things. For a wart you tied a horsehair from a horse's tail around the wart until it would fall off. You could also take a dirty dishrag and bury it then the wart would fall of.

Q: How were wedding celebrated?

A: My sister ran away and got married. My brother got married by the Justice of the Peace. My little brother had a Catholic wedding – it was an all day thing with lots of food. My wedding, I was in charge of. She didn't do anything about weddings. She wasn't well at my wedding. She was there, but she wasn't well.

Q: Did she teach you any childhood rhymes and games?

A: Yes. She taught us all the rhymes. We played "Kick the Can" and "Run, Sheepie! Run!" With "Run, Sheepie! Run!", what you'd do is you'd get in teams. The captain of the team would hide a group of people somewhere (his "sheepies"). He would go back to the other team and draw a circle and tell where his "sheepies" were. You'd have to go find them. When you found them you'd have to yell something. You had to get back before the "sheepies" got back. A lot like "Kick the Can", except you hit in a group. Hopscotch, jump rope and jacks – I was good at jacks. I was the champion in grade school. My mom taught me to play jacks. Tricky bars were a big thing – we did it with dresses on. My mom taught me how to embroider – pillow cases and runners.

Q: Tell me a little bit more about when your mom was older and you were married – what was your relationship like then?

A: I called my mother everyday of my life. I would tell her what my children were doing because she cared. Nobody else really cared – their kids were doing the same things. She was good to listen. I called her everyday – everyday that I was married until she died. Then when she died it took me six months not to go call her. The kids would do something and a few times I would get to the phone and I'd remember. Before she died we used to visit her on Sundays. We used to go over for dinner occasionally.

Q: Tell me the story of when you and dad were fighting and you went back to your mom?

A: We fought all the time. I had watched my dad rule over my mom and when I got married and Ralph kind of had a tendency to be in control of me, we would fight all the time. He worked nights and I worked days. This one night we had a terrible fight. The next day I went to my mom's after work. (I used to go to my mom's after work cause I was alone during the evening.) This one night I went over there, we were watching TV and we had had something to eat and it was getting a later – maybe nine – and my mother said, "What time are you going to go home?" I said, "I'm not going home." She said, "Why?" I started crying and told her how mean Ralph was and how he just wasn't nice to me – the whole thing. My mother looked at me very seriously and said, "Norma, you are welcome here for dinner. You are welcome here to watch TV. You can come whenever you want, but when it's time to go to bed you go home to bed. You made your bed now you go lie in it." I was just crushed. Then she said, "I don't know what Ralph did, but I've known you for 19 years and I know you. It can't be all Ralph's fault." I went home thinking my mother had taken Ralph's side and of course we got over it. Best thing she ever did for me.

Q: What happened when your mom died?

A: I was working at Albertson's and they had told us that she was going to die many times. It was to the point where I thought she was indestructible. My dad called me at Albertson's and said, "Norma Jean, your mother's dead." That was it. I said, "Where is she?" He told me where she was. She was at Holy Cross. I hung up the phone and went running to the back to get my coat and my purse. I said to the baker, "I've got to go my mother died." I guess I was really distraught. I've always been one to do it myself. One of the bakers grabbed me and said, "You can't go home like this. I'll take you home." I think I'd taken my bike to work cause I didn't have a car. So he brought me home and I came in and told Ralph what had happened and we went up to the hospital. Before my mother died my sister had called that day. My mother was always "fine". Matter of fact, she was sick all her life, but if you asked her how she was doing she'd say, "Oh, I'm doing fine." My little sister had called and asked, "How's mom doing?" My dad said, "Well, she's a little tired today. She's in bed. Hazel how are you doing?" She said, "Oh, I'm fine." And when he got off the phone she was dead. Her last words were, "I'm fine." That's who she was. She didn't ever tell you much. You never knew when she was in pain. I'm sure if she could write her journal she had a lot of pain in her life, but you'd of never had known it.

Lucious Snow Rosenbaum

Father: Morris David Rosenbaum
Mother: Abigail Harriett Snow
Born: 23 June 1882
Place: Brigham City, Utah, USA
Married: October 1903 (Cecelia Hazel Marcroft)
Place: Salt Lake City, Utah, USA
Died: 19 December 1945
Place: Salt Lake City, Utah, USA

Lucius Snow Rosenbaum

Lucius Snow Rosenbaum was the seventh of eight children born to Morris David Rosenbaum and Abigail Harriet Snow. He arrived June 23, 1882 in Brigham City, Box Elder, Utah. His father was a merchant by trade and a convert to the Church of Jesus Christ of Latter-day Saints. His mother was the daughter of the Church President Lorenzo Snow.

Lucius grew up in Brigham City. His father had two wives due to the practice of polygamy, and a total of 22 children. Since his youngest sister, Lena, died when she was only 2 years old, Lucius was considered "the baby" of the family. They use to call him Lutie. He had his share of chores to do around the house, chop the wood and fetch water. He attended church meetings on Sundays and went to school during the week. He completed a fifth grade education. When he reached the age of accountability his parents saw to it that he was baptized a member of the Church of Jesus Christ of Latter-day Saints.

When he was 16 years old he ran away from home. He traveled to San Francisco, California for a short while before he returned home to Brigham City. When Lucius was 17, he left home again. This time he settled in Salt Lake City, Utah. Sometime during the next four years, he met and fell in love with Cecelia Hazel Marcroft. She was five years younger than he. They were married sometime in June 1903. He was 21 and she was 16. Together, they had 10 children.

Ruth Marie arrived September 21, 1904 followed by Clifford born October 21, 1907. Unfortunately, his stay in mortality was a short one. He died two months later on December 18, 1907. Lucius was not a man to express his feelings verbally, but he did like to jot his feelings and emotions down on paper. Often he would write a poem and then he would throw it away. His daughter, Marie, kept this one describing the loss of his son:

> Baby has gone to the land of rest.
> The baby you loved and held to your breast.
> God gave you that baby and took it away.
> He was in need of an angel that very same day.
>
> The speaker was good, the music was fine
> The prayers that were rendered are deep in my mind.
> Your friends shared your sorrow,
> They took it to heart,
> To know that our baby had to depart.
>
> God will protect it, Believe what I say,
> The baby he gave and then took away.

Joy came into their home once more when Cora May arrived safe and sound November 10, 1909. But tragedy struck a second time when their fourth child arrived May 16, 1910. He was almost four months old when he died (September 10, 1910). His death certificate simply read, "Baby Boy Rosenbaum".

The family was in Brigham City, Utah when Kenneth Morris was born the following year on May 16, 1911. They were back in Salt Lake City, Utah again when Claude Eugene arrived on July 23, 1913. For some reason, the family was in Pinguine, Idaho when Fred Leroy arrived July 5, 1915. Pinguine was a small town that was later called Caldwell. Today, it is a ghost town. The family then returned to Salt Lake City, Utah where the last three children were born. Hazel Maude arrived September 6, 1917, June Louise arrived August 27, 1921 and Donna Viola was born October 19, 1924. Thus his family was complete.

His son, Morris, recalls that their family was a poor one. Both parents had to work in order to support their large family, yet they barely made ends meet. Both Lucius and his wife were employed at the Royal Laundry. He did all sorts of jobs. He ran the laundry machines, acted as a night watchman and even worked his way up to a foreman position.

His daughter, Marie, remembers that because she was the oldest, she was expected to take care of the children and clean the house. Morris was in charge of chopping the wood. Whenever it was possible the children would walk along the railroad tracks collecting coal. The coal was used for fuel in the old coal stove in the kitchen.

On Sunday mornings, her mother did the washing. On Saturdays, her mother would bake a weeks worth of bread and other baked items and then place them in a locked closet. The baked goods were then used during the remainder of the week. When her mother came home from work at night she would stop at the store and buy something to go with the baked items for dinner such as a bottle of pickled pigs feet, or a can of pork and beans or a can of sardines. Sometimes on Sundays, the family would take their dinner to Liberty Park and then stay for the band concerts. Morris especially enjoyed the "Pig in the Jacket" his mother use to cook. It was like a meat pie where in you roll hamburger into the bread dough and bake it. Marie liked her mother's homemade soup. Donna and June both remember how wonderful the homemade bread used to taste. Despite the fact their mother was a good cook food was limited. Morris felt that the best meals they ate were when relatives invited them to dinner. Morris admits he use to swipe food at Liberty Park and take school milk out of the window when he'd get hungry during the week. On occasions, he even tried to pick the lock on the food closet door. Marie describes a typical weekday meal to consist of one piece of bread and ½ of a sardine, or one piece of bread with deviled ham on it or one piece of bread with pork and beans.

Morris said they lived in a two-story house at 142 Lucy Avenue (Salt Lake City). He recalls the bathroom had a toilet and a faucet but no sink. Later, after their mother's death, the family moved to a home located on 2nd North between 1st and 2nd West on the east side of the street.

The children could play after school at home. Their parents were home by 6:00 PM at which time dinner was served. Afterwards the kids could run and play again but they had to be home by 9:00 PM or else they would get a spanking with a green willow switch (stick).

Marie notes the children wore hand-me-down clothes most of the time. Her mother would sit up nights sewing new clothes so the children could wear a new outfit for Washington's Birthday, the 4th of July and Christmas. Each payday her parents would buy several pairs of shoes for the kids. That way, the children got a new pair of Buster Brown shoes each month. Marie never liked the shoes so she tried her best to wear them out so she could get a new pair.

Marie felt that their parents loved them by the sacrifices they made and the things they did for them.

Five years after Donna was born, Lucius lost his wife. Cecelia passed away December 15, 1929. This was a very heartbreaking experience for him to endure. Sometime after his wife's death, Lucius wrote the following poem:

> Everything's against me no matter what I do
> When I look at the cedar chest, it sure makes me feel blue
> When I look at Donna's dresser and kiss her little skirts
> My thoughts go back to her mother and oh how it hurts.
> I look at grandma's picture and my wife's face I see
> And wonder why God took her instead of taking me.
> Then I look into the dresser and certain things I find
> I cry and cry until I am almost blind.
> Many times I've kneeled at her bed and offered up a prayer
> And asked the Lord to be good to her while she is in his care.
>
> (Lucius was basically an inactive member of the church, yet his relationship to God was reflected in his poetry.)

When his wife died, Lucius had a difficult decision to make. According to the law, when a wife dies and there are both girls and boys in the family that you had to separate the girls from the boys until the father could properly provide a woman in his home to care for them. So Hazel, age 12, was sent to live in Boise, Idaho with Cecelia's mother Susan Walkey O'Brien and her husband Patrick while Donna, age 5, and June, age 8, went to live with an Aunt in Brigham City, Utah (her name was Maud Sorenson). Marie and Cora were both married.

According to Morris, the aunt in Brigham City wanted June and Donna to live with her permanently. She offered to give the girls $85,000.00 each when they reached the age of 21 if she could keep them with her. Lucius found a live-in-housekeeper by the name of Elizabeth Bexstead Webb, a widow, to care for the children so Hazel,

Donna and June all came back to Salt Lake City to live with their father again. The children were happy to be reunited as a family.

The children all called the housekeeper "Beth" for short. She became a substitute mother for the girls. Donna recalls that Beth was the only mother she could really remember. Beth was described to be a large boned, heavyset, boisterous woman who seldom smiled. She was a strict woman but she was a good cook and a tidy housekeeper with an excellent talent for crocheting and knitting items. She didn't allow pets in the house except canary birds.

Donna recalls that her father always wore suit pants and a shirt to work all the time. If he went out dancing at the Old Bluebird Dance Hall, he'd put on a tie, suit jacket and wear a hat. After a hard day at work, her father liked to drink quietly at home or go dancing with the girls at the dance hall. She remembers one dancing partner he particularly liked by the name of Grace Homestead.

Marie recalls that Lucius could hold his liquor well. He didn't drink beer, just whiskey. He could walk a straight line no matter how much he drank. The only way the children would tell he had been drinking was if his eyes were red.

He'd been described to be about 5'10" tall weighing about 180 pounds. He was medium build but not heavyset. He developed a tummy through the years like we all do. Donna says he was a muscular man who enjoyed flexing his muscles. Lucius was a quiet, sensitive man who rarely did a lot of talking. He preferred to listen to a conversation rather than participate. Morris recalls his father had a sense of humor. He'll never forget how his father use to rub onions on his baldhead in hoped of restoring his receding hairline. He was a good man even though he didn't go to church. She remembers watching him roll his own cigarettes.

When Marie got married her father wrote her a very special letter. In it he told her many things. The following are a few of his comments:
> "We have never missed you so much as we do now ... Happy is such a nice and wonderful thing, money doesn't make one happy ... I have said I wouldn't give a penny for another me and I wouldn't sell anyone I have for all the love, happiness or money in the world."

On one occasion Lucius wrote the following poem to Marie:

> Thanks for remembering me on Father's Day
> And thanks for the token of love
> I'll put it away in my little cedar chest
> Then take it with me up above.
> I'll show it to mother and tell her it's from our daughter Marie.
> And I know it will make her happy because you gave it to me.
>
> I'll pick this little token up many times after I put it away
> And I won't forget the one that gave it to me on Mother's Day.

Yes I'm only a dad and only in the way
Because I am getting old and my hair is turning gray.
But when I go to mother and your feeling blue and sad
Remember I was your mother as well as only a dad.
First I lost you Marie, then from Cora I had to depart
Then I lost you mother, It almost broke my heart.
It seemed as though bad luck wasn't satisfied in taking away you three
It came back to my door and stoled my boy from me –
Yes, only a dad!

In time Lucius finally decided to marry his housekeeper, Beth. According to Donna, they were married in 1945 the same year he died. Sometime before his death, he also wrote the following poem:

Your mother is calling me to another station
I've heard her say, "Oh, Luke" so often I know it's not my imagination
Last Sunday while down to Cora's, I heard: "Oh, Luke" so plain
That's the reason I never went out last night for fear she would call again
I didn't think she's satisfied there, maybe something she wants to say
I know it's her that's calling me, for I've heard her twice today.

Lucius Snow Rosenbaum died of a heart attack at home, December 18, 1945. He was 63 years old. He was buried beside his beloved wife in the Salt Lake cemetery.

SOURCES:

1)   Family group sheets
2)   Personal knowledge of Marie Easthope – daughter
3)   Personal knowledge of Morris Rosenbaum – son
4)   Personal knowledge of Donna Bowman – daughter
5)   Personal knowledge of June Williams – daughter

Compiled – June 1979 by: Elizabeth J.O. Williams
Ogden, Utah

Cecelia Hazel Marcroft

Cecelia & Hazel (daughter)

Father: Hyrum Taylor Marcroft
Mother: Suzan Walkey
Born: 1 March 1887
Place: Salt Lake City, Utah, USA
Married: October 1903
(to Lucious Snow Rosenbaum)
Place: Salt Lake City, Utah, USA
Died: 17 December 1929
Place: Salt Lake City, Utah, USA

Cecelia, Viola (sister), LeRoy (brother) ?

Cecelia Hazel Marcroft

Cecelia Hazel Marcroft was born in Salt Lake City, Utah, March 1, 1887. She was the oldest child born to Hyrum Taylor Marcroft and Susan Walkey. When she arrived, she was born with an enlarged heart. In her early years, she also developed a problem with her goiter gland.

In 1895 she was baptized a member of the Church of Jesus Christ of Latter-day Saints. Her father was a very missionary conscious man who served several four-year missions in Australia. Her mother was a convert from Australia who wanted to pursue a career as an actress rather than one as a wife and mother. Consequently when her father was in Australia, her mother would leave the children alone nights. According to her father's biography her mother "would leave the children (Cecelia, Viola and LeRoy) to the mercy of anyone's care." As a result, her parents got a temple divorce. The children went with their mother. This really had quite an impact upon Cecelia because the one concept she tried to instill within her children was that of "No Divorce" once your married. According to her daughter, Marie, "Cecelia knew what it was like to come from a divorced family and she didn't want that type of a life for her children or for her children's children."

Cecelia helped support the family by working at the American Linen Company. When she was 15 years old, her mother left her in the care of an aunt while she traveled with the Max Senate Acting Circuit. Cecelia continued to work until she fell in love and got married at the age of 16. She married Lucius Snow Rosenbaum, in 1903.

On September 21, 1904, Cecelia became a mother for the first time when a mid-wife helped deliver Ruth Marie at home. She was only 17 at the time. Three years later a doctor helped deliver her son, Clifford, on October 21, 1907, but unfortunately he died (December 18, 1907). Two years later, on November 10, 1909, Cora May arrived safe and sound with the help of a mid wife. Six months later a doctor helped deliver another son but he died. The two times a doctor brought her children into the world they died. The rest of her children were delivered by a neighborhood mid-wife at home. Kenneth Morris arrived May 16, 1911 followed by Claude Eugene born on July 23, 1913, and Fred LeRoy arriving July 5, 1915. Cecelia had three more lovely daughters after that. Hazel Maude was born September 6, 1917 and was named after her mother. June Louise arrived August 27, 1921 and Donna Viola was born October 19, 1924. Donna was named after her mother's sister, Viola.

Supporting a large family was not an easy task so Cecelia's husband helped her get a job working for the Royal Laundry Company also. When Cecelia left work at night she would walk to the grocery store, purchase a few simple items for dinner and come home. After dinner, she would sew clothes for the children until it was time to go to bed. There were only three times a year that the children were given new clothes to wear, and that was Washington's Birthday, the 4th of July and Christmas Day. Marie recalls how her mother must have liked the colors pink and blue, because those were the colors she chose in making the girl's dresses. Her mother also enjoyed putting a lot of lace and frills on their dresses.

At Christmas time a typical Christmas list would look like this:

Marie	Cora	Morris
A doll	A doll	A toy
A dress	A dress	An outfit
A pair of shoes	A pair of shoes	A pair of shoes

And so on down through the children.

According to Marie, her mother not only sewed well but she also did a lot of tatting and embroidery work.

Because she worked, Cecelia would do the family wash and bake bread and other items on the weekends. She was considered a good cook by her family. Marie especially liked the way she would cut up kidneys and fry them with potatoes and onions and put gravy over them. Morris liked his mother's "pig in the jacket". That's where you bake hamburger in bread dough and eat it. Some of Cecelia's favorite foods to buy were sardines and pickled pigs feet. These were items she'd buy at the store on the way home from work.

Because of their family situation Cecelia didn't go out much. When she was first married, she and her husband used to ride the bus to Sara Sota Springs and go swimming. While her family was growing up, she liked to attend the Sunday band concerts at Liberty Park. They would take dinner and just relax. When Marie got married, her parents would go out to dinner with them on paydays. But before Cecelia would go out with her husband, he would have to be clean-shaven and well groomed. She used to rub his whiskers and call him Santa Claus if he didn't shave each day. She even gave him a haircut when his hair started to curl at the ends so he would look nice.

She didn't live in a big house, just one that was large enough for their needs. Outside the house in the summertime, Cecelia would raise a small vegetable garden. She liked flowers but she didn't have the time to properly care for them, but she would raise vegetables to eat. Marie remembers that whenever her mother needed vegetables, she would take the children's little red wagon and walk to the vegetable market, purchase the items she wanted and return trailing the little red wagon behind her.

Cecelia saw to it that her children had a new pair of shoes to wear each month, yet she herself wore "shabby shoes that were worn down badly on each side". She used to sew clothes for her children but never anything for herself. She basically wore hand-me-down clothes furnished by her sister, Viola, and her mother. Marie commented, "Some of the clothes looked brand new or hardly used at all when her mother received them. Some of her dresses were made from a fancy crepe material and when her mother wore them, she looked out of place in her shabby shoes going off to work."

Marie describes her mother as a very plain, unselfish woman with brown eyes and brown hair. "She was a small boned, thin woman who loved her children. Their needs always came before her own. She didn't go to church much. She didn't take to other people. She preferred to be alone at home with her family. She was a quiet, shy lady who liked living in a clean house. She was a hard worker who seldom complained."

Marie recalls how her mother didn't care much for pets around the house. Marie used to find stray cats and bring them home. Her mother would tell her to let them go, she couldn't keep them. But on one occasion, she found a beautiful Persian cat and she brought it home only to have her mother tell her she couldn't keep it. When she told her father, he helped her find the cat and together they brought it home. An argument resulted but the cat stayed. Marie also recalled that her mother didn't get angry very often buy when she did, she had a violent temper.

Marie felt her mother loved her very much although she could not express her feelings in words. She showed her love through the sacrifices she made and her everyday actions all said, "I love you". It used to bother Cecelia when the other children used to tease her children and call them "Jews". Her children didn't like it.

Sometime in December 1929, at the age of 42, Cecelia developed a serious heart problems and had to undergo heart surgery. According to Morris, complications set in after her surgery and his mother had to undergo surgery a second time. She was much too weak to survive and so she died, December 15, 1929, in the County Hospital in Salt Lake City, Utah of a bad heart condition.

When she died, she left six children for her husband to care for. They ranged all the way from age 18 to 5. Her husband wasn't a man to openly express his feelings but he did write his thought in poetry. The following poem describes his feelings for his wife and children:

Back in the days of my childhood, in the days when I was young,
I met your wonderful mother who I claimed as my chum.
There is not a mother that was sweeter and I am not going to look anymore
I will never find any one better if I looked the whole world over
She had helped me many times and helped me through life's weary road.
She stood by me in sorrow and grief and helped me carry my load.
As I sit here alone a dreaming, thinking of things of the past,
A dreaming of you wonderful mother and wonder why she didn't last.
I am blue over our troubles and sorrow that we two
Had once in a while but smile behind my tears with you
Until they turn into smiles
I will always remember your children through sorrow and fun
As I go through life in the future to know that your hearts I had won.

Written by: Lucius Snow Rosen Baum

Special Note:
Her oldest daughter, Marie, recalls that she really hesitated doing her mother's temple endowments in the Salt Lake Temple. She prayed about it and finally decided to go ahead and do it (on November 25, 1932). During the endowment, Marie was still wondering whether or not she was doing the right thing, when she felt three fingers upon her left shoulder. She thought the lady behind her must be touching her, but when she looked, no one was touching her – yet, she could still feel the three fingers on her shoulder. She felt it was her mother reassuring her that it was all right – that she wasn't to worry. After her father passed away, Marie saw to it that her parents were sealed for time and eternity on January 17, 1955.

SOURCES:

1)   Family group sheets
2)   Hyrum Taylor Marcroft's biography
3)   Personal knowledge of Kenneth Morris Rosenbaum – son
4)   Personal knowledge of Ruth Marie Easthope – daughter
5)   Poem by Lucius Snow Rosenbaum in the possession of Marie Easthope
Complied by: Elizabeth J.O. Williams, August 1979

Morris & Abigail Rosenbaum

Morris David Rosenbaum
Father: David Rosenbaum
Mother: Sharah Barnes
Born: 11 July 1831
Place: Fordon, Prussia
Married: 2 April 1858 (to Alice Neibaur)
Place: Brigham City, Utah, USA
Married: 10 August 1867 (to Abigail Harriett Snow)
Place: Brigham City, Utah, USA
Died: 8 August 1885
Place: Mink Creek, Idaho, USA

Abigail Harriett Snow
Father: Lorenzo Snow
Mother: Harriett Amelia Squires
Born: 16 July 1849
Place: Mount Pisgah, Pttwt, Iowa
Married: January 17 1864 (to Thomas Caldwell)
Place: Brigham City, Utah, USA
Married: 10 August 1867 (to Morris David Rosenbaum)
Place: Brigham City, Utah, USA
Died: 9 May 1914
Place: Brigham City, Utah, USA

Life and Travels of Morris D. Rosenbaum.

Original Handwriting Sample of M.D.R.

Morris
David
Rosenbaum

Alice Neibaur
(Morris' 1st Wife)

Life and Travels of Morris David Rosenbaum
(Taken from M.D.R.'s personal account of his life)

July 11, 1831 Morris D. Rosenbaum only son of David Rosenbaum and Sarah Barnass was born in Fordon, Kingdom of Prussia, Germany July 11, 1831. Of my early youth I can say but little.

My Father was a hard working man and generally occupied in trading. He was a man of good morals and he exerted himself dilligently by example as well as precept to instill into the mind of his children every principle of honesty, honor and virtue.

My Mother was a very good and pious women, and devoted a good deal of her time in explaining the Bible to her children especially to myself her only son. She was President of a charitable Institution and her spare time was occupied in visiting the sick and needy, administering to their wants.

As my parents were of the Jewish faith I was sent at an early age to a Rabbi to study hebrew in connection with the commen school which I attendet for 6 years in succession.

1840 When about 9 years old while skating on the river Vistula I fell and broke my right tigh. I was carried home the doctor sett it, this accident Kept me about 4 weeks in bed, during that time it growed together as good as ever it was.

1842 When about 11 years of age I commenced to study the hebrew Bible, the old Testament only, and was taught by my teacher that this is the original language spoken by Adam and Eve, that the jewish religion is the only true one in existance, that the new Testament is a fable, Christ an imposter, all the human familie have gone astray and will be dammed except the Jews, the only chosen people of the Lord. I remember of asking my Teacher, why is it that our people are so scattereth in the world, why we have no Prophets or inspired men, no Temples, and why we are like sheep without a sheppard. Oh said he, Prophets, inspired men and Temples are no longer needet, Moses and the Prophets we read about are our patterns and law givers, the old Testament is complete, we are the chosen people of the Lord, there is no further need of this things, therefore they ceased.

I thought to myself, can it be possible that my Teacher is corect, that the Lord is so unmericiful as to damn millions of his children, and not given them a chance to embrace the true religion. Can it be possible that our forefathers have rejected and slain the savior our Messiah, and are therefore scattereth among all nations, and no longer favored with Prophets, inspired men and Temples.

1844 At the age of 13 I went clerking in a store and stopped there nearly 6 years.

1850 When about 19 years of age, I left my native country for America, went to Hamburg by Rail, and from there in a sailing ship to New York, this trip lasted 74 days. After resting a short time I bought a few dollars worth goods and went out peddling with a basket in the outskirts of New York. This was very hard task, as I could not talk nor understand the English language, but after a few weeks I got along very well. Then I traveled along the Hudsen River to the Catskils and returned to New York, and from there to Philadelphia, the Eastern and Southern states and to New Orleans. From there I took passage in a steamer, John L. Steavens, via Havana, Aspinwal, Panama and Acapolca to San Francisco.

1856 There I bought a horse, saddle & C and goods and went peddling through the northern mines.

1857 During this summer I heard of a mormon settlement in Carson Valley, and was greatly impressed to visit them to learn for myself what Kind of people they are and learn some of their doctorine.

I remember well when first seeing their settlement of hearing a voice. "There is a people which you never leave." Arrived at the valley, I stopped at the first house with Joseph Mordnah all night. I was anxious and enquired of him about Mormonism, but he seemed to be scaret to talk to me about it and said, there is no use in preaching to a Jew, because he cannot believe the gospel.

I traveled on and stopped at noon with a man by name of Simon Baker. I enquired and he argued with me about Mormonism untill midnight, but seemingly making very little impression on my mind. But his earnestness and pain taking in declaring and instructing me in the pincipels of the gospel sett me to thinking and searching the scriptures.

I traveled through their settlement several times, and found them the best people I ever came in contact with. My desire to be with this people increased and as they moved en masse for Salt Lake Valley this fall, I made up my mind to travel with them, stop there during the winter, and return to my native country the following Spring.

September 27 Left Carson Valley with the mormon company, Mr Wm Smith captain, I rode in his company the most of the way ahead of the train to find camping places. We came by the northern route, arrived at Brigham City, November 2 of this month, and I stopped with Mr Sammel Smith a short time.

Then went to Salt Lake City and boardet there with Mr. George Nebecker, he was one that came in our campany from Carsen Valley. Went to school during this winter to Mr Isaac Bowman in the 17. ward. I remember well going to a meeting the first time in the Tabernacle with Brother Nebecker, Brother H.C. Kimball preached. I listened attentively and it seemed to me I heard that serman before, because during his remarks I could tell beforehand what he was going to say and was convinced of its truthfullness. On our way home Br Nebecker asked me how I liked the sermon, my reply was, I like it very well and I remember of hearing that serman before, he said if you did it was before you came into this world.

300

Brother Nebecker informed me there is a german Jew Mr. Neibaur, a Matchmaker, living in the 13 ward, and one day after school hours I startet to visit him, as I turned the corner and saw his sign I imagent of hearing a voice like this. "You are going to get married in that house." I went in the house and found Mr Neibaur, his wife and several children. I was treated very Kindly and after several visits Mr Neibaur began to talk to me about Mormonism, at first I could not believe and differed with him in some of principels of the Bible, but in a short time found that I was in error, and became interested in the principels of the gospel, a peaceful and teachable spirit wrought mightily in me commending the ancient gospel to my conscience.

1858 I read the Book of Mormon from beginning to end in connection with the Bible prayerfully, and arose from its perusal with a strong conviction on my mind, "this Book was written by inspiration". Dreams and Visions which I had at that time began to have great efect on my mind, but when I listened to my selfish thoughts it seemed to me I was deceived, I hated Mormonism in my heart, and regretted ever hearing it. Whenever I made up my mind to have nothing more to do with it, my mind was darkened, tribulation and danger seemed to be near me and I felt surroundet by evil spirits.

Whenever I studied the Book of Mormon and went to meeting hearing the Elders preach I felt a peacefull influence by day and during the dark hours of the night I felt surroundet and was instructed by an unseen power in the principels of the gospel. During several successive nights I could see plain the following words of the prophet Isaih before me. "Wash you make you clean, put away the evil of your doings from before mine eyes, Cease to do evil," & C. I felt convinced of the truth of The Book of Mormon and the preaching I heard of the principles of the gospel and made a strong resolution in my mind, "I can and I will embrace the truth regardless of consequences".

I remember well of hearing Brother Neibaur bearing his testimony to the truth of the everlasting gospel to me. I asked him, Mr Neibaur why can not I have such a testimony? he replied, Mr Rosenbaum I promise you in the name of Israels God you will, if you obey the principals of the gospel, repent and be babtised for the remission of your sins, and then ask prayerfully your heavenly Father for it. Such a promise I longed for, in a few days I went to Bishop Thomas Calister and asked to be babtised for the remission of my sins.

1858 March 27 This day I was babtised by Br John Tingey, a Teacher in the 17 ward Salt Lake City.

April 1 This day I was confirmed.

April 2 This day I paid my first tithing to the Bishop Calister amounting to 140 Dollars in coin.

1858 April 2 This evening I married Alice Neibaur of Salt Lake City. Her Father performed the ceremony at his house. About this time my Father died.

April 28 Today I was called and started to Echo canjon in company with others to assist in defending the people, stopped there about 3 weeks and returned to Salt Lake City.

May 17 Today I started to travel south with my wife and stopped at Provo during the great Move, returned to Salt Lake last of June.

June 4 Today I was ordainet an Elder by Pres. D. Hunt in the fifth quorum of seventies. I wrote several Letters to my Mother and Sisters, explaining the principals of the gospel and the history of the church to them and was in great hopes and almost certain, that they would examine and accept its principels as I did. But in this I am disapointed up to the present time.

1858 A short time afterwards I received Letter from my Mother, she was awfull mad because I joined the church said she, I have 3 children laying in the graveyard and would rather have you there, then hearing you have forsaken our holy religion & C –and asking me if it was my intention when I left home to apostatise and join such a degradet people as the Mormons.

In my answer I told her when leaving home I did not Know what I was going to do, but now I know for a fact that I am in the hands of the Lord and have confidence in him, that I have not forsaken the jewish religion, I believe in the God of Abraham, Isaac and Jacob, but I accepted more truth. I told her I could answer your questions by asking another and asked her, When the sons of Jacob sold their Brother Joseph to the Egyptions, did they expect that he would ever be a savior to his Fathers house?

1858 About this time I went to bed one night contemplating on the principals of the gospel and wondering if my mother or any of my relations ever would join the church. I dreamt of traveling in a Carriage through a large city and seeing a large number of men and women repairing the streets, in the crowd I saw my mother and invited her to come in and ride with me, pleadet with her for a long time but she would not come with me. I told the driver to go ahead, he started but I stopped him again in a few moments and called my mother again, and entreated her to come with me, told her how much better it would be for her to come and ride with me then to work on the public street, but she refused and would not come with me, so I told the driver to go ahead and left her.

1859 September 23 My wife Alice gave birth to a girl and we named here Sara, after my mother.

1859 December 3 This day I received my endowments, and my wife Alice was sealed to me by President Brigham Young, this night I received a testimony of this work which I hope and desire never to forget.

1860 February 24 Moved to Farmington, Kept a store there for about 9 months, then moved back to Salt Lake City and bought a house and a lot in the 8 ward.

1861 March 11 My wife Alice gave birth to a Boy and we named him David after my father.

April 10 Moved to Brigham City, rented a house from Brother John Gibbs on Main Street and opened a store there. Sold my place in Salt Lake City and bought the place in Brigham City.

1862 Built an addition in front of my place and moved my store there.

November 17 My wife Alice gave birth to a girl and we named her Ellen after her mother.

1863 This year I built a rock store on the south side of my place, Watson Bro done the mason work, moved into it November 4

1864 November 6 My wife Alice gave birth to a girl and we named her Fanny. This spring I shipped 600 sacks Flour to Helena, Montana, and lost nearly 6000 Dollars on it.

1865 This spring I send 4 teams of my own to Boise City, Idaho loadet with Flour, Butter, Eggs and C and returning lost 12 head of Mules on rock creek.

1866 January 22 My wife Alice gave birth to a girl and we named her Alice. October 21 Our child Alice died.

1867 July 30 My wife Alice gave birth to a Boy and we named him Morris.

August 10 Abigail Snow Caldwel was sealed to me.

1868 September 7 Our child Sarah died at Salt Lake City where we took her to the Doctor.

1869 March 2 My wife Abigail gave birth to a girl and we named her Harriet.

July 10 Received my certificate of naturalisan at Salt Lake.

September 13 My wife Alice gave birth to a Boy and we named him Alexander.

1871 August 5 Our child Harriet died.

August 19 My wife Abigail gave birth to a Boy and we named him Moses.

October 17 My wife Alice gave birth to Boy and we named him Aaron.

1873 October 14 My wife Abigail gave birth to a girl and we named her Henrietta.

1874 January 21 My wife Alice gave birth to a Boy and we named him Joseph.

July 18 Our child Joseph died.

July 20 Our child Moses died.

1875 May 3 My wife Abigail gave birth to a girl and we named her Alice.

1877 March 3 My wife Abigail gave birth to a Boy and we named him Morris.

1877 August 18 My wife Alice gave birth to a girl and we named her Margereth.

1879 April 21 Our child Margareth died.

November 16 My wife Alice gave birth to a girl and we named her Leah.

1880 March My wife Abigail gave birth to a girl and we named her Minna.

March 26 Received the following letter from President John Tayor.

Salt Lake City
March 25, 1880
Elder Morris Rosenbaum
Brigham City

Dear Brother

Your name has been suggested and accepted as a Missionary to Germany. The work of the Lord is progressing in the nations, and faithfull, energetic Elders are needet in the ministry to promolgate the everlasting gospel openings for doing good appearing in numerous directions. Yourself with others having been selected for this mission; should there be no reasonable obstacles to hinder you from going, we would be pleased to have you make your arrangements to start as early a date as April Conference. Please let us Know at your earliest convenience what your feelings are with regard to this call.

Your Brother in the Gospel
John Taylor

1880 March 28 I wrote the following letter to President Taylor.

Dear Brother,

I received your letter of the 25th yesterday informing me that my name has been sugested and accepted as a Missionary to Germany, and you wish to Know my feelings in regard to this call. I am happy to inform you that I feel proud to be worthy of such a call although I never preached a sermon in my life, yet bliving the Lord is able to qualify his servants, I am willing to go. But there is one obstacle which will hinder me for a short time as I can not get ready by April Conference. I am County Assessor and can not complete my work until the 1st of June, and as this labor is necessary for me to do in order to get means for my journey and provide for my families, I would like to have you to extend the time, providet it don't conflict with other arrangements.

Your Brother in the Gospel.

April 1 Received the following answer.

Salt Lake City
April 1, 1880

Dear Brother,

Yours of the 28th received, I am directed to say, take the amount of time necessary to close your Business.

Yours & C
L. John Nuttal, Secy

May This month I was busy engaged closing up my business and until I left.

1880 June 11 Left Brigham City by R.R. in company with John Mcalister arrived at Chicago on the 14th. We stopped at the Moulten House, the next day we visited several business houses in company with Moses Thatcher who went to New York on business, we stopped 2 days here.

June 17 Left for New York arrived there on the 19th and stopped at the Steaven House. Here we walked through Broadway and other streets and rode on the elevated Rail Road through the City, bought our Tickets for Liverpool.

Sunday, we crossed the river to Brooklin and heard H.W. Beecher preach, he is a very eloquent speaker but only a form without the power of God. After meeting we went to Greenwood Cemetery which is said to be the finest in the world, it contains 450 acres, length or carriage avenue 18 ½ miles, length of paths 17 ½ miles, fare only 25 cents to go all around it. Here we saw Monuments which costs 10,000 Dollars.

Monday We went in company with Br Staines to Wall Street Exchange up Broadway, then we went to see the Steamer which we were to sail in, and in the evening visited Br Moses Thatcher and wife at the Hotel and stopped with them until 11:30 PM.

June 22 Left New York for Liverpool in the steamer Wisconsin at 5 PM nothing unusual happened until the 26th when all at once it began to turn cold and very foggy, we could not see 20 feet ahead, all the sailors were on duty as there is danger in foggy weather, the engines yelled loud and long so that ships may not come too close, our steamer stopped and we saw several mountains of Ice, one of them close by us said to be 60 feet high, 300 feet long and about 10 times that size under water. We traveled very slow all that day and night, I heard experienced sailors say that this was the greatest danger they seen for 25 years. I was sea sick about 4 days and felt better after that.

July 1 Today we began to see Land and Lighthouses, several Ships and fishing vessels, and passed Queenstown in the night.

July 2 Today we landet at Liverpool was met on the landing by Bros Budge, Nicholsen, Cope & Martinew, and after our baggage was examind went with them to the office 42 Islington. I felt happy and thanked the Lord for his goodness and protection by Land and Sea and prayed for a continance of the same.

July 3 At Liverpool wrote Letters to my families, and then walked with McAlister through several streets, went to the museums, and other public places.

1880 July 4 Went to the L.D.S. meeting, was called on and spoke a short time, then went to the office for dinner, then to the Park to an open air meeting. Bros Cope, and Anderson preached, then went to evening meeting, then walked with McAlister until 10 p.m.

July 5 Cloudy day, went to the office to see Pres Budge, he counselled me to go to Berlin and report to Brother Kinke President of the Branch there, afterwards went with McAlister and bought a Coat and Vest for myself.

July 6 Was invited to the office for breakfast. Brother Budge went with me to the Ticket office and I bought a Ticket for Hull, left Liverpool at 11:15, arrived there at 5 p.m. bought a Ticket for Hamburg and took my satchel on board, then walked through the town untill after supper, and the Steamer was advertised to start at 5 next morning I went on board and slept there.

1880 July 7 At Hull on steamer Albano, started at 5:30 for Hamburg, got sea sick about noon went to bed and stopped there all night.

July 8 On the north sea felt a little better this morning eat a very light breakfast went on deck began to see land about 3 p.m. and 3 Pilots came on board during the day but we could not read Hamburg that night on account of the tide being against us, we anchored about 15 miles this side until 1:30 a.m. and arrived there next morning.

July 9 At Hamburg, I felt tired and sleepy and concludet to stop and rest today, wrote Letters to my families, and took a walk in the afternoon through the City.

July 10 At Hamburg, left by R.R. at 7:30 a.m. for Berlin, and arrived there at 3 p.m. hired a Hack and went to a Hotel. I enquired for the street where the President of the Branch lives, and had no difficulty in finding it. As soon as I entered the room and told him I came from America he Knew who I was and wanted me to stay with him, but I declined on account of my satchel which I left at the Hotel. Eat supper with him, then he went with me to the Hotel and promised to come after me next morning. I went to bed early being tired and sleepy and slept good all night.

July 11 At Berlin, rose early this morning and after shaving the washing myself, offered up the following prayer to him who lives forever.

Great and allmighty God, my heavenly Father. In obedience to the councel of the authorities of the church and Kingdom upon the earth, I left my mountain homes and all those that are near and dear unto me for the purpose of coming to this land and proclaim the everlasting gospel to the people. I pray the Lord to parden and forgive all my sins and transgressions up to the present time, let them be rememberet no more before thee. I acknowledge my weaknesses and imperfections, Knowing I am liable to err and go estray. Therefore O Lord I pray thee in the name of Jesus Christ that thou willst grant unto me a double portion of thy holy spirit that my tongue may be loosened, my memory strengthened, and I may be able to see of things to come that I may be an instrument in thy hand in doing much good in my day. I pray thee my heavenly Father to prepare the hearts of the people unto whom I may come by dreams and visions, that they may Know that I dont come in my own name but in thine, and they be prepared to received me as a servant of God, and let thy great Kindness conquer and subdue the unbelief of thy people. Heavenly Father, I pray thee to bless Zion and all her stakes, especially those in authority, that they may have wisdom to lead thy people in truth and rightiosness. Bless all the honest in heart among the nations, may the time speedely come when they shall be gathered from Babylon that they may escape the wrath and indignation that will pass over the land.

I pray thee to remember and bless the sick and needy of thy people, comfort their hearts and may their wants be supplied from time to time. I pray thee in the name of Jesus Christ to remember and bless my families, and all those that are near and dear unto me with goodly portion of thy holy spirit, that they may be comforted by day and by night that the angels of thy presents may be around about them, and if they need any assistance it may come in time, if any of them should get sick or an accident befall them, if they call on the Elders of thy church and the ordinances of the gospel be administered in their behalf. I pray that their prayers may be heard before thee, and they may be restored to helth, strength, and peace of mind, strengthen their desires to serve thee and Keep thy commandments, that they may not do anything to grieve the holy spirit, that peace and contentment may dwell in their habitations.

Now o Lord, I dedicate and consecrate myself and all I possess to thy service, praying thee to accept and let the Angels of thy presents be around about me that I

307

may be protected day and by night. I pray thee o Lord that thou wilt make a speedy work among the nations, that the door may be opened for preaching the Gospel, confound all those who oppose thy servants, and spare our lives to return home in safety. All this favors and blessings I humbly ask in the name of Jesus Christ, Amen.

1880 July 12   At Berlin, The local president Schakowsky came after me this morning, I hired a hack and went home with him at Skalitzer Str N.

This is sunday and after dinner we went to meeting which was in a private room by one of our Brethern, there I met Brother Kienke from Nephy who is president of the North german mission. He was very glad to see me, as he had not seen a man from Utah for 8 months and made many inquires, our meeting commenced, he introduced me to the congragation about 20 in all and I made a short speech to them in german. Our meetings here must be held in secret, as it is against the law of the land for more than 25 persons to meet in one place without a policeman being present, religion here must be acknowledged by Government and established according to law.

After meeting I went with Brother Kienke to Friedrichburg just outside of Berlin and administered to a sick child, then we walked through the streets and had a pleasant time until went to bed.

1880 July 13   At Berlin, took a walk with Br Kienke took a likeness of my son David to get a few copies taken, then went to Mr Newbaur with a Letter that my father in law Br Neibaur gave me as an introduction to his coseng, he was very glad to see me and introduced me to his wife a very intelligent Lady she aked me a good many question about Utah and the Mormons, and Mr Newbar went in a corner of the room and cried.

She invited me to stay to dinner but as Brother Kinkey was waiting outside for me, I begged to be excused and promised to return in a day or two.

July 15   Today I went to Mr Newbaur for dinner had a very good time and a good dinner, he invited me to make my home there as long as I stay in Berlin, I promised to come and visit them again when I return from visiting my sisters.

July 16   Left this morning for a visit to the place of my birth at 10:30 by R.R. for Bromberg, arrived there at 5:30 pm and as the stage don't leave till next morning I stopped here all night.

July 17   At Bromberg, the stage dont leave until 10:45 so I took a walk through the City noticed great improvements in the Buildings since I left here, but not in the customes of the people, saw several men pulling a large canal boat on the river harnessed something like Horses, men and women barefooted and half clad working in the fields like slaves, while Overseers standing there and hurry them to work. Left here at 10:45 for Fordon by stage, arrived there at 12.n. stopped at a Hotel, it did not take me long to find where my sistor Fanny lives, as I entered her house I saw her in the Hall and recognised her at first sight, told her I came from America and Knew her Brother, she invited me in and be seated, and after speaking to her for a few minutes I asked her if she would know her brother if she should happen to see him, she became excited and said, I never expect to see him any more in this life. I noticed tears in her eyes.

I could no longer Keep the secret from her, and told her I am Mority her long absented Brother. She was overcome with Joy and Kissed me, her husband who was present arose, bid me welcome and Kissed me too, invited me to stay with them. But I could see more sorrow than Joy in their faces, they supressed it as well as they could, this was on account I joined the church. They send for sister Minna who lives close by she came in a few minutes and I could see the same feelings in her coutenance.

After answering a great many questions about my familie I had to go home with sister Minna to dinner which she left to come to see the stranger from America. My sister Fanny soon came there too and we talked together untill evening, as this was Friday, all the Jews went to the Synogoge to pray, I went with them, for the first time in 30 years. This meetings are not interessing as the prayers are in hebrew just as they were 1000 years ago. After meeting I went home with Levin Rosenar my sister Fannys husband, where I stopped.

July 18 at Fordon, today I saw the house where I was born, the schoolhouse where I received my first education and a good many old relations and aquaintenses, went with my sisters and Brother in laws to the graveyard and saw the graves of my Father, Mother, Sisters and relations. Took the genaology from the tombstones as far as I could get them.

July 20 At Fordon, My Brother in law Morris Cohn, my sister Tinas husband came after me and I went home with him. He lives about 10 miles from here, here I received about the same reception as with my sisters, stopped 3 days with then, they Keep a public house and a store, I was well treated here, answered a great many questions, but they would not listen to the gospel. Returned to Fordon July 22.

1880 July 23 at Fordon. Visited my sisters and families tryed several times to preach to them the gospel but they would not listen to me, it seems they will not or can not believe.

Left Fordon on the 25 in company with my sisters and their daughters in their team for Bromberg, I bought each of them a Dress pattern and left them there in the hands of the Lord, as I could not do anything more for them as far as their spiritual welfare is concerned at present, but am in hopes I may in the future.

Left Bromberg at 5:53 for Posen arrived there at 10 p.m. stopped here all night.

July 26 at Posen. Left here this morning by R.R. for Bonns arrived there at 1 p.m. got dinner here and then hired a team to go to Wollstein arrived there at 5 p.m.

stopped at a hotel, went to a Lawyer to look up Documents about Br Neibaur Legacy, but could not obtain them then.

July 27 at Wollstein, this forenoon I went to the lawyers office, he showed me all the Documents about Br Neibaurs legacy, there was nothing left for him. I got a copie of all the proceedings and how the property was dividedt and brought it home with me, spent about 15.00 in traveling expenses and lawyers fees.

July 28 at Wollstein, left by stage for the rail road station, arrived there at 11:30 bought a Ticket for Berlin, left at 12. m. and arrived there at 5 p.m. hired a Droshke and went to my lodging place at Brother Schakowsky.

July 29 at Berlin. In company with Br Kinkey. We visited the Museum and other public Buildings held meeting twice a week and done all we was able to magnify our callings.

August 13 Bros. Baliff, Budge, Moroni Snow and Martinew arrived here on a visit, we held a conference. The first latterdays saints conference ever held at Berlin. Brother Kienkey was released from his mission to return home and I was appointed to take his place to preside over the north german mission with headquarters at Berlin.

1880 Aug 19 at Berlin. Bros Budge, Snow and Martinew left to day for Liverpool. This evening we held a meeting in the upper room by one of our Brethern when 3 Policemen entered the room and commandet all the male members to follow them to a police station. We had here a pleminary examination which resulted in all our native brethern being allowed to go home for the present and Bros Baliff, Kinkey and myself were held as prisoners, that night they took us to the central station (Molkenmarkt) here our pockets was searched, all papers, money, & Hats & C taken from us and we were put in a room under Guard, where we had to set on hard benches, one in each corner of the room and forbedding to talk, this seemed to me the longest night I ever saw, but the time passed of in contemplating about those who were in similar circumstances. I felt proud and rejoiced of being worthy to be put in prison for the gospels sake.

1880 August 20 at Berlin in Prison. This morning we were asked weather we want for our breakfast prison or hotel fare, we told them that we wanted hotel fare the best that could be got, as we had plenty money to pay for it. They brought to us a good breakfast, and at about 7 a.m. our trial commenced, they tryed one at a time, and Kept it up untill 3 p.m. The charges against us was preaching Mormonism and assisting people to emigrate.

They could not prove anything against us never the less at about 3 p.m. sentence was passed upon us, we were banished from the Kingdom of Prussia with orders to leave next day at noon, and if ever found again in the Kingdom of prussia, a heavy fine, imprisonment and be transported over the Prussian line would be our lot. We had to sign a Document that we understook the decree and would act accordingly.

While in prison about 100 secret detectives came to look at the mormon apostels as we were called there.

After our sentence was passed they gave us our papers, money and all they took from us the previous night. We had a friendly talk with the policemen, Lawyers and Judges and we bore our testimony to them of the truth of the everlasting gospel.

August 21 at Berlin. Today we bid good bye to all our Brethern and Sistors we could see, Brother Kienkey left towards Liverpool. I and Brother Baliff left at 12. m. by R.R. for the Kingdom of Bavaria travelled all day and stopped all night at Eisenach.

August 22 at Eisenach. Left by R.R. this morning for Frankfort a/m arrived there about 4 pm

August 23 at Frankfurt on Maine. Left here this afternoon for Mayence, arrived there in evening, it was Br Baliffs intention to leave me here to introduce the Gospel, but the newspapers related all about our arrest, and we thought it would not be safe for me to stop here, but we stopped all night and the next day.

August 25 at Mayence. Left here this morning for Ludwigshaven arrived there about 2 p.m.

August 26 at Ludwigshafen, here we have a branch, alson one in Manheim which is over the river Rhyn, a large Bridge divides the two Kingdoms one is Baden, the other Bavaria. Brother Baliff left for Switzerland and I was left here in company with Brother Schram from Payson to preside over the two Branches. We can do but very little good seemingly at present, as we are forbidden to preach, hold meetings or babtize, but we can visit and explain our principles in private, sometime we held regular meetings but allways in fear of being detected.

September 24 My teeth got so bad that I could scarcly use them so I made up my mind to get me a new sett made while here, so I went to the Dentist today had all my decayed teeth pulled and ordered a new sett.

1880 Oct 12 Left Ludwigshafen in company with Brother Schram to Manheim for a visit to Stuttgard left Manheim by R.R. at 9:45 arrived at Kalsrnhe at 11:45. This is the capitol of the Kingdom of Baden, the King and royal familie reside here in a large Palace. We went to see it, there is a large and beautiful garden in front ornamented with Statues, Fountains, Walks, and good many gas lamps. We walked through the principal streets, stopped there about 3 hours and left at 3 p.m. for Calw arrived there at 6 p.m. I went with Bro Schram to visit his mother, she received us not very Kindly, as she is not a member of our church, but quarreld with her son and opposed our principels so much that I was glad to leave her and went to a Hotel.

Oct 13 At Calw in Baden, cloudy morning, this is a smal city suroundet by high mountains, we walked this morning nearly to the top of a mountain and there

Kneeled praying the Lord for protection and blessings for ourselves and for our families at home. Left by R.R. at 11:25 arrived at Nagold at 12.m. Here we went to see a familie recommendet to us as wishing to hear the gospel, we talked with them about 2 hours explaining the gospel to them, but they could not see the neccesity of changing their religion. We left there about 2:30 and walked over a high Mountain to a village Walddorf, here lives a sister which joined the church about 2 years ago, but her husband and father opposed our principels so much, that I expected they would order us to leave the house, but after a short time they cooled off and invited us to stay all night.

October 14 at Walddorf in Baden. It rained last night the road was muddy weather cold which suited me, as we had to walk again over high mountains to another village to visit a familie which was recommended to us. We found them, the man profess to believe, but would not be babtized on account of his wife which opposed us, we left some of our Books and told them to instruct his famielie. We left them and walked again over mountains back to the rail road station.

This mountain country is thickly setteld with poor people, we saw villages every 2 or 3 miles the ground is cultivated to the very top of the mountains where there is no Timber, we saw men, women and childern working on them, some carry on their heads baskets filled with manure, while others digging the ground with spades and picks, as it is too steep for animals to clime up.

There are a few rich people living here in fine Palaces while the majority are poor and like slaves live a miserable life with no expectation of ever bettering their condition. We arrived at Calw this evening at 8. p.m.

October 15 at Calw, this morning we visited several families, spoke to them about the principals of the gospel, but could not make any impression on them, as they are steeped in sin, and nothing short than the power of God will awake them. Left at 2:15 by R.R. for Stuttgart, this road goes over high mountains and through several long Tunnels, and while passing though them it was darker then the darkest night I ever seen. We arrived there at 5:30 pm went with Br Schram to his sitor got supper there but as they had no bed for me I went to the Hotel.

October 16 at Stuttgart in Wurtemberg, this is a large city of about 100,000 inhabitans the Kapital of the Kingdom, celebrated for its high schools, Book printing establishments & C & C. We went to see the Kings Palace, Museum, Picture Gallery and to the Theatre in the evening.

Oct 17 at Stuttgart, rainy morning, went with Br Schram to his sistor for lunch. Then we went to see the garden by the Kings palace which has a large round Fountain in the centre, suroundet with Statues, beautiful plants, flowers & C. Brother Schram left the city about noon to visit some of his relations in the country, and I started back at 2:10 for Manheim arrived there at 8:30 pm. Walked to Ludwigshaven arrived there at 9 pm.

October 18   at Ludwigshaven. it rained here every day for about 4 weeks in sucession and on account of that the river Rhein went over its Banks doing a great deal of damage, a good many Warehouses near the river, and thousands acres of Land is under water in several instances, the farmers could not gather their crops, the flood came so sudden on them.

November 1   Today I wrote the following lines to my daughter Nelly in answer to the last of hers.

My dear daughter Nelly (Ellen R. Tippetts)
I did not mean to mistrust you And though you where out at night,
While I am in Germany preaching the Gospel I belive that you Know it is not right.
I only done my duty to warn you To be carefull and not be led astray,
That you may grow up in purity As your Father and Mother allways pray.
For Satan will not fail to tempt you And try you to consent what is not right,
But allways pray for His holy spirit Which will guide and direct you aright.
You know I am absent, yes your Father Has gone and left you all alone.
Is my name ever mentioned By my loved ones at home?
Do they miss my Kind attention, Miss their Fathers warm embrace,
Oft forgetful I am absent Run to greet to see my face?
When the hours of day are numbered And the evening Lamps they light,
When they seek their peacefull slumbers Do they miss my Kind, good night?
Do they miss me in the morning When draws near the hours of prayer.
At our table, at our meeting Do the miss me everywhere.
Why does Father go and leave us Seems I hear the children say.
He must Know that it will grieve us When he stays so long away.
We have playmates and their Father Never think to leave them so,
But when next he comes to see us Mother do not let him go.
Stop my childern be not angry With your Father Kind and true.
For it is not for wordly pleasure That he has bid his home adieu.
Let us take the holy Bible Over its sacred pages look,
Read the words of Christ our Savior Which is written in that Book.
He that leaveth Father Mother Wife and children for my sake,
To go forth and preach the gospel Of my glory shall pertake.
But while we are seperated. O how good you must try and be,
Seek to make each other happy And should never disagree.
You must ask your heavenly Father To protect him as his way,
And as God loves his childern He will hear you when you pray.
My mind leaps backward for a little while As my memory oft retraces,
I see at the window as I pass by A group of smiling faces.
Thy Kiss there hands as I seem to go To labor, thus made light,
Mans lot in this world must be hard and drear When not by children made bright.
I thank thee o Lord for my children That cluster around my heart,
In virtues path may they ever be found, From goodness never depart.
Now my dear daughter Ellen, if you Be obedient to your Mother and allways true,
Kind and obliging to your sistors and brothers The blessings of heaven will rest on you.
I hope you will answer this soon Because I have pleasure allways to learn,
Good news and tithings from home Especially from my daughter Ellen.

November 10   I felt very lonesome for some time, not because I am so far away from my home but I can do so little good here which I am not use too, I would like to travel more, and be an instrument in the hand of the Lord to bring people to a Knowledged of the truth, but this our Elders are prohibited by this government. We were forbidden to assemble and hold meetings, forbidden to preach in public and in private, and forbidden to babtise. Yet in spite of all this, we assemble, preach and babtise, but allways in fear of being detected and arrested.

But we have a satisfaction in Knowning the Lord is with us, and our ennimis will be permitted to go so far, and no further. A few nights ago I dreamt that we held a meeting on sunday and while we were in about the middle of it a policeman came in and ordered us to follow him, in the excitment I awoke. I told this dream to several of our people and advised them to be on their guard. Last sunday we assembled in a house outside the town, nearly all the member where there, then we discovered an aposte watching, watching for all to come so he can inform the police about, which he treatened for some time. But we left that place and met in another part of the city by one of our people. Here is a testimony that the Lord is with his people, protected us and showed us things to come, a promise which we have to encourage and strengthen us in our most holy faith.

I pray that I and my familie may allways so live, as to be worthy of His protection and blessings all the days of our lives. I allways feel my weaknesses and imperfections, but have faith in the Lord that He will be with me, protect and give me strength according to my day, if I had not this hope and faith abiding within me I would never have left my home depending on my own strength.

This mission is a great trial on my patience, as we have the promise to be tryed in all things this is one. I expect when I be tryed sufficiently in this, the Lord will try me in something else, but I hope and pray that He will bless me, and give me strength at all times that I may be able to overcome, and have a right to claim the blessings of eternal life. Amen.

1880 December 11 at Ludwigshafen, Kingdom of Bavaria. It is six months this morning since I left my mountain homes, and all that is dear and near to me for the purpuse of proclaiming the gospel to those that sett in darkness.

I have tryed in my weak and imperfect way to do this to the best of my ability, and I pray that I may receive aid from on high so as to be able to magnify my calling and to hold out faithfull all the days of my life. When I reflect how Kind my heavenly Father has been towards me, I feel thankfull for his protecting care, for He has guarded and protected me from danger and accidents, seen and unseen by land and on the sea. I have had good health and peace of mind, and allthough very lonesome at times I feel that I am in the service of God, I learn to appreciate the Book of Mormon as I never did before. Whenever I feel inclined to be lonely, low spirited or home sick, I read some in its sacred pages, and receive consolation, new strength, peace and satisfaction enters my spirit. When I read of the great trials these people were willing to undergo for the salvation of men, what are my little difficulties compared with their afflictions which they had to endure.

314

If I expect to share the glory for which they contendet, I see that I must labor in the same spirit. I have had thus far plenty of time for meditation and to review all the events of my life and to think of my beloved ones at home from whom I am so far seperated, how wonderfully I was led to join the church of God, blessed with Wifes and childern which are good and true, blessed with good comfortable homes and all that can make life desirable, I cannot find words to express my gratitude to my heavenly Father for all those blessings.

This mission is quite a trial on my patience, as I am not use to be so quiet and so long away from home. But on due reflection we can indeed have patience, when we Know our reward is sure, that the cause we advocate will stand, and that the principels for which we suffer will exist after our persecuters shall have met their deserts at the hands of justice. Knowing their miserable faith and contrasting it with our glorius prospect we can say with our savior, Father forgive them for they Know not what they do.

Thos were some of my reflections this morning and thinking they would be interessting, I wrote them down and send them to my families.

December 15 at Ludwigshaven, wrote today Letters home and the following lines to my daughter Nellie. I was very much pleased to receive your Letter of November 24th, and read with pleasure those beautiful lines. In answer to those, I hope you will always gather And seek wisdom from on high, praying to your heavenly Father Who will grant you a rich supply.

God be thy light thy teacher be, Inspire thy words with truth, And your reward will be when you see The progress in thy youth.

God bless my children, forever bless Over them thy spirit throw, And may their lives for ever express The gratitude they owe.

Affectionately your father,

1881 January 5 Wrote to my children and at the closing of my Letter the following lines.

Let us prove by our acts and good feelings, As we mingle with friends day by day,
That we gladly remember Gods blessings And try his commands to obey.
Let us try to make our friends happy, Let us seek to have love in our homes,
For it is good to have friends all around us, When a day of adversity comes.
Then let us be up and be doing, Improve ourselves in all good we can see,
The Kingdom of Heaven ought always And onward our watchword should be.

1881 January 14 at Ludwigshaven, wrote the following Letter and lines to my daughter Nellie.

Your interesting lines of December 16 I received a few days ago, they gave me much pleasure and enjoyment on account of the good sentiment, faith, and hope expressed therein.

I feel much obliged to you for the same, and wish you may continue to write inlines to me because I can see an improvement every time. It takes much practise to write in verses, but you must remember, "There is no excellency witout labor". I will try to answer your lines, with lines, if able to do so, and time permits.

I wish you and all my children could fully realize the blessings they enjoy in having their lot cast among the pleasant homes and peaceful valleys of Utah.

I wish they could appreciate, the intervention of their heavenly Father in their behalf, while there are thousands of childern scattered through the world who have not bee so favored and who could they change positions with the childern of Zion, would think themselves highly blessed. In this country and in all nations around about, the children are not teached the principals of the gospel, exept what they learn from the elders of Zion, and there is only a small number who are willing to obey, because of the wickedness of their parents, and the cunning and craftiness of their priests.

They are bound for destruction, there will soon be in their midts of famine and pestilence, war and spreading death.

Therefore be thankful that you are in a place where your heavenly Father desires you to be.

And should you feel at times to complain of your lot, just contrast the misery existing in the world, with the blessings you enjoy in your own happy homes, and you will find sufficient cause to be thankful.

In answer to your last lines, I say,

I try at any time day or night, To do things I Knew are right, The many miles that part us makes no difference to me, I Know in whom to trust, and whose servant I be.

Christmas has come and gone, you see That Santa Claus had not forgotten thee, You will find him always good and true, If you try your best his will to do.

You say, we miss you sadly, miss you At home here on the farm, But we grieve not and we weep not, We Know you are protected from all harm.

This is right, you need not grieve nor fear, Because I am in His service and He is always near, When dangers or troubles in my path should apear, That He will protect, bless and make my way clear.

I can always tell if that or this, Of paths I meet the right one is, I try to have His Keeping care, Then I can journey safely anywhere.

If dark the day or way may be, Or rough, Ah what is that to me, God leads and will control the storm, And Keep His faithful ones from harm.

Who trust in Him the victory wins, Before temptations fray begins, This is my hope and my defence, I trust and wield Omnipotence.

1881 February 1 at Ludwigshaven, wrote the following lines

My Mountain Home

I love the still my mountain home, Though in distant lands I am called to roam,
From my humble cot near the Rail Road station Neath the rugget hill that was cut by donation.
I love each tree with its grateful shade, Each flower and plant that the Lord had made.
And the healthful breezes that gently come, From the mountains down to my peaceful home.
I love my home up on that hill, Where an industrious people work with a will.
Where Shops and Factories are erected By the counsel of him whom God ordainet.
I love each man that works on that hill, When he does his duty and works with skill.
When he obeys the counsel of those that are sett, To lead them, to teach, instruct and direct.
I have traveled there in the stilly night, When the moon shone bright with her silvery light,
Over field and groove, and hill, and dale, And seen Bear Lake in the distant vale.
The whispering wind from the mountain height, Was coming down with all its might.

I was cold and chilled as I swiftly came, To Bear Lake Valley, from my mountain home.
As I returned, on the mountain side My rapturous gaze extended wide.
Over distant plains, fields and grooves, To see Bear River in its winding coves.
And further still the Promontory laves, Its southern wing in the sparkling waves.
Oh Great Salt Lake, whose briny foam, I love to see from my mountain home.
I have traveled since then over Land and Sea, To go where I am at present be.
I left my wives, childern, friends, To preach the gospel in foreign lands.
I have been in Prison like men of old, For the word of God which we have told.
The enemys of truth will rage and foam, Untill judgements reach them, from my mountain home.
Guide me my Father with Thine hand, While traveling through this wicket land,
Guide me, I pray along the way, That Thou wouldst have me go to day.
Give me thy spirit that I may, Do my duty day by day,
Protect and bless me while I roam, Untill I return to my mountain home.
This scenes I love and will cherish yet, In memory dear each found regret,
As I wonder forth I will bear in mind, Those loved ones dear I have left behind.
My fervent hope and constant prayer, Shall be for those I have cherished there.
Wives, childern and friends, where ever I roam, I love you still, and my mountain home.

1881 February 10 at Ludwigshaven. Extract from a letter written to my wife.

I am thinking a great deal about you of late, I know it must be a great trial, and you must have a great deal on your mind to govern and control such a large familie, allthough I believe they are not so hard to control as a good many others, but nevertheless there must be a great anciety on your mind concerning them.

But I feel comforted in my reflections that the Lord is with you through his holy spirit. He will strengthen you according to your faith and good desires. He will send His guarding Angels to comfort, bless and protect you and our beloved childern. This feeling and Knowledge which I possess gives me in my lonesome hours joy and consolation which I am unable to describe. You say you never seen such dark times in the church at the present and that something must come to wake people up.

You dont begin to see such dark times in Utah as in this old world. While visiting last week one of our members, I saw a woman with her baby coming in begging for a piece of bread, she told a sorryfull story, her husband has been out of employment all winter, they had nothing to eat for several days, she has two more children at home famishing for something to eat, and they expected to be thrown out doors by the Landlord as they are unable to pay rent.

And this only one case in a hundred thousand, the Newspapers are full with cases where people take their own lives, and the lives of others, driven by desparation of actual starvation.

The elements here are dark as well as the people, the weather is dark and gloomy, it seems that the sun refuses to shine, and here we can plainly see that darkness covers the earth, and gross darkness the minds of the people.

Last week was an earthquake at Bern in Schwitzerland which set the people there thinking the last days are at hand. It shock there several times, ruined a great many building, and thrown down 300 chimneys. This is only a fore taste of what is to come over the nations, for they have Killed the prophets and many people of God, and consequently their days are numbereth.

I hope and pray that we may allways be found contending for the truth, and be able to overcome all our failings and weaknesses, and that we may be worthy to

317

come forth in the morning of the first resurection with our childern and posterity and inherit eternal lifes. Amen.

I have not received answer yet with permission to go home, but I expect one before long. On account of my teeth, and sore gums, I can not speak disstinkly, but I dont expect to leave without permission.

I been yesterday in Manheim visiting the saints and held meeting in the evening, as we dare not assemble in the day time because the police are after us, and if they should find us assembled, they would arrest, and perhaps put some of us in prison, fine and banish us, because some of our apostates informed that we held meetings, which privileged the chief of police forbid us.

There is the same spirit here against the saints as there was in Nauvoo. But we are not afraid, for the Lord has promised to take care of us, and we are satisfied He is able to do it. If it was not for this faith which is witin us we could not exist here. For the devil holds great power over the hearths of this people, they are willing to serve him because they are a wicket and adultories people, and are nearly ready for distruction. Still there are a few honest people among them, and on account of them I believe the Lord delayed his judgements a little while longer.

At our meeting last night a man that we cut of the church about 3 months ago for adultery according to his own confession, spoke and said that he had repented, is willing to make restitution, and renew his covenant and live a better life, he said since he was cut off, he had no rest day nor night, the agonies of hell are always before him. He cried and wished to be prayed for.

I told him not to give away to evil spirits, to show his repentance by his works, and after while he could be rebabtized and again become a member in the church of God. This was a scene that I never witnessed before, and I hope will be a warning to others in this country.

This meeting closed at 10:30 p.m. so late on account of our members being at work at the Factories untill 7. p.m. and we can not commence our meeting til 8. p.m. then I had to walk home, about 2 miles in a snow storm the wind blowed terrible.

1881 March at Ludwigshaven, Kindgom of Bavaria. Wrote the following lines, To my dear Alice,

As I read that Poetry you have sent to me I thought of the many changes since I first you see,
Then I was a stranger in a foreign land. A stranger to the Gospel, which I could not understand.
I was traveling eastward to my native land, From the golden shores on the Pacific's strand.
I was an Unbliver in the word of God, Did not believe our Savior was His Son our Lord.
There I found a people, good, Kind and true, And to my astonishment the gospel was there too.
There I was instructed by a man I never Knew, and I never expected would be "my father in law".
He took great pains to teach, and so instructed me, That the everlasting gospel I may be able to see.
I listened, examined and prayed day and night, That my mind may get enlightened, so I could see the light.
The Lord in His kindness was merciful to me, And by dreams and visions the necessity I could see.
To repent, be babtized, and thus to gether in with all the faithful saints, who have conquered sin.
As I became a saint, I could see very soon, That it is not good for man "to be alone".
I did not loose much time to explain this unto you, Asked you to become my wife, We never shall be two.
It did not take much coaxing, we were filled with mutual love,
Pure as the dews from heaven descending from above.
You wished for time to consider, I thought it right and smart,
At last you said, "Yes, I will be yours with all my heart".
We were married in a short time, now twenty three years.

318

The Lord was merciful unto us, He has heard our prayers.
We have always lived peaceful and on virtues side, Unconsious that Angels had always been our guide.
We have been blessed and prospered winter and summer.
We also have Boys and Girls too, yes quite a number.
We should be thankful to Him, and praise His name,
For all blessings and pray We may continues the same.
I pray that all our children be good, and pure in heart, Always be found faithful, from virtue never depart.
That the be kept from evil, and from doing every wrong,
Till changed to life immortal and join the ransomed throng.
We also had some ups and downs which are needful changes.
They all come from above, from Him who our lot arranges.
Let us seek the highest good, not for wealth or pleasure,
They have wings and fly away, we must seek a better treasure.
At present among the wicket I was called to roam, And for a short time to leave my mountain home.
I have been abiedient, done the best I could, But his wicket people refuse the word of God.
I am not discouraged, think not my task is hard, I am trying to be faithful, that I may reap a sure reward.
And with that faithful number of that immortal band, to sing the songs of Zion, and on mount Zion stand.
I expect the Letters will be few, I write for Germany, Because in a short time I hope to cross the sea,
And return to those which are deares to me. Then all the wealth of Europe, great as it appears to be.
They are doomed for destruction according to His word,
For they have rejected the gospel of the Son of God.
They will be visited with famine, wars, and earthquarkes dire,
And they will be wasted by Gods consuming fire.
Then let us be faithful and endure the test, The plan of our heavenly Father is sure the best.
He Knoweth if our hearts are always pure and true,
Of sins or wickedness, they are not hidden from His view.
When you at times feel lonely and the weight of care,
Believe that there is comfort and great help in prayer.
Your words not your tears shall unnoticed fall, Our heavenly Father will answer, yes before you call.
It seems the time had sooner come, Then I expected, to see my mountain home,
I have been protected, blessed, had all I stood in need, Have good health in body, all but my teeth.
I have great faith in a short time to be. Through Gods blessings with our childern and thee.
That God who has always protected me, Will not fail to be my guard by land and sea.

1881 March 5 at Ludwigshaven. Today I received a letter from President Baliff of Bern informing me that on account of my sore gums and not being able to talk distingly, I was released from my mission to return home with the first company, which will leave Liverpool April 16.

Wrote several Letters to my Brother in laws and sistors explaining to them the principals of the everlasting gospel, and informing them of my early return to America.

March 23 Received a Letter from home enclosed a draft of 50.00 which was thankful received.
Brother Baliff requested me if I possible could to pay the passage for a young man named Ludwig Kinchley from Speier, he joined our church about one year ago, and appearingly a faithful member in the church. I answered him and told him, I will try and do so.

1881 April 4 at Ludwigshaven. Extract from a Letter I wrote to my daughter Nellie.

> I perfectly agree with you
> That my home is the dearest spot on this earth for me,

Especially when I find peace and happiness in my families.
I will also write a few lines to you, to answer yours.
When over the dark waters I was called to go
I did not grumble, although felt very weak,
I had faith in the Lord and prayed also
For His spirit to be with me, I felt very meek.
His spirit has been with me, is yet my constant guide,
I pray it may never leave me wherever I may be.
I have been blessed, protected, when danger was near my side,
And I will try to keep it on land or on the sea.
When you get this lines I expect to be,
Far away from here on the Atlantic sea.
This country and all Europa has no charms for me,
And in a short time it will be full of misery.
Because they will not listen to the warning voice,
And have enacted laws that people have no choice,
To repent, be babtized, and do as we propose,
To gather them to Zion, and life eternal choose.
I know it is through His goodness
Which He has shown me from above,
That I am spared to see His goodness,
And witness His unchanging love.
Let us ever be truthful, let others fence,
And like hypocrites trim their words for pay.
In pleasant sunshine of pretence,
Let others spend their day.
Let us face the wind, though safer seem
In shelter to abide.
We were not made to sit and dream,
The safe must first be tried.
We must be true to our inmost thought,
And as our thought our speech,
What we have not by experience bought,
We can not undertake others to teach.
In a short time I expect to see,
My mountain home, and all that is dear to me.
There I hope to find all inpeace and harmony,
Wives, Childern, friends as well as thee.
I pray to God who always protected me,
To be my guard by land and on the sea.
To give me health, strength and prosperity,
And life eternal in eternity.

Your affectionate father.

1881 April 10 at Ludwigshaven, left this morning by steamboat down the Rhein to Rotterdam.

Memo:
The above has been taken from a copy of the original handwritten journal of Morris David Rosenbaum. We have tried to keep the grammer, puctuation and spelling the same as his original writing. Some words were difficult to read and might not be accurate.   Var Rosenbaum, Pason, UT

Sandringhaven of 11th(?) Oct 7, 1880.

My dear Daughters Nelly & Fanny

I was very glad to receive Lines & Letters from you, and I wish you write every time your mother sends me a Letter, it will do you good as it will give you practice in writing Letters, and will be a benefit to you in time to come.

You asked me to write something about this country, and as the place where I am now is not very attractive I will write about Berlin the place I like so well on account of being honored with police guarding me about 18 hours.

Berlin is the capital of the Kingdom of Prussia and the residence of the Emperor of the german Empire, situated on the river Spree between the rivers Elbe and Oder, almost in the centre of Europe. It has about 600 Streets, 60 Spaces and 48 Bridges, and is divided in 18 districts, which have in all about 20,000 houses the most of them 4 stories high with over one million and fifty thousand inhabitants among which are 50,000 Soldiers and 5000 Police men.

Industry and commerce have increased in such

2

a wonderful way, that it can be said every article of trade is not being manufactured in this Capital.

There are a great many curiosities in this City, I you to like to go to the promenade "Under den Linden" a beautiful avenue planted with trees on both sides and bordet with magnificent palaces, large and elegant stores, brilliant Hotels, Coffee Houses &c &c. here can be seen the palace of the Emperor, Palace of the Crown prince, Opera House "H. Hedwigs" Church, the Academy of Architecture &c the University, the Arsenal, the principal guard, and in the Lustgarten a beautiful garden and the Museums, Bilder galleries, and Statues.

A few Blocks from here is the (Kaisergallerie) which is a splendid passage leading to another street a magnificent construction, it is said that for splendor and elegance it surpasses all the galleries in Europe. it is about 80 feet high, has a glass roof and both sides crowded with stores.

Here is the (Panopticum) Wachs works galleries. I went to see that twice, there are about 500 figures in wachs, life size and just at naturel, that when I entered the first time I thought they where

322

alive, there are Emperors, Kings, Queens and their
children, Lords and men and women of renown, as
well as Murders, Thieves and criminals of all
Kinds &c. &c. it takes a whole day to go through the
different rooms. I also went to the Museum
and Picture galleries, which are filled with statues,
of ancient and modern Warriors, Kings, Princes &c.
the stair case which forms the centre of the Museum measures 50 feet in length, 22 feet wide and 40 feet high.
there are celebrated pictures painted on the walls representing the principal events in history, the Tower of
Babel, the time of Greece, destruction of Jerusalem, &c
&c. &c. I can not begin to tell or write all there
is to be seen there, but it takes several days to see
everything understandigly.
I visited the Jewish Synagogue, it is a fine large
building of square rocks the interior is very richly
decorated and contains 3000 seats. In the evening
during meeting it is splendidly illuminadet with
gas lamps which gives a grand effect to the eye.
In walking down the street "Under den Linden"
we passed under the Brandenburger (Thor) Gate
which is 200 feet wide, and 75 feet high. the top is

4

ornamented with the (Quadriga) a celebrated piece of
Art, it is a large carirage drawn by 8 Horses, and
is made of copper. Next is the (Thiergarten) a grand
park with splendid walks, drives, Statues, avenues, &c.
containing 240 acres of Land. On the right is the
Kömigsplatz, here is the (Siegessäule) or victory monument
erected in 1873. It is a magnificent Monument 200 feet
high, consisting of a square granite base highly polished
with relief figures cast in bronze, representing various
scenes in the late war. on the top of this colum is
a large bronze figure of Victory, a female with imense
wings, holding in her left hand a spear, and in her
right a laurel wreath. this figure is cast from
material captured from the enemy is 40 feet high,
and weighs 24700 pounds, it is gilbet over with gold.
A winding stair within leads to the top of the colum,
wich we accendet and obtained a grand view of Berlin.
There are 30 Theaters, and gardens for concerts by the
score. I can not begin to describe all there is to be seen
in this city, I bought Photographs of the most of the places
and when I return you can see them.
Hoping this will find you all in good healt, and praying the
Lord to bless you all, I remain your father A. I. M

324

Letter Written by Morris David Rosenbaum to His Daughters
During His Mission in Prussia (Germany)

Ludwingshafen Oct 7, 1880

My dear Daughters Nelly & Fanny,

I was very glad to receive Lines & Letters from you and I wish you write every time your mother sends me a Letter, it will do you good as it will give you practise in writing Letters, and will be a benefit to you in time to come.

You asked me to write something about this country, and as the place where I am now is not very attractive. I will write about Berlin, the place I like so well on account of being honored with police guarding me about 18 hours.

Berlin is the capital of the Kingdom of Prussia and the residence of the Emperor of the german Empire situated on the river "Spree" between the rivers Elbe and Oder, almost in the center of Europe. It has about 600 streets, 60 Squares and 48 Bridges, and is divided in 18 districts, which have in all about 20,000 houses the most of them 4 stories high with over one million and fifty taused inhabitants among which are 50,000 Soldiers and 5000 Police men.
Industry and commerce have increased in such a wonderful way, that it can be said every article of trade is now being manufactured in this Capital.

There are a great many curiosities in this city. I (?) like to go to the promenade Under den Linden a beautiful avenue plantet with trees on both sides, and borderet with magnificent palaces, large and elegant stores, brilliant Hotels, Coffee Houses & C & C, here can be seen the palace of the Emperor, Palace of the crown prince, Opera House, St. Hedwigs Church, The Academy of Architecture & C, the University, the Arsenal, the principal guard, further on is the Lustgarten, a beautiful garden and the Museum, Bilder galleries, and Statues.

A few Blocks from here is the (Kaisergatten) which is a splendid passage leading to another street, a magnificent construction, it is said that for splendor and elegance it surpasses all the galleries in Europe. It is about 80 feet high, has a glass roof and both sides crowded with stores. There is the (Tasapticum) Masks works galleries. I went to see that twice, there are about 500 figures in masks, life size and just as natural, that when I entered the first time I thought they where alive, here are Emperors, Kinds, Queens and their children. Lords and men and women of renown, as well as Murderers, Thieves and Criminals of all Kinds & C & C it takes a whole day to go through the different rooms. I also went to the Museum and Picture galleries, which are filled with statues, of ancient and modern Warriors, Kinds, Princes & C. The staircase which forms the center of the Museum measures 50 feet in length, 22 feet wide and 40 feet high. Here are celebrated pictures painted on the walls representing the principal events in history, the Tower of Babel, the time of Greece, destruction of Jerusalem, & C & C & C. I cannot begin to tell or write all there is to be seen there, but it takes several days to see everything understandingly.

I visited the Jewish Synagogue, it is a fine large Building of square rocks the interior is very richly decorated and contains 3000 seats. In the evening during meeting it is splendidly illuminadet with gas lamps wich gives a grand effect to the eye.

In walking down the street "Under den Linden" we passed under the Brandenburger/Ther gate wich is 200 feet wide, and 75 feet high. The top is ornamented with the (Quadriga) a celebrated piece of Art; it is a large carriage drawn by 8 horses, and is made of copper and victory riding in the car. Next is the (Thiergarten) a grand park with splendid walks, drives. Statues, avenues, & C containing 240 acres of Land. On the right is the Kinigsplatz, here is the (Linegessule) or victory monument erected in 1873. It is a magnificent Monument 200 feet high, consisting of a square granite base highly polished with relief figures cast in bronze, representing various scenes in the late war. On the top of this colum is a large bronse figure of Victory, a female with immense wings, holding in her left hand a spear, and in her right a laurel wreath. This figure is cast from material captured from the enemy is 40 feet high and weighs 24,700 pounds, it is gildet over with gold. A winding stair within leads to the top of the colum, wich we ascendet and obtained a grand view of Berlin.

There are 30 Theaters, and gardens for concerts by the score. I cannot begin to describe all there is to be seen in this city. I bought Photographs of most of the places and when I return you can see them.

Hoping this will find you all in good health, and praying the Lord to bless you all, I remain your father M.D.R.

326

Life Story of Morris David Rosenbaum

Morris David Rosenbaum, only son of David Rosenbaum and Sarah Barnas was born in Fordon Kingdom of Prussia, Germany, July 11, 1831.

My father was a hard workingman and generally occupied in trading. He was a man of good morals and he exerted himself diligently by example as well as precept. To instill into the minds of his children every principle of honesty, honor, and virtue. My mother was a very good and pious woman and devoted a good deal of her time to explaining the Bible to her children, especially to myself, her only son. She was president of a charitable institution and her spare time was occupied in visiting the sick and needy, administering to their wants. As my parents were of the Jewish faith, I was sent at an early age to a rabbi to study Hebrew in connection with the common school, which I attended six years in succession.

In 1842 when about 11 years of age I commenced to study the Hebrew Bible. The Old Testament only, and was taught by my teacher that this is the original language spoken by Adam and Eve, that the Jewish religion is the only true one in existence, that the New Testament is a fable, Christ and imposter, all the human families have gone astray and will be damned except the Jews, the only Chosen People of the Lord.

I remember asking my teacher, "Why is it our people are so scattered in the world, why we have no prophets or inspired men, no temple, and why we are like sheep without a Shepard?"

"Oh!" said he, "Prophets, inspired men and temples are no longer needed. Moses and the prophets we read about are our patterns and lawgivers. The Old Testament is complete; we are the Chosen People of the Lord. There is no further need of these things, therefore they ceased."

I thought to myself, can it be possible that my teacher is correct? That the Lord is so unmerciful as to damn millions of his children and not give them a chance to embrace the true religion? Can it be possible that our forefathers have rejected and slain the Savior, our Messiah and are therefore scattered among all nations and no longer favored with prophets, inspired men and temples?

1844, at the age of 13, I went clerking in a store and stayed there for 6 years. In 1850, when about 19 years of age, I left my native land, Germany, for America. Went to Hamburg by rail and from there in a sailing ship to New York. This trip lasted 74 days. After resting a few days I went out peddling on the out skirts of New York with goods in a basket carried from door to door. This was very hard because I neither spoke nor understood the English language. But still I got along very well.

Then I traveled along the Hudson River to the Catskills and returned to New York and from there to Philadelphia, the Eastern and Southern states and to New Orleans. From there I took passage in a steamer, John L. Steavens, via Havana, Aspinual, Panama and Acapolea to San Francisco. Here I bought a saddle horse, saddle etc. and goods and went peddling through the settlement in Carson Valley and was greatly impressed to visit them and learn for myself what kind of people they are and learn some of their doctrine. I remember well when first seeing their settlement of hearing a voice say, "There is a people which you will never leave."

Arriving in the valley, the first house I stopped at was Joseph Morduck. I inquired of him about Mormonism. He seemed afraid to talk to me about it. He said there is no use in preaching to a Jew because he cannot believe this gospel.

I traveled on and stopped at noon with Simon Baker, he argued with me about Mormonism until midnight but made very little impression on my mind. But it set me to thinking and searching the scriptures. I traveled through their settlement many times and found them the best people I ever came in contact with. My desire to be with these people increased and as they moved in mass to Salt Lake Valley, I made up my mind to travel with them, stop there during the winter, then return to my native land the following Spring.

1857 September 27, I left Carson Valley with the Mormon company, William Smith as Captain. I rode my saddle horse with others in his company most of the way ahead of the train to find camping places. We came by the Northern route arriving at Brigham City on November 2, 1857, and I stopped with Samuel Smith a short time, then went to Salt Lake and boarded with George Nebecker and went to school there in the 17th Ward, Isaac Bowman Teacher.

I remember well going to a meeting the first time with Brother Nebecker and heard that sermon before, because during his remarks I could tell beforehand what he was going to say and was convinced of its truthfulness.

On our way home Brother Nebecker asked me how I liked the sermon. I replied, "Very well. I remember of hearing that sermon before." He said, "If you did it was before you came to this world." Brother Nebecker also informed me there is a German Jew, Alexander Neibaur, a matchmaker, living in the 13th Ward, Andas. I went to visit him and saw his sign. I imagined hearing a voice like this, "You are going to get married in this house."

I went in the house and met Mr. Neibaur, his wife and several children. Mr. Neibaur talked much on the principles of the gospel with a peaceful and teachable spirit. I was treated very kindly by this family and after several visits Mr. Neibaur began to talk about Mormonism. At first I could not believe and differed with him in some of the principles of the Bible, but in a short time found I was in error, and became interested in the principles of the gospel. A peaceful and teachable spirit wrought mightily in me commending the ancient gospel to my conscience.

I read The Book of Mormon from beginning to end in connection with the Bible prayerfully and arose from its perusal with a strong conviction on my mind, "This book was written by inspiration."

Dreams and visions which I had at that time began to have great effect on my mind, but when I listened to my selfish thoughts, it seemed to me I was deceived, I hated Mormonism in my heart and regretted ever hearing of it. When I made up my mind to have nothing more to do with it, my mind was darkened, tribulation and danger seemed to be near me and I felt surrounded by evil spirits. Whenever I studied The Book of Mormon and went to meeting hearing the Elders preach, I felt a peaceful influence by day and during the dark hours of the night, I felt surrounded and was instructed by an unseen power in the principles of the Gospel. During several successive nights, I could see plain the following words of the Prophet Isaiah before me, "Wash you. Make you clean. Put away the evil of your doings from before mine eyes. Cease to do evil etc." I felt convinced of the truth of The Book of Mormon and the preaching I heard of the principles of the Gospel and made a strong resolution in my mind, "I can and will embrace the truth regardless of consequences." I remember well of hearing Brother Neibaur bearing his testimony to the truth of the Everlasting Gospel to me. I asked him, "Why can not I have such a testimony?" He replied, "Mr. Rosenbaum, I promise you in the name of Israel's God, you will if you obey the principles of the Gospel, repent and be baptized for the remission of your sins, and then ask prayerfully your Heavenly Father for it." Such a promise I longed for. In a few days I went to Bishop Thomas Calister and asked to be baptized for the remission of my sins.

March 27, 1858 I was baptized by Brother John Tingey. April 1st I was confirmed. April 2nd I paid my first tithing to the Bishop Calister of $140.00 in coin. That same evening I married Alice Neibaur daughter of Alexander her Father performing the ceremony at his house.

April 28, 1859 – Today I was called and started to Echo Canyon in company with others to assist in defending the people. Stopped there about 3 weeks and returned to Salt Lake City. May 17, 1859 -- Today I started to travel south with my wife and stopped at Provo during the great move. Returned to Salt Lake the last of June. July 4 – I was ordained an Elder by President D. Hunt in the 5th quorum of Seventies. I wrote several letters to my mother and sisters explaining the principles of the gospel and the history of the church to them and was in great hoped and almost certain that they would examine and accept its principles as I did, but in this I am disappointed up to the present time.

A short time afterwards I received a letter from my mother, she was awful mad because I joined the church. Said she, "I have 3 children lying in the graveyard and would rather have you there than having you forsake our holy religion and etc." And asking me if it was my intention when I left home to apostatize and join such a degraded people as the Mormons.

In my answer I told her when leaving home I did not know what I was going to do but now I know for a fact that I am in the hands of the Lord and have confidence in Him, that I have not forsaken the Jewish religion. I believe in the God of Abraham, Isaac and Jacob, but I accepted more truth. I told her I could answer her question by asking another one and I asked her, "When the sons of Jacob sold their brother Joseph to the Egyptians, did they expect that he ever would be a Savior to his father's house?" 1858 – about this time I went to bed one night contemplating on the principles of the gospel and wondering if my mother or any of my relations ever would join the church. I dreamed of traveling in a carriage through a large city and seeing a large number of men and women repairing the streets. In the crowd I saw my mother and invited her to come ride with me, pleaded with her for a long time but she would not ride with me. I told the driver to go ahead. He started but I stopped him again in a few moments and called my mother again and entreated her to come with me. Told her how much better it would be for her to come and ride with me than to work on the public streets, but she refused and would not come with me, so I told the driver to go ahead and left her.

1859 September 23 – my wife Alice gave birth to a girl we named here Sara after my mother. 1859 December 3 – I received my endowments and my wife Alice was sealed to me by President Brigham Young. This night I received a testimony of this work which I have and desire never to forget. My father died about the time of my marriage and was buried at Fordon Germany.

330

1860 February 24 – Moved to Farmington and kept a store there for 9 months, then moved back to Salt Lake and bought a house and a lot in the 8th Ward. 1861 March 11 – my wife Alice gave birth to a boy. We named him David after my father. April 10 moved to Brigham City rented a house from Brother John Gibbs on Main Street and opened a store there. Sold my place in Salt Lake and bought the place in Brigham. 1862 – Built an addition in front of my place and moved my store there. 1862 November 17 – my wife Alice gave birth to a girl we named her Ellen after her mother. 1863 – this year built a rock store on the South side of my place. Watson Brothers did the mason work, moved into it. November 4th 1864 my wife gave birth to a girl we named her Fanny.

I shipped 600 sacks four to Helena, Montana lost $6,000.00 on it. In 1865 sent 4 teams of my own to Boise City, Idaho loaded with flour, butter, eggs, etc. Returning lost 12 head of mules on Rock Creek.

1866 January 22 – my wife Alice gave birth to a girl. We named her Alice. She died October 21, 1866. Another son, Morris, was born July 30, 1867. August 10 Abigail Snow Caldwell was sealed to me. 1866 September 7 Sara died. 1869 March 2, Abigail gave birth to a daughter named Harriet. September 13 Alice gave birth to a son name Alexander, July 10, 1869 received my naturalization certificate. 1871 August 5 Harriet died. 1871 October 17 Alice gave birth to son Aaron. 1873 October 14 Abigail gave birth to Henrietta. 1874 January 21, Alice gave birth to Joseph who died July 18, 1874. July 20, 1874 Moses died. 1875 May – Abigail gave birth to Alice. 1877 March 3 Abigail gave birth to Morris. 1877 August 18 Alice gave birth to Margarete, who died April 21, 1879. 1879 November 16 Alice gave birth to Leah. 1880 March – Abigail gave birth to Ninna. 1880 March 25 was called to go on a mission to Germany I as county assessor at the time and asked for an extension of the time until my work as assessor could be completed which request was granted and after closing up my business left Brigham City by rail road June 11, 1880 with my companion John Mcalister. June 22 – Left New Jersey for Liverpool in the steamer Wisconsin. The sea was very foggy and mountains of ice. The sailors said this was the most dangerous journey they had had for 25 years. We were met on the landing by Brothers Budge, Nicholson, Cape and Martineu.

We asked to go to Berlin to report to Brother Kinke. Arrived there July 10, 1880. Started out tracting the following day after offering up a prayer to Him who lives forever:

"Great and Almighty God, My Heavenly Father, in obedience to the council of the authorities of the church and in the Kingdom upon the Earth. I left my mountain homes and all thus that are near and dear unto

me for the purpose of coming to this land and proclaiming the Everlasting Gospel to the people. I pray the Lord to pardon and forgive all my sins and transgressions up to the present time. Let them be remembered no more before Thee. I acknowledge my weaknesses and imperfections knowing I am liable to err and go astray. Therefore, O Lord, I pray Thee in the name of Jesus Christ that Thou whilst grant unto me a double portion of Thy Holy Spirit that my tongue may be loosened, my memory strengthened and I may be able to see of things to come. That I may be an instrument in Thy hand in doing much good in my day. I pray Thee my Heavenly Father to prepare the hearts of the people unto whom I may come by dreams and visions that they may know that I don't come in my own name, but in Thine and they be prepared to received me as a servant of God. And let Thy great kindness conquer and subdue the unbelief of Thy people. Heavenly Father I pray Thee to bless Zion and all Her stores. Especially those in authority that they may have wisdom to lead Thy people in truth and righteousness. Bless all the honest in heart among the nations may the time speedily come when they shall be gathered from Babylon that they may escape the wrath and indignation that will pass over the land. I pray Thee to remember to bless their hearts and may their wants be supplied from time to time. I pray Thee in the Name of Jesus Christ to remember and bless my families and all that are near and dear unto me with goodly portion of Thy Holy Spirit and they may be comforted by day and night. That the angels of Thy presence may be around about them and if they need any assistance it may come in time. If any of them should get sick or an accident befall them if they call on the Elders of the church and the ordinances of the Gospel be administered in their behalf. I pray that their prayers may be heard before Thee, and they may be restored to health, strength and peach of mind. Strengthen their desires to serve Thee and keep the commandments that they may not do anything to grieve the Holy Spirit. That peace and contentment may dwell in their habitations. Now, O Lord, I dedicate and consecrate myself and all I possess to Thy service praying Thee to accept and let the angels of Thy presence be around about me that I may be protected day and night. I pray Thee, O Lord, that Thou wilt make a speedy work among the nations that the door may be opened for preaching the Gospel. Confound all those who oppose Thy servants and spare our lives to return home in safety. All these favors and blessings I humbly ask in the name of Jesus Christ, Amen."
(Typed 1966 by Reuben L. Prescott, corrections made 6 October 1992. Ready to sent to Salt Lake City, Utah)

ADDRESS BY MORRIS D. ROSENBAUM
SON-IN-LAW OF LORENZO SNOW
(Given as a tribute on Lorenzo Snow's 70th birthday)

I've come, responsive to your call, dear friend,
And heartfelt tribute cheerfully extend
On this, your seventieth anniversary,
And gladly honor this, your jubilee.

I fain would cherish all men's noble deeds,
Without regard to nations or their creeds:
I'll never harbor malice in my heart –
From truth and virtue I will not depart.

In the grand cause of truth, and human right,
You've labored long – you've worked with all your might,
In aiming Zion's children to unite;
The Lord has blest you with unrivaled light.

You've traveled much abroad o'er land and sea –
The Gospel standard raised in Italy;
Journeyed in Asia's far-off sunny clime,
And testified to men in Palestine.

A sacred record, by the ancients written,
You once presented to the Queen of Britain;
In various ways you've worked for Zion's cause,
Withal assisted framing Utah's laws.

You long have known that truth alone will stand;
You know God's kingdom yet will fill the land;
You see it rolling forth in might along,
And yearly in these mountains growing strong.

You've bravely toiled through many joys and fear,
Until your age o'erreaches seventy years;
On this occasion I rejoice to see
You thus enjoy your well-earned jubilee.

Since nightly rest is unto labor given,
And one day set apart in every seven,
'Tis right that you should have a jubilee
Of rest, and bless your own posterity.

I wish a thousand blessings and good cheer
To you, with all your family now here,
For what you've done and what you've suffered too,
With life so pure, and with a heart so true.

In fervent prayer I ask the God of grace
To smooth your pathway in your onward race;
And unto you may special grace be given
To help you walk the "narrow-way" to heaven.

May many years of true prosperity
Be added on to your past seventy,
With peace and plenty in your mountain home,
Is the wish of your friend,

333

Abigail Harriett Snow

Abigail Harriett Snow was born July 16, 1847 at Mount Pisgah, Iowa (USA). She was the first-born child of Lorenzo Snow and his second wife Harriett Amelia Squires. As a child, she experienced many of the unpleasant situations the early saints were forced to endure. When the saints began their trek westward she was just a baby. Her father became Captain of the 2nd Company of Brigham Young traveling west. Her family traveled by means of covered wagon. When they arrived in the valley (of the Great Salt Lake) in 1848, Brigham Young sent their family to help settle the territory known as Brigham City, Utah.

At the age of nine, she was described as having large brown eyes, with long beautiful hair that hung in ringlets down to her waist, and she was small for her age. She used to attend private school at home, with her Aunt Lenora as a teacher.

She had a flare for dramatics and became a member of the Dramatic Association of Brigham. At the age of 14, she landed a staring role in one of their productions, which lasted for several years.

Abigail met and married Thomas Caldwell on January 17, 1864. He was the son of General Caldwell. They became the parents of three children. Twin boys, Sylvanus and Sylvester (born 5 February 1866 in Brigham City, UT) and a daughter, Hazel. This couple was sealed for time and eternity before her husband was later killed by the Indians. She was a widow at the age of 18. Abigail remained a widow for a long time before she decided to remarry again.

She married Morris David Rosenbaum April 5, 1868. He was a merchant who had come to Brigham City selling goods along the way. He already had one wife by the name of Alice Neibaur and 13 Children. But this did not stop the newlyweds from adding nine more children of their own to take care of. Harriett was born March 2, 1869, and she died 2 years later on August 2, 1871. Moses was born August 19, 1871 and he too died when he was almost three years old on July 22, 1874, Nettie May arrived October 13, 1873. Alice Maude was born May 4, 1876, Morris Snow was born March 3, 1878, Minnie

Mabel arrived March 19, 1880 and Lucius Snow was born June 23, 1882. They called him Lutie for short. We also found a death record confirming the fact this couple had a ninth child by the name of Lena born February 17, 1885 but unfortunately, their daughter died August 5, 1887 at the age of two. Abigail and her second husband were also sealed together for time and eternity on July 16, 1864. This apparently must have been a legal procedure at the time, thus giving Abigail her choice of husbands for eternity.

Abigail was a good mother with very strong religious convictions. She saw to it the children attended their church meeting and that each of her living children were baptized when they reached the age of eight years of age.

As time passed, she became widowed for the second time. She took up dressmaking orders to support her family.

In 1878, the first Primary Association was organized in the 2nd Ward. Abigail served as the Primary President until 1881 at which time she was made President of the Box Elder Primary Stake Board.

Marie Rosenbaum Easthope, a granddaughter, recalls: "I remember when I was about six years old, I wanted to live with my grandmother in Brigham City. My mother let me go to live with her. She had had a stroke before I went to live with her and she wasn't very well. She lived alone in an old adobe house on Main Street (in Brigham City, Utah). The house was so old it was ready to fall down. The upstairs was all gone. There were bats that came out at night and my cousin and I used to chase them with long sticks.

Grandmother lived in two rooms of the house. Her fingers were paralyzed. She would let me rub her fingers with oil and that would relax them. She could hold a spoon to eat and a pencil to write, like a child, between her middle fingers.

She was very religious and always one hour before bedtime, she would read her Bible and tell stories. And I would kneel down by her knees and lay my hands on the Bible. She would put her hands on top of mine, as she told me what to say in my prayers.

I can remember, I walked on the top of a new fence in the back yard. Grandmother told me not to, but I did anyway. A bee flew in my face and I slapped at it. It went down my neck and stung me twice before grandmother came to me. I cried like I was killed. She put mud on it to take away the sting. When I quit crying, grandma told me to sit down on the porch while she talked to me about right and wrong. She told me that when we did bad things or didn't do what we were told, God would punish us, like the bee stinging me. The sting of the bee was like religion, it left its mark. And that we should always do what we were told and never do wrong. Our Heavenly Father loved us and didn't want us hurt. And the bee sting was like our conscience. We know good from bad. God was good and Satan was bad. I never forgot her words."

Marie also recalls that, "Grandma had some chickens and that one of the hens would lay an egg out in one of the buildings. I would get the egg and clean it. How happy I was when my grandmother would give me the egg so I could take it to the store and get five cents worth of candy in exchange for the egg."

Marie also adds, "My grandmother left some wonderful memories for me. I hope I can always be like her. I remember the last time I saw her alive. She told me one golden rule. To be like the three wise monkeys, to live like them: 'See No Evil, Hear No Evil and Speak No Evil.' I have always tried. I love the three monkeys she gave me. I always want to live her teachings. When I was eleven years old my grandmother had another stroke that took her life."

Abigail Harriett Snow Caldwell Rosenbaum died, May 9, 1914, in Brigham City, Box Elder County, Utah. She was almost 67 years old.

Compiled by: Elizabeth J.O. Williams; November 1978
SOURCES:
1)   Family group sheets
2)   Personal knowledge of her granddaughter, Marie Rosenbaum Easthope as fo
      in a brief history outline submitted to the Daughters of the Utah Pioneer Soc
      in March, 1963.
3)   Information obtained from Elaine Kay Rosenbaum Christensen.

Hyrum Taylor Marcroft

Ada May Walkey, Hyrum & Lou Walkey

Father: John Marcroft
Mother: Charolette Whitehead Taylor
Born: 10 August 1860
Place: Salt Lake City, Utah, USA
Married: 19 January 1887 (to Susan Walkey)
Place: Salt Lake City, Utah, USA
Married: 31 October 1905 (to Jeannie Campbell)
Place: Salt Lake City, Utah, USA
Died: 24 July 1938
Place: Salt Lake City, Utah, USA

Hyrum Taylor Marcroft

Hyrum Taylor Marcroft was one of the finest men to walk this earth. Born at home (338 West 8th South), August 10, 1860, in Salt Lake City, Utah, he was the 10th child of Joseph Marcroft and Charolette Whitehead Taylor. Six of his older brothers and sisters died as children so he only got to know and enjoy his brothers: John, Robert and Joseph while he was growing up. They were a very close-knit family. In fact, they were so close that when they got married, Hyrum built his own adobe brick home at 334 West 8th South, his brother, Joseph, lived on the east side of Hyrum and his brother Robert, lived to the rear. It's interesting to note that the home located on the east side of Joseph's home belonged to the John Page family. Joseph and Robert both married girls belonging to the Page family. Their wives were sisters. Joseph married Lydia and Robert married Mary Ann. When Hyrum was a young boy he used to herd pedigree livestock (cows) that were entrusted to his care. He used to take them almost to the Oquirrh Mountains. Many times it would take him from sun up to well past sundown to bring the livestock home. Each day when it came time to cross the Jordan River, he would remove his clothes and stuff them under his hat until he had crossed the river. Then, he would redress before they resumed their journey. On those occasions when the livestock gave him trouble, he would not be able to go home at all. Instead, he would have to find a shady safe place to stay until he could return home.

On 25 August 1868, Hyrum was baptized a member of the Church of Jesus Christ of Latter-day Saints. He was baptized in the Jordan River. He recalled that the water was very cold this particular day, even more so than when he would swim across with the cattle.

Hyrum discovered how to create and make the first adobe bricks made in the Salt Lake Valley. He built the first adobe brick by stacking mud, etc. in a pan, then he made some boxes the size he felt would be about perfect and tried the mixture out. Thus he created something new to build with, something that had not been used in building before. His adobe bricks could withstand the wind, rains and any strong destruction that came their way. He even built his own home from the product he created. These bricks were far stronger and more dependable than the bricks they use today (1978). This became his business for many years. (Later Hyrum was employed by the Utah Light and Traction Company. He held this position of supervising foreman for 49 years).

The railroad used to pass by his door on 8th South. On 2nd West, there were poles in the middle of the street where he later supervised the laying of all the tracks for the change from street car trolleys that moved the street cars to rail tracks, that have now been removed or covered over by pavement surfaces in order for our modern bus transportation to travel more comfortable routes.

During his 49 years with the Utah Light and Traction Company, he was never absent from work. He was a very dependable employee who was loved and respected by all those he worked with. Hyrum was a hard worker. He worked 12 hours a day and received $1.25 a day. He got paid extra for overtime and he took all the overtime he could get.

Hyrum married twice in his lifetime. He first married Susan Walkie on June 1, 1886, but this marriage ended in a temple divorce. It seems that while he was serving a mission in Australia, Susie would leave there children to the mercy of anyone's care while she left them in the night to pursue her own pleasures. This union produced four children, one of which was Cecelia Hazel Marcroft born 1 March 1887. (One of their children died as a baby and not much is known of the other two children.) After the divorce was granted, Hyrum maintained the custody of their three living children.

In time, Hyrum married Jeannie Cambell, October 31, 1905. They were later sealed for time and eternity, January 20, 1918. She was a lovely mother of six children who had also obtained a temple divorce from her first husband, one James Henry Young. She mothered Hyrum's three children along with her own and loved them equally as well. They were a happy family living in a home where love and peace reigned continually. This couple was blessed with a son, Arnold Taylor Marcroft, born 19 April 1907. Unfortunately, the Lord called their son home shortly after he was ordained a deacon at the age of 12 on September 18, 1919.

Hyrum used to raise a nice vegetable garden, plus care for rabbits, chickens, etc., to help keep his food table filled. He did his best to keep all the children's mouths fed, and shoes and clothing on them.

There were 14 loaves of bread baked every other day. Ten lunches had to be put up every day, plus the breakfast meal and evening meal to prepare. Huge meat pies were made and every bite was eaten at one meal. A roast was always prepared for the Sunday meal along with other goodies. Jeannie's pies and cakes melted on ones mouth and there were always plenty of cookies for the weeks lunches.

Hyrum never left his home without praying for the day's blessings upon his home and loved ones knowing full well that the Lord would answer his prayers. The Marcroft family attended all their church meetings. Hyrum served the Lord faithfully and humbly as a result the family was blessed beyond measure. Both parents had beautiful singing voices and they sang in the 5th Ward Choir for many years. Hyrum held the office of a High Priest, and he was a faithful block teacher for many years. Hyrum would also place a sack of wood or a sack or coal or a sack of flour or a large bag or two of groceries on the porches of people in need of heat or food and leave without anyone knowing that he was the one who left it. Only his wife and God knew where the gifts came from. That was the type of man he was.

He helped to heal the sick with the help of the Lord. On one occasion, he anointed a man who was possessed with the evil spirit and commanded it to leave this man's body. It took six men to hold this sick man down in his bed while the evil spirit left his body. That's how powerful the evil spirit was. As the spirit left, the man's body became weak and his normal strength had been reduced to the strength of a young child. In time the man became well and later testified of his experience with the power of the Priesthood and related many blessings that had come into his life as a result of his experience.

Hyrum witnessed many spiritual experiences. While serving a mission in Pago Pago (South Sea Islands), he and his partner came to a home with a sign on the gate that said, "Beware of Vicious Dog, Do Not

Enter". His missionary companion, Elder Dunkworth, was afraid to go into the yard. Hyrum prayed to his Heavenly Father and asked if this was the place they should go into. He received his answer, opened the gate and the huge vicious dog that was taller than Hyrum (when he was standing on his hind legs) lunged for Hyrum's throat. Hyrum raised his hand and commanded the dog to stop. The dog was in the air by then, but it howled and fell immediately to the ground – helpless. The lady of the house then came outside. She was afraid to look at the missionaries for fear the dog had wounded one of them. When she saw what had taken place, she went to her dog and stroked him. The dog was helpless to move so Hyrum pulled him over on the grass. The missionaries were then invited inside the home to give their message. Their message was warmly received. The people treated them kindly. When it came time to leave they had to use the same entrance and the dog was now back on his feet. The dog walked over to the missionaries and licked Hyrum's hand while it wagged its tail. Then he quietly laid down while the missionaries opened the gate and left.

Hyrum used to say that, "if I ever take ill, it will surely be my last days, because God has blessed me with good health always." True to his prediction at the age of 77 he became ill and was taken to the St. Marks Hospital (Salt Lake City). Ten days later, on July 4, 1938, he passed away. Thus ended the mortal existence of Hyrum Taylor Marcroft.

Compiled by: Elizabeth J.O. Williams
               November 1978

Susan Walkey

Cecelia (daughter), Cora & LeRoy (grandchildren), & Susan

Susan with her
great grandchildren
Judy, Norma & Raymond

Marie, Cora, Susan, Hazel, & June
All granddaughters

Father: Henry William Walkey
Mother: Mary Moss
Born: 2 December 1865
Place: Little Durham, NSW, Australia
Married: 19 January 1887 (to Hyrum Taylor Marcroft)
Place: Salt Lake City, Utah, USA
Married: (to "Mr. Young")
Place: ?
Married: (to Patrick O'Brien)
Place: ?
Died: August 1950

Susan Walkie

Susan Walkie was born in Sydney, Australia about 1862. She was the daughter of John Walkie.

Not much is known of her early life except that she achieved about a third grade education. While living in Australia, she became a convert to the Church of Jesus Christ of Latter-day Saints. According to Marie Easthope, a grand daughter, Susan was converted by her future husband, Hyrum Taylor Marcroft. She was baptized sometime between 1881 and 1885. She then migrated to the United States and settled in Utah. After Hyrum returned from his mission in 1885, the couple courted awhile before they were married in the temple for time and eternity, June 1, 1886. Ten months later a daughter, Cecelia Hazel was born, March 1, 1887. Later on, another daughter, Viola, and a son, LeRoy, joined the family.

According to Marie, Susan enjoyed participating in church plays. She and her husband used to both participate in the different church activities. Susan seemed to have a natural acting ability. The more she participated in plays the better she became. Eventually she wanted to become a professional actress. Naturally her husband refused. He felt her place was at home taking care of her family. He did not approve of a wife pursuing a career on the stage. Susan had other ideas. According to Hyrum's biography, "while he was serving another mission in Australia, Susan would leave the children at home alone nights, leaving them to the mercy of anyone, while she pursed her own pleasures."

As a result when he returned home, the couple ended their marriage in a temple divorce. Susan took the children and tried supporting them as an actress on the stage in the old Salt Lake Theatre. Later on she became a member of the Max Senate Acting Circuit and traveled from city to city presenting their minstrel shows. Susan left her children with an aunt while she was traveling around. She used to blacken her hands and face and tell funny jokes and stories. According to Marie, she didn't sing or dance. She mainly told jokes and acted out parts.

While on tour she met and married a younger man by the name of Mr. Young. He was also a member of the acting profession. This marriage didn't last long before he left her for a younger actress. When the circuit reached Boise, Idaho, some years later, Susan finally quit the world of show business and started her own Millenary Shop. She sold fancy hats and ladies fine lingerie. Some of the hats she made herself.

In time, Susan married for a third time. This time to a fine man by the name of Patrick O'Brien. They lived in a nice home with a large yard. Susan loved flowers. She raised a beautiful variety of flowers in her back yard.

Marie recalls that when she visited her grandmother, that she enjoyed eating her homemade buttermilk hot cakes made from sour milk. She also recalls that there was a pet squirrel by the name of Pete that used to live in the tree in her backyard. Pete used to climb down the tree and climb up on Grandpa O'Brien's shoulders in order to eat food out of his shirt pocket.

When her daughter, Cecelia, died (December 15, 1929) Susan graciously let her grand daughter Hazel Maude, age 12, come live with her until her father could provide a proper woman to care for his family.

Marie describes her grandmother as a large busted woman with dark eyes and dark hair. She was a very stylish woman who enjoyed wearing the latest styles of her time. She especially liked satin dresses and jewelry. She used to curl her hair in the latest styles with a curling iron and a can of heat. She was a pretty lady with a funny sense of humor. She used to tell jokes and amusing stories about her theatrical adventures.

According to Marie, her grandmother lived a long life and that she died sometime in 1941. Thus ended the colorful life of Susan Walkie.

SOURCES:
   1)   Hyrum Taylor Marcroft's biography
   2)   Personal knowledge of Marie Easthope – granddaughter

Compiled by: Elizabeth J.O. Williams
              August 1979

Uncle Hyrum and Aunt Susie's Divorce
By: Sarah Edna Marcroft

Aunt Susie was a woman that we children were all afraid of. Her own three children were afraid of her. I never knew of any children that were deprived more of love and affection than they were. They were whipped more than any children I know of – they got so they expected it. When Hazel (Cecelia) was a big girl her mother would turn up her clothes and whip her in front of anyone. The ice house and Lemps Bottling Co. were close and they would all see her whip her. The reason I mention this is that it was so much more severe than the usual punishment. Uncle Hyrum didn't seem to do anything about it.

They both used to take part in ward dramatics, that is, when they became friendly with Mr. And Mrs. Young. They used to go out to parties. There were several couples that used to meet at each other's homes.

Uncle Hyrum was called on a mission. They used to call married men at that time. It was my understanding that she encouraged him to go, although she knew she would have to work at dressmaking to get along. They used to go without purse or script. He went to Australia. He hadn't been gone very long when some of the "Young" children (Aunt Jennie's children) were sick with diphtheria. They were quarantined – that is when Mr. Young came to stay at Aunt Susie's. No one thought anything of it because they were good friends. Just a short time after "Young" went home, his wife (Aunt Jennie) wondered why he didn't come home one night. Then she investigated and found he had taken all his clothes and left, leaving her almost penniless.

A very short time later Aunt Susie was sick. She called mother and Aunt Annie over. She seemed terribly sick. She asked mother if she would look after the children till Uncle Hyrum got home if anything happened to her. Mother and Aunt Annie thought she meant she was afraid she was going to die. They were very worried. In a few days she left without saying a word. She left her children to the mercy of anyone who would take care of them. She went to "Young". As I remember mother took Hazel and Viola and Aunt Annie took Roy, till Uncle Hyrum came home. The Church sent him home. He didn't know till he landed in New York just what the trouble was – he thought she was sick or had died.

When he came home he tried to take care of the three children. Hazel had never been taught anything and she was quite a problem. Uncle Hyrum used to pay me to wash and iron their clothes, although Hazel was older than I was.

We were all surprised when Aunt Susie came home. She asked Uncle Hyrum to take her back. He told mother after that he felt that he should take her back. He wanted to find out for himself if she was guilty. She was only home a very short time when she told Uncle Hyrum she wanted to go back to Young, that she loved him – so Uncle Hyrum sold the back part of his lot to Mr. Lester and gave her the money to go away on. I guess she and Young were married. They fooled around in theatricals for awhile. They didn't live together very long. She stayed in Boise, he went to California.

In the meantime Hazel was married very young – had a baby very young. I helped take care of the baby. Hazel lived there for quite awhile after the baby was born. Uncle Hyrum was good to them. Her mother didn't care anything about her.

Uncle Hyrum and Mrs. Young started going out together. Everyone though it was nice. Uncle Hyrum got a temple divorce and Mrs. Young got a temple divorce, soon they were married in the temple and she became "Aunt Jennie." She had a large family. They all came to live at Uncle Hyrum's. Roy and Viola were also there and later they had a child Arnold. He died when he was about 12 years old. All of Aunt Jennie's children thought a great deal of Uncle Hyrum.

Later, Roy and Viola went to Boise where their mother was. They were old enough to take care of themselves. Aunt Susie later married a man named Pat O'Brien.

Hazel had her children quite fast. She had a big family. 11 children I think. She had a hard life, not knowing how to take care of a home and family, and her husband drinking so heavy, and no mother to help her at all. It was a pitiful situation. I don't know what the trouble was between Hazel and her father or what Hazel expected, buy anyway, she took very sick and I guess the poor girl suffered a lot. Anyway, she told her father when she died she didn't want him to come to her funeral. Well, when she died he did not go to her funeral. But anyway Aunt Susie and Viola were there and they carried on just terrible because he didn't go, which of course was an awful thing. But it made me sick the way Aunt Susie carried on at the funeral because he wasn't there, but my thoughts went back to the time when she deserted them as helpless children and I know how he tried to take care of them then.

I know Uncle Hyrum's grandchildren all feel hard towards him, but they don't understand the situation.

I think Hazel's children have turned out pretty good as far as I know. Hazel's children's names were Marie, Cora, Claud, Roy, June, Morris, Hazel, Lute. I know she buried one baby. I can't remember the other names. One thing about Hazel – wherever she went she took her children. She used to chase in saloons after him, but her children were always close by. I never knew Hazel to ever drink, or go out with any man.

Roy was a wonderful worker. Roy was burned badly in a fire in the projection room of a theatre in Boise. He was running the films. This resulted in his death, he was married had two other sons. A clipping I have said he was survived by his widow and two sons living in Monterey, California. He died in Portland, OR on his way to California for his health. He was 42 years old when he died. His sons may be living somewhere in California. Their names are LeRoy and Marvin Marcroft.

Walkey.

"Argent on a bend engrailed Gules between
two gryphons' heads erased of the last each
holding in the beak a trefoil vert, three
cinquefoils of the first" — Burke's Peerage
1962 Edition, page 1066

Research: Judy   Artwork: Alec

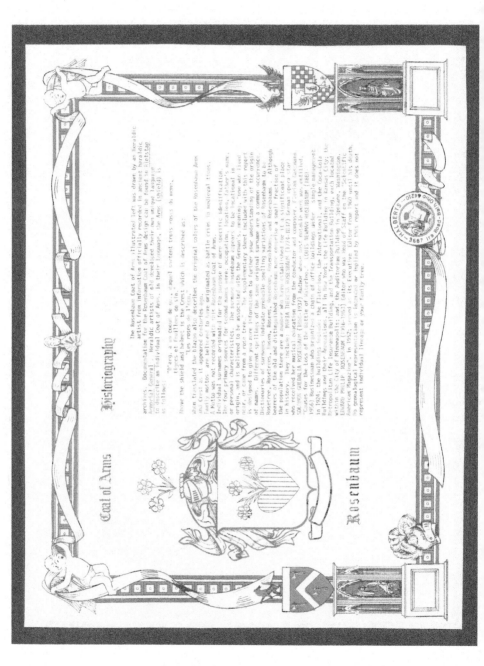

Coat of Arms

Historiography

The Rosenbaum Coat of Arms (illustrated left) was drawn by an heraldic artist from information officially recorded in ancient heraldic archives. Documentation for the Rosenbaum Coat of Arms design can be found in Rietstap Armorial General. Heraldic artists of old developed their own unique language to describe an individual Coat of Arms. In their language, the Arms (shield) is as follows:

"D'arg. a un coeur de gu., duquel sortent trois roses du meme, tiges et feuilles de sin."

When translated the blazon also describes the original colors of the Rosenbaum Arms as the shield and helmet is the crest which is described as:

The four primary sources for surnames or family names are: occupation, location, father's name, and crest as it appeared centuries ago.

Individual surnames originated for the purpose of more specific identification. The surname Rosenbaum appears to be locational in origin, and it is believed to have originated with this report which includes with this report of name. Different spellings of the same original surname are a common occurrence. Dictionaries of surnames indicate probable spelling variations of Rosenbaum to be Rosenroe, Rosetroes, Rosen, Rosers, Rosenbau, Rosenblaum, and Rosenbaums. Although the population there are a number who have established for it a significant place in history. They include: MARIA THERESA ROSENBAUM (1774-1837) German opera star who is noted for her medical education from the Conductor and composer; Austrian musician SON VON GREBALIA ROSENBAUM (1874-1937) Austrian musician, but further your information two further spelling variations of the origin of name. "Guides for the Loss of the battle of Waterloo. (LOUIS BERNING ROSENBAUM (1881-1968) Businessman who organized a chain of office buildings under single management in 1924, the buildings include: the Flatiron, the International, and the Coca-Cola Building, and their Annexations, all in New York; the Life Building in Kansas City; the Metropolitan Life Insurance Building, and the Transportation Building, each located within the city of Minneapolis; and the Auditorium Building in Spokane, Washington. EDWARD PHILLIP ROSENBAUM (1916-1963) Editor who was Head of Staff on the Scientific American Magazine. In 1962, served as its Executive Editor from 1960 until his death. No genealogical representation is intended or implied by this report and it does not represent individual lineage or your family tree.

Rosenbaum

David Rosenbaum
Father: Jude Rosenbaum
Mother: Meta Lister
Born: 1797
Place: Fordon, Prussia
Died: 23 August 1857
Place: Fordon, Prussia

Sharah Barnes
Father: Samuel Barness
Mother: Hannah Liser
Born: 1802
Place: Fordon, Prussia
Married: 1820
to David Rosenbaum
Place: Fordon, Prussia
Died: 1860-1880
Place: Fordon, Prussia

David Rosenbaum

David Rosenbaum was born in 1797, in Fordon, Kingdom of Prussia, Germany. He is the son of Jude Rosenbaum and Meta Lister.

He married Sharah Barnes about 1820 and together they raised a family of seven children, six girls and one boy. Fanny was born July 20, 1823, Hannah was born about 1825 and died November 1, 1843 at the age of 18, Linah was born about 1827 and died November 26, 1846 at the age of 19, Hulda was born about 1829 and died December 17, 1858 at the age of 21. His only son, Morris David, was born July 11, 1830, Minna arrived about 1832 and Ernstina arrived about 1833.

Morris David described his father as a hard workingman who was generally occupied in the world of trading. "He was a man of good morals, and he exerted himself diligently by example as well as precept to instill into the minds of his children every principal of honesty, honor and virtue."

David was raised in the Jewish religion and he tried to raise his children to embrace the Jewish faith as he himself did. It must have saddened him when his only son began to question the Jewish beliefs. When Morris was only 11 years old, he wanted to know why the Jewish people were so scattered in the world. He wanted to know why the Jews had no prophets, or inspired men and why they no longer had temples. Morris couldn't accept the teaching that Jesus Christ was an imposter and that all human families had gone astray and would be damned except the Jews who were the only chosen people of the Lord. He questioned how the Lord could be so unmerciful as to damn millions of his children without giving them a chance to embrace the true religion.

David was a good husband and father. He saw to it his son began early in life to prepare for his role as a provider when he grew up. At the age of 13, Morris began clerking in a store for six years before he decided to leave home and travel to America.

It must have been hard for David to bury two daughters and then say goodbye to his only son, knowing full well that he would never see him again in this life. Morris left home in 1850, and his father died eight years later in the Spring of 1858. (We actually have a written record of David Rosenbaum's death as occurring 8/23/1857)

Compiled by: Elizabeth J.O. Williams
                    December, 1978

SOURCES:
   1)   Family Group Sheets
   2)   Morris David Rosenbaum's diary entitled: "Life and Travels of Morris David Rosenbaum"

Sharah Barnes

Sharah Barnes or Barness was born about 1802 in Fordon, Kingdom of Prussia, Germany. She is the daughter of Samuel Barness and Hannah Liser.

She married David Rosenbaum about 1820 and together they raised seven children in a good home. She named her children: Fanny, Hannah, Linah, Hulda, Morris David, Minna and Ernstina.

Her son Morris David describes his mother as "a very good and pious woman" who "devoted a good deal of her time in explaining the Bible to her children." She spent extra time making sure her only son understood the teachings in the Bible. She taught basically from the Old Testament because the Jews believed the New Testament was only a fable.

Because his parents were both strongly converted to the Jewish faith, they were desirous that their only son was properly raised in the Jewish religion. Morris David was sent at an early age to a rabbi to study Hebrew in connection with the common schools for six years in succession.

It must have proved a big disappointment to Sharah that at the end of Morris David's extensive religious training to find that instead of embracing the Jewish beliefs, he questioned them. He could not accept in full her many explanations in defending her beliefs.

But she was a good woman who loved her family. On one occasion, when Morris was nine years old, he fell while ice-skating on the River Vistual and broke his right thigh. He was in bed for four weeks while his leg healed and Sharah made sure he was well taken care of while his leg was mending.

Morris David also recalls that Sharah "was an unselfish person because she was the president of a charitable institution and that her spare time was occupied in visiting the sick and needy administering to their wants."

Morris' family all spoke the German language. He recalls how hard it was for him to learn English when he left home and arrived in America at the age of 19.

It wasn't easy for Sharah to say good-bye to her son when he left. She had already lost two daughters who had passed away as well as both of her parents. Hannah died at the age of 18 (November 1, 1843) and Sharah's mother also died sometime in 1843. Linah died at the age of 19 (November 26, 1846) and she lost her father, Samuel Barness, sometime in 1850.

Morris left home in 1850. She never saw him again as long as she lived. But she enjoyed her three remaining children as she watched them marry and continue to raise their children to be strong members in the Jewish religion.

She lost her dear husband in the spring of 1858 and on December 17, 1858, her daughter, Hulda, died at the age of 21. Sometime between 1860 and 1880, she joined them again in death. The exact date was never recorded.

Compiled by: Elizabeth J.O. Williams
                    December 1978

SOURCES:
1)   Family group sheets
2)   Morris David Rosenbaum's diary

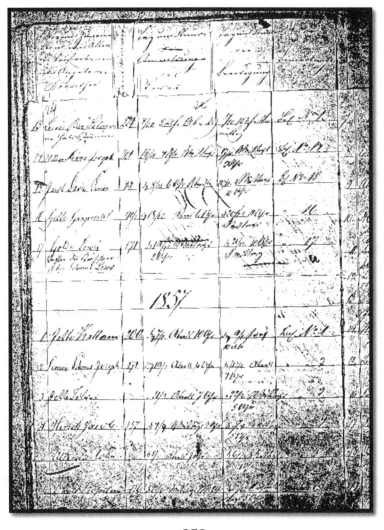

Lorenzo Snow

LORENZO SNOW HIGHLIGHTS
(1814 – 1901)

Date	Age	Event
Apr 3, 1814	--	Born in Mantua, Ohio
1831	17	Mother joins Church; he hears Joseph Smith speak
1835	21	Enters Oberlin College; sister, Eliza R., joins Church
1836	22	Baptized
1837	23	Serves mission to Ohio
1838-39	24-25	Moves to Far West, serves mission Midwestern states
1840-43	26-29	Serves mission to GB; presents BofM to Queen Victoria
1845	31	Marries
1846-48	32-34	Crosses plains
1849	35	Ordained apostle
1849-52	35-38	Serves mission to Europe
1853	39	Presides over colonization of Brigham City
1872-82	58-68	President, Utah Territorial Council
1872-77	59-63	Counselor to Brigham Young
1885	71	Serves mission to Indians in NW United States
1886-87	72-73	Serves 11-month prison term on plural marriage charge
1889	75	Becomes President, Council of the Twelve
1893	79	Becomes President, Salt Lake Temple
1898	84	Sustained the 5th President of the Church
1899	85	Initiates tithing emphasis
Oct 10, 1901	87	Dies

LATTER-DAY PROPHETS

Joseph Smith 1832–1844

Brigham Young 1847–1877

Gordon B. Hinckley 1995–

John Taylor 1880–1887

Wilford Woodruff 1889–1898

Lorenzo Snow 1898–1901

Joseph F. Smith 1901–1918

Heber J. Grant 1918–1945

George Albert Smith 1945–1951

David O. McKay 1951–1970

Joseph Fielding Smith 1970–1972

Harold B. Lee 1972–1973

Spencer W. Kimball 1973–1985

Ezra Taft Benson 1985–1994

Howard W. Hunter 1994–1995

The home of Oliver and Elizabeth Snow in Portage, Ohio
Cemetery containing some members of the Snow Family.

Lorenzo Snow

Father: Oliver Snow
Mother: Elizabeth Phillips
Birth: 3 April 1814
Place: Mantua, Portage, Ohio, USA
Marriage: 1845 (to Mary Adaline Goodard)
Place: Nauvoo, Hancock, Illinois
Marriage: 21 April 1845 (to Sarah Ann Prichard)
Place: Nauvoo, Hancock, Illinois
Marriage: 1845 (to Eleanor Houtz)
Place: Nauvoo, Hancock, Illinois
Marriage: ? (to Mary Houtz)
Place: ?
Marriage: 17 January 1846 (to Harriett Amelia Squires)
Place: Nauvoo, Hancock, Illinois
Marriage: Jan 1846 (to Charlotte Squires)
Place: Nauvoo, Hancock, Illinois
Marriage: 9 October 1853 (to Caroline Horton)
Place: Place: Salt Lake City, Utah, USA
Marriage: 4 April 1859 (to Phoebe Amelia Woodruff)
Place: Salt Lake City, Utah, USA
Marriage: 12 June 1871 (to Sarah Minnie Ephramina Jensen)
Place: Salt Lake City, Utah, USA
Died: 10 October 1901
Place: Salt Lake City, Utah, USA

Harriett Amelia Squires

Father: Aaron Squires
Mother: Elizabeth Prichard
Born: 13 September 1819
Place: Aurora, Geauga, Ohio, USA
Marriage: 17 January 1846 (to Lorenzo Snow)
Place: Nauvoo, Hancock, Illinois, USA
Died: 12 May 1890
Place: Brigham City, Utah, USA

Patriarchal Blessing of Lorenzo Snow
Given 15 December 1836 in Kirtland Temple
Given by Joseph Smith, Sr.

Brother Snow. In the name of Jesus Christ, and by the authority of the Holy Priesthood, I lay my hands upon thy head, and give to thee a Father's Blessing. I ask God to have mercy upon thee, who art but a youth. Thou hast been diligent in thy application to learn; God has looked upon thee from all eternity and has been bountiful in gifts. He has given thee intelligence, talent, and great faculties of mind, that thou might be useful in His cause. Thou hast a great work to perform. God has called thee to the ministry. Thou must preach the gospel to the inhabitants of the earth. Thou shalt become a mighty man. Thou shalt have great faith, even like the brother of Jared. Thou shalt have power to translate thyself from one planet to another. And power to go to the moon, if thou desire; power to preach to the spirits in prison; power to render the veil and see Jesus Christ at the right hand of the Father. There shall not be a mightier man on earth than thou. Thy faith shall increase and grow stronger, until it shall become like Peter; Thou shalt restore the sick; the diseased shall send to thee their aprons and handkerchiefs, and by thy touch, their owners shall be made whole. Thou shalt have power over unclean spirits. At thy command the powers of darkness shall stand back, and devils shall flee away.

If expedient, the dead shall rise, and come forth at thy bidding – even those who have long slept in the dust. Thou shalt have long life – live to the age of Moses, yet shall not be old. Age shall not come upon thee. The vigor of thy mind shall not be abated, and the vigor of thy body shall be preserved. Thou shalt have power to stand in the flesh and see Jesus Christ come in the clouds. No power on earth shall be able to take thy life, so long as thy life shall be useful to the children of men. Thou shalt preach the gospel as long as there is an ear to hear, or a head to bless. Thou must open thy mouth and the Lord will fill it with arguments. Thy voice shall cause the earth to tremble. Thou must pray for thy kindred and be diligent and they shall all receive a Celestial Glory.

Thou art the seed and lineage of Abraham thru the loins of Joseph and Ephraim and thou art entitled to these blessings. God will give thee a companion of thy hearts desire, and thou shalt have prosperity. Thy sons shall be large and mighty men, even large in stature. Thou shalt sit in council with the One Hundred and Fifty Four Thousand and be able to sing the songs. This is thy blessing, of the Holy Priesthood, I seal thee up to eternal life.

Amen and Amen.

Taken from the family records of Lillion Melba Duke Yeats.

Compiled by: Elizabeth J.O. Williams, December 1978

Lorenzo Snow

Lorenzo Snow was the fifth of seven children born to Oliver Snow and Rosetta Lenora Pettibone, April 3, 1814, at Mantua, Prtg., Ohio.

As a boy, he spent much of his time working on his father's farm. He had four older sisters and two younger brothers so the majority of the chores became his responsibility. One wintry day as Lorenzo was passing thru the pasture, he was attacked and chased by a very unpleasant bull. He scurried up a strong oak tree and hung on for dear life. The bull charged the tree and refused to go away. Lorenzo was forced to stay in the tree all day. Night was coming on, his hands were numb and he felt he could no longer survive in the tree. Just then, his father rode up on his horse and rescued his son. It was an experience he never forgot.

Lorenzo worked so hard, that he had to give up going to school, except for three months in the wintertime. He wanted to have more education. One day he told his favorite sister, Eliza, or his great desire to make the army his career. It was a desire he had since he was very small and had watched the army drill and he had listened to the military band. Eliza felt her brother was too fine a young man to waste his good qualities upon the battlefield. He answered her by saying: "Our country needs a well trained army and I am no better than anyone else." She agreed to help break the news to their father. He wanted Lorenzo to follow in his footsteps as a farmer. Eliza thought her father would finally let him have his way, and he did.

Lorenzo knew that if he were going to be successful in the army, he would have to further his education and get a college degree. He sold his share of the family's property and went to Oberlin College in Ohio. On route, he met David A. Patten, an Apostle of the Church of Jesus Christ of Latter-day Saints who was returning from a mission in England. They sat discussing religion. Lorenzo was so interested and so convinced by the Spirit and earnestness of the man, that he was determined to learn more about this new religion.

Before he graduated from college, Eliza wrote her brother that she had joined the Church. She asked him to come to Kirkland, Ohio upon graduation so he could study Hebrew under a well know scholar. This he did. While he was here, he met the Prophet Joseph Smith. Lorenzo said: "As I looked upon him and listened to him, I thought to myself that a man bearing such a wonderful testimony as he did and having such a countenance as he possessed, could hardly be a false prophet."

Lorenzo studied the scriptures, talked to other church members, prayed and was finally baptized in June 1836. Afterwards, he was disturbed. He knew the Holy Ghost was promised to those baptized and he felt he had not yet received it. He wondered if he had done something wrong. He decided to pray. His prayer was answered with a wonderful vision that revealed to him that Jesus was a Son of God, and that Joseph Smith was a true prophet of God. The Holy Ghost descended upon him and his prayer was answered.

Because he was a college graduate, the Prophet asked Lorenzo to teach school. The class he was asked to teach consisted of the rowdiest students in school. The students had succeeded in driving away every teacher asked to take this position. Lorenzo hesitated. He decided he could be a good teacher if he could teach with love. This he did and he encountered very few problems as a result.

When the Prophet Joseph Smith was a political candidate for President of the Untied States, Lorenzo helped distribute literature in support of his friend. It was while he was busy campaigning for the Prophet that he received word that Joseph Smith had been killed, so he returned home to his family.

Lorenzo did not marry his first wife until he was 31 years old. (He had a total of nine wives altogether). The wife we are related to was Harriett Amelia Squires. She and Lorenzo were sealed January 17, 1846, in the Nauvoo Temple at 5:25 PM by Brigham Young. He had held off getting married as he felt he could better serve the Lord as a missionary if he were single. He realized married men could fill missions too, but he felt if he didn't have a family to care for, he could devote his entire time to missionary work. He planned carefully for his first mission. He started out all alone without purse or script. This was difficult for him because he was used to paying his own way. He visited many of his relatives in Ohio and preached the gospel to them. As a result, he successfully baptized many of them.

After his first short mission, he did missionary work in other parts of the United States of America. He suffered many hardships and was often ill, yet he was able to carry out the plans he had made. Later on in his lifetime after he was married, he served a mission in England where he had the honor of giving Queen Victoria a copy of the Book of Mormon. He was put in charge of the London Branch. Before he was released to return home the number of saints had increased to 400. He was then called to initiate missionary work in Italy. He also served a mission in Japan and in Hawaii (Sandwich Islands). Later, he visited the Nez Perce Indians and the Bannock Indians in Idaho to make preparations for the missionaries who would take the gospel to them.

He was also a pioneer. He and his families were driven from Nauvoo in February 1846. They spent winter in a camp known as Pisgah. Come spring, he was called to preside over the camp and the church there. The saints were in serious condition. There was not enough food or clothing for the saints and many of the people were sick.

Lorenzo organized men into companies. Some of these companies were sent to work in other towns to earn money. Some of the companies repaired covered wagons for the trek westward. Some built items such as churns, chairs and tables, to sell for money. He also sent men to ask for contributions from wealthy non-members to assist the saints in their trek westward. These men raised $600.00. He also recognized the need for recreational activities to keep his people physically fit and in a healthy mental and spiritual condition. Therefore, he organized games, socials, parties and plays.

In the spring of 1848, he went to Winter Quarters, a town on the banks of the Missouri River, where the saints gathered to make final preparations to go west. Here, he organized a company of 25 families, including his own, and came west. At Elk Horn, on May 31, 1848, he was made captain of 100 people. He arrived in the Great Salt Lake Valley, September of 1848 with no serious accidents.

A year later, in 1849, he was made an Apostle and was called to go to Brigham City, Utah to preside over and strengthen the saints in that settlement. Fifty families accompanied him there. Already, 200 people were living at the fort.

He first had to get the people there to let him purchase land and water for irrigation because the country was so dry. He taught the people to work together. He knew that when people work together, that they can accomplish much. He helped erect buildings such as the Tabernacle and the courthouse.

He again recognized a need for recreational activities for his people. He turned his home into an amusement or cultural hall and organized a dramatic association to put on plays. He also planned for dances and other types of entertainment.

A few years later, in 1853, he organized the Brigham City Cooperative Association. Under the direction of this organization, industries were begun – a tannery, a butcher shop, a boot and shoe store and a woolen factory. The association also had a herd of sheep, a farm and a dairy. The people under his leadership prospered.

While President of the Quorum of the Twelve Apostles, he realized that he was probably next in line to become the next president of the church when President Wilford Woodruff died. He was 84 years of age at the time and he felt the responsibility would be more than he could assume. A short time before President Woodruff's death, Lorenzo, knowing how seriously ill the President was, went into a small room in the Salt Lake Temple to pray to his Father in Heaven. He prayed that the life of the President be spared because he couldn't assume the leadership of the Church. He concluded his prayer by saying: "Thy will be done." In answer to his prayer, he received a vision. Jesus appeared to him and instructed him concerning the reorganization of the First Presidency. He told him: " – to organize the Presidency of the Church at once." He also revealed to him who his counselors were to be.

Lorenzo had faith that his Heavenly Father would bless him and give him the strength he needed to fulfill his duties as president of the church. He made a habit of seeking the Lord in prayer. And then, he planned and organized to carry out the Lord's will regarding the church.

When he was made president of the church in 1898, he spoke to the congregations and said: "Now brethren, this much I say, and I say it in the name of the Lord. I will endeavor to be devoted to your interests of the Kingdom of God. I will serve you to the best of my knowledge and understanding, in reference to that which will promote your interests in connection with the interests of the Almighty. I will do this, the Lord being my helper."

This was his guide throughout his life. He became president at a very critical time in church history. The church was suffering from a financial crisis. Much church property had been confiscated because of polygamy. Leaders had been imprisoned. During his presidency, he emphasized the commandment to pay tithing.

In the spring of 1899, Saint George, Utah encountered a severe draught. In May the Spirit prompted Lorenzo to go there. He promised the people of St. George that if they obeyed the law of tithing that they could plant crops and expect a good harvest despite the drought. If the saints would be faithful in paying honest tithes, the clouds would gather and the rains of heaven would descend and they would reap a bounteous harvest. The saints did as they were asked and Lorenzo's prediction came true.

Also at this time, individual saints had become heavy in debt. Lorenzo promised that if these saints would pay an honest tithing, that they would be free of their obligations and that they would become a prosperous people. The saints responded to his words and by 1900, great progress had been made. The people prospered. Lorenzo's promise had come true.

Getting the saints to pay an honest tithing was the most noteworthy contribution he made as president of the church.

He died in Brigham City, Boxy Elder County, Utah, at the age of 87 on November 10, 1901. He was indeed a remarkable man.

Compiled by: Elizabeth J.O. Williams
                      November 1978

SOURCES:
   1)   Family group sheets
   2)   The book, <u>A Child's Story of the Prophet Lorenzo Snow</u>
   3)   The book, <u>Lorenzo Snow's Biography</u>, by Thomas C. Romney

REMARKABLE MANIFESTATION IN TEMPLE TO LORENZO SNOW

By: Le Roi C. S

For some time President Woodruff's health had been failing. Nearly every evening President Lorenzo Snow visited him at his home on South 5th East Street. This particular evening the doctors said President Woodruff was failing rapidly and they feared he would not live much longer.

Lorenzo Snow was then President of the Council of the Twelve and was greatly worried over the possibility of succeeding President Woodruff, especially because of the terrible financial condition of the Church. Referring to this condition President Heber J. Grant has said: "The Church was in a financial slough of despond, so to speak, almost financially bankrupt – its credit was hardly good for a thousand dollars without security."

My father went to his room in the Salt Lake Temple where he was residing at the time. He dressed in his robes of the Priesthood, went into the Holy of Holies, there in the House of the Lord and knelt at the sacred alter. He plead with the Lord to spare President Woodruff's life that President Woodruff might outlive him and that the great responsibility of the church leadership would never fall upon his shoulders. Yet he promised the Lord that he would devotedly perform any duty required at his hands. At this time he was in his eighty-sixth year.

Soon after this President Woodruff was taken to California 1898. President George Q. Cannon at once wired the sad information to the President's office in Salt Lake City. The telegram was delivered to him on the street in Brigham City. He read it to President Rudger Clawson, then president of Box Elder Stake, who was with him, went to the telegraph office and replied that he would leave on the train about 5:30 that evening. He reached Salt Lake City about 7:15, proceeded to the President's office, gave some instructions and went to his private room in the Salt Lake Temple.

President Snow put on his holy temple robes, repaired again to the same sacred alter, offered up the signs of the Priesthood and poured out his heart to the Lord. He reminded the Lord how he had plead for President Woodruff's life and that his days might be lengthened beyond his own; that he might never be called upon to bear the heavy burdens and responsibilities of church leadership. "Nevertheless," he said, "Thy will be done. I have not sought this responsibility but if it be Thy will, I now present myself before Thee for Thy guidance and instruction. I ask that Thou show me what Thou wouldst have me do."

After finishing his prayer he expected a reply, some special manifestation from the Lord. So he waited – and waited – and waited. There was no reply, no voice, from the Lord.

He left the alter and the room in great disappointment. He passed through the Celestial room and out into the large corridor leading to his own room where a most glorious manifestation was given President Snow. One of the most beautiful accounts of this experience is told by his granddaughter, Allie Young Pond:

"One evening when I was visiting Grandpa Snow in his room in the Salt Lake Temple, I remained until the doorkeepers had gone and the night-watchman had not yet came in, so grandpa said he would take me to the main, front entrance and let me out that way. He got his bunch of keys from his dresser. After we left his room and while we were still in the large corridor, leading into the Celestial room. I was walking several steps ahead of grandpa when he stopped me saying: 'Wait a moment Allie, I want to tell you something. It was right here that the Lord Jesus Christ appeared to me at the time of the death of President Woodruff. He instructed me to go right ahead and reorganize the First Presidency of the Church at once and not wait as had been done after the death of the previous presidents, and that I was to succeed President Woodruff.'

365

Then grandpa came a step nearer and held out his left hand and said, `He stood right here, about three feet above the floor. It looked as though he stood on a plate of solid gold.'

Grandpa told me what a glorious personage the Savior is and described His hands, feet, countenance and beautiful, white robes, all of which were of such a glory of whiteness and brightness that he could hardly gaze upon Him.

Then grandpa came another step nearer me and put his right hand on my head and said: `Now granddaughter, I want you to remember that this is the testimony of your grandfather, that he told you with his own lips that he actually saw the Savior here in the Temple, and talked with Him face to face.'

Then we went on and grandpa let me out of the main, front door of the temple."

During the M.I.A. June conference in 1919 at the officers' testimony meeting in the Assembly Hall I related Allie Young Pond's experience and testimony. President Heber J. Grant immediately arose and said: "In confirmation of the testimony given by Brother Le Roi C. Snow quoting the granddaughter of Lorenzo Snow, I want to call attention to the fact that several years elapsed after the death of the Prophet Joseph Smith before President Young was sustained as the president of the Church; after the death of President Young, several years elapsed again before President Taylor was sustained, and again when he died several years elapsed before President Woodruff was sustained.

"After the funeral of President Woodruff the Apostles met in the office of the First Presidency and Brother Francis M. Lyman said: `I feel impressed although one of the younger members of the quorum to say that I believe it would be pleasing in the sight of the Lord if the First Presidency of the Church was reorganized right here and now. If I am in error regarding this impression, President Snow and the senior members of the council can correct me.'

"President Snow said that he would be pleased to hear from all the brethren upon this question, and each and all of us expressed ourselves as believing it would be pleasing to the Lord and that it would be the proper thing to have the presidency organized at once. President Anthon H. Lund and myself are the only men now living who were present at that meeting.

"May the Lord bless and guide us by his spirit continually and may the testimony that we possess of the divinity of the work ever abide with us and may our faithfulness be an inspiration to lead others to a knowledge of the gospel, is my prayer and I ask it in the name of Jesus Christ. Amen."

In a few days after the M.I.A. Conference, in an interview with President Lund in his office he retold the incident to me as given by President Grant regarding the meeting in the office of the First Presidency, which was held Tuesday morning, September 13, 1898, at which time President Snow was chosen President of The Church. President Lund also told me that he heard my father tell a number of times, of the Savior's appearance to him. After he had dressed in his temple robes, presented himself before the Lord and offered up the signs of the Priesthood.

I related this experience in the Eighteenth Ward Sacramental service. After the meeting Elder Arthur Winter told me he also heard my father tell of the Savior's appearance to him, in the temple instructing him not only to reorganize the First Presidency at once but to select the same counselors who had served with President Woodruff, President George Q. Cannon and Joseph F. Smith.

RAISING THE DEAD

In the early part of 1891, in Brigham City, Utah, Lorenzo Snow's nineteen-year-old niece Ella Jensen contracted scarlet fever. Within a few weeks was near death being attended by her concerned family and helpful neighbor volunteers. After a particularly bad day Ella asked for her comb and brush explaining, "They are coming to get me at ten o'clock." When asked who was coming, she answered, "Uncle Hans Jensen and some messengers, I am going to die..."

Assuming that this improbable story was merely the jumbled thoughts of a fevered mind, her nurse combed her hair for her to calm her. Ella then called for her parents and bid them farewell and told them about the messengers who were coming. Her parents too were disbelieving as Hans Jensen had died sometime before. Ella called for all the family to come in so she could wish them good-bye and all came in, all but Grandma Jensen who came in a short while. While she was wishing her grandmother good-bye she quietly died.

Her father, Jacob Jensen, decided to contact Lorenzo Snow, who had married Sarah E. Minnie Jensen, his sister. Elder Snow was then speaking at a meeting in the Brigham City Tabernacle. Jacob hitched up his team and drove to town as fast as he could, jumped from his buggy and ran into the tabernacle. He quickly wrote a note and had it placed on the pulpit. President Snow read the note, excused himself and went to speak to his brother-in-law. After a moment of meditation, he sent for Elder Rudgard Clawson who was on the stand and the three of them left the tabernacle and rode the mile and a half to the Jensen home.

On arriving, they found that the sisters had made initial preparations for burial and were washing and dressing the body. The men came in and President Snow stood for a while in deep meditation and then asked for some consecrated oil. This surprised the Jensen's, as Ella had now been dead for two hours, nevertheless complied with the request. Lorenzo handed it to Brother Clawson, requesting that he anoint the girl, which he did. Then the two of them laid their hands on Ella's head and said in part, "Dear Ella, I command you, in the name of the Lord, Jesus Christ, to come back and live, your mission is not ended. You shall yet live to perform a great mission." He said she should live to rear a large family and be a comfort to her parents and friends, then in a commanding tone said, "Come back Ella, come back. Your walk upon the earth is not yet completed, come back." Then shortly after they left the home. Ella's body remained lifeless for more than an hour, then as her parents sat near her bedside, Ella suddenly opened her eyes.

"She looked about the room," her father reported, and said, "Where is he? Where is he?" We asked, "Who?" "Why Brother Snow," she replied, "He called me back."

At first Ella was not happy about being called back. She explained to her weeping parents and amazed friends that she had visited the world of spirits.

"I entered a large hall. It was so long that I could not see the end of it. It was filled with people ... I passed on through the room and met a great many of my relatives and friends ... Everybody appeared to be perfectly happy. I was having a very pleasant visit with each one that I knew. Finally I reached the end of that long room. I opened a door and went into another room ..." It was a smaller room filled with children, who were being supervised by Eliza R. Snow. While listening to the singing of these children, Ella heard the voice of Lorenzo Snow calling her back to mortality. Obedient to that command, Ella walked back through the large hall, advising relatives along the way that she was going back. "It was very much against my desire," she later wrote, "as such perfect peace and happiness prevailed there, no suffering, no sorrow. I was taken up with all I saw and heard; I did hate to leave that beautiful place."

Ella Jensen married Henry Wight, and they had eight children. She lived to be eighty-six and died on October 23, 1957.

(Details of this story found in LORENZO SNOW by Francis M. Gibbons, Young Women's Journal 4:164-164 and Improvement Era, October 1929 pp. 973-974)

Harriet Amelia Squires
Written by her granddaughter, Maude R. Sorenson

Harriet Amelia Squires, daughter of Aaron and Elizabeth P. Squires, was born September 13, 1819, in Aurora, Geauga County, Ohio. Her parents were very religious and were strict disciplinarians.

She attended the schools in Aurora and when eighteen years of age, began to teach school, a profession she followed for several years. During the summer months, she worked in a tailor shop and learned the tailor trade, becoming an expert buttonhole maker and a very efficient tailor or "tailoress".

It was while teaching school that she met Lorenzo Snow and he converted her to the L.D.S. faith.

In the Nauvoo Temple, January 17, 1846, Harriet Amelia Squires was sealed to Lorenzo Snow for time and all eternity by President Brigham Young. The marriage was witnessed by Willard Richards and Amasa M. Lyman.

The Snow family left Nauvoo early in the spring of 1847 and Lorenzo Snow was called to preside over a settlement of saints at Mt. Pisgah, Iowa. It was while here that Lorenzo was taken seriously and dangerously ill with fever and lay at the point of death for many days. This illness was brought on by exposure and lack of nourishing food. He was restored to health by faith and prayer and the nursing and care given him by his wives and sister Eliza.

Harriet was an excellent nurse and knew the healing qualities of many roots and herbs and when any of the family were ill, she was always the one on whom they called.

When Lorenzo Snow was in Italy on a mission, one of his wives, Caroline, was very ill and grandmother had her brought to her home where she nursed her for several months. She gave birth to twins, a boy and a girl, and died two weeks later. She left a girl, Clarissa, age two and Franklin, two weeks old. Grandmother reared these two children to manhood and womanhood.

While crossing the plains, it was the custom whenever the company came to a stream or pond of water, for the women to have a washday. On one occasion they came to a pond late in the afternoon and grandmother took her three-month old baby, laid her under the willows and proceeded to do her washing. She was so busy that she didn't hear the company leave and she and the baby were left alone on the plains. It was beginning to get dark but she didn't dare make a fire for fear it would attract the Indians or wild animals, so she wrapped the babe and sat under a large sagebrush until morning. Food was scarce and was rationed, and she hadn't eaten anything since breakfast the day before. In looking around, she found an old cowbell and after cleaning it thoroughly she filled it with water, which she heated and made some sage tea for her meal. She made a fire by rubbing two sticks together. About noon, two men from the company, who had been searching for her found her bathing the baby. She told them she felt sure someone would find her, so was not worried or upset. Grandmother had a very calm, cool disposition and never seemed to get excited. She was very efficient and thorough in everything she undertook.

She was the mother of five children, three girls and two boys. Twins, a boy and a girl, died when only a few months old. The eldest child, Abigail, was born July 16, 1847 at Mt. Pisgah, Iowa, and was only a few months old when they left for the West (1848).

For many years, Harriet Snow was President of the Ward Relief Society at Brigham City and President of the general monthly meetings of the four (branch) wards. When the Stake Relief Society was organized, she was ordained Stake President, a position she held for many years.

I remember when a child, of going with her to the Relief Society granary, which is still standing on the high school grounds, where she set and emptied mouse traps in an effort to rid the place of mice as the Relief Society grain was stored there. When the granary was built, the children of Box Elder stake gathered old glass, which was broken in fine tiny pieces and mixed with the mortar. This was supposed to keep the mice from making holes in the building.

In one of her large upstairs rooms, she raised silk worms and gathered enough silk to make many yards of silk cloth. I remember helping pick mulberry leaves to feed the silk worms or cocoons.

Grandmother died May 12, 1890 at Brigham City and is buried in the Snow Family plot.

Information about Harriet Amelia Squires

Her Parents:

Father:		Mother:
Aaron Squires	AND	Elizabeth Prichard
B. 29 Sep 1795		B. 10 Apr 1796
Ludlow Massachusetts		Great Barrington, Berks, Mass
(then Hampshire, later Hampton)		
D. 4 Feb 1881 probably in Ohio		D. 2 May 1875

1.	Harriet Amelia	13 Sep 1819
2..	Lorenzo	22 Jan 1821
3.	Alonzo	16 Jan 1822
4.	John Prichard	30 Mar 1824
5.	Franklin	15 Feb 1826
6.	Henry (twin)	16 May 1829
7.	Henrietta (twin)	16 May 1829
8.	Edward	30 Oct 1831
9.	Adeline Cordelia (twin)	4 Mar 1833
10.	Emaline (twin)	4 Mar 1833
11.	Lorinda E.	14 Mar 1835

This seems to have been a pioneer family from the very first, as the first eight children were born in Aurora County in Ohio, one of the most western States of the Union. The last three children were born in Bainbridge of Geauga County in Ohio. This County borders on Lake Erie and is on the northern border of the State.

Of this large family only Emaline, the tenth, is recorded as having died as a baby (13 Dec 1833) which was quite unusual for those days.

Aaron Squires and his wife were remembered as being the strong and rugged people who could withstand the hardships of the frontier territory of their day. See the Introduction page for more of the life of the subject of this book, Harriet Amelia, the eldest child of the family.

INTRODUCTION
(Written by Valoie Rosenbaum Hill)

As a child in Utah, I often sat quietly in the shadows in the evenings; my relatives were visiting, to hear them talk of our Pioneer ancestors. The story I liked best was the one of a lady with a little baby who somehow had been left behind her group on the plains, when our Church members had been forced to leave Illinois, and were coming to the Utah desert. She was a very brave woman, and kept a little fire going with grass and twigs she gathered. When she was hungry, she heated water in an old cow bell she found, and made sage tea. She had nothing else for many hours.

When I grew older I learned this Pioneer woman was my own Great Grandmother Snow! Her name was HARRIET AMELIA SQUIRES, and she was born 13 Sep 1819 in Aurora, Geauga County, Ohio. She grew up to be a fine young lady there. She was a schoolteacher and a seamstress by the time she met and married my Great Grandfather, Lorenzo Snow.

He had been sent to Ohio to campaign for the Prophet Joseph Smith, as a Presidential Candidate. The prophet felt he could put his views before more people of the United States, by doing this. Lorenzo had already filled other missions for the Church of Jesus Christ of Latter-day Saints. He was 32 years old and she was 27.

Soon after their marriage in the temple at Nauvoo, Illinois, they were driven West, due to persecutions of the church. At Mount Pisgah, in Iowa, her husband was appointed to preside, and helps the people grow gardens to leave for the Saints when they came later, to harvest. He also directed the groups when they came to this point of their journey. It was late in 1848 when it was his turn to come to the gathering place. He was put in charge of the 2nd Hundred of the Brigham Young Company of that year. It was at this time that the incident I had often heard of took place. A few years ago I wrote a dramatic Vignette from this incident as it was researched by my sister Lucille R. Hillyard.

In the early days of Utah's history, Harriet took care of her growing family while her husband fulfilled a mission to Italy. After his return in 1853 he was called to settle some families north of Salt Lake in the Box Elder area, where he presided many years. In this move, twin children were born and died.

372

Besides often using her teaching talents, Harriet did sewing for local tailors. She was called to serve her church in positions of responsibility in Stake Relief Society and Primary. She died 12 May 1890 in Brigham City, where she is buried near her husband.

Harriet Amelia Squires Marriage to Lorenzo Snow
(excerpts taken from chapter 9 of the biography of Lorenzo Snow by ?)

"...One important concern was the completion of the temple. Lorenzo joined enthusiastically to contribute his slender means and his labor to complete this beautiful building. He was acutely aware that a principal ordinance to be performed in the temple was the sealing of husbands to wives in an eternal union. Given his total commitment to the church and its doctrines, the counsel he had received from the Prophet Joseph Smith about polygamy, and his advancing age, we may be sure that as the temple neared completion Lorenzo became increasingly conscious of the need to marry. The depth of his feelings may be gauged by the fact that in 1845, at age thirty-one, he was sealed to four women in the Nauvoo temple: Mary Adaline Goddard (his cousin, who had three sons by a former marriage, Hyrum, Orville, and Jacob); Charlotte Squires; Sarah Ann Prichard; and Harriet Amelia Squires. When the new husband accompanied his wives to the altar, one of the temple officiators, impressed by the dignified appearance of this unusual quintet, was heard to comment; "And his train filled the temple."

On the face of things, Lorenzo seems to have bridged the gulf between celibacy and family life with hardly a break in his stride. Much of the credit for this must be given to his wives, whom Eliza described as "stately appearing ladies." These able women were fired with the same convictions and zeal that burned with such intensity in the heart of their husband. And they shared with him the goal of exaltation, the door to which had been opened for them by the sacred ordinances performed in the temple.

If either Lorenzo or his wives thought that the road leading to their objective would suddenly become smooth and straight, they were jolted out of that misconception within a few months after receiving their blessings in the temple. As winter descended upon Nauvoo at the close of 1845, it became increasingly apparent that the Mormon exodus, originally planned for the spring of 1846, would have to be accelerated. Spurious charges of counterfeiting brought against Brigham Young and other leaders of the Church, and disturbing reports that the government was sending a military force up the Mississippi to confront the Latter-day Saints, caused the change in plans. So, instead of an orderly and more leisurely departure in the spring, the Saints were forced to cross the Mississippi in the dead of winter and to plunge westward toward the mountains in search of a haven from persecution.

When the Twelve sounded the call for the exodus, Lorenzo and his family responded promptly. This was not done, however, without some misgivings, especially on the part of the wives, who had to leave their comfortable homes. All the clothes and furnishings it was feasible to take, together with a tent and foodstuffs, were stowed in two wagons Lorenzo had acquired. With pots and pans and other miscellaneous gear hanging on the exterior of the wagons, and with the family cow tethered behind, the Snows set out on the great adventure that would ultimately take them to the high mountain country in Utah.

They crossed the Mississippi on February 12, 1846 ...”

The Children of Lorenzo Snow and Harriet Amelia Squires

1. Abigail Harriet Snow (F)
   Born: 16 Jul 1847 in Mount Pisgah, Pottawattamie, Iowa
   Died: 9 May 1914 in Brigham City, Box Elder, UT

2. Lucius Aaron Snow (M)
   Born: 11 Dec 1849 in SLC, UT
   Died: 3 Oct 1921 in Brigham City, Box Elder, UT

3. Alonzo Henry Snow (M)
   Born: 15 Feb 1854 in SLC, UT
   Died: 1 Nov 1854 in SLC, UT

4. Amelia Henrietta Snow (F)
   Born: 15 Feb 1854 in SLC, UT
   Died: 30 Oct 1854 in SLC, UT

5. Celestia Armeda Snow (F)
   Born: 2 Dec 1856 in SLC, UT
   Died: 13 Mar 1938 in SLC, UT

John Marcroft

Father: John Marcroft
Mother: Isabell Scholes
Born: 6 February 1812
Place: Middleton, Lancashire, England
Married: 1835 (to Charolette Whitehead Taylor)
Place: Middleton, Lancashire, England
Died: 16 October 1898
Place: Salt Lake City, Utah, USA

Charolette Whitehead Taylor

Father: Robert Taylor
Mother: Mary Whitehead
Born: 17 March 1817
Place: Sattleworth, Yorkshire, England
Married: 1835 (to John Marcroft)
Place: Middleton, Lancashire, England
Died: 16 May 1887
Place: Salt Lake City, Utah, USA

John Marcroft
Written by: Sarah Edna Marcroft

Born Middletown, Lancashire, England February 6, 1812. Came to Utah 1859. Died October 16, 1898, Salt Lake City, Utah.

I can remember Grandpa Marcroft a little. He was a slender man, sandy complexion – that is where we get our red hair. One thing that I remember, he used to go to the tithing office and get some of his food. I remember he especially brought honey home and I remember he kept it in a trunk along with other food. But he would always give us children some honey. When I remember him he lived in one room of a two-room adobe house, west of Uncle Hyrum's house. Uncle John and his wife Aunt Rellie and their adopted daughter, Little Rellie, lived in the other room. Grandpa lived in the front room and Uncle John's family in the back room. The house had two outside doors facing the east. Grandpa used to be the babysitter for mother and Aunt Annie. I know he used to made what they called "sugar tits" to satisfy the babies – that was some sugar put in a cloth and tied with a string, then wet it, and the baby would suck on it.

As I remember Grandpa he was a very even-tempered man. I guess I've heard mother say that he was. To me Brother Bob Russell looks more like grandpa than anyone in the family. Grandma Marcroft died before I was born. I remember him coming over to our house and looking at the enlarged picture of grandma (he called her his Charolette). He dearly loved grandma. She was inclined to be a little strict with him, so I have heard mother say. Mother tried to keep grandpa's cloths washed and mended; of course, this was after grandma died. I remember how putout mother said she was once when grandpa tried to hide the holes in the seat of his pants by wearing a coat. She said she made him take them off and she mended them.

I remember when grandpa took sick I saw his lying in a big wooden bed. We used to take things over for him to eat. I remember Lottie made him an eggnog and he enjoyed it so much – then she made him another one later and he couldn't drink it. I remember the day grandpa died – how we children used to run and meet him – don't remember too well, but I do remember him.

He married Charolette Whitehead Taylor in 1835. The record shows they had 10 children – two were born in St. Louis – they must have been buried in St. Louis or near there. They must have joined the church when the first missionaries were sent to England. My father was born in 1849 and he said they joined the church 6 or 7 years before he was born. This is the story as I have heard it. Grandma was the first. I always thought she became interested before she was married, that she was working out, and that she attended several meetings. Her half-sister's husband, (John Easthope) and Grandpa Marcroft, who was her sweetheart, found out about it and were very angry. They followed her one night to a meeting, intending to make a fuss about it, but instead they became interested. Grandma was blessed with the gift of tongues. In England they used to call the Mormons "The Dippers." In grandma's older years she must have been sort of short and heavy. I've heard she wasn't much of a housekeeper, but was very clean in person, that she wouldn't go to ward meeting unless she was clean from skin out. Mother always said grandma was of different temperment than grandpa.

This is a story I heard Aunt Annie tell – said it taught her a lesson. Grandpa always divided everything with his son, Uncle John and his wife, Aunt Rellie. Aunt Annie gave him 50 cents she told him to spend on himself. He turned to her and said, "Thee tell me how to spend the money – thee keep it."

In grandpa's old age he was broken-hearted about Uncle Hyrum. There was some trouble over property. I don't think Uncle Hyrum spoke to his father. I know he didn't go to his funeral or see him before he died. Aunt Susie influenced him a great deal.

I don't know what offices grandpa held in the church, but in my father's diary he tells of he and his father administering to the sick. Grandpa was a weaver by trade – also a glass blower. There was not much work at his trade. For many years he used to garden with a man by the name of Harrow on Harrow's land. It was on 8th South between 3rd and 4th West. They raised all the celery – or most of it – that was sold in Salt Lake.

Grandpa was 86 years old when he died, grandma was 69 years old. Grandpa must have been a very active old man. I am sure he wasn't sick very long. Grandpa and grandma are buried in City Cemetery – same lot as Aunt Annie and Uncle Bob.

Children born to Grandpa and Grandma

> James Marcroft – died a baby
> William Marcroft – died a baby
> Sarah Marcroft – died a baby
> John Marcroft, Jr.
> Robert Marcroft
> Joseph Marcroft
> Thomas Marcroft – died at 3 years old
> Benjamin Marcroft – died a baby
> Mary Ellen Marcroft – died a baby
> Hyrum Taylor Marcroft

John Marcroft

John Marcroft was born February 6, 1812 in Middletown, Lancashire, England. He was the son of John Marcroft and Isabell Scholes. He is described as being a slender, sandy complected man who was very even tempered and kind to everyone.

He married Charolette Whitehead Taylor in 1835. He loved his beautiful wife very much. It was said she was a little strict with her husband, but he seemed to like this trait in her. In time God blessed this couple with a son that they named William. He arrived in August 1835. Unfortunately, he died the same year. In May 1836, another son was born. His name was James and he died a baby in 1837. Then about 1840, a daughter by the name of Sarah arrived only to join her brothers beyond the veil. Needless to say, this young couple was depressed and seeking for some source of comfort.

It was about this time that they first heard of the "Mormon" religion. They investigated and finally joined the Church of Jesus Christ of Latter-day Saints in 1842.

Life seemed to hold new meaning for them now. They continued to try and have a family. John Jr. arrived April 25, 1843, Robert arrived February 28, 1846, Joseph arrived April 9, 1849 and Thomas came May 1, 1852.

Because of their religion, they left their home in England and sailed for America. They arrived in America in 1852. They traveled to St. Louis, Missouri where they lived for 5 years. While living here, a set of twins were born. Benjamine and Mary Ellen arrived May 1855. Unfortunately, sadness came into their lives again when not only the twins passed away, but their 3 year old son Thomas did as well. About a year later, the Marcroft family began their long walk, pushing a handcart across the plains in order to join the saints in the Salt Lake Valley. They arrived in Salt Lake City September 1, 1859.

By trade, John was a very skilled glass blower and a weaver. But there was not much work to be found using these skills in their new home so he became a fine gardener. He secured work gardening a farm belonging to a Brother Harrows located at 8th south between 3rd and 4th West (Salt Lake City). He worked hard and helped raise most of the celery produced in the Salt Lake Valley at this time.

About a year after they arrived in the valley, John took out his endowments (March 28, 1860) and was sealed to his beloved wife the same day.

While living at 338 West 8th South (Salt Lake City) their 10th child, Hyrum Taylor Marcroft, was born on August 10, 1860. He was a strong healthy child. He was the fourth child to survive infancy and grow up to become a fine young man.

John used to go to the Tithing Office to get some of his food. He was very fond of honey. He would place the container of honey in a special truck where he saved special food items and whenever the grandchildren came for a visit, he would bring out his special truck of goodies and share the food items with the children.

He loved to baby sit his grandchildren. For when they stayed with him, he would make a special treat called "sugar tits". He did this by placing some sugar in a rag and then forming the rag into a ball. Then he would dip the ball into water and let the small children and babies suck on them. This was his secret for keeping the children happy and content until their parents came to claim them.

He was a good man who stayed close to the church all his life. He helped instill a strong desire for his living children to follow in his footsteps. He found pleasure in serving the Lord, as did his family.

He was well remembered and loved long after he passed away (October 16, 1898) at the age of 86. He was buried beside his loving wife in the Salt Lake Cemetery in 1898.

Compiled by: Elizabeth J.O. Williams
              November 1978

SOURCES:
  1)   Family group sheets on file at the Genealogy Library
  2)   Computer Index File
  3)   Temple Index Cards
  4)   Information found in Hyrum Taylor Marcroft's biography

Charolette Whitehead Taylor

Charolette Whitehead Taylor was born March 17, 1817 in Sattleworth, Yorkshire, England. She was the lovely daughter of Robert Taylor and Mary Whitehead.

Not much is known about her early life except that she was born with the gift of tongues, a gift given to few people.

She used to work for a living before she got married. The story is told of how her half sisters husband, John Easthope, and John Marcroft, her future sweetheart, followed her one night to find out where she was going. They intended to make a big fuss about it, but instead John became interested and decided to get to know Charolette better.

Sometime in 1835, when she was about 18 years old, she married John Marcroft and they lived in John's hometown of Middletown, Lancashire, England. She's described as being a beautiful woman who was very neat personally. She was a good wife and mother. She was a great lover of the gospel. And she was somewhat strict with her husband. This was a trait he seemed to enjoy however.

About nine months after they were married a son by the name of William arrived in August 1835. Unfortunately, he died the same year. Nine months after William Arrived, another son came in May 1836. His name was James and he also passed away in 1837. About four years later, she bore a daughter called Sarah and she too passed away in infancy.

Loosing three children in a row was a deep loss. It wasn't until she embraced the Gospel of Jesus Christ that she found the courage needed to try and start having a family again.

Both Charolette and John became converts to the "Mormon" Church. She was the first one however to be baptized, on March 13, 1842.

After their son John Jr. arrived April 25, 1843, there home was filled with the laughter of children. Robert followed on February 28, 1846, Joseph arrived April 9, 1849, and little Thomas joined the family May 1, 1852.

It was after Thomas arrived that the family left their home in England and sailed to a new life in America. They temporarily settled in St. Louis, Missouri for approximately 5 years. During this time, a set of twins blessed their family in May 1855. Unfortunately, God called Benjamin and Mary Ellen home again shortly after they arrived in this world. That same year, baby Thomas, who was only 3 years old, died also.

Despite their hardships and sorrows, they decided to take their three living sons and join the pioneers in their trek westward. They traveled by handcart until they were able to join the saints in the Great Salt Lake Valley on September 1, 1859.

On March 28, 1860, while expecting their 10th child, Charolette took out her endowments and was sealed for time and eternity to her dear husband.

Now in the "Valley of the Saints" in Salt Lake City, they settled in a fine new home located at 338 West 8th south and this is where their newest son, Hyrum Taylor Marcroft, was born. It was on August 10, 1860. He was a fine healthy child. God had blessed them once more.

It was not an easy life pioneering in Utah but it was a good life. Charolette saw to it that all four of her living sons were baptized members of the Church of Jesus Christ of Latter-day Saints. She raised them to be faithful members who loved the Lord and had strong personal testimonies of the truthfulness of the gospel.

She was indeed a good woman, a choice daughter of our Father in Heaven. She lived a good life for 69 years, then it was time to rejoin her other six children. She passed away May 16, 1887, and was buried in the Salt Lake Cemetery. Nine of her children were sealed to her for eternity on January 24, 1917. Hyrum, of course, was the only child to be born under the covenant.

Compiled by: Elizabeth J.O. Williams
            November 1978

SOURCES:
    1)   Family group sheets on film at Ogden Genealogy Library
    2)   Temple index cards
    3)   Temple index file
    4)   Information from Hyrum Taylor Marcroft's biography

Henry William Walkey

Father: Joseph Walkey
Mother: Susana Colin
Born: 17 April 1835
Place: St. Catherine, Jersey Island, England
Married: ? (to Mary Moss)
Place: ?
Died: 20 May 1898
Place: Heber, Utah, USA

Tid bits about Henry William Walkey and Mary Moss

Henry William Walkey was born to Joseph Walkey and Susana Colin on April 17, 1835 at St. Catherine, Jersey Island, England. Mary Moss was the oldest child of John Moss and Emma Foster, born on the 9th of March 1845 in Durham, New South Wales, Australia. Mary Moss was baptized as an infant into the Church of England on 8 June 1845.

There is a story that talks of an orphan (possibly Joseph Walkey) who left the Church of England and signed his name as "Walkey". No records show a Walkey as joining the Church of England or any others in the area. The story goes on to say three brothers (not necessarily from the original Walkey) left England for the United States. Upon arrival in New York one brother (possibly Henry William Walkey) had some legal problems (ie: a fight or equivalent) and in order to avoid jail joined the merchant marine and shipped out to Australia. They say that when Henry was a sailor as a young man he would jump ship when his ship would come to port in Australia. This is where he met Mary Moss.

Henry and Mary were married in the early 1860's and had four children in Australia: Susanna Walkey (2 December 1965), William Henry Walkey (11 June 1867), Mary Louise Walkey (11 September 1869) & Joseph Walkey (2 May 1872). Then sometime in 1872 they met the missionaries for The Church of Jesus Christ of Latter-day Saints and were converted and baptized. Mary's parents (John and Emma Moss) were also baptized and left for Utah in September of 1873 and Henry and Mary Walkey came with them. They settled in Moroni, Utah where they had four more children: Emma Jane Walkey (24 June 1875), John Walkey (23 Feb 1878), Cecilia Matilda Walkey (1 Jan 1879) & Lily Mae Walkey (13 April 1881). Of these four children only Emma Jane made it to adulthood all the others died under the age of two.

Somewhere in between 1881 and 1883 the family moved to Salt Lake City, Utah and there they had two more children: Emily Ada Walkey (2 Feb 1883) and Henry Herbert Walkey (28 Feb 1886). Of the ten children Henry and Mary had only 5 made it to adulthood. Three died in Moroni as babies and William Henry Walkey died at 7 years of age and Joseph Walkey died at 18 years of age.

Henry William Walkey died 20 May 1898 and is buried in the Salt Lake City Cemetery.

Mary Moss moved to Aetna, Alberta, Canada around 1906 where she owned a home (see picture) and lived out the rest of her life. She died and is buried in Aetna on January 4, 1920.

Mary Moss

Mary's first house she had in Aetna, Canada about 1906.
Henry Herbert Walkey (son) by the window

Father: John Moss
Mother: Emma Foster
Born: 9 March 1845
Place: Durham, NSW, Australia
Married: ? (to Henry William Walkey)
Place: ?
Died: 4 January 1920
Place: Aetna, Alberta, Canada

Tid bits about John Moss and Emma Foster

John Moss was born in Proud, Preston, Lancashire, England on the 28th of November 1809. He married a young girl in England (Emma Prestridge) and was disowned by his parents for marrying a commoner. Emma had a baby and both of them died. Then he went to Australia where he met Emma Foster, an orphan at 14 years of age, she was also born in England on the 9th of May 1825. They were married about 1844 and had 10 children (all born in Australia):

Born	Date	To whom	Died
1)Mary Moss	9 Mar 1845	Henry William Walkey	4 Jan 1920 (75)
2)John Moss	abt. 1848	Jane Mason	June 1901 (53)
3)Caroline Moss	15 Sept 1851	William Jeffs, Jr.	?
4)Joseph Moss	21 Sept 1853	?	31Mar1874 (21)
5)George Moss	9 Apr 1856	?	18Mar1874 (18)
6)Emma Moss	18 July1859	Ira Ernest Egan	11Sept1907(48)
7)Fredrick Richard Moss	18 Feb 1860	Caroline Christensen	23Apr1927 (67)
8)Eliza Katherine Moss	1 Jan 1863	John James Haight	24Feb1931 (68)
9)Robert Thomas Moss	abt. 1866	?	Mar 1874 (8)
10)Elizabeth Moss	5 Nov 1869	John Hancock	3 Aug 1940 (69)

Elder John Sharp and Elder Robert Beicham were the missionaries for The Church of Jesus Christ of Latter-day Saints who baptized the Moss family. All of the family came to Utah in September of 1873 except John and his family. John Moss (senior) died in Moroni, San Pete County, Utah of pneumonia on 21 Jan 1874. He was a painter. Emma remarried William Jeffs in 1875.

John Moss (junior) was killed in Australia. Mary H. Walkey died in Aetna, Alberta, Canada. Caroline M. Jeffs died in S.L.C., Utah. Joseph, George and Robert all died of scarlet fever in 1874. Emma M. Egan died in Smithfield Utah of heart trouble, 14 years after they arrived to Utah. Fredrick died in Moroni, Utah, some of his family is still there. Eliza died in S.L.C. and is buried in Wasatch Lawns Cemetery. Elizabeth died in California; her body is buried in Utah at Wasatch Lawns Cemetery. She was only 4 when they arrived from Australia to Utah.

Emma Foster

Father: ?
Mother: ?
Born: About 1825 - 28
Place: Nothingham or Norwick, England
Married: 1844 (to John Moss)
Place: ?
Died: June 1901
Place: Provo, Utah, USA

Made in the USA
Las Vegas, NV
26 February 2022

44651227R00214